I think I'm becoming addicted to photo composition. For someone like me, who as a kid always scribbled on pictures of famous people in my schoolbooks, the PC is a cool toy!! I want to learn more about it and create a collection of surreal photo compositions!! ...Naturally, this is after my serial is completed.

—Kentaro Yabuki, 2004

Kentaro Yabuki made his manga debut with *Yamato Gensoki*, a short series about a young empress destined to unite the warring states of ancient Japan and the boy sworn to protect her. His next series, *Black Cat*, commenced serialization in the pages of *Weekly Shonen Jump* in 2000 and quickly developed a loyal fan following. *Black Cat* has also become an animated TV series, first hitting Japan's airwaves in the fall of 2005.

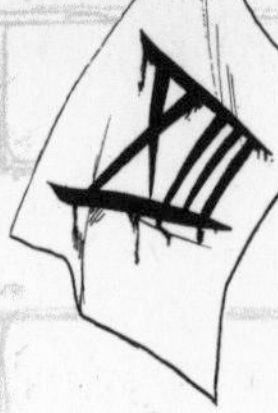

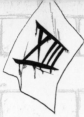

BLACK CAT VOL. 18

The SHONEN JUMP Manga Edition

STORY AND ART BY
KENTARO YABUKI

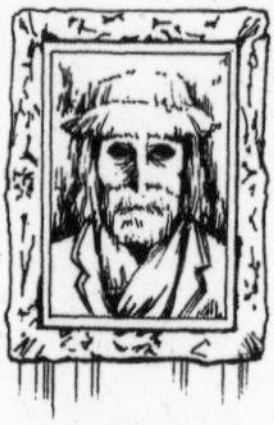

English Adaptation/Kelly Sue DeConnick
Translation/JN Productions
Touch-up Art & Lettering/Gia Cam Luc
Design/Courtney Utt
Editor/Jonathan Tarbox

Editor in Chief, Books/Alvin Lu
Editor in Chief, Magazines/Marc Weidenbaum
VP, Publishing Licensing/Rika Inouye
VP, Sales & Product Marketing/Gonzalo Ferreyra
VP, Creative/Linda Espinosa
Publisher/Hyoe Narita

A CIP catalogue record for this book is available from the British Library.

Printed in the U.S.A.

Published by VIZ Media, LLC
P.O. Box 77010
San Francisco, CA 94107

SHONEN JUMP Manga Edition
10 9 8 7 6 5 4 3 2 1
First printing, January 2009

SHONEN JUMP MANGA EDITION

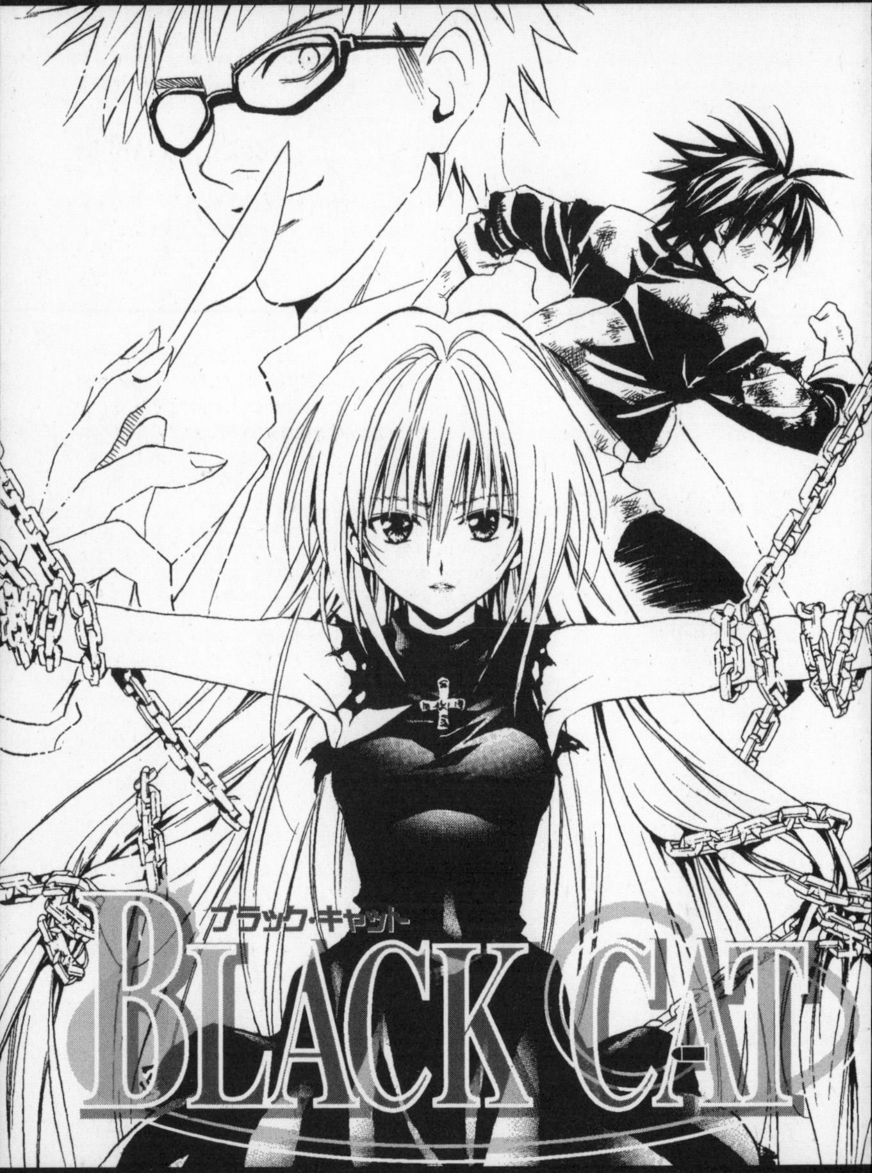
ブラック・キャット
BLACK CAT

VOLUME 18

GUIDING LIGHT

STORY & ART BY KENTARO YABUKI

SVEN VOLLFIED

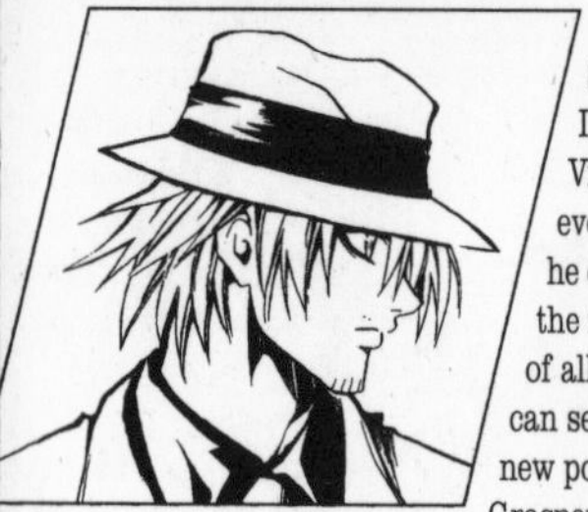

Train's partner Sven, a former IBI agent. His Vision Eye has evolved, and now he can slow down the movement of all objects he can see with his new power, the Grasper Eye.

SEPHIRIA ARKS

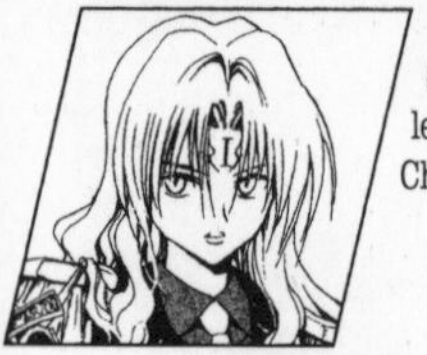

As Number I, Sephiria is the leader of the Chrono Numbers.

BELZE ROCHEFORT

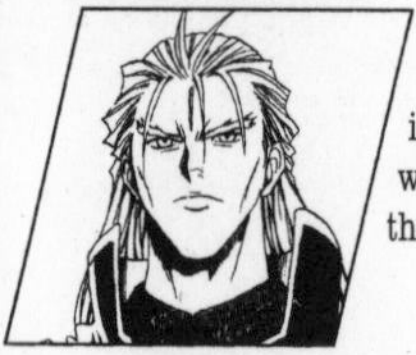

As Chrono Number II, Belze is equally adept with the pen and the sword.

JENOS HAZARD

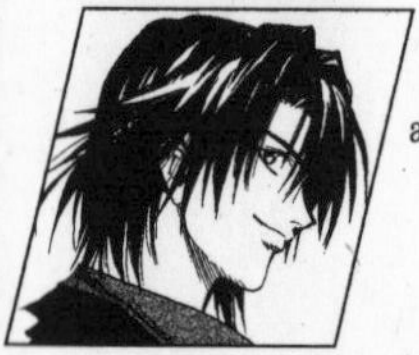

Chrono Number VII manipulates wires... and women.

LIN SHAOLEE

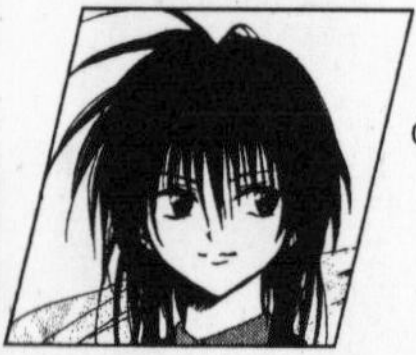

Chrono Number X is a master of disguise.

TRAIN HEARTNET

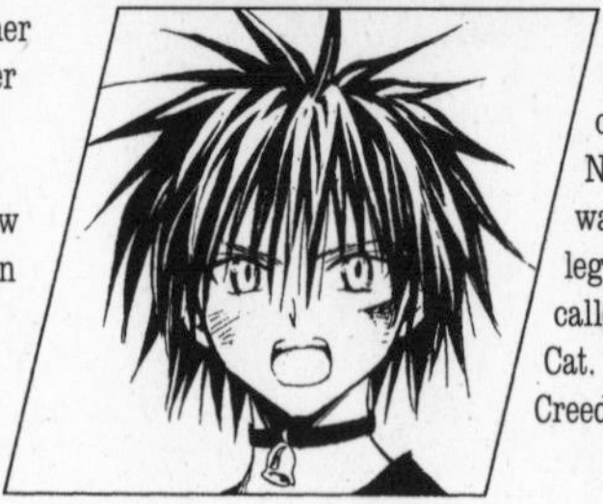

Formerly Number XIII of the Chrono Numbers, Train was once a legendary eraser called the Black Cat. He now pursues Creed as a sweeper.

EVE

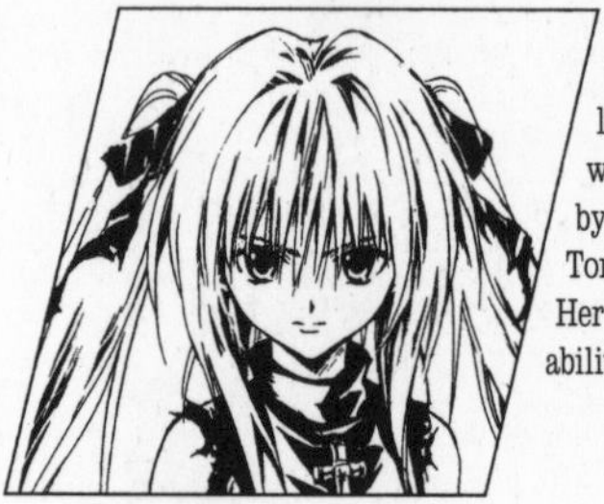

Part bio-weapon and part little girl, Eve was manufactured by weapons dealer Torneo Rudman. Her power lies in her ability to transform.

RINSLET WALKER

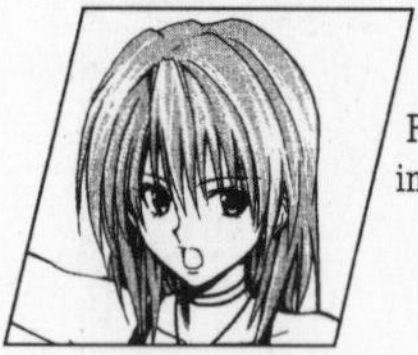

A self-styled thief-for-hire, Rinslet is fiercely independent.

KYOKO

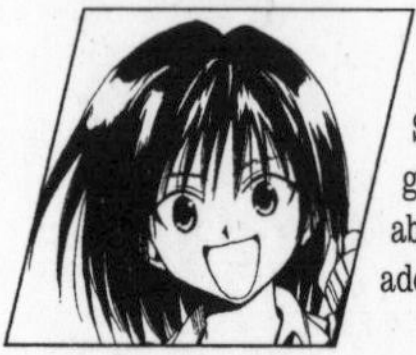

Member of the Apostles of the Stars. A young girl who absolutely adores Train.

SAYA MINATSUKI

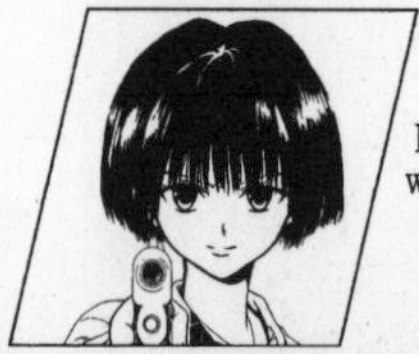

Saya is an important woman from Train's past who was fatally wounded by Creed.

A fearless "eraser" responsible for the deaths of countless men, Train "Black Cat" Heartnet was formerly an assassin for the crime syndicate Chronos. Train betrayed Chronos and was supposedly executed for it, but now, two years later, he lives a carefree wanderer's life, working with his partner Sven as a bounty hunter ("sweeper") and pursuing Creed Diskenth, the man who murdered his dear friend Saya Minatsuki.

Creed finally turns up, determined to lead a revolution against Chronos. He tries to convince Train to join his Apostles of the Stars, but fails at that and escapes once again.

Train decides Creed must be stopped, and for the first time, he tells his friends the story behind Creed and Saya.

In an effort to close the door on Train's past, he, Sven and Eve head out with a new resolve. They hook up with an elite band of bounty hunters to form a Sweeper Alliance and infiltrate Creed's island hideout. Once there, they confront formidable Apostles wielding the power of Tao.

Train teams up with Eve and enters Creed's hideout. Quickly they are confronted with the Shooting Star Unit and the mysterious Doctor. Before they know what's happened, they are transported to a bizarre other world.

CREED DISKENTH

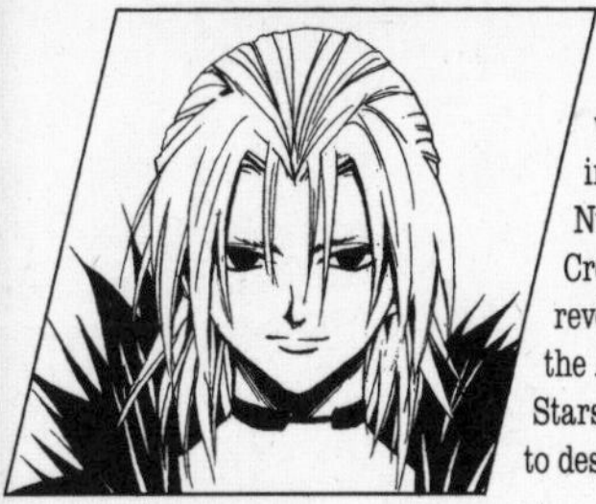

Though he and Train were associates in their Chrono Numbers days, Creed now heads the revolutionary group the Apostles of the Stars, whose goal is to destroy the world.

DOCTOR

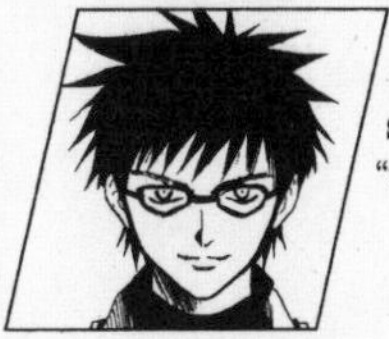

Little is known about Creed's spokesman, "the Doctor."

ECHIDNA PARASS

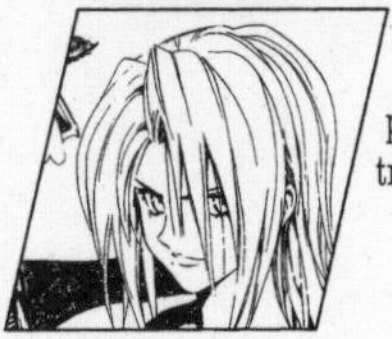

Echidna has the power to create portals in space and travel through them.

BALDORIAS S. FANGHINI

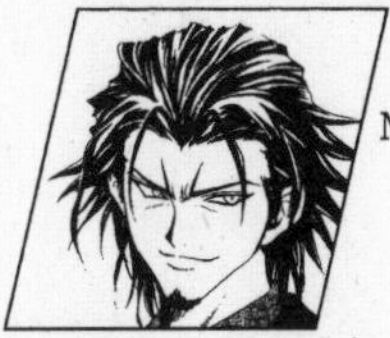

Nurtured by Chronos to fight as Chrono Number VIII.

KRANTZ MADUKE

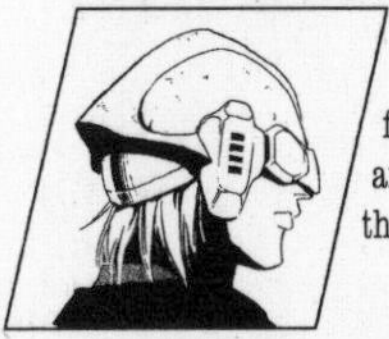

Blind warrior Chrono Number IV fights using sound and his keen sense of the air around him.

BLACK CAT

VOLUME 18 GUIDING LIGHT

CONTENTS

CHAPTER 159: NOWHERE WORLD

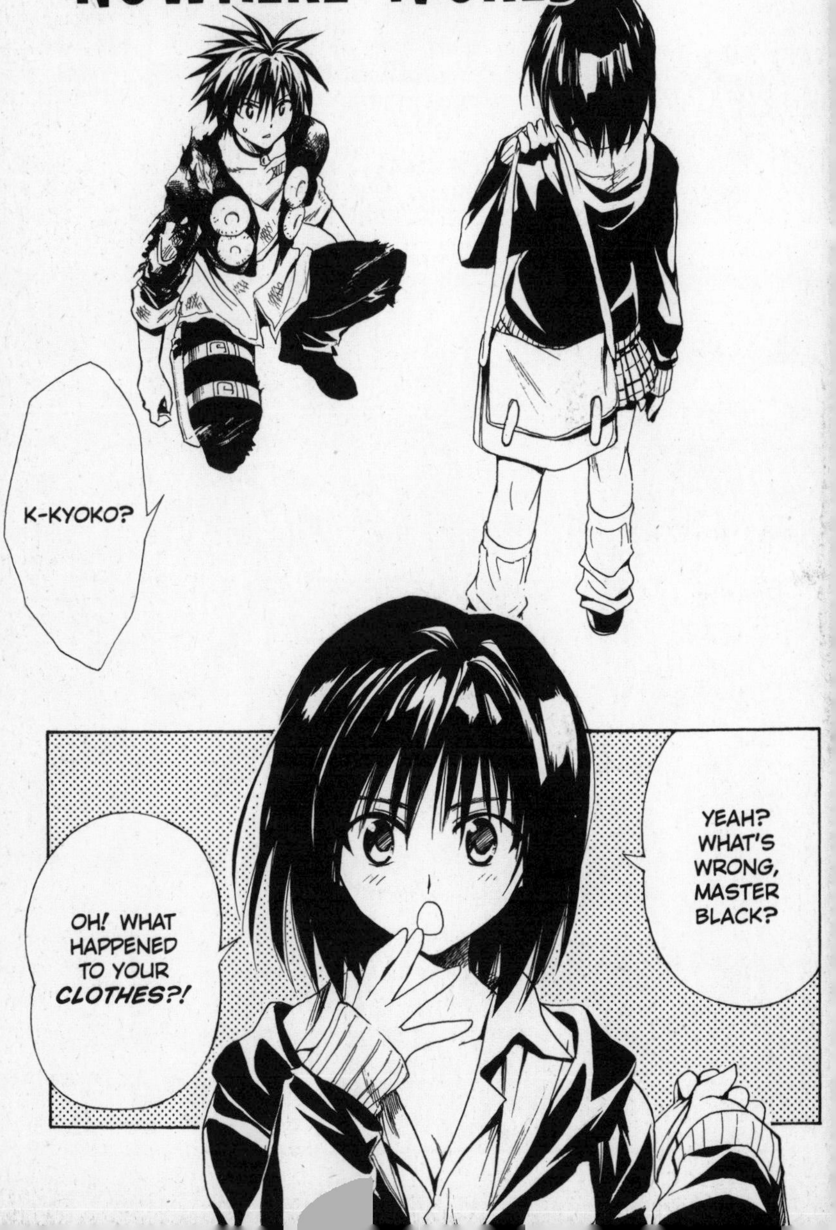
K-KYOKO?
YEAH? WHAT'S WRONG, MASTER BLACK?
OH! WHAT HAPPENED TO YOUR *CLOTHES?!*

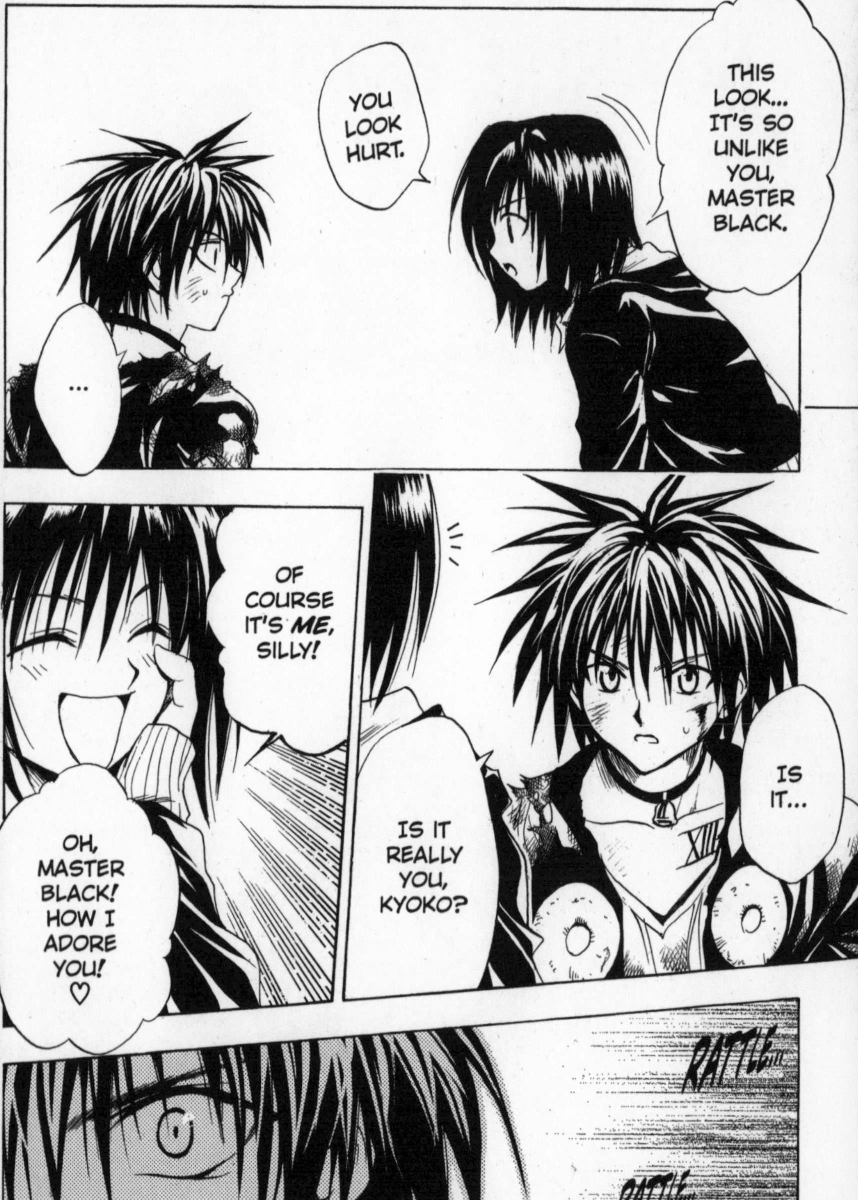
THIS LOOK... IT'S SO UNLIKE YOU, MASTER BLACK.
YOU LOOK HURT.
...
IS IT...
IS IT REALLY YOU, KYOKO?
OF COURSE IT'S *ME*, SILLY!
OH, MASTER BLACK! HOW I ADORE YOU! ♡
RATTLE...
RATTLE...

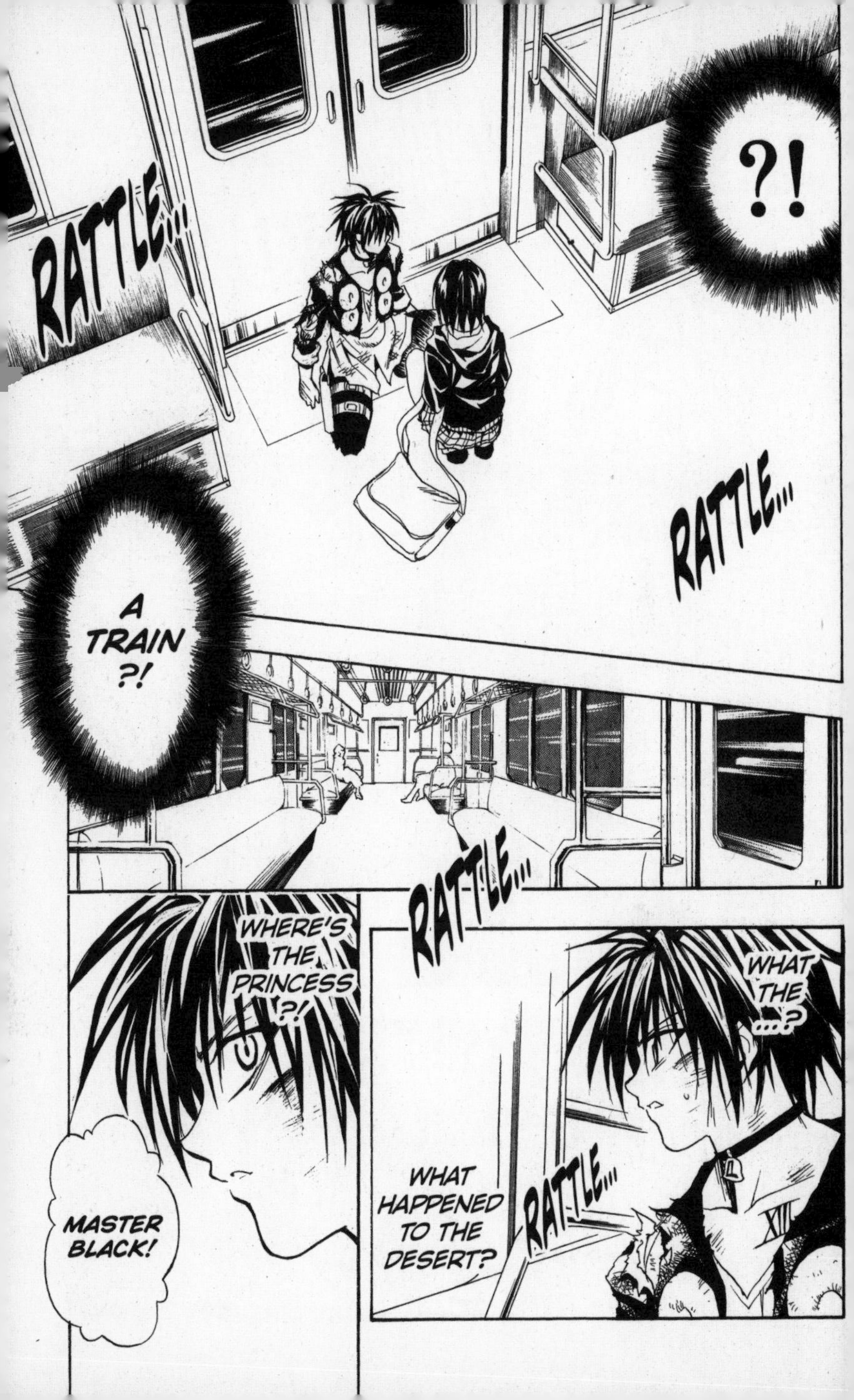
?!
RATTLE...
RATTLE...
A TRAIN ?!
RATTLE...
WHAT THE ...?
WHAT HAPPENED TO THE DESERT?
RATTLE...
WHERE'S THE PRINCESS ?!
MASTER BLACK!

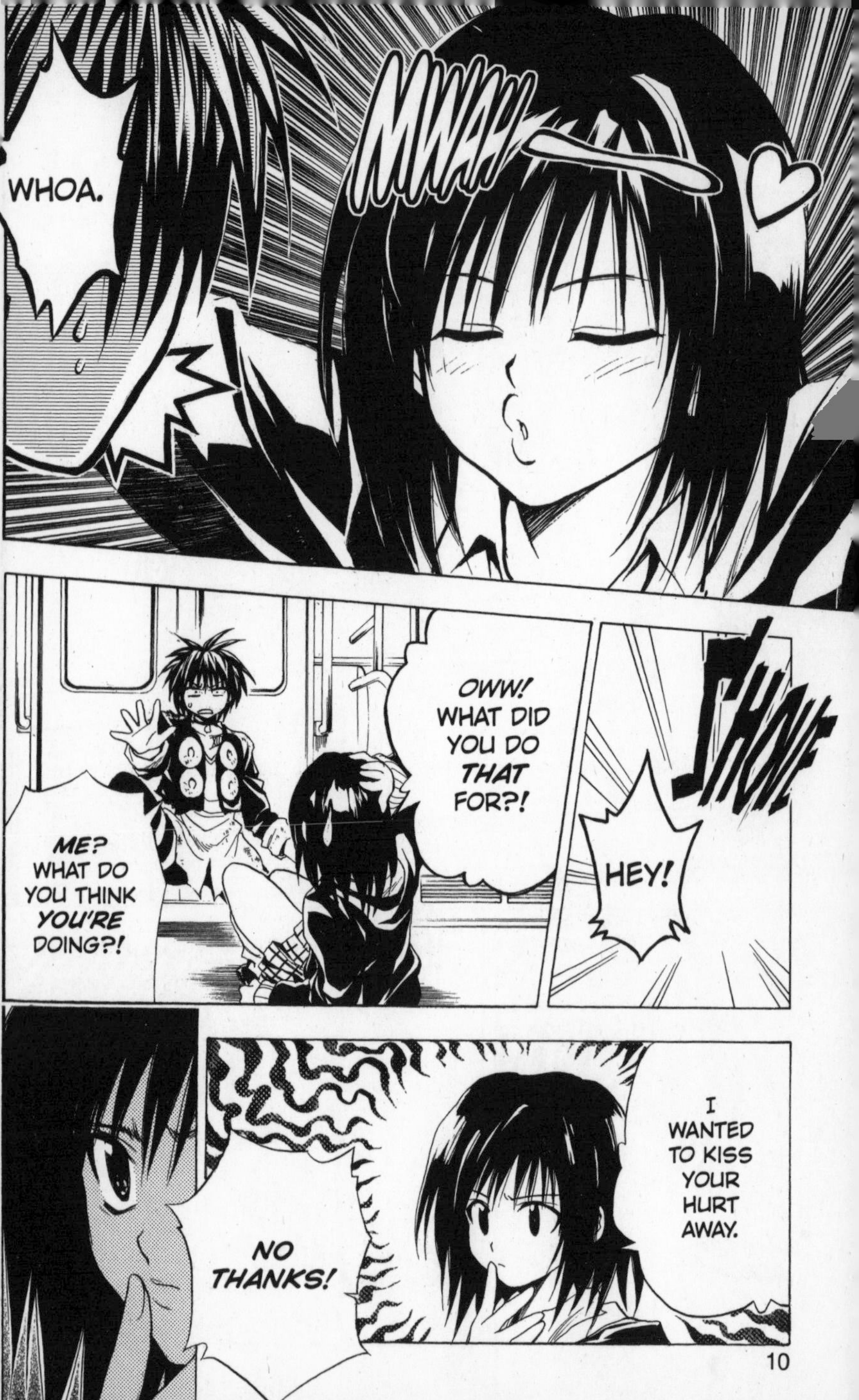
MWAH!
WHOA.
HEY!
OWW! WHAT DID YOU DO THAT FOR?!
ME? WHAT DO YOU THINK YOU'RE DOING?!
I WANTED TO KISS YOUR HURT AWAY.
NO THANKS!

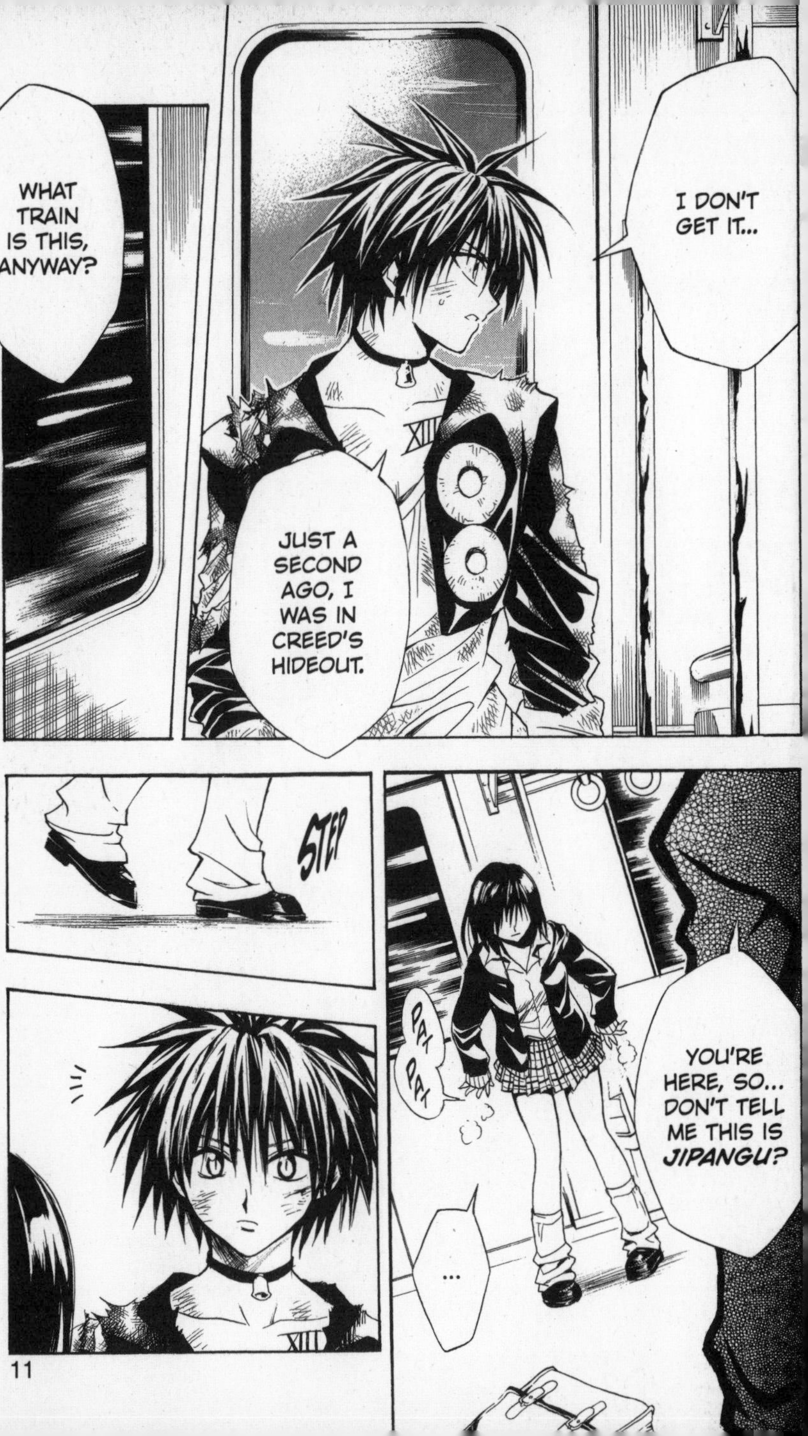
I DON'T GET IT...
WHAT TRAIN IS THIS, ANYWAY?
JUST A SECOND AGO, I WAS IN CREED'S HIDEOUT.
YOU'RE HERE, SO... DON'T TELL ME THIS IS *JIPANGU?*
PAT PAT
...
STEP

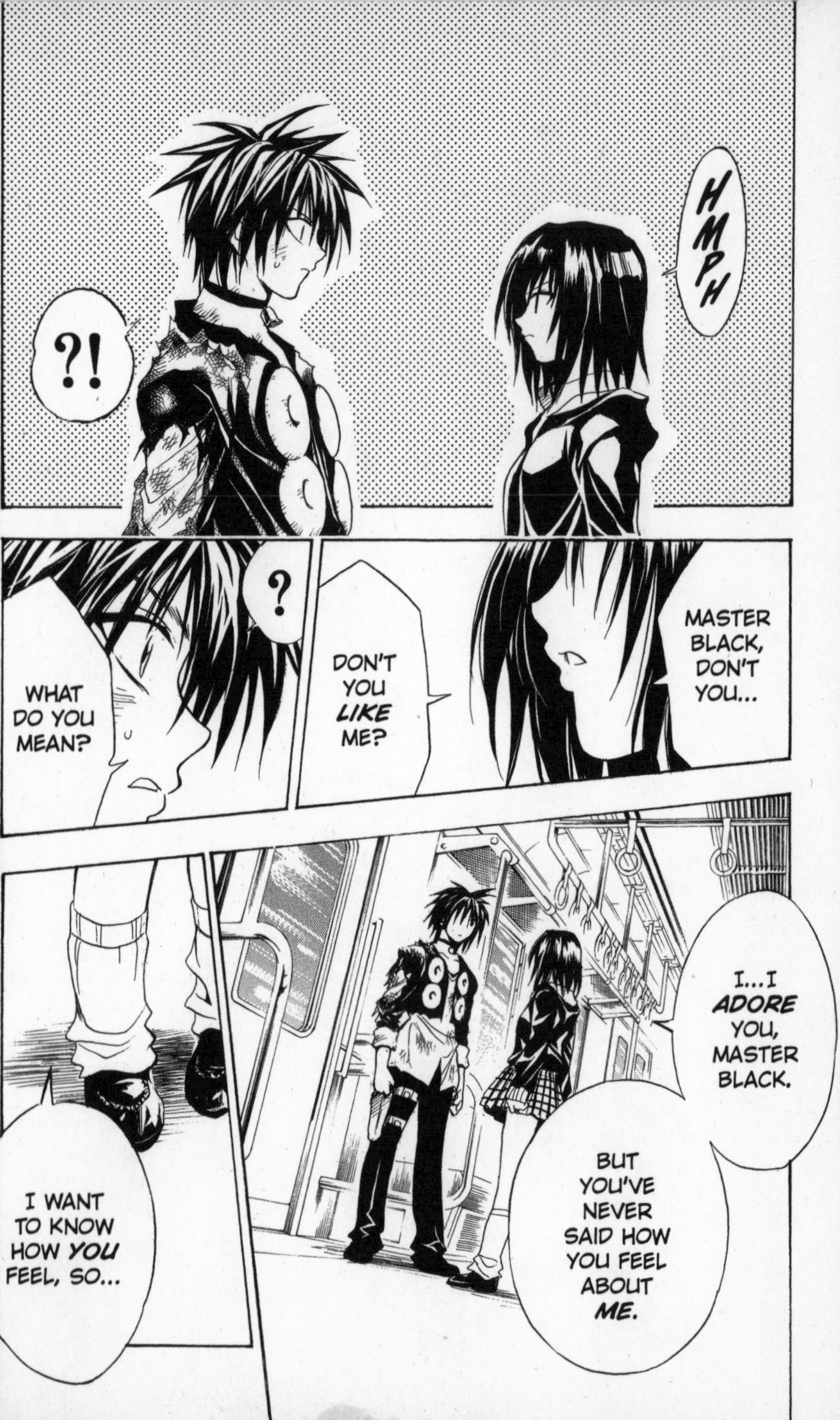
HMPH
?!
MASTER BLACK, DON'T YOU...
DON'T YOU *LIKE* ME?
?
WHAT DO YOU MEAN?
I...I *ADORE* YOU, MASTER BLACK.
BUT YOU'VE NEVER SAID HOW YOU FEEL ABOUT *ME.*
I WANT TO KNOW HOW *YOU* FEEL, SO...

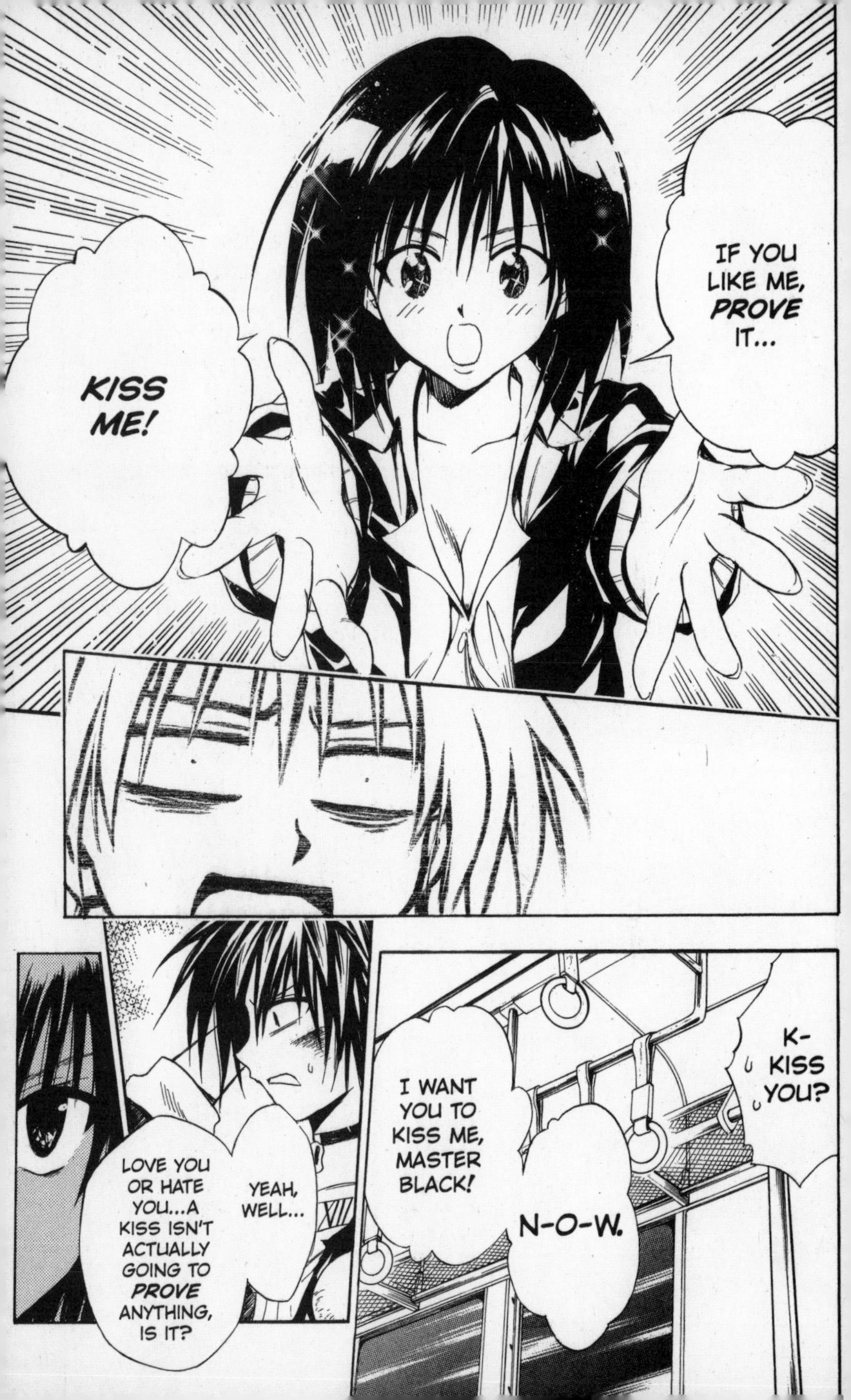
IF YOU LIKE ME, *PROVE* IT...
KISS ME!
K-KISS YOU?
I WANT YOU TO KISS ME, MASTER BLACK!
N-O-W.
YEAH, WELL...
LOVE YOU OR HATE YOU...A KISS ISN'T ACTUALLY GOING TO *PROVE* ANYTHING, IS IT?

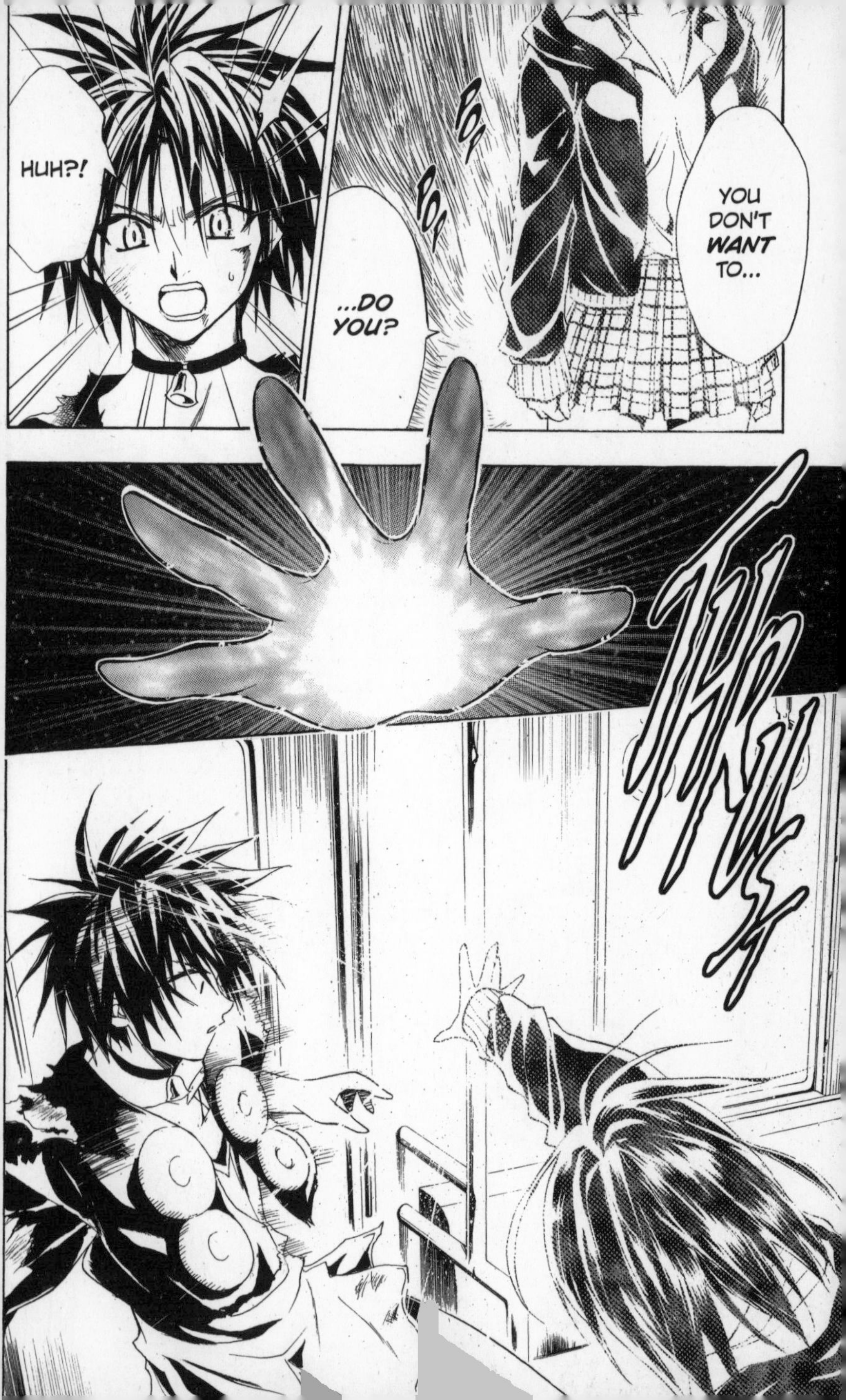
YOU DON'T WANT TO...
...DO YOU?
HUH?!

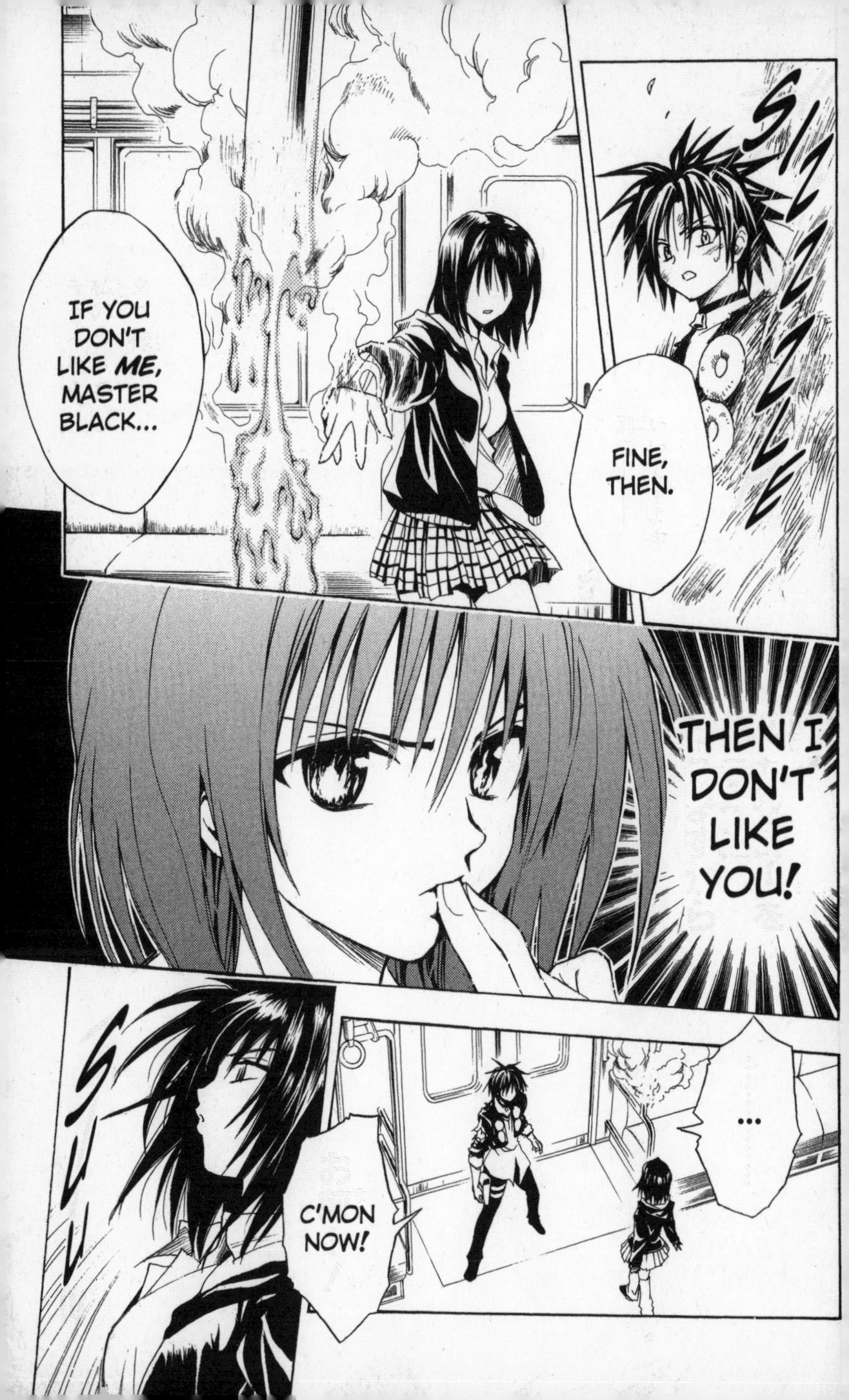
FINE, THEN.
IF YOU DON'T LIKE *ME*, MASTER BLACK...
THEN I DON'T LIKE YOU!
...
C'MON NOW!

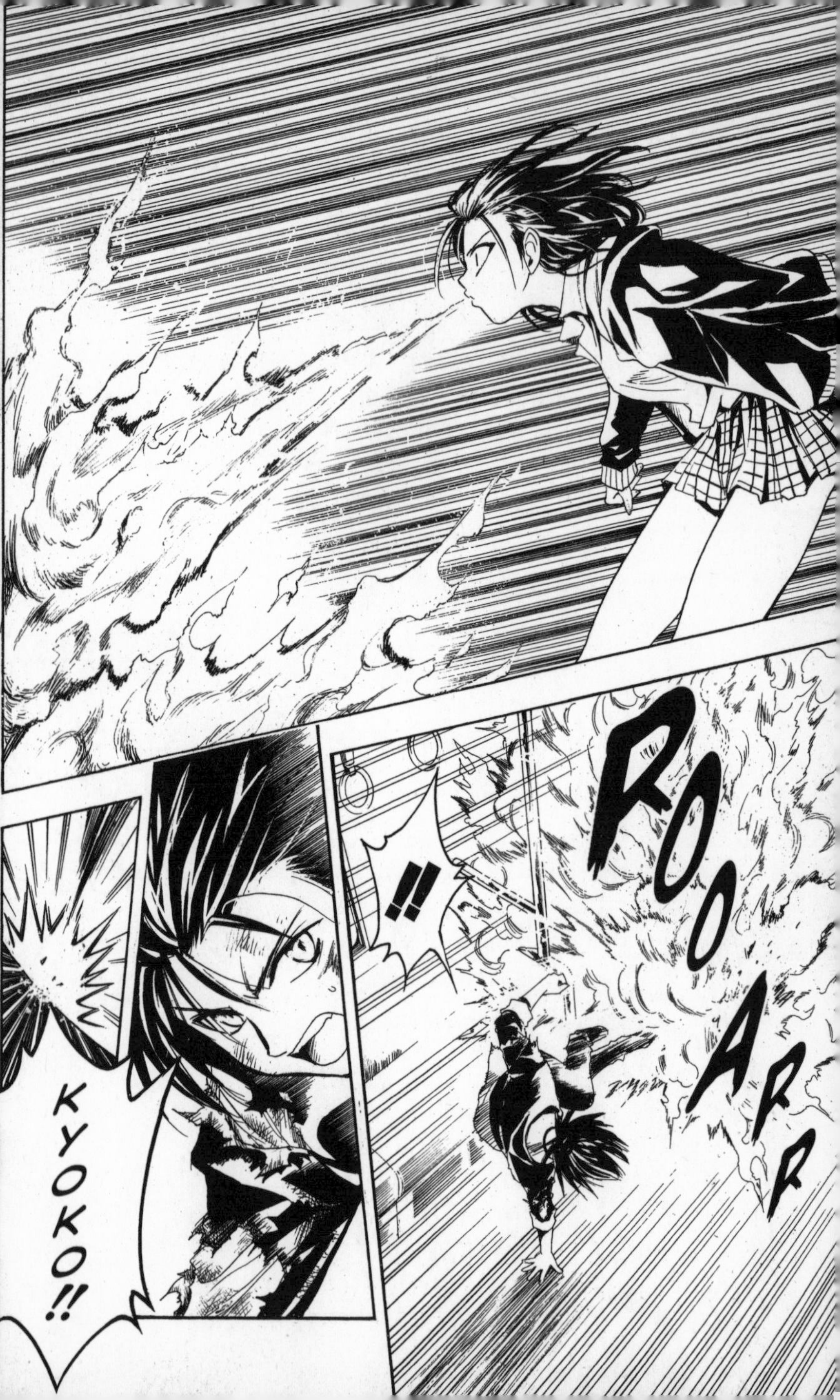
ROOARR
!!
KYOKO!!

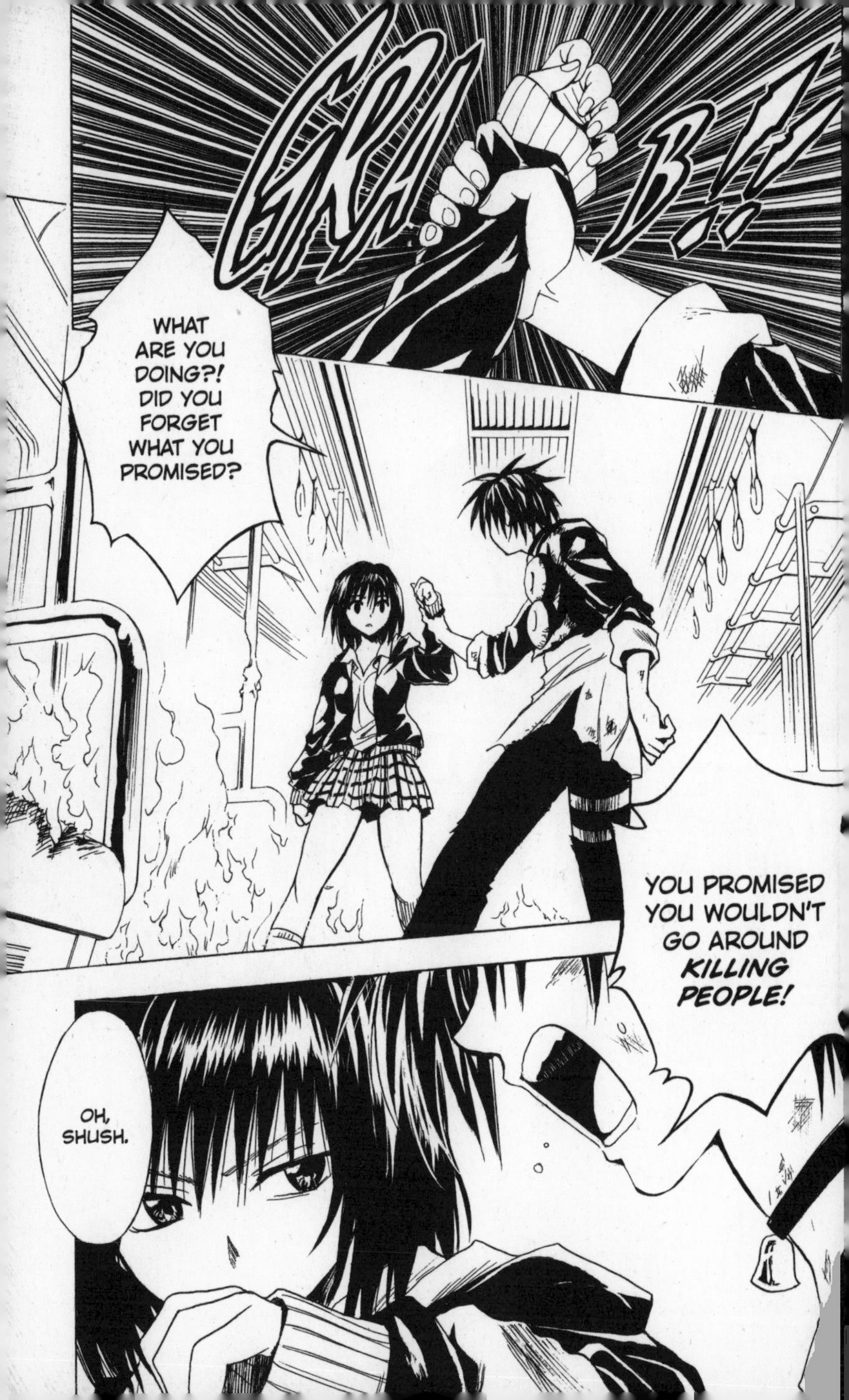
GRAB!!
WHAT ARE YOU DOING?! DID YOU FORGET WHAT YOU PROMISED?
YOU PROMISED YOU WOULDN'T GO AROUND *KILLING PEOPLE!*
OH, SHUSH.

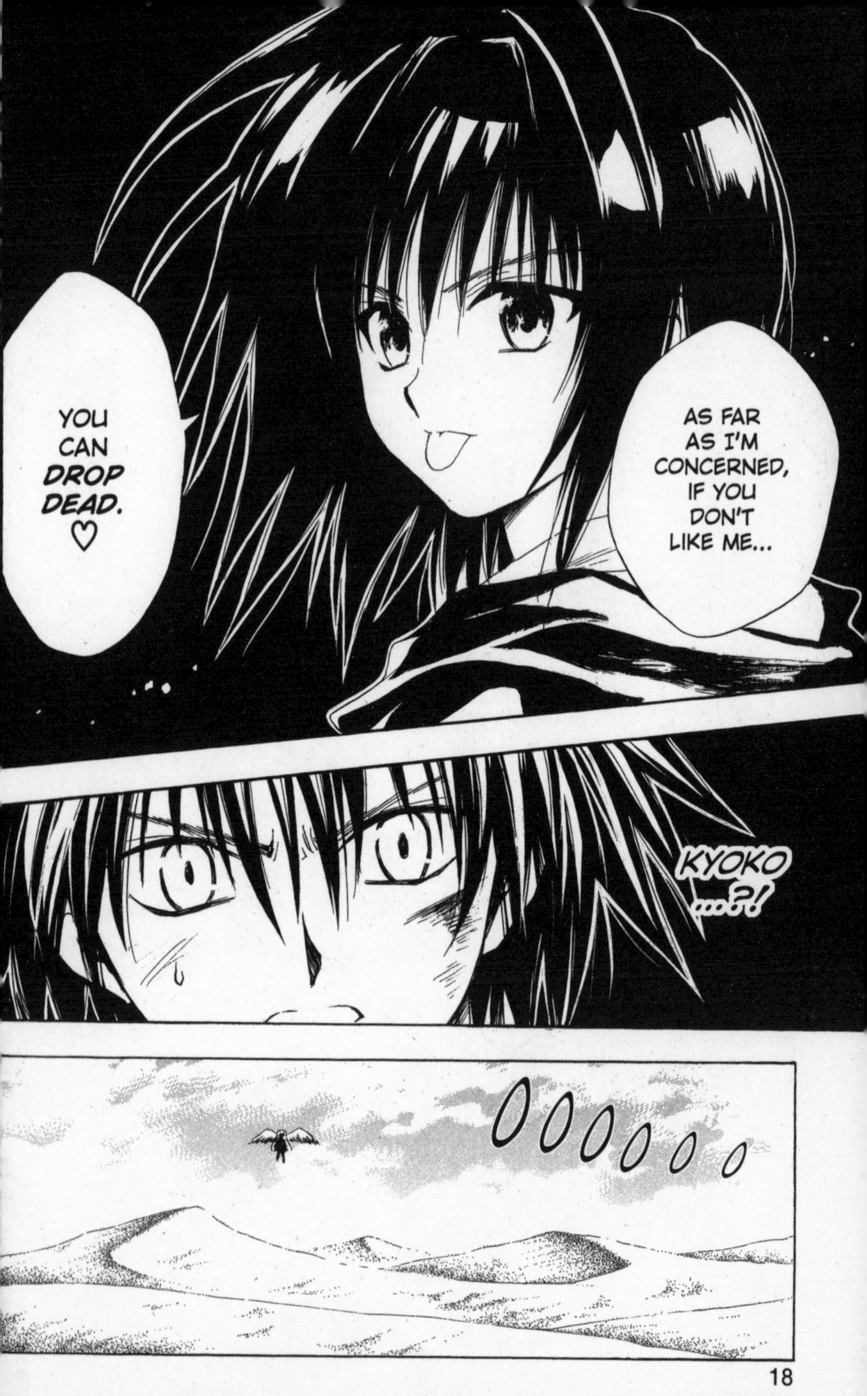

AS FAR AS I'M CONCERNED, IF YOU DON'T LIKE ME...
YOU CAN DROP DEAD. ♡
KYOKO ...?!
OOOOOOO

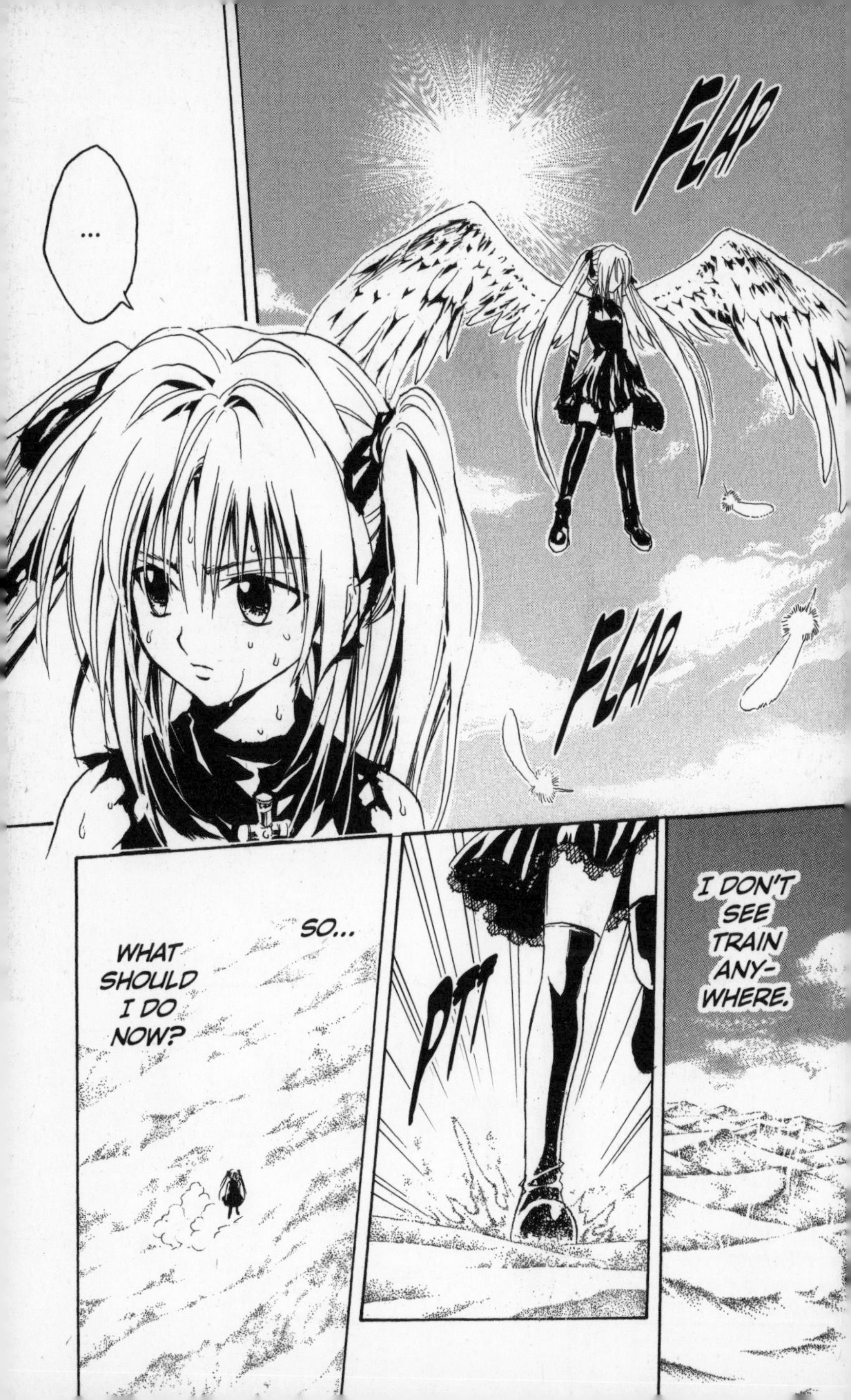
FLAP
FLAP
...
I DON'T SEE TRAIN ANY-WHERE.
PTT
SO...
WHAT SHOULD I DO NOW?

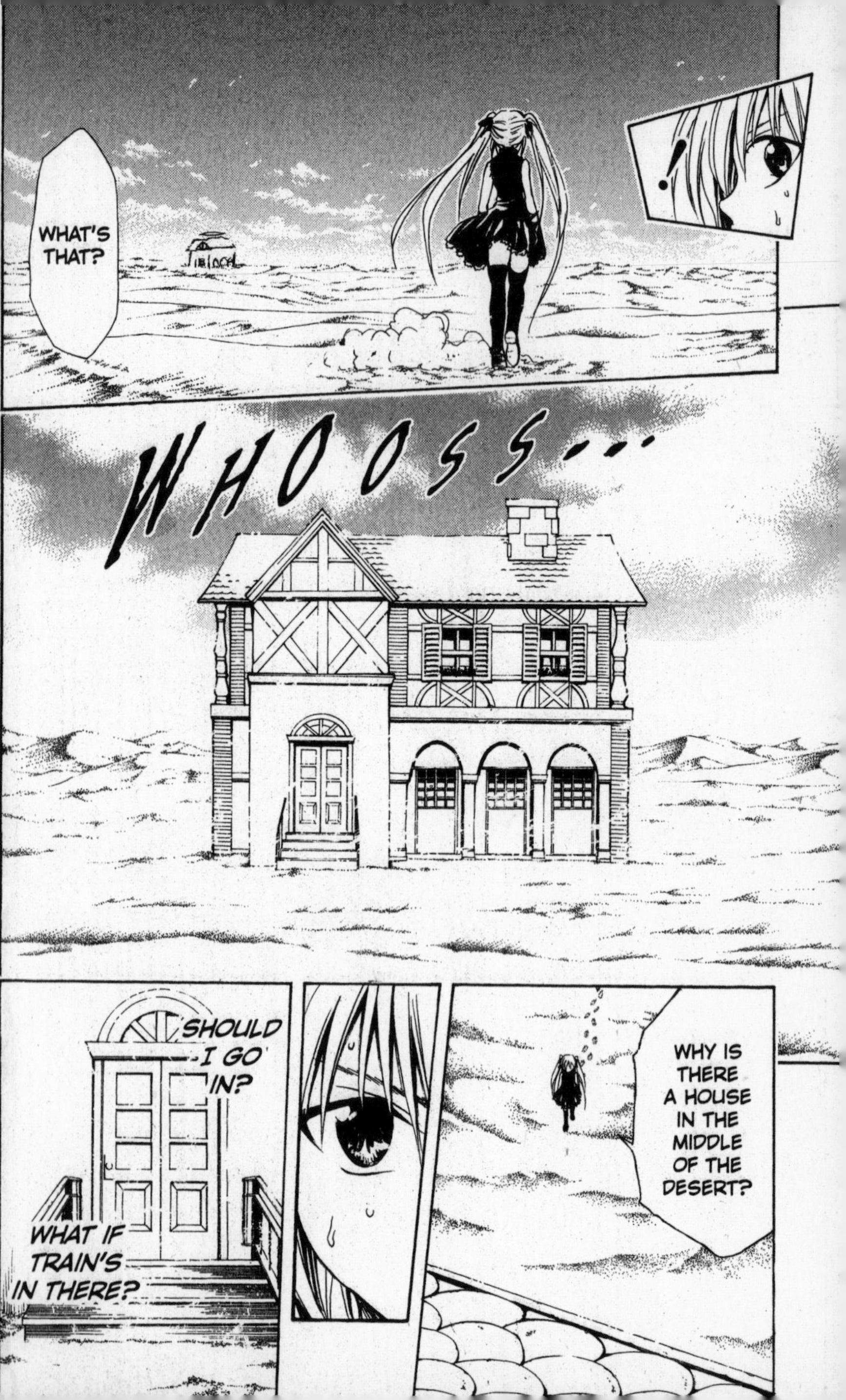
!
WHAT'S THAT?
WHOOSS...
WHY IS THERE A HOUSE IN THE MIDDLE OF THE DESERT?
SHOULD I GO IN?
WHAT IF TRAIN'S IN THERE?

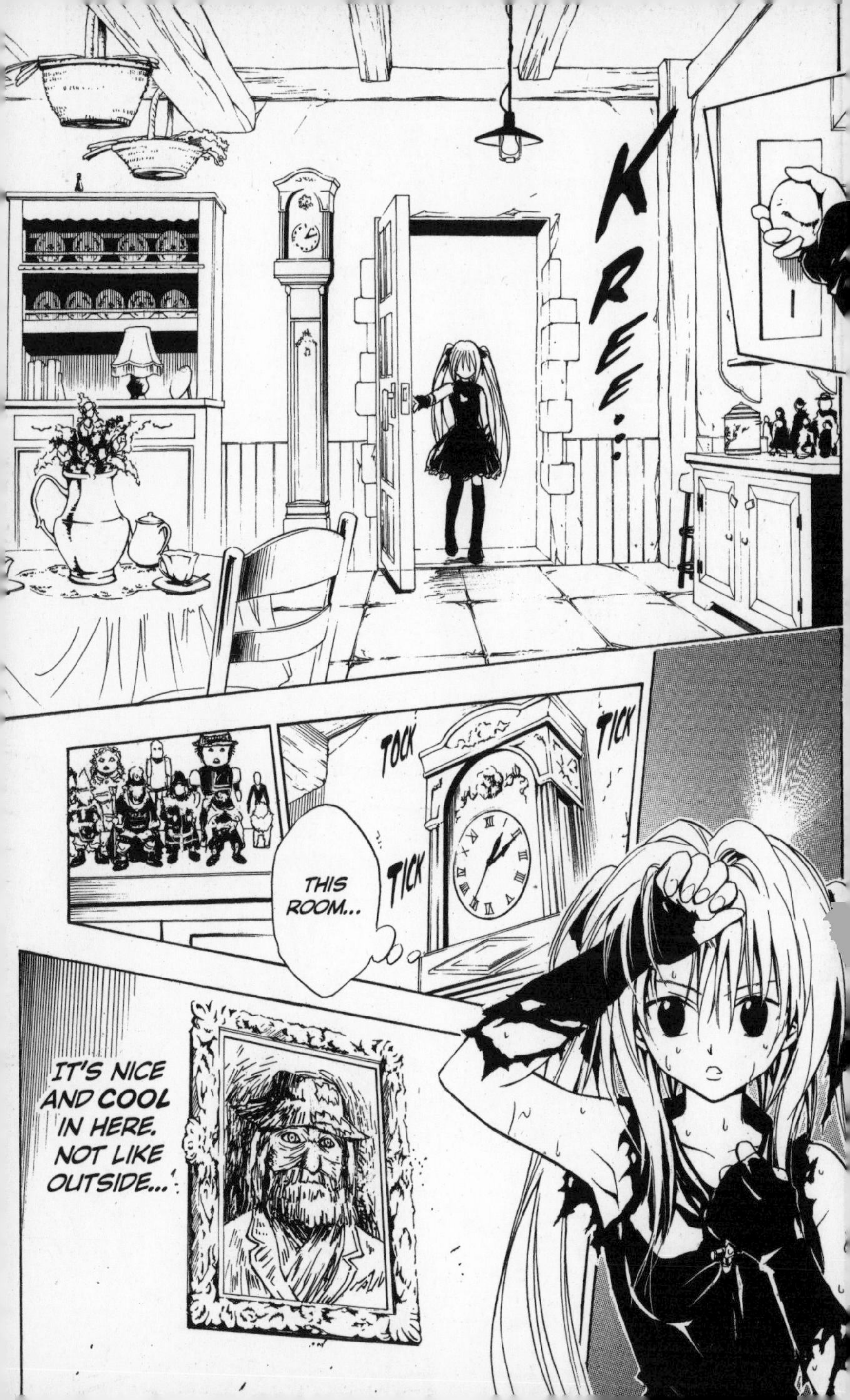
KREE...
TICK
TOCK
THIS ROOM...
TICK
IT'S NICE AND COOL IN HERE. NOT LIKE OUTSIDE...

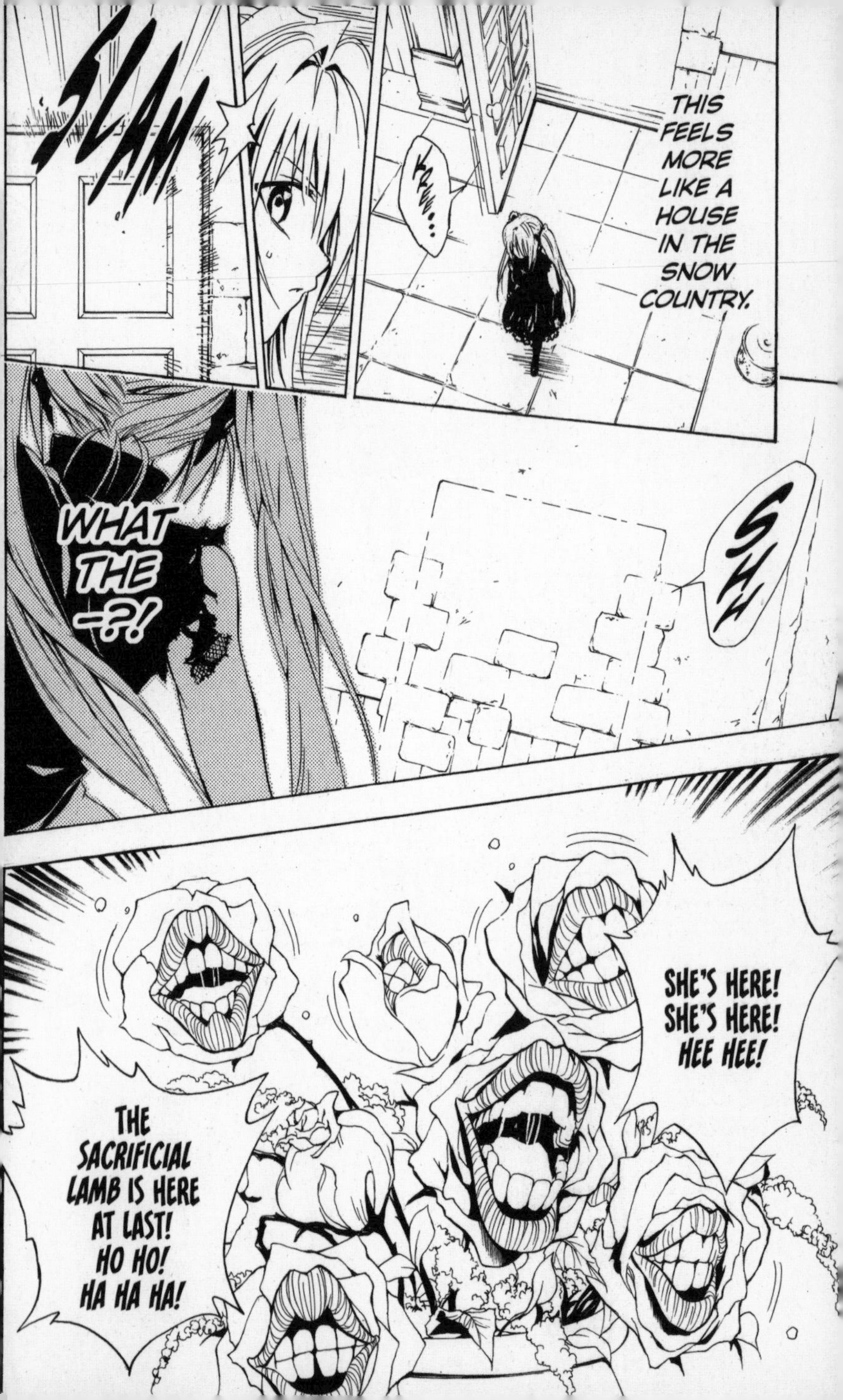
THIS FEELS MORE LIKE A HOUSE IN THE SNOW COUNTRY.
KREEE...
SLAM
SHH
WHAT THE -?!
SHE'S HERE! SHE'S HERE! HEE HEE!
THE SACRIFICIAL LAMB IS HERE AT LAST! HO HO! HA HA HA!

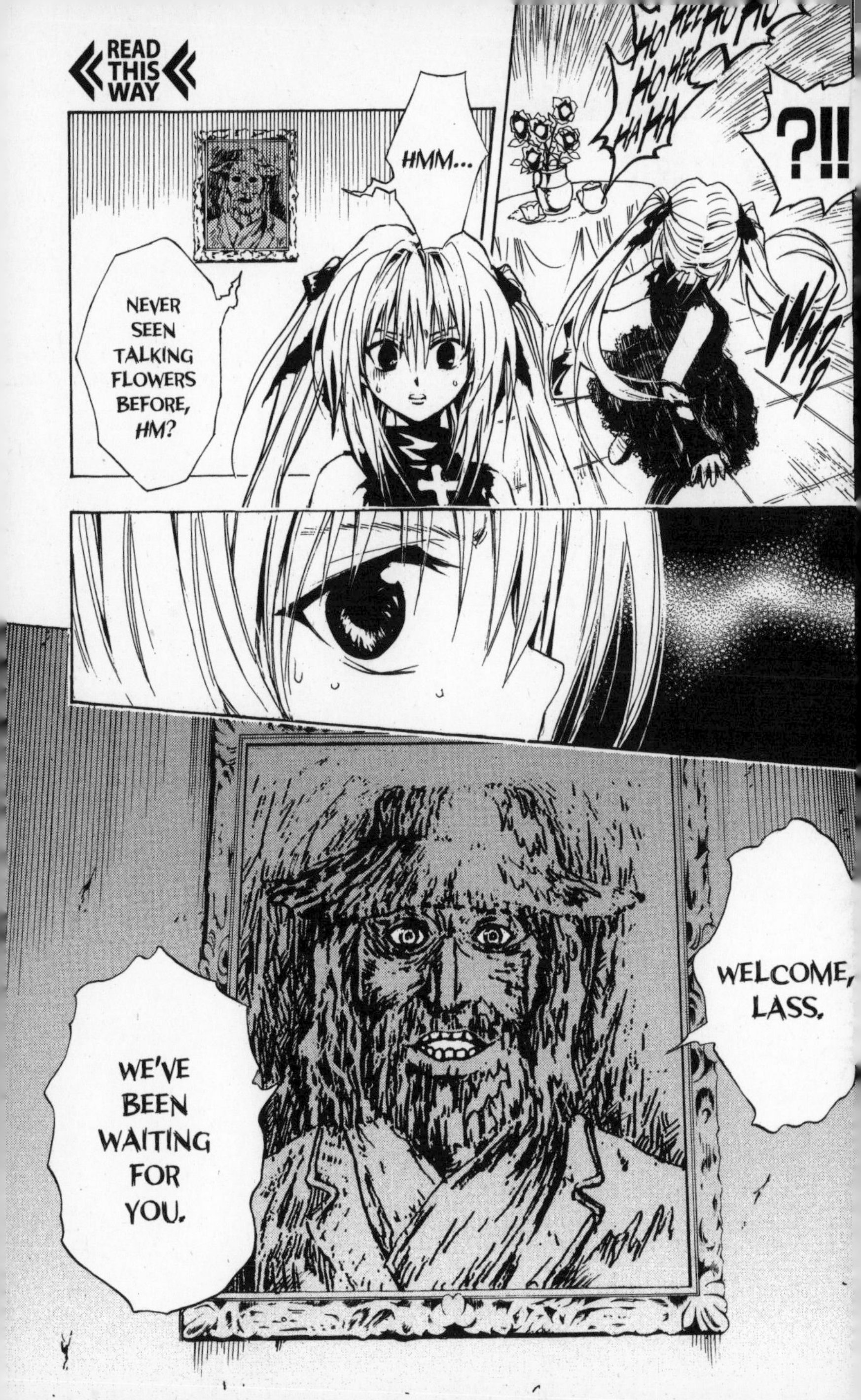
READ THIS WAY
HO HEE HO HO HO HEE HO HA HA
?!!
HMM...
NEVER SEEN TALKING FLOWERS BEFORE, HM?
WELCOME, LASS.
WE'VE BEEN WAITING FOR YOU.

SKETCHES: NUMBER 1

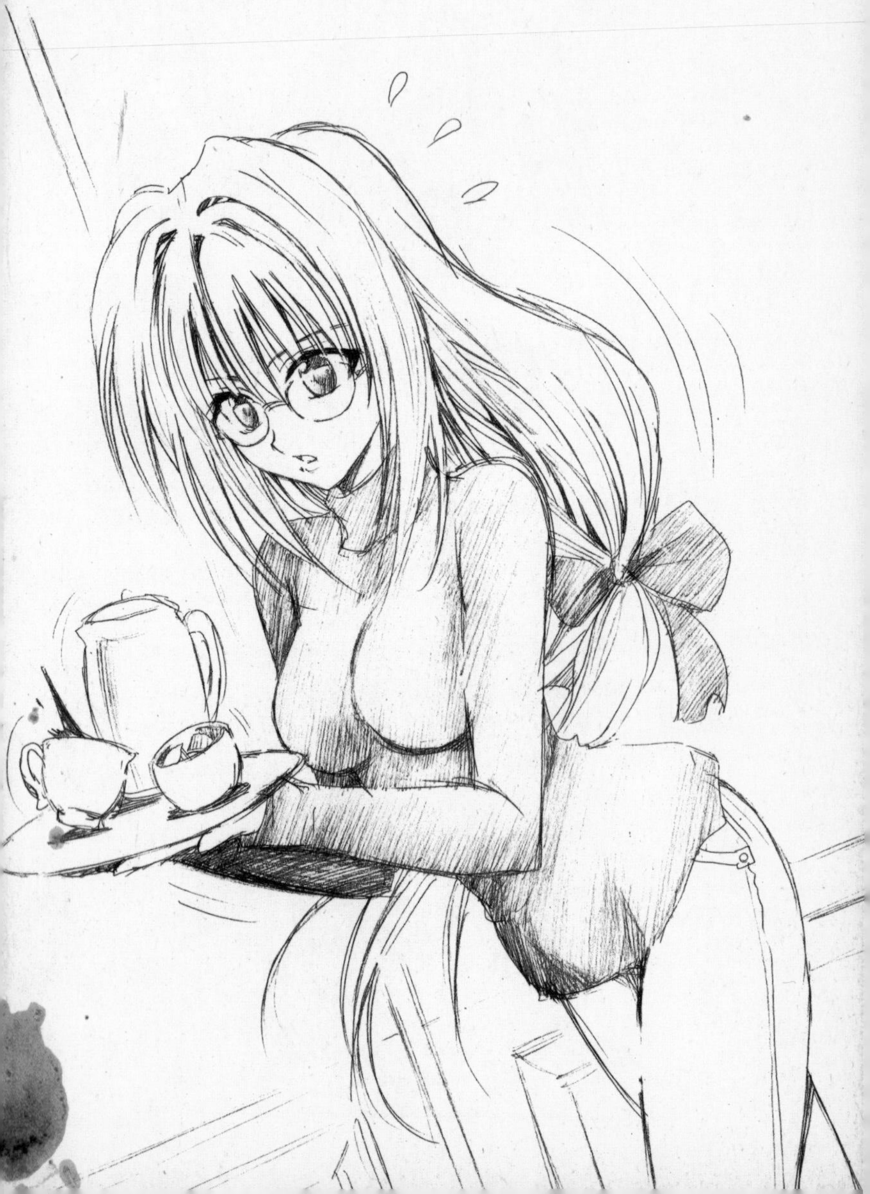

Chapter 160: Room of Fear

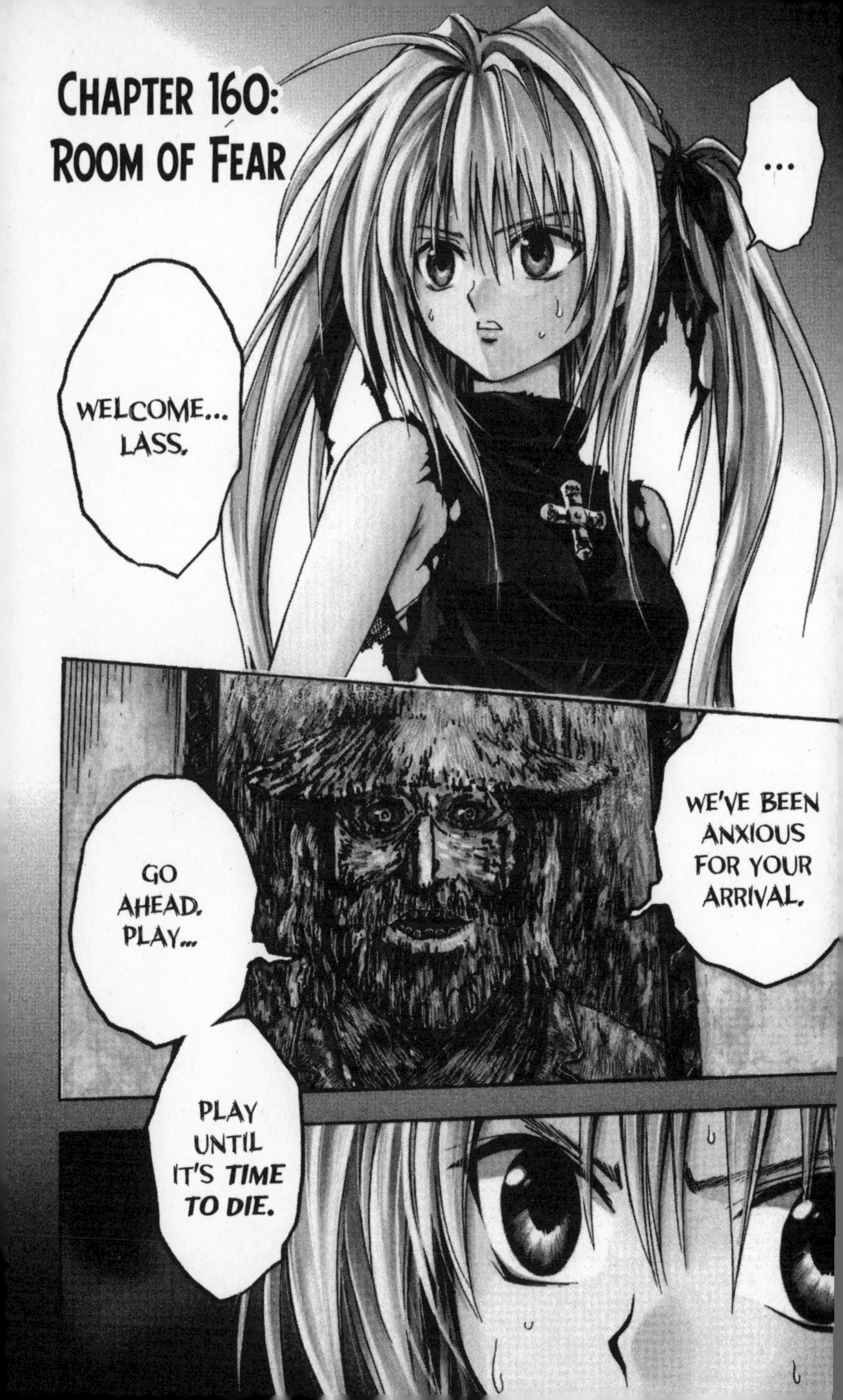
...
WELCOME... LASS.
WE'VE BEEN ANXIOUS FOR YOUR ARRIVAL.
GO AHEAD. PLAY...
PLAY UNTIL IT'S *TIME TO DIE.*

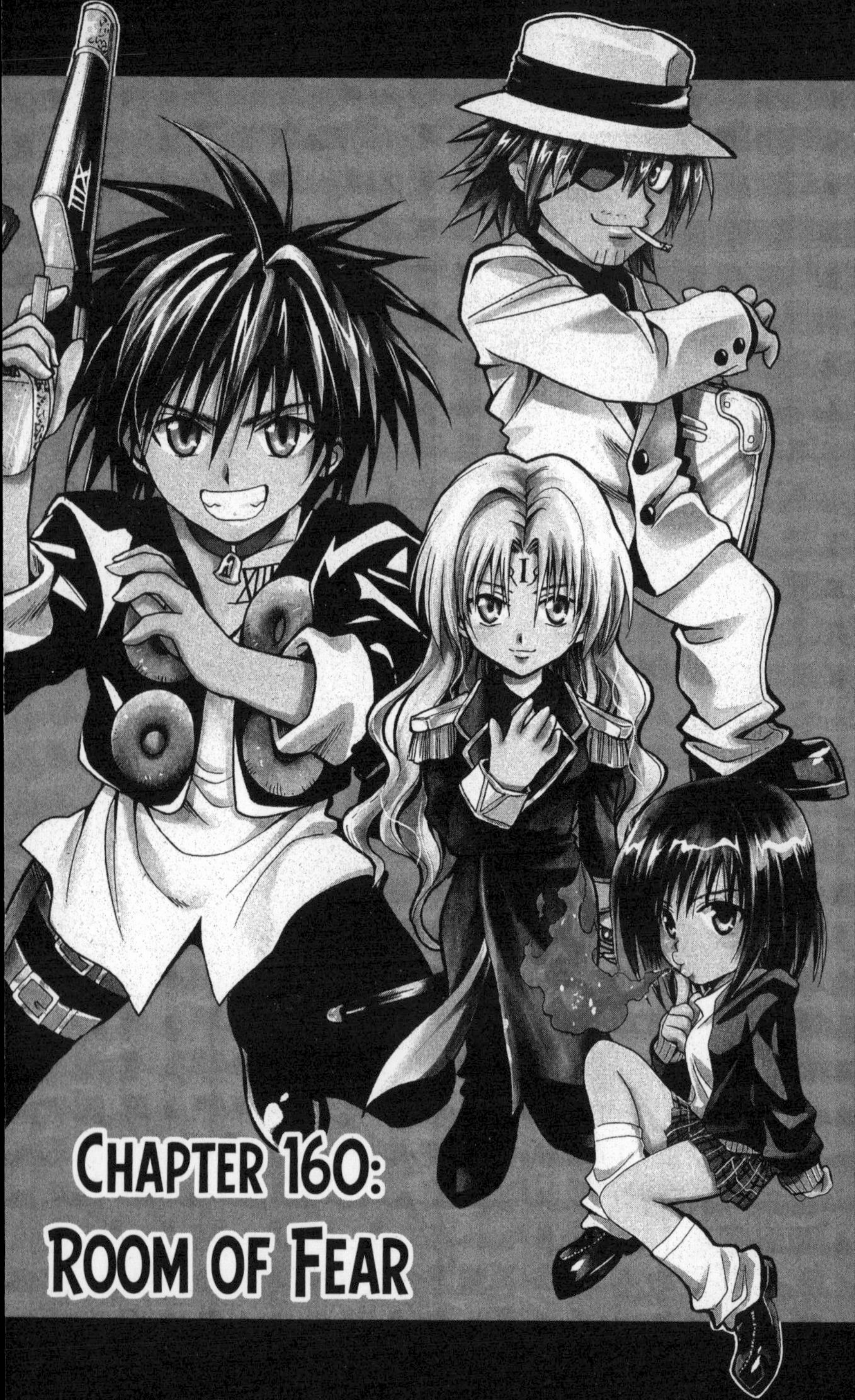

Chapter 160: Room of Fear

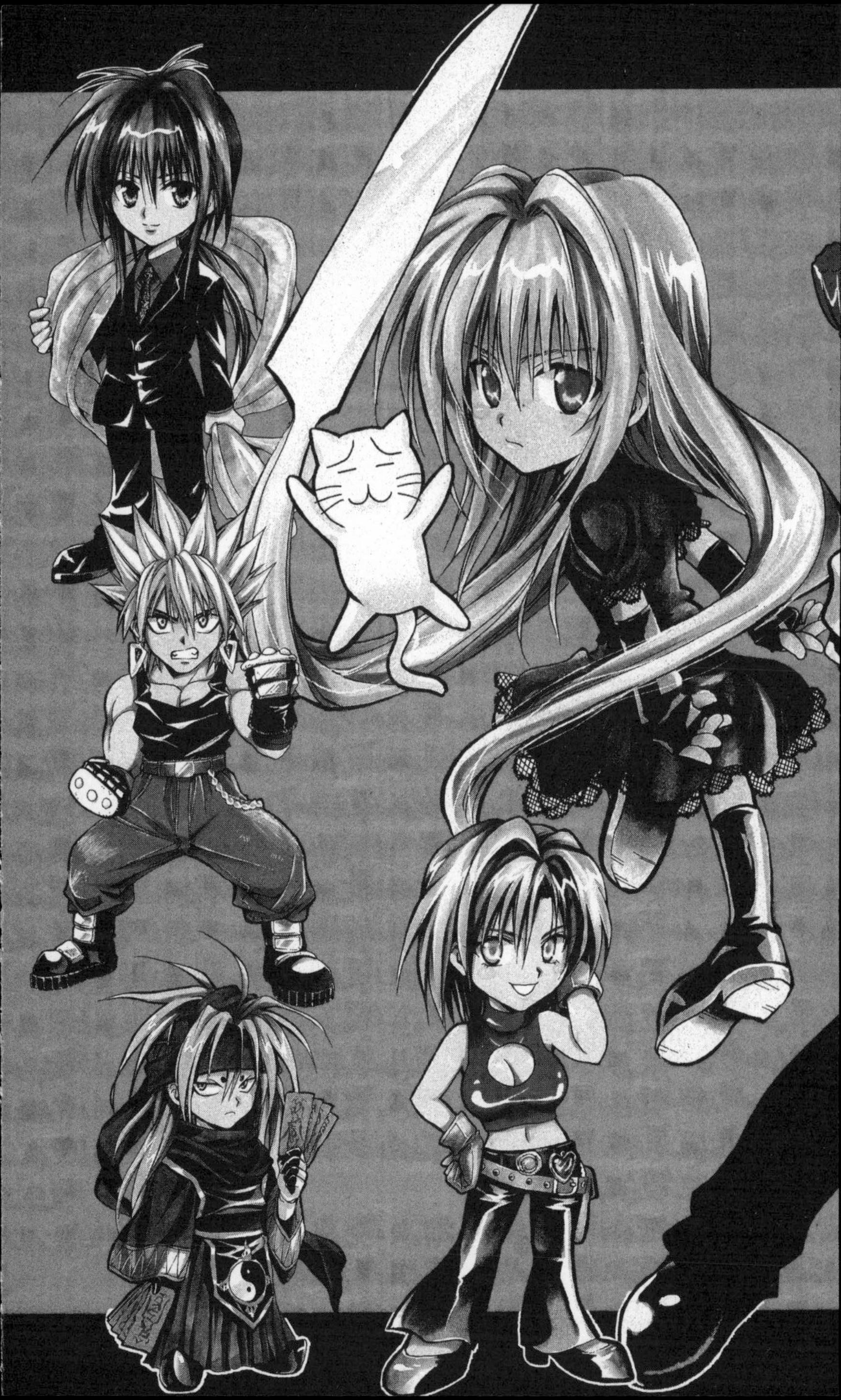

ブラック・キャット

BLACK CAT

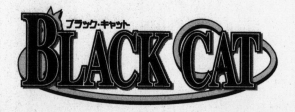

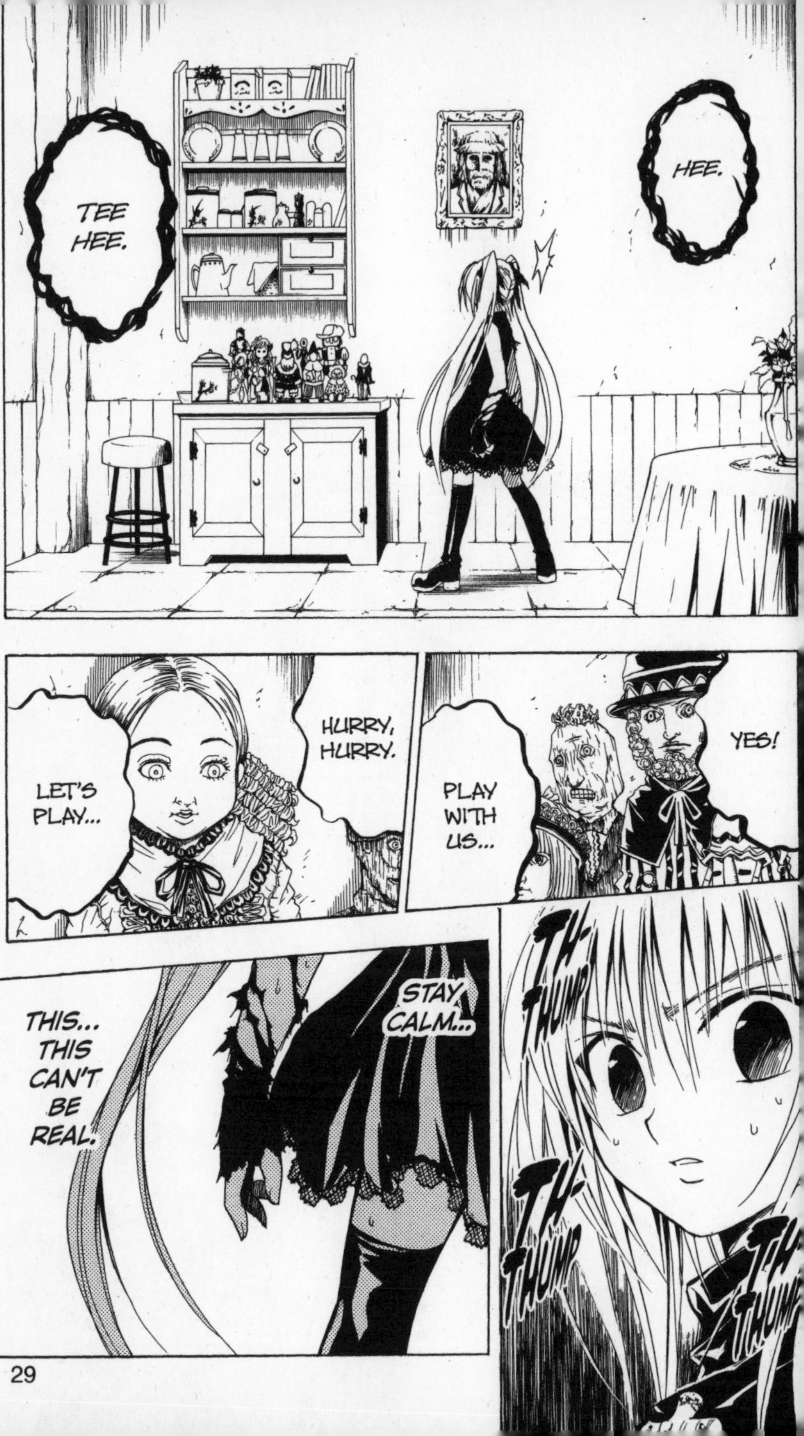
HEE.
TEE HEE.
YES!
PLAY WITH US...
HURRY, HURRY.
LET'S PLAY...
TH-THUMP
TH-THUMP
TH-THUMP
STAY CALM...
THIS... THIS CAN'T BE REAL.

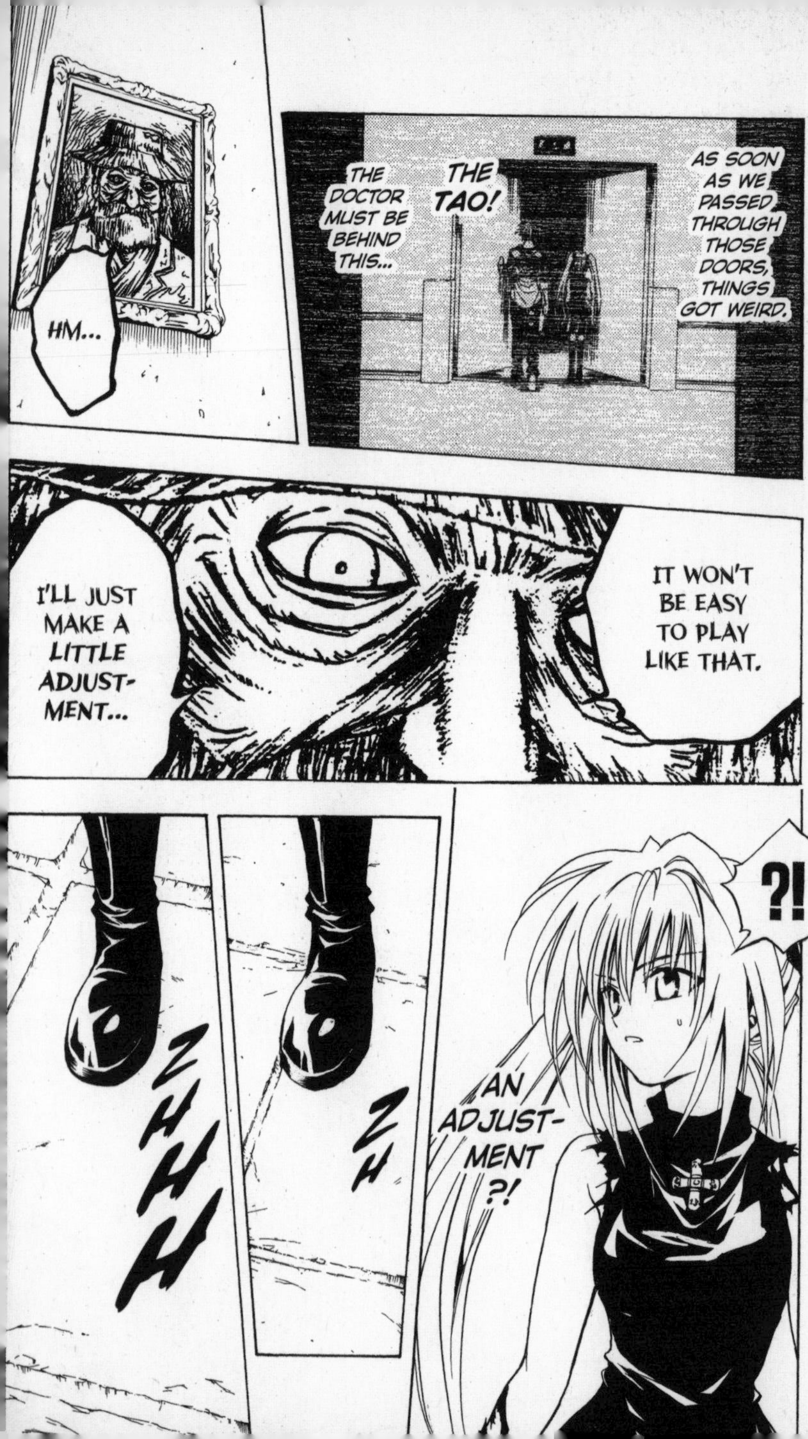
AS SOON AS WE PASSED THROUGH THOSE DOORS, THINGS GOT WEIRD.
THE TAO!
THE DOCTOR MUST BE BEHIND THIS...
HM...
IT WON'T BE EASY TO PLAY LIKE THAT.
I'LL JUST MAKE A LITTLE ADJUSTMENT...
?!
AN ADJUSTMENT?!

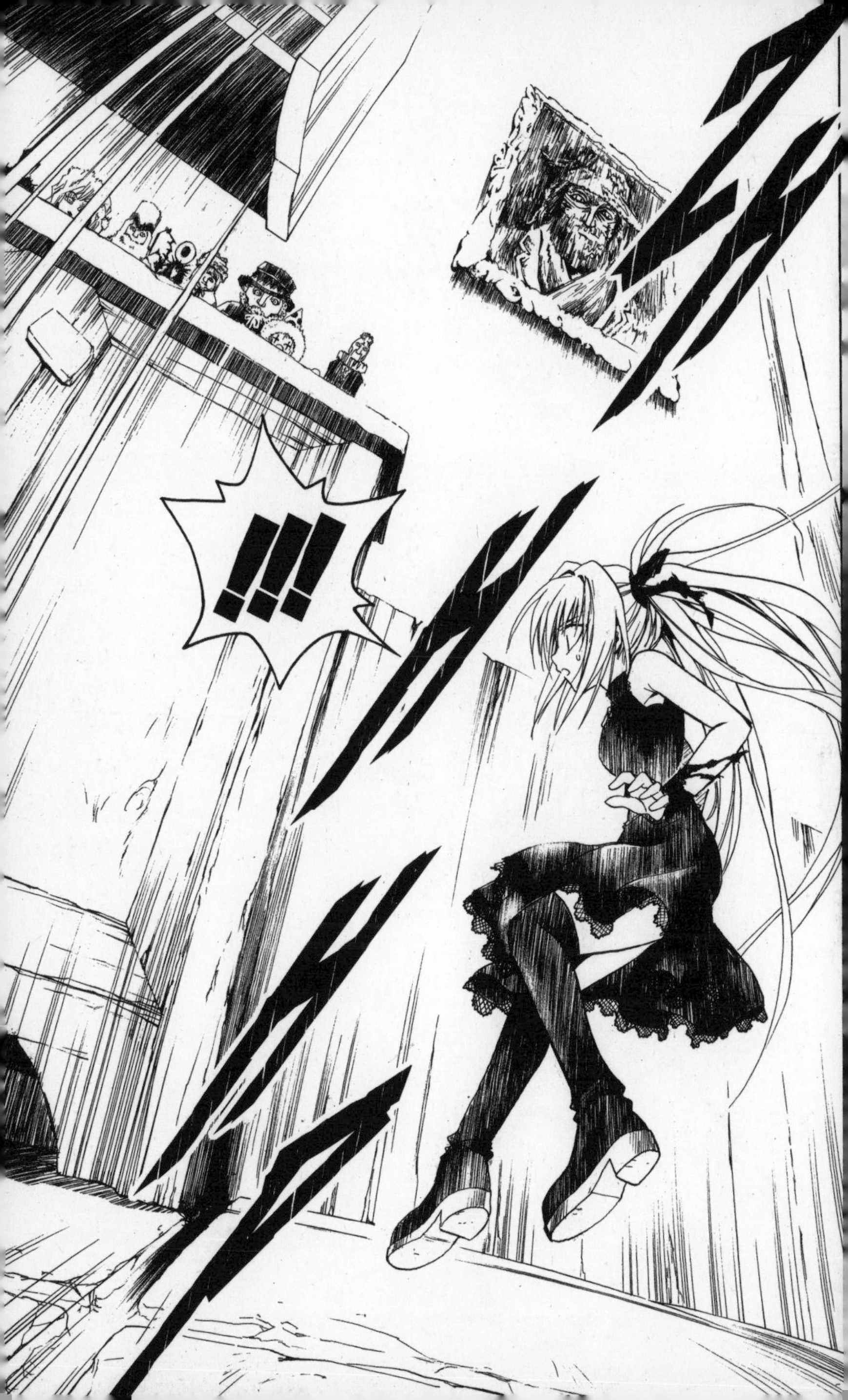
!!!

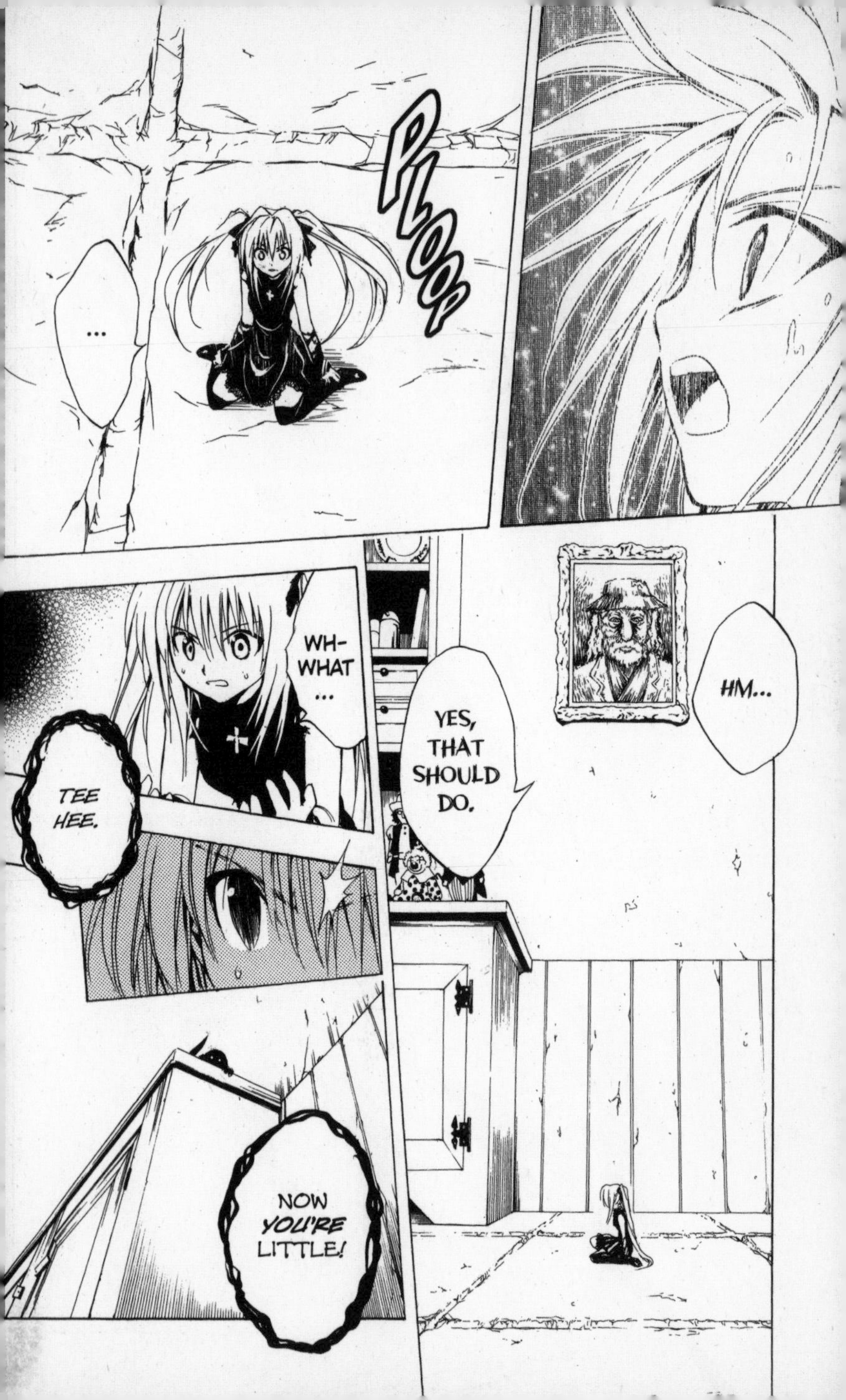
PLOOP
...
HM...
YES, THAT SHOULD DO.
WH-WHAT...
TEE HEE.
NOW *YOU'RE* LITTLE!

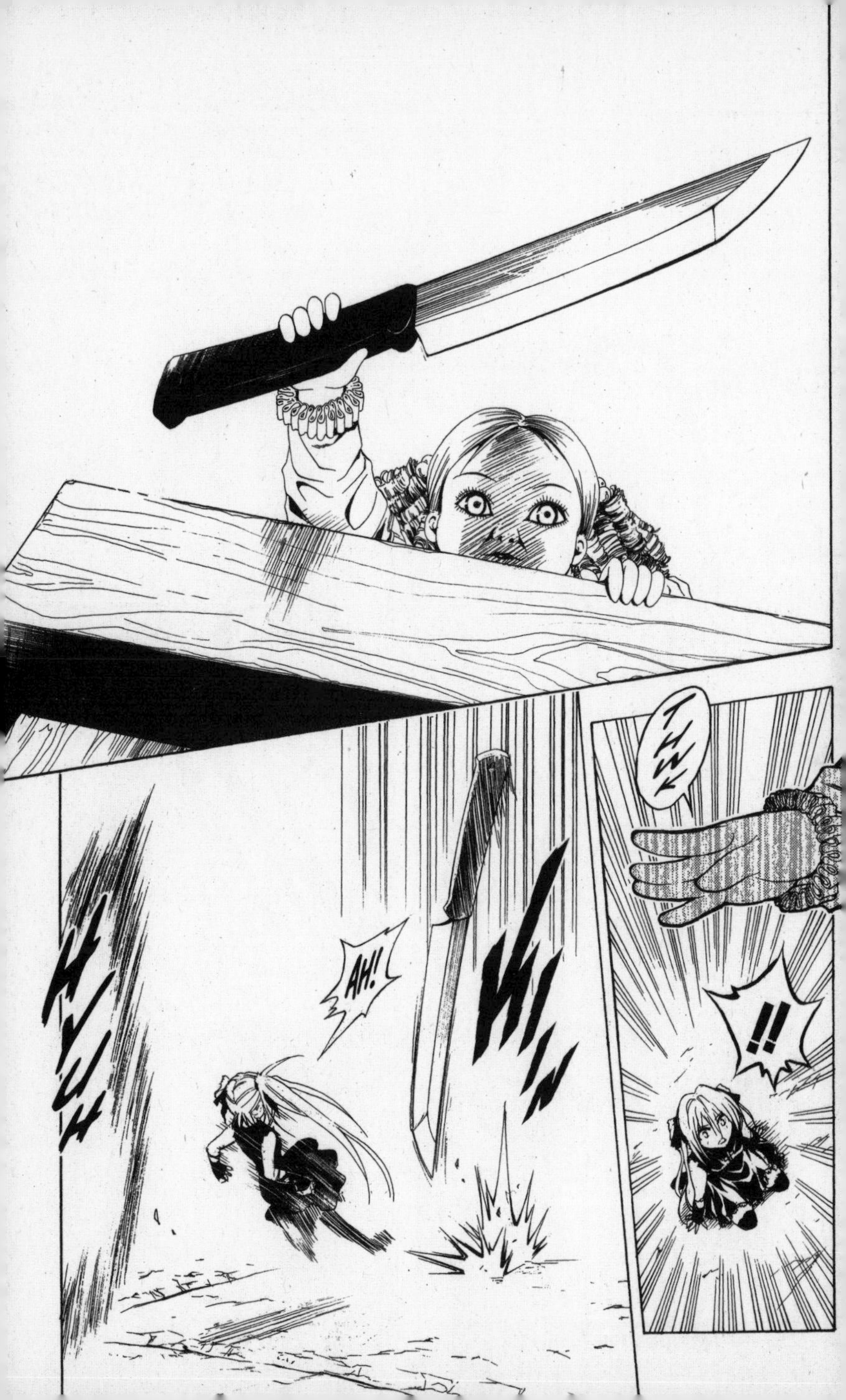
THWK
!!
AH!

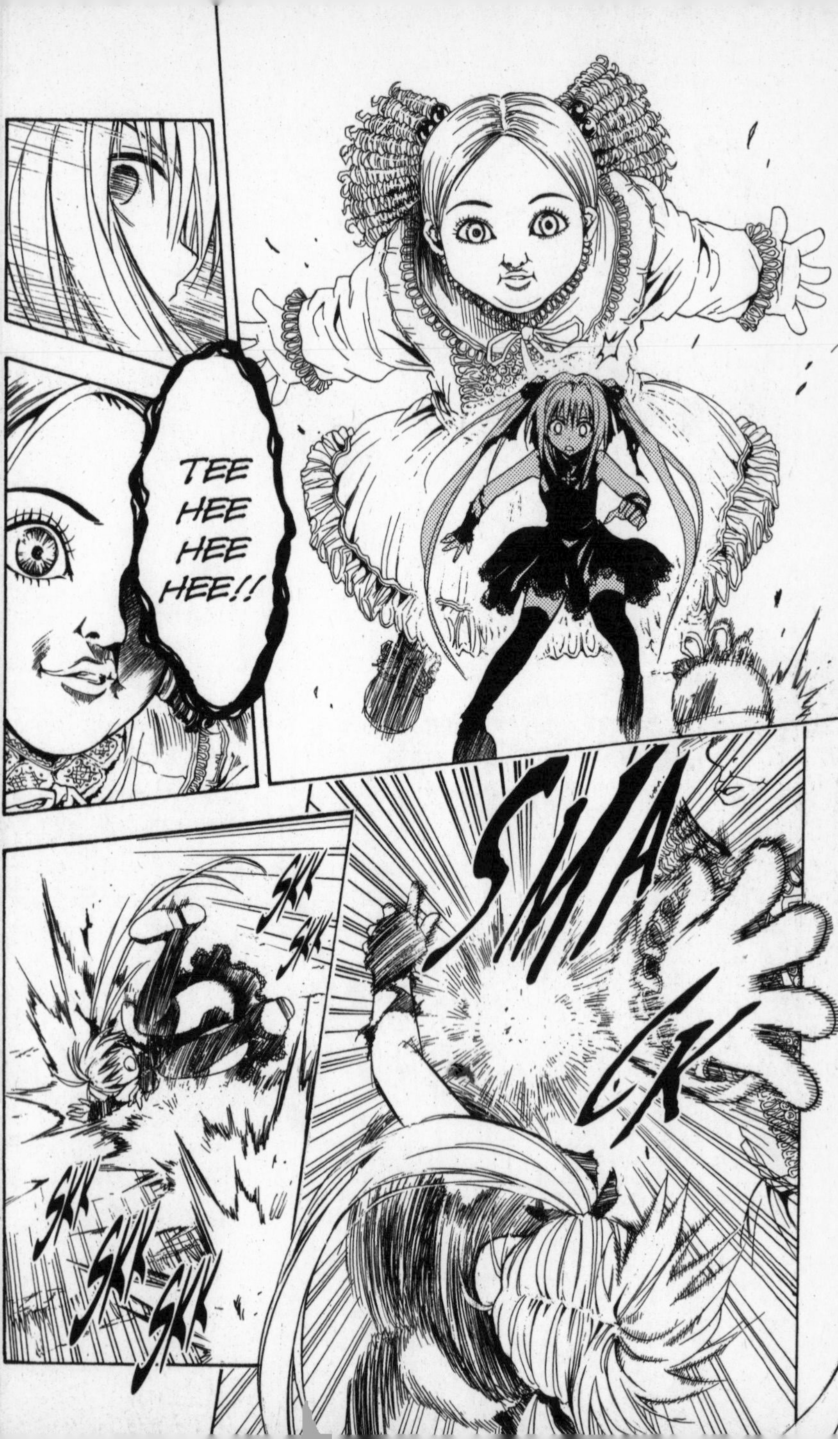
TEE HEE HEE HEE!!
SMACK
SHK SHK
SHK SHK SHK

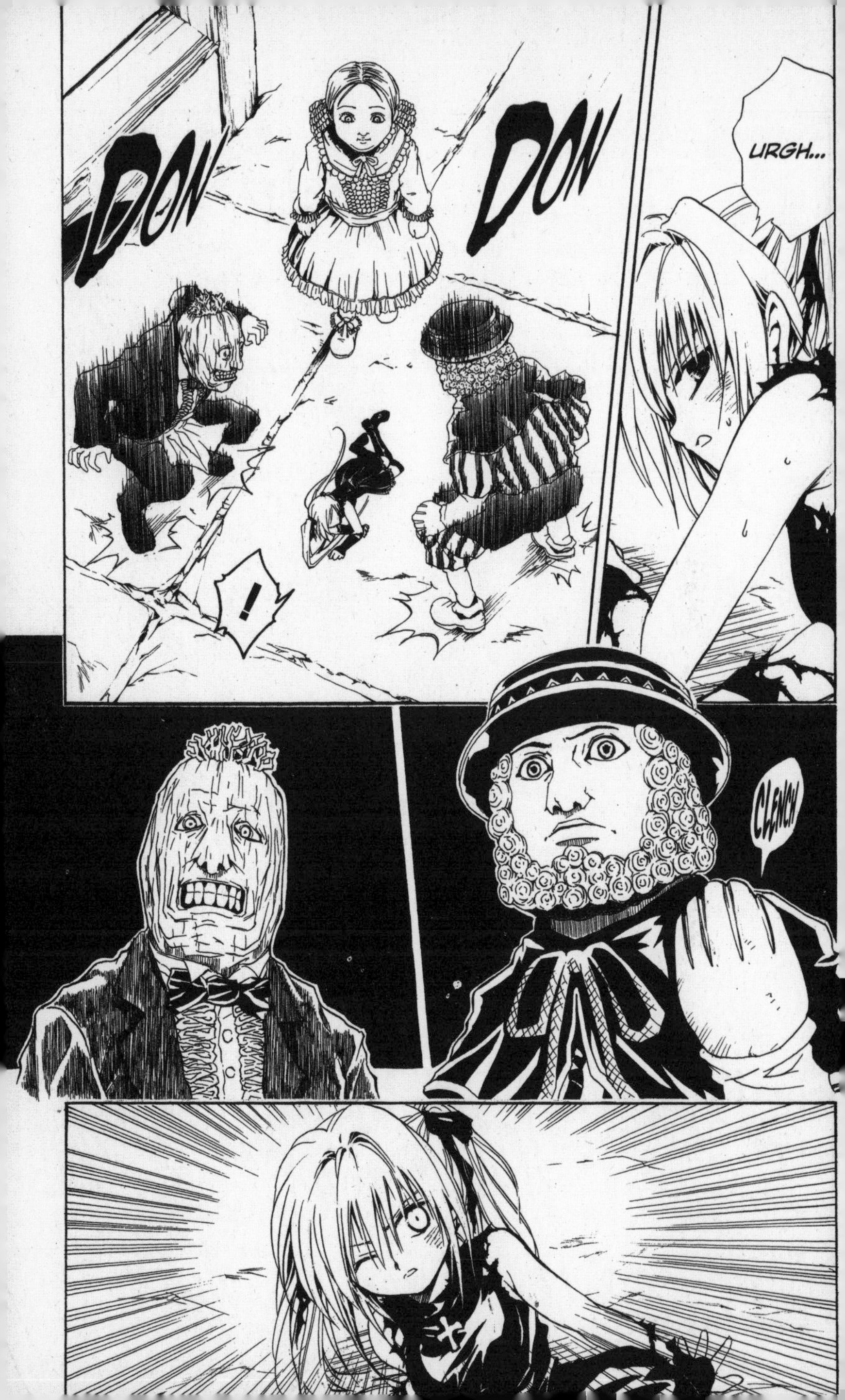
URGH...
DON
DON
!
CLENCH

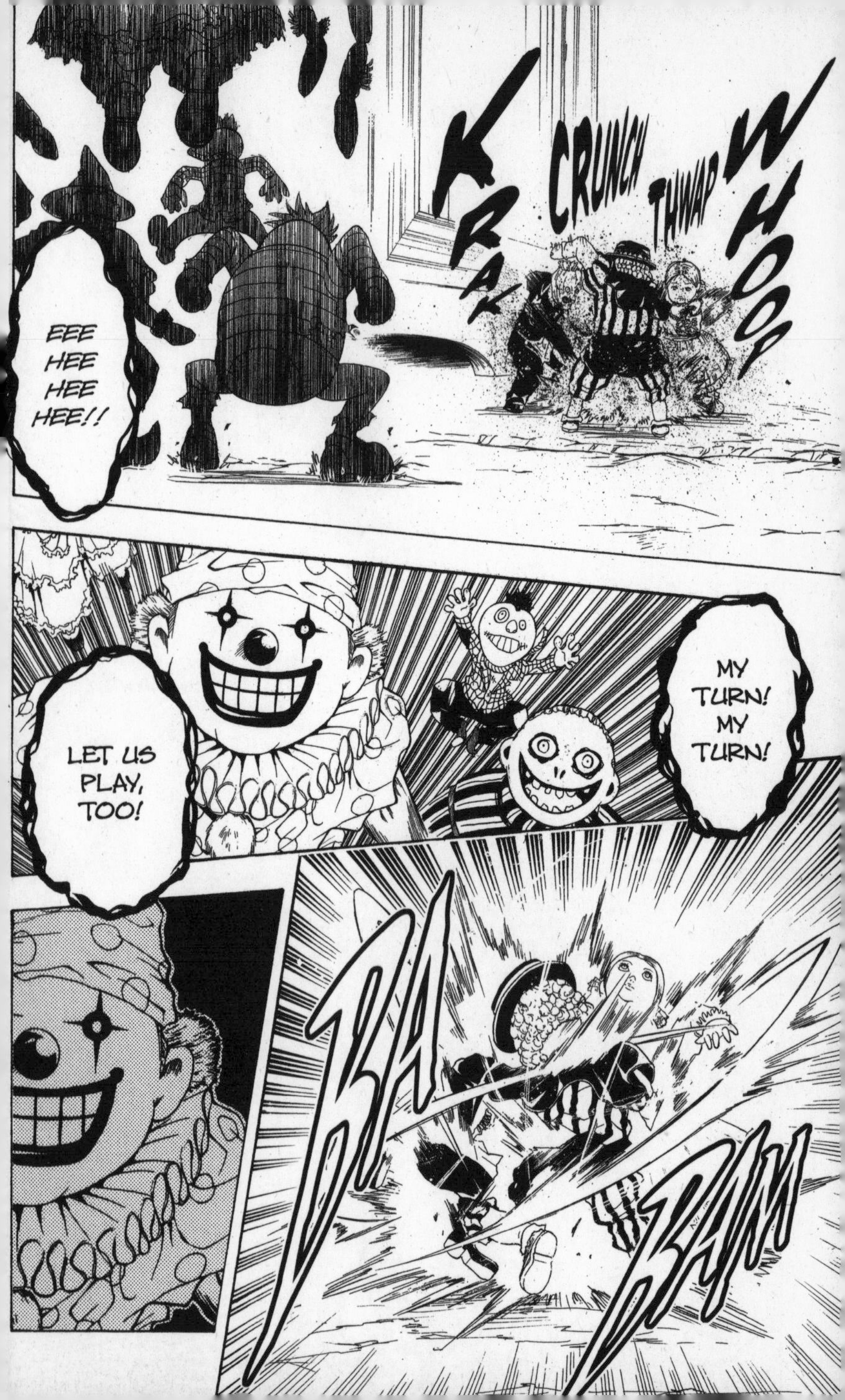
WHOOM
THWAP
CRUNCH
KRAK
EEE HEE HEE HEE!!
MY TURN! MY TURN!
LET US PLAY, TOO!

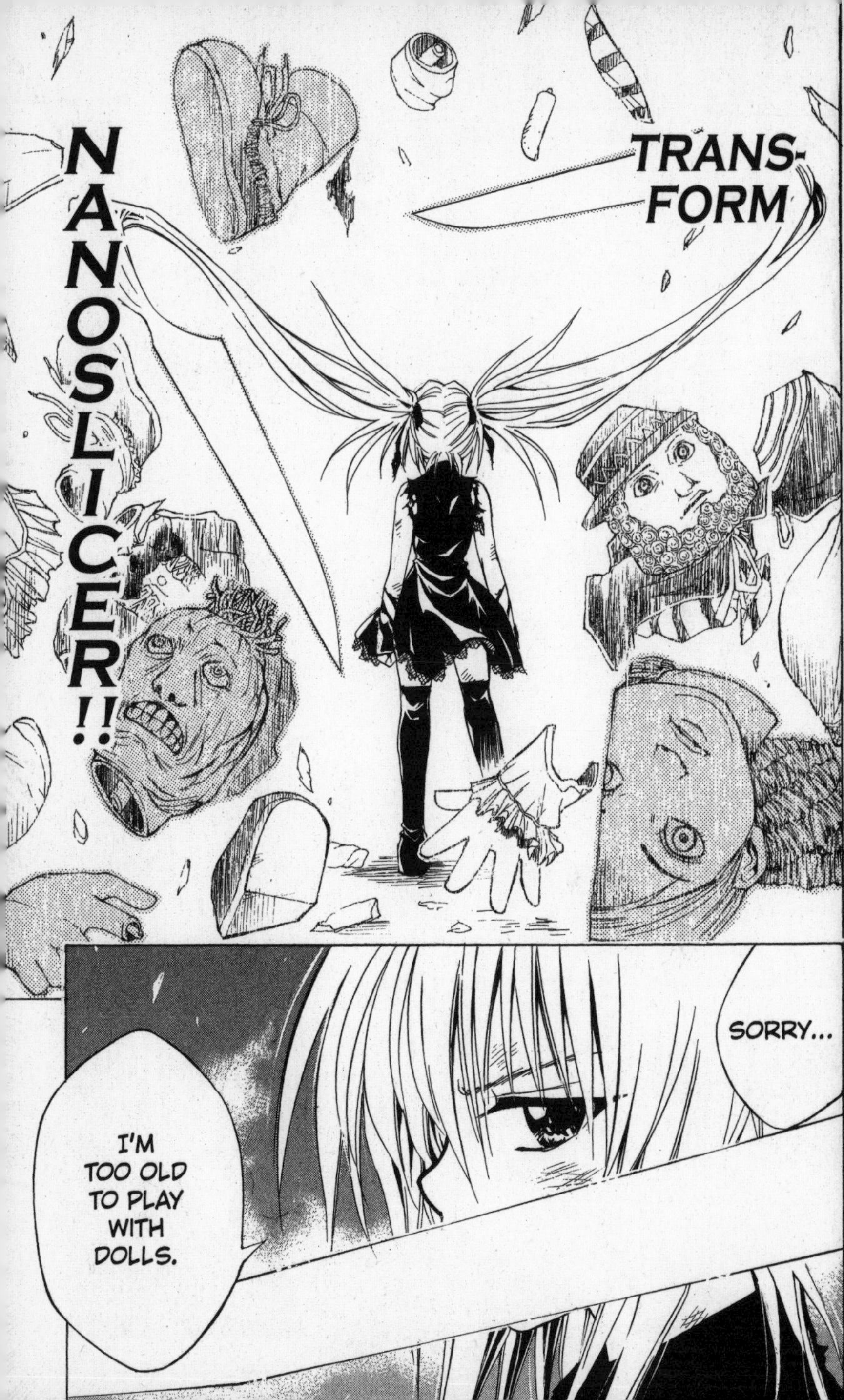
TRANS-FORM
NANOSLICER!!
SORRY...
I'M TOO OLD TO PLAY WITH DOLLS.

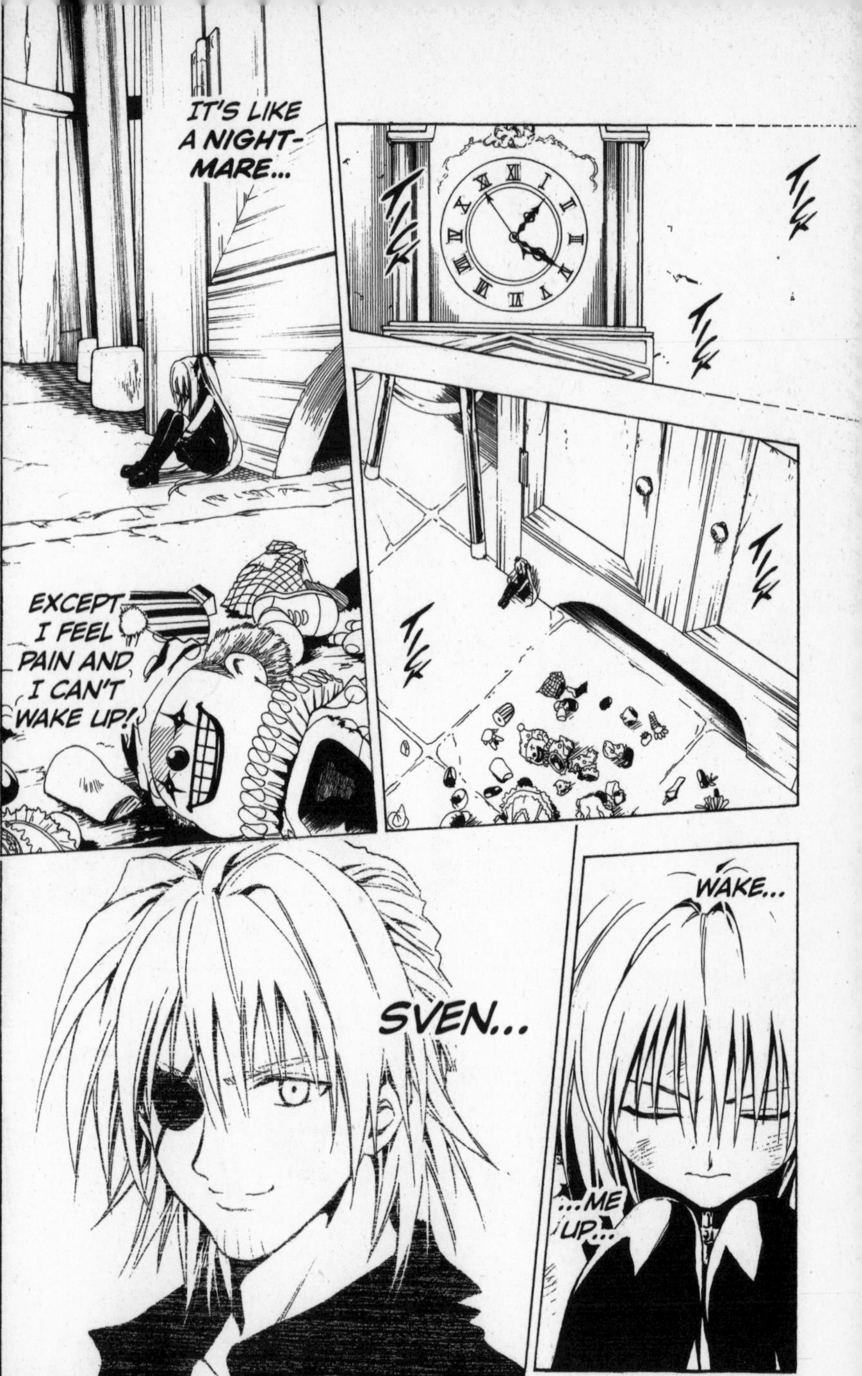
TICK
TICK
TICK
TICK
TICK
IT'S LIKE A NIGHTMARE...
EXCEPT I FEEL PAIN AND I CAN'T WAKE UP!
WAKE...
...ME UP...
SVEN...

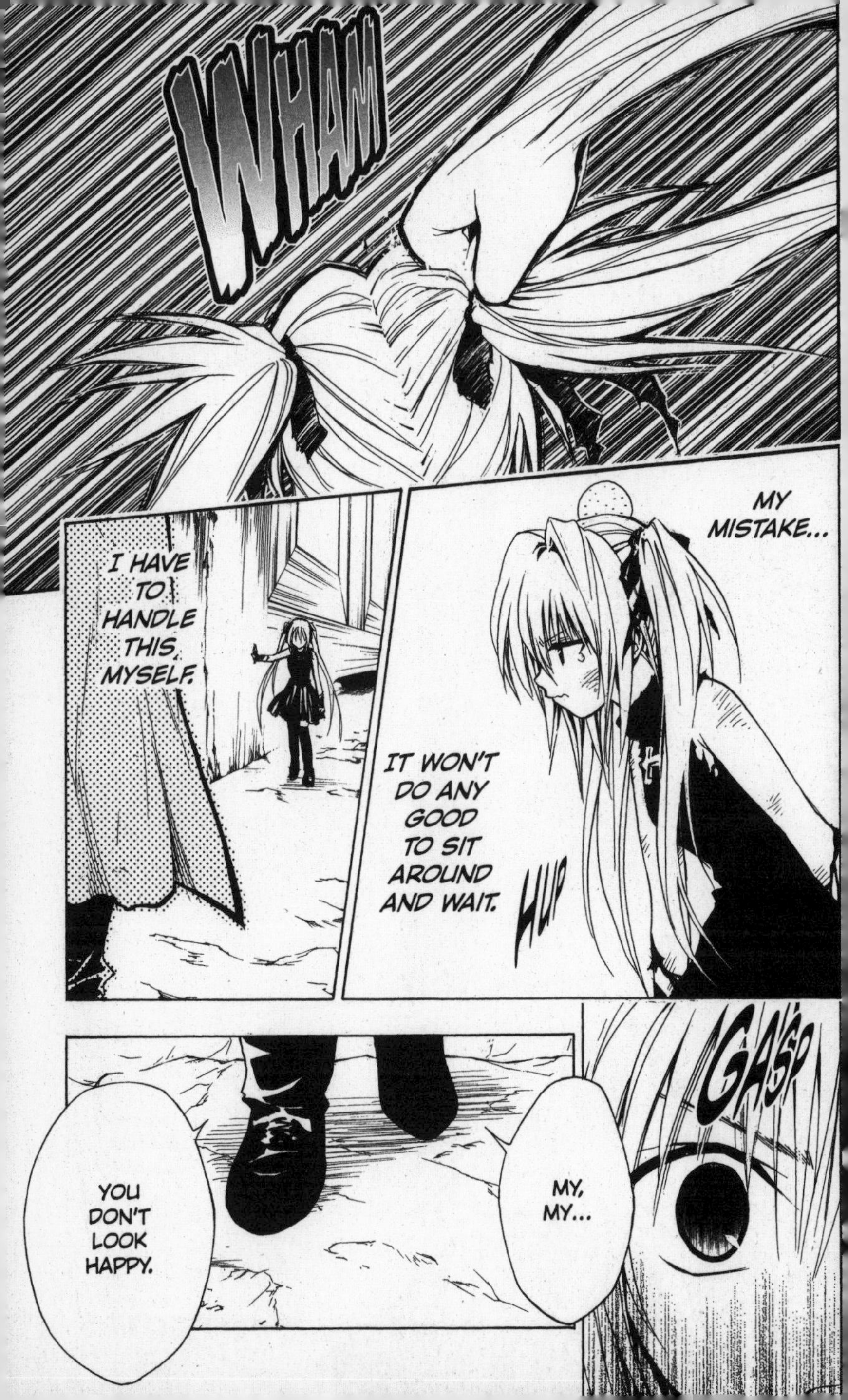
WHAM
MY MISTAKE...
IT WON'T DO ANY GOOD TO SIT AROUND AND WAIT.
HUP
I HAVE TO HANDLE THIS MYSELF.
GASP
MY, MY...
YOU DON'T LOOK HAPPY.

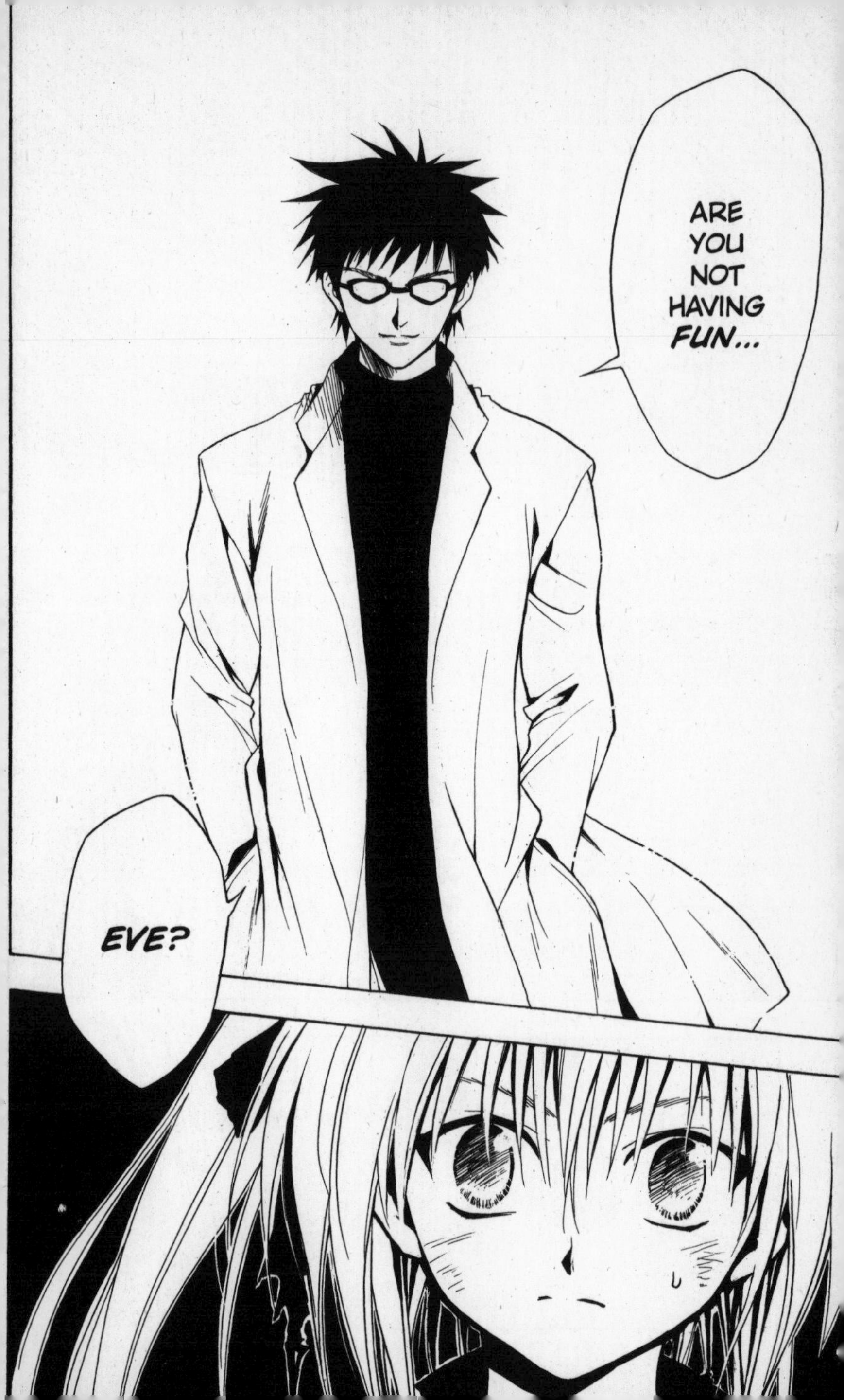
ARE YOU NOT HAVING FUN...
EVE?

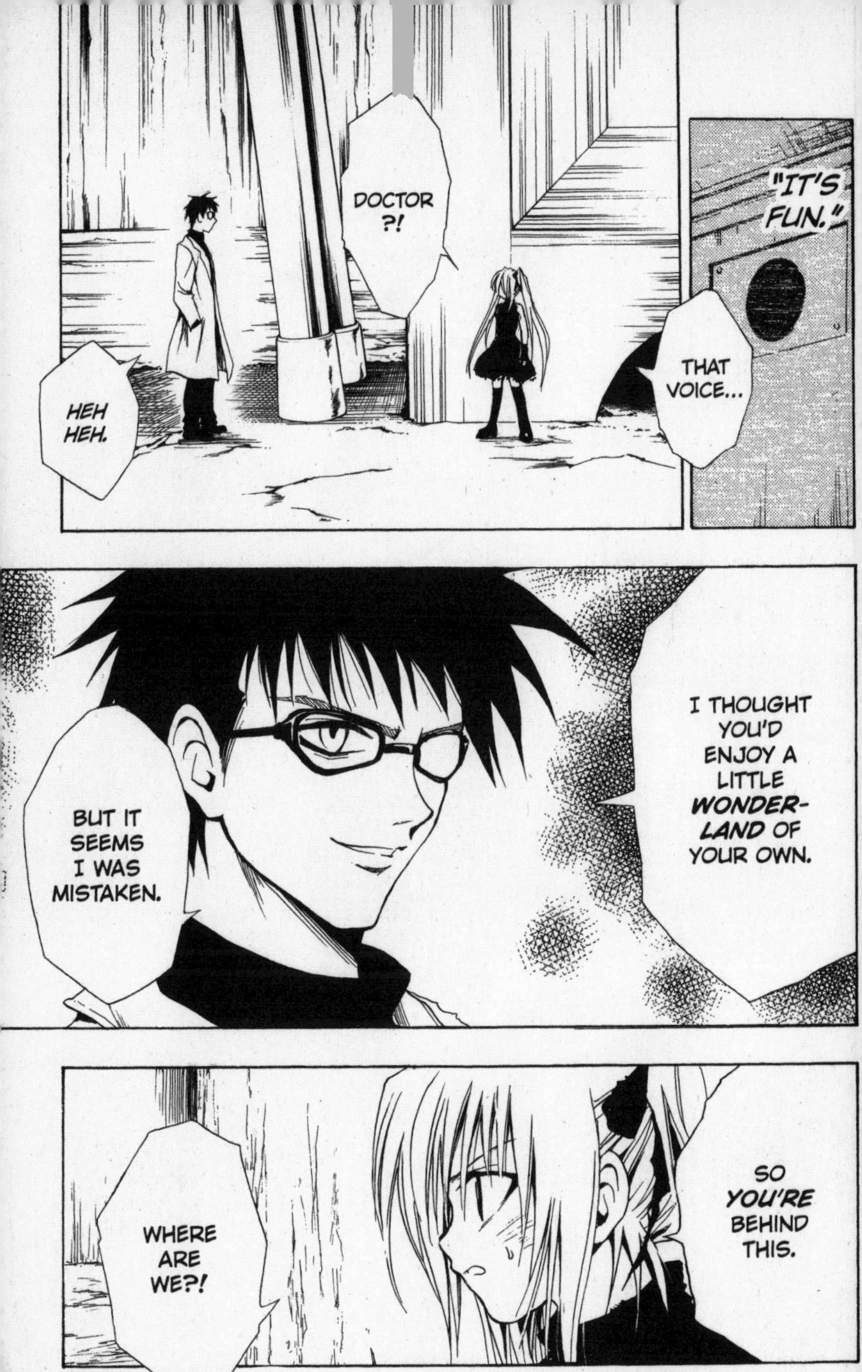
"IT'S FUN."
THAT VOICE...
DOCTOR ?!
HEH HEH.
I THOUGHT YOU'D ENJOY A LITTLE *WONDERLAND* OF YOUR OWN.
BUT IT SEEMS I WAS MISTAKEN.
SO *YOU'RE* BEHIND THIS.
WHERE ARE WE?!

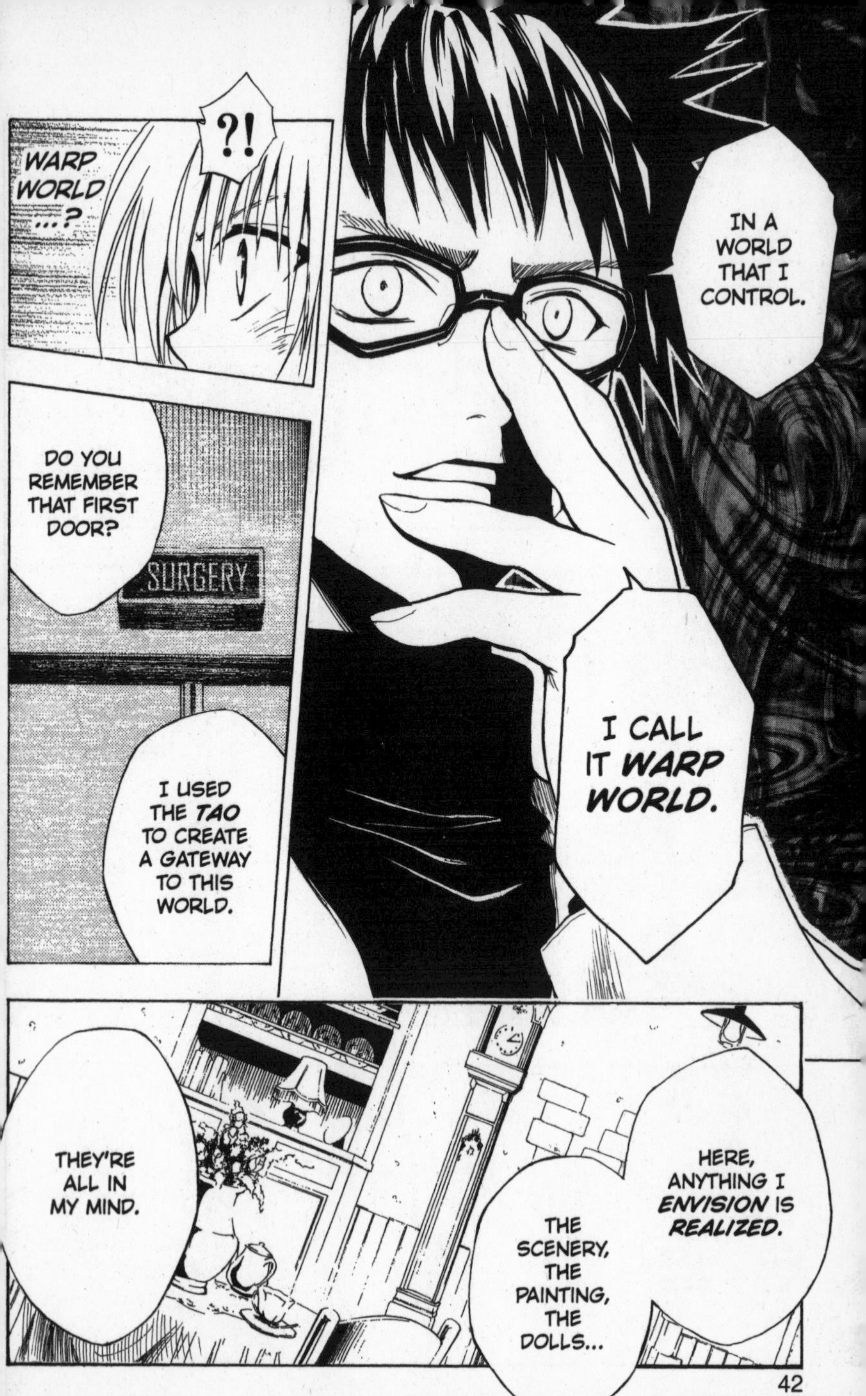
IN A WORLD THAT I CONTROL.
I CALL IT *WARP WORLD.*
?!
WARP WORLD ...?
DO YOU REMEMBER THAT FIRST DOOR?
SURGERY
I USED THE *TAO* TO CREATE A GATEWAY TO THIS WORLD.
HERE, ANYTHING I *ENVISION* IS *REALIZED.*
THE SCENERY, THE PAINTING, THE DOLLS...
THEY'RE ALL IN MY MIND.

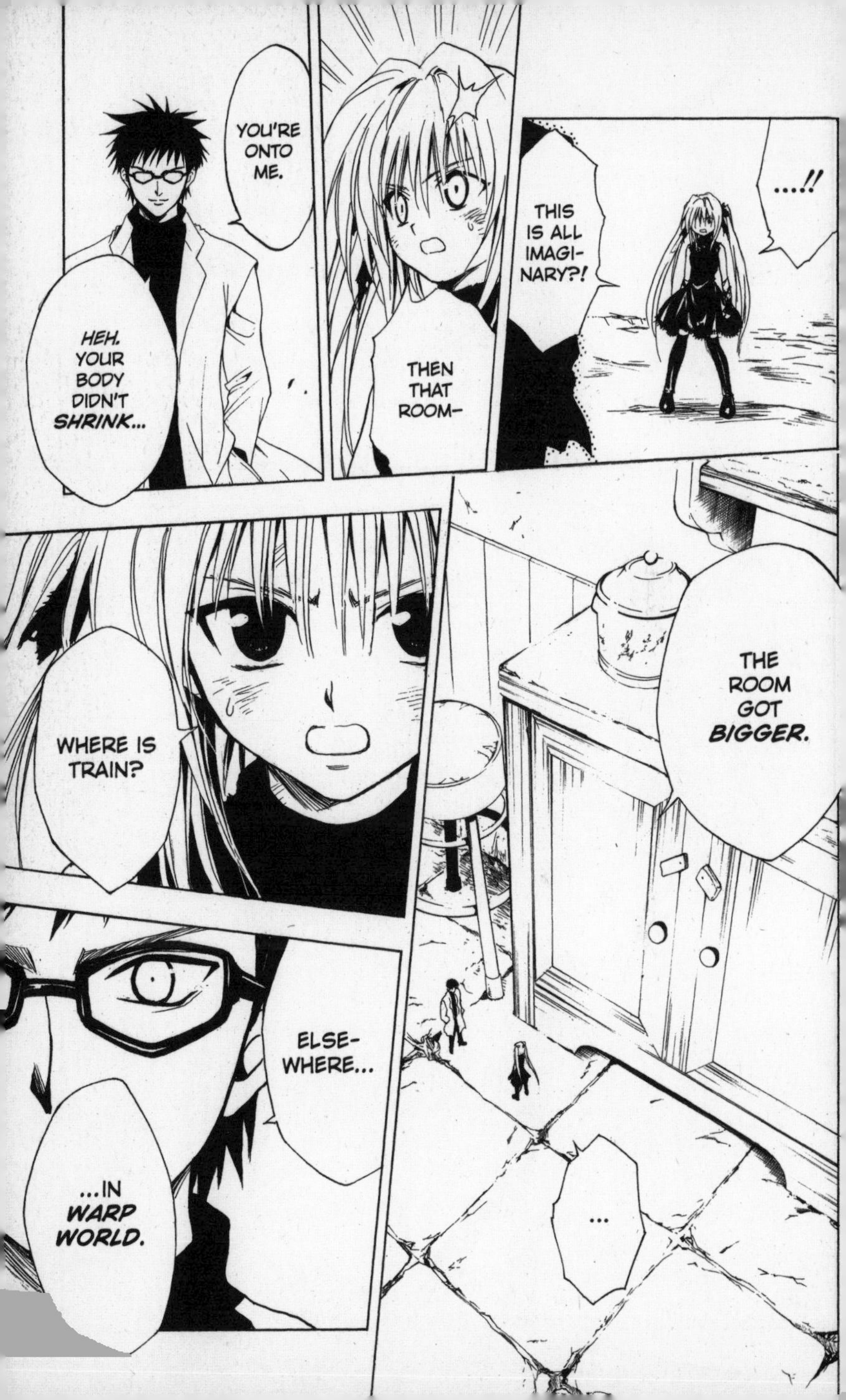
....!!
THIS IS ALL IMAGINARY?!
THEN THAT ROOM-
YOU'RE ONTO ME.
HEH. YOUR BODY DIDN'T *SHRINK*...
THE ROOM GOT *BIGGER*.
...
WHERE IS TRAIN?
ELSE-WHERE...
...IN *WARP WORLD*.

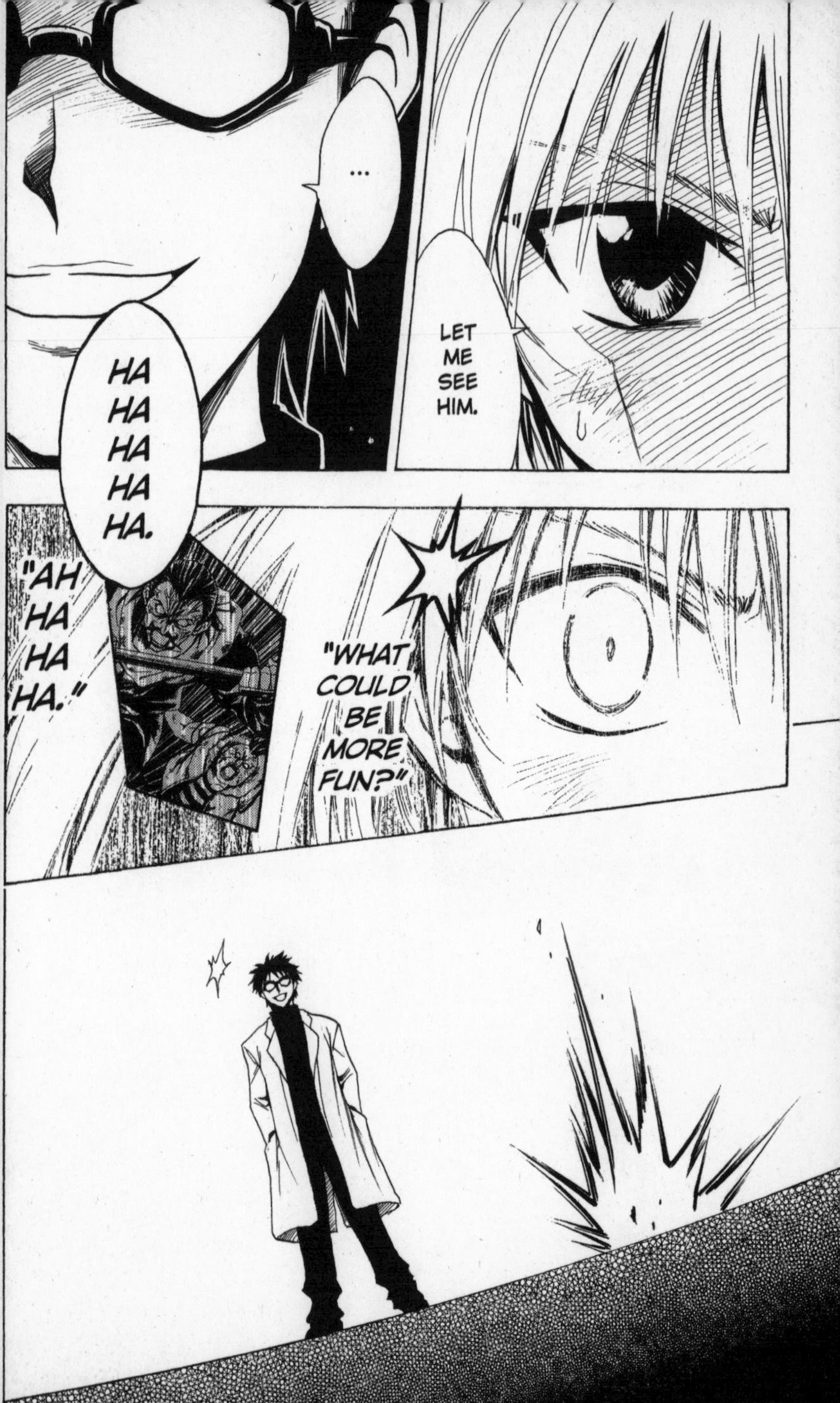
LET ME SEE HIM.
...
HA HA HA HA HA.
"WHAT COULD BE MORE FUN?"
"AH HA HA HA."

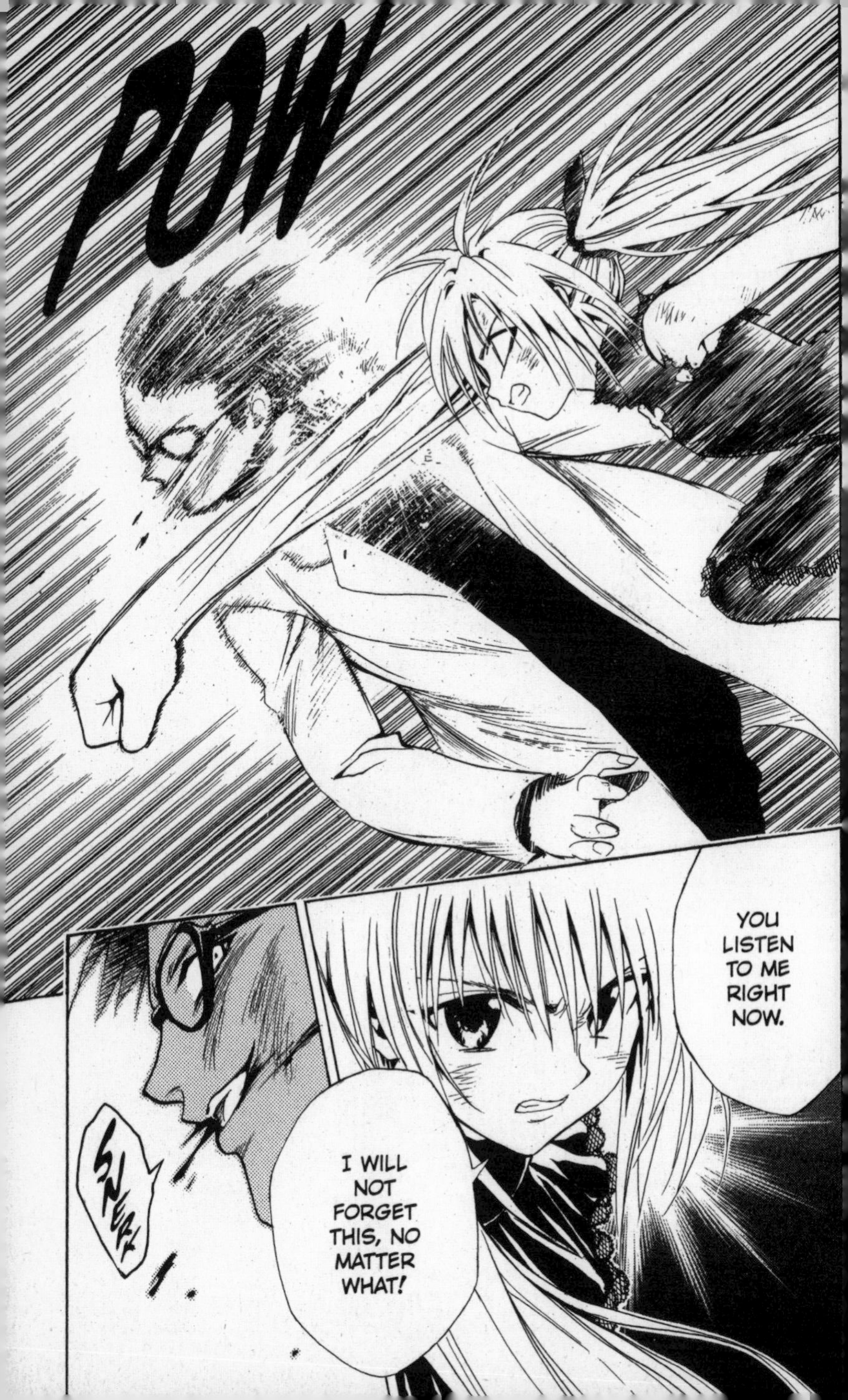
POW
YOU LISTEN TO ME RIGHT NOW.
I WILL NOT FORGET THIS, NO MATTER WHAT!
SNERK

OFFICE DIARY BY TAKASHI MORIMOTO

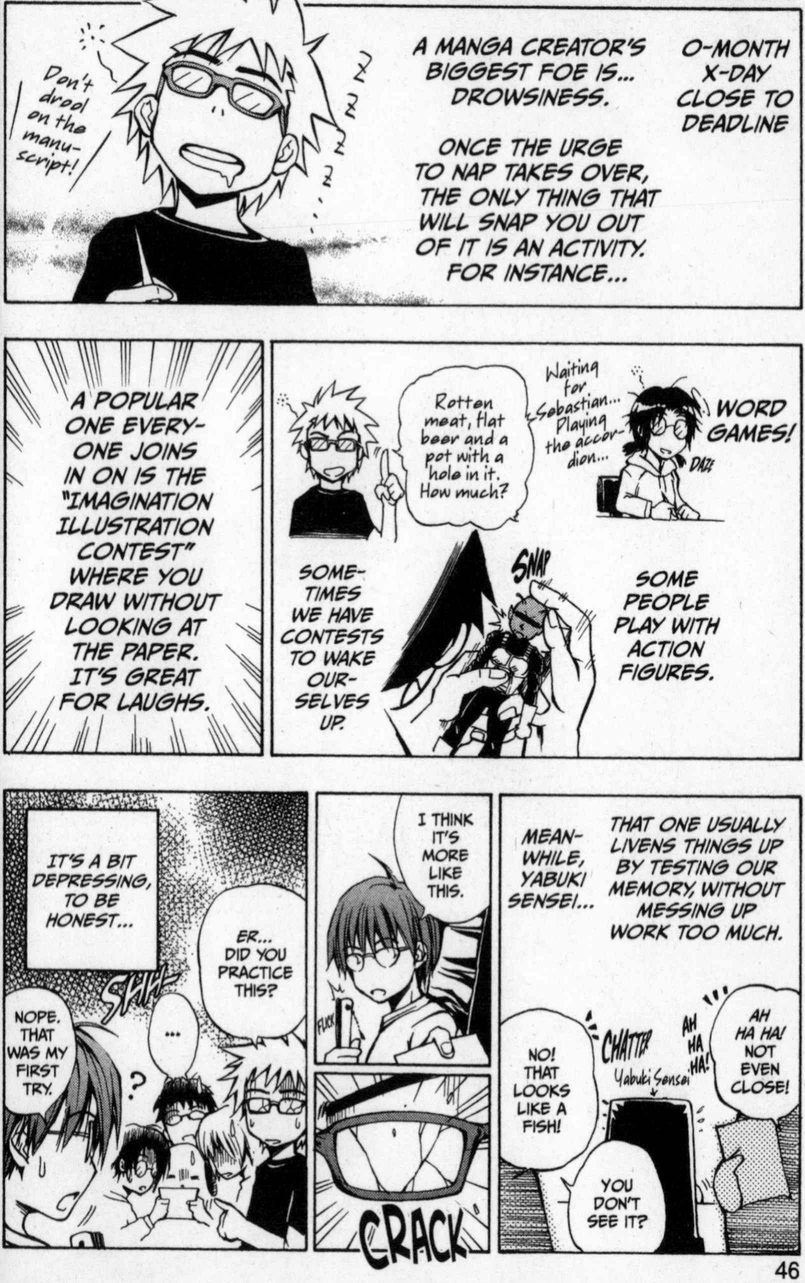
O-MONTH X-DAY CLOSE TO DEADLINE
A MANGA CREATOR'S BIGGEST FOE IS... DROWSINESS.
ONCE THE URGE TO NAP TAKES OVER, THE ONLY THING THAT WILL SNAP YOU OUT OF IT IS AN ACTIVITY. FOR INSTANCE...
Don't drool on the manuscript!
WORD GAMES!
Waiting for Sebastian... Playing the accordion...
Rotten meat, flat beer and a pot with a hole in it. How much?
SOME PEOPLE PLAY WITH ACTION FIGURES.
SNAP
SOMETIMES WE HAVE CONTESTS TO WAKE OURSELVES UP.
A POPULAR ONE EVERYONE JOINS IN ON IS THE "IMAGINATION ILLUSTRATION CONTEST" WHERE YOU DRAW WITHOUT LOOKING AT THE PAPER. IT'S GREAT FOR LAUGHS.
THAT ONE USUALLY LIVENS THINGS UP BY TESTING OUR MEMORY, WITHOUT MESSING UP WORK TOO MUCH.
MEANWHILE, YABUKI SENSEI...
AH HA HA! NOT EVEN CLOSE!
AH HA HA!
CHATTER
Yabuki Sensei
NO! THAT LOOKS LIKE A FISH!
YOU DON'T SEE IT?
I THINK IT'S MORE LIKE THIS.
FLICK
CRACK
IT'S A BIT DEPRESSING, TO BE HONEST...
ER... DID YOU PRACTICE THIS?
...
NOPE. THAT WAS MY FIRST TRY.
?

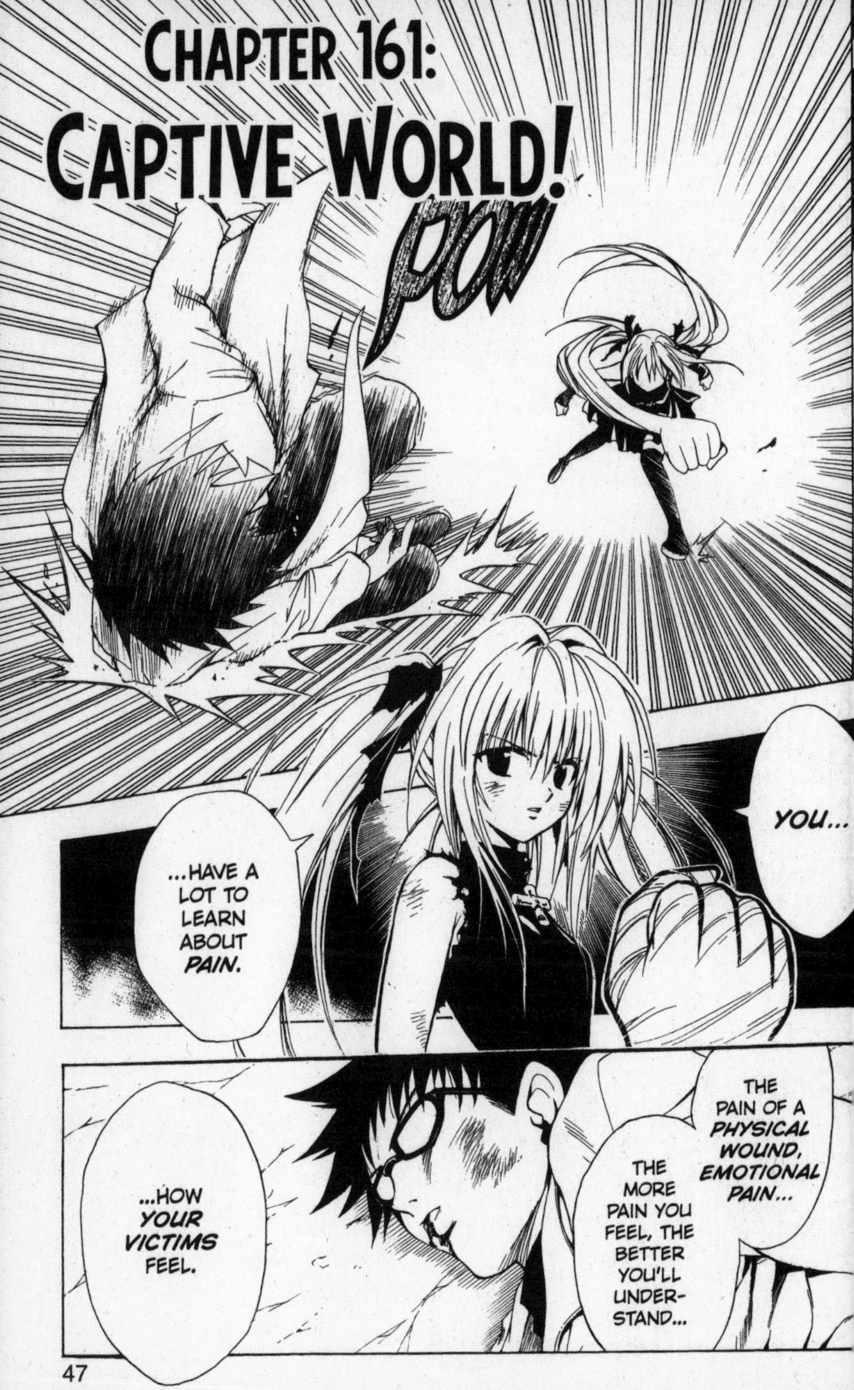
Chapter 161:
Captive World!
POW
YOU...
...HAVE A LOT TO LEARN ABOUT PAIN.
THE PAIN OF A PHYSICAL WOUND, EMOTIONAL PAIN...
THE MORE PAIN YOU FEEL, THE BETTER YOU'LL UNDER-STAND...
...HOW YOUR VICTIMS FEEL.

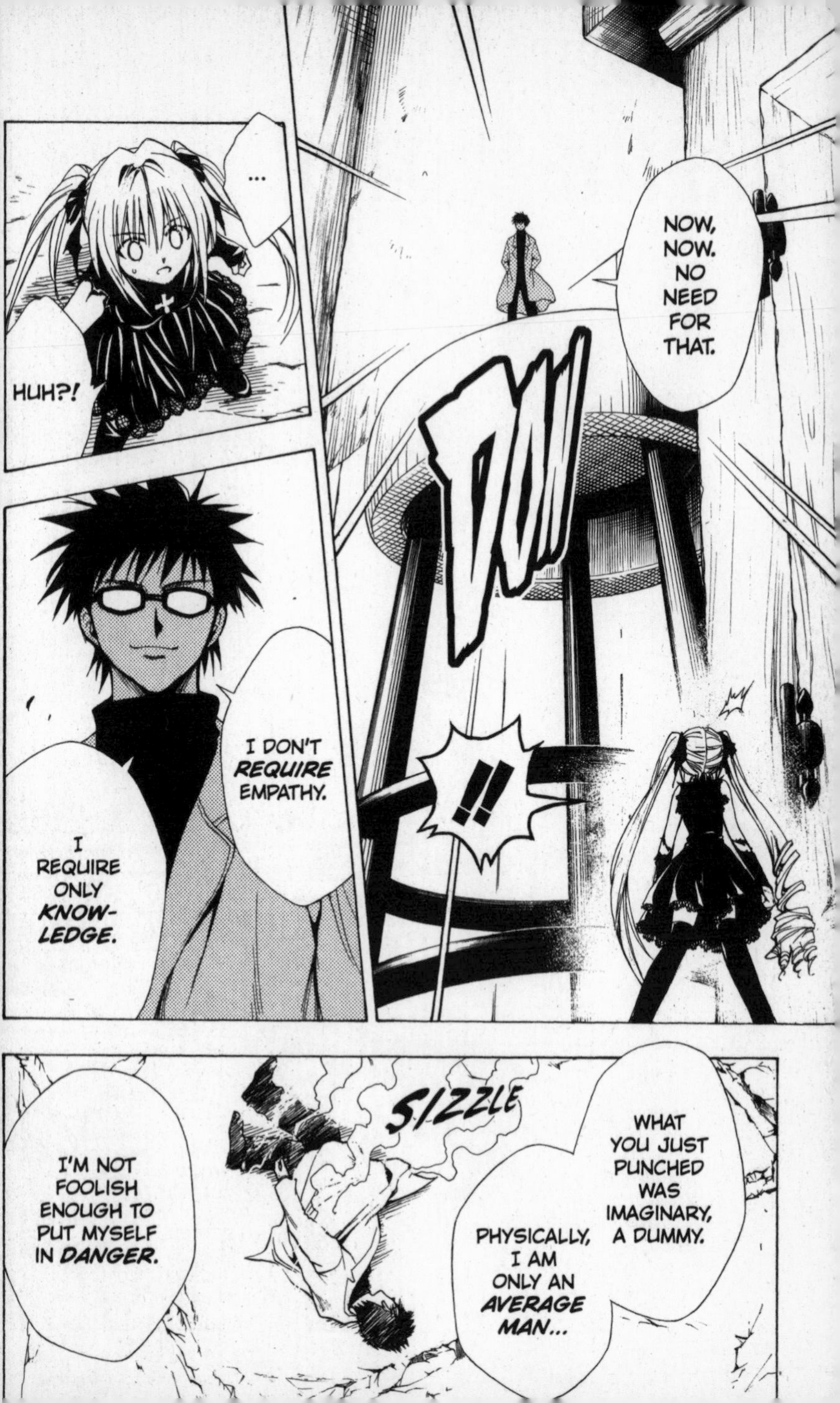
NOW, NOW. NO NEED FOR THAT.
!!
...
HUH?!
I DON'T REQUIRE EMPATHY.
I REQUIRE ONLY KNOWLEDGE.
SIZZLE
WHAT YOU JUST PUNCHED WAS IMAGINARY, A DUMMY.
PHYSICALLY, I AM ONLY AN AVERAGE MAN...
I'M NOT FOOLISH ENOUGH TO PUT MYSELF IN DANGER.

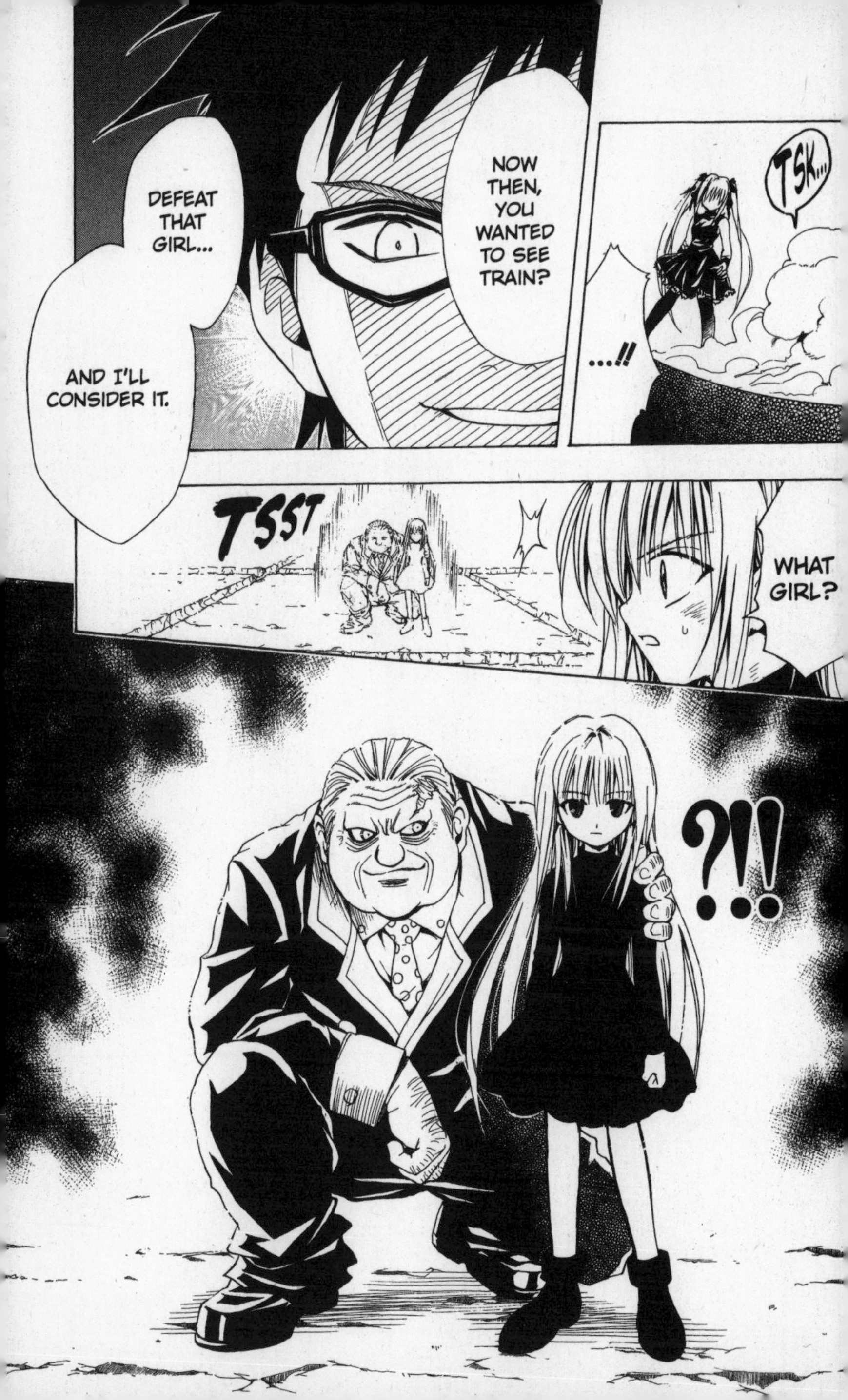
TSK...
...!!
NOW THEN, YOU WANTED TO SEE TRAIN?
DEFEAT THAT GIRL...
AND I'LL CONSIDER IT.
WHAT GIRL?
TSST
?!!

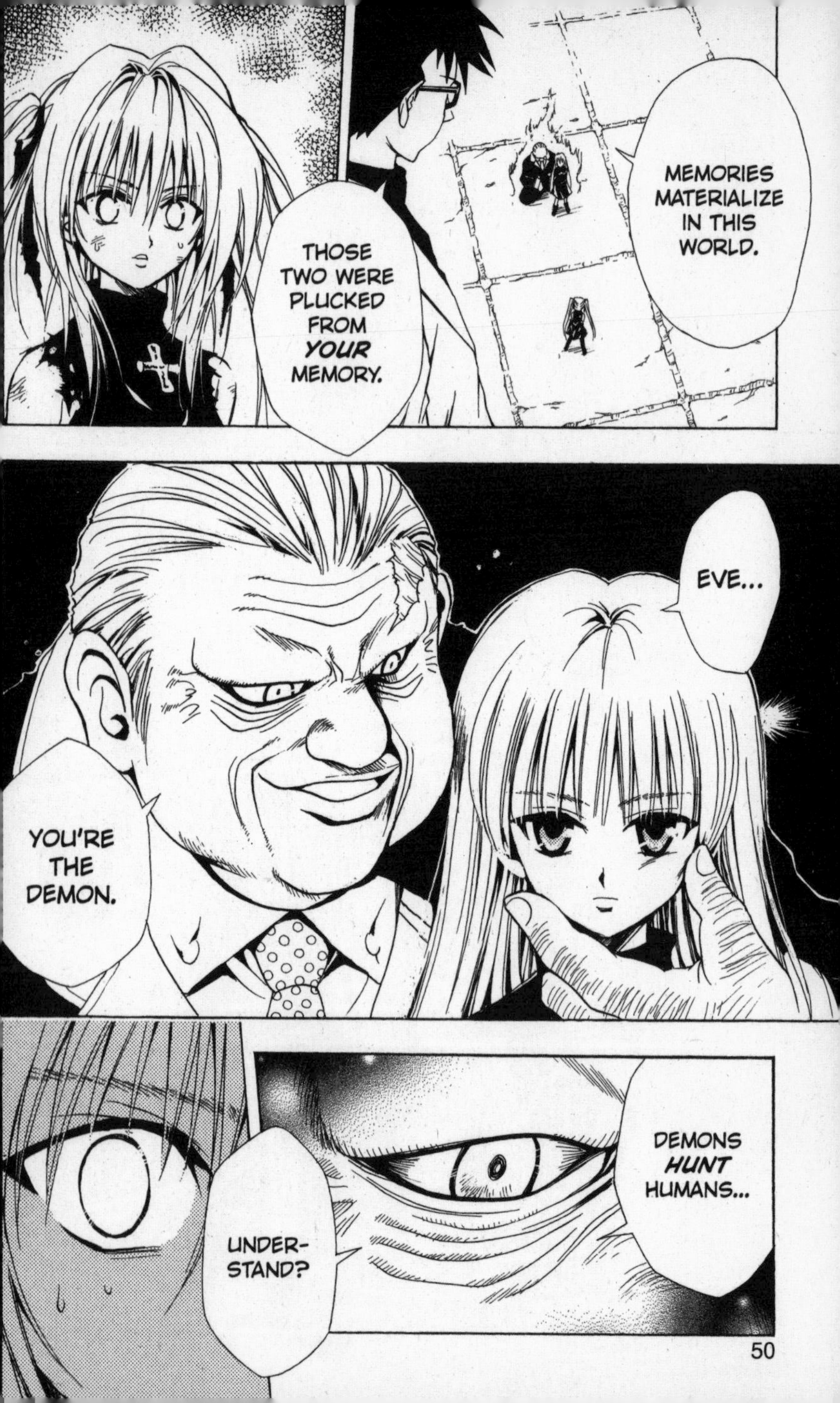
MEMORIES MATERIALIZE IN THIS WORLD.
THOSE TWO WERE PLUCKED FROM *YOUR* MEMORY.
EVE...
YOU'RE THE DEMON.
DEMONS *HUNT* HUMANS...
UNDER-STAND?

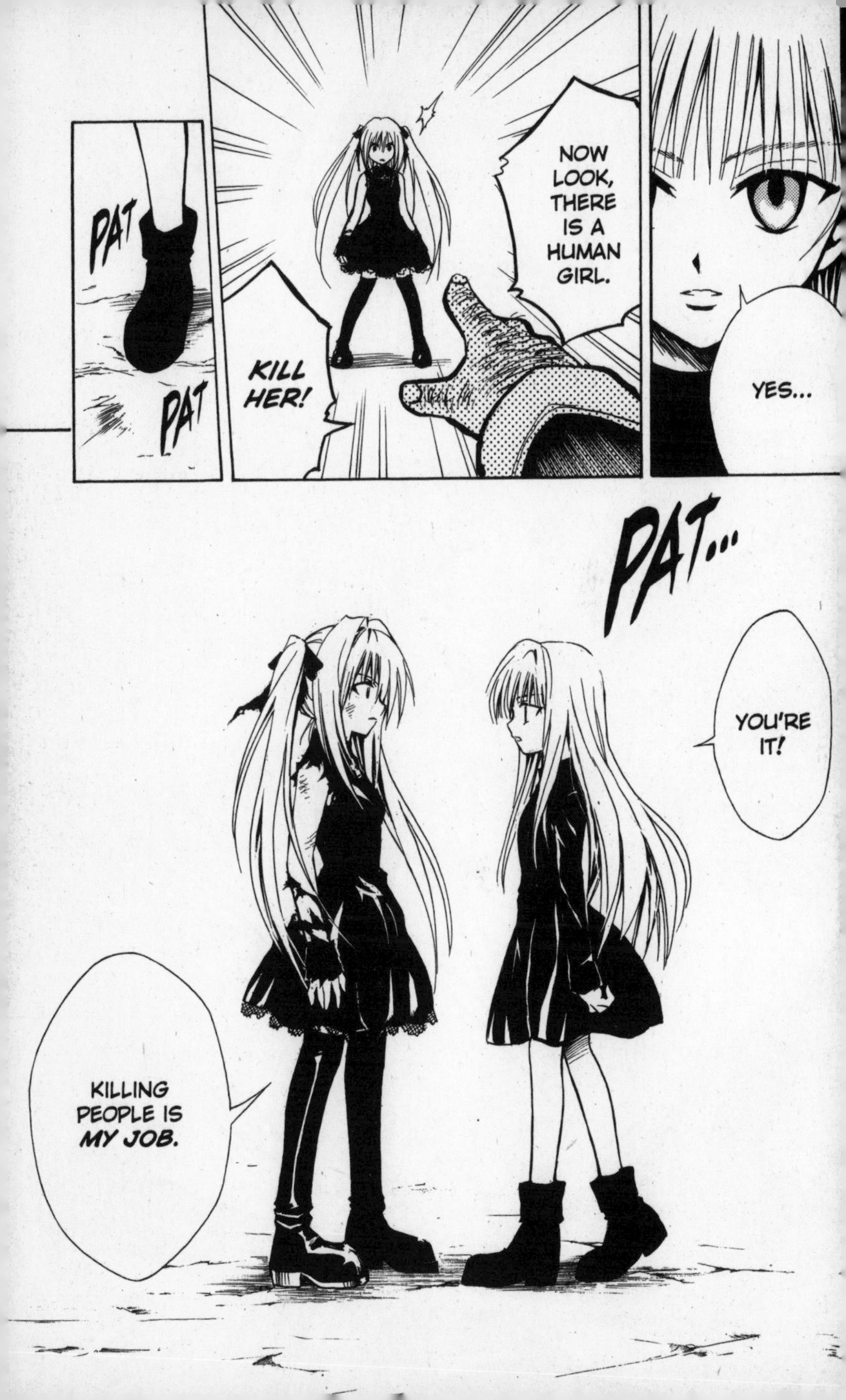
YES...
NOW LOOK, THERE IS A HUMAN GIRL.
KILL HER!
PAT
PAT
PAT...
YOU'RE IT!
KILLING PEOPLE IS MY JOB.

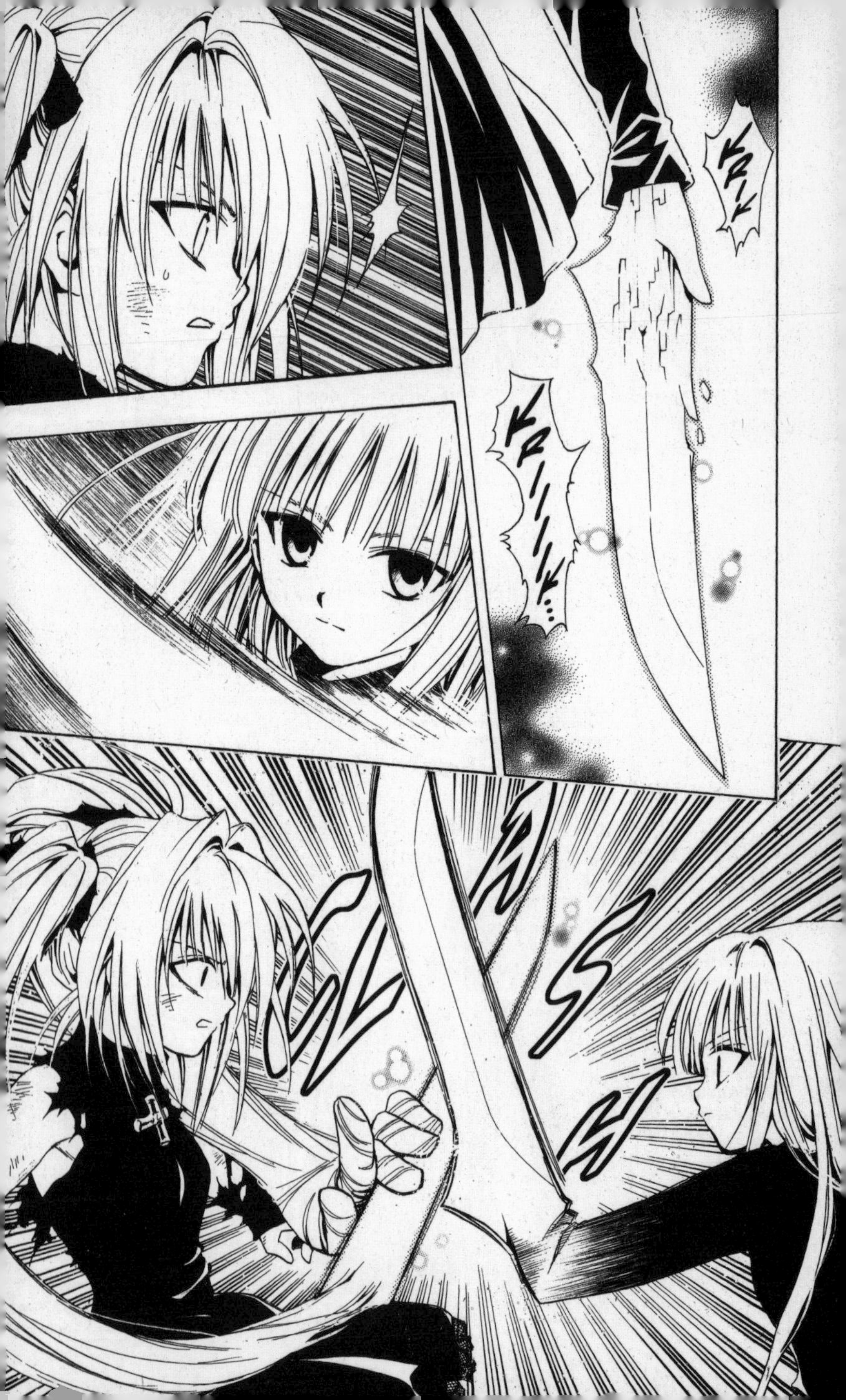
KRIK
KRIIIIK...

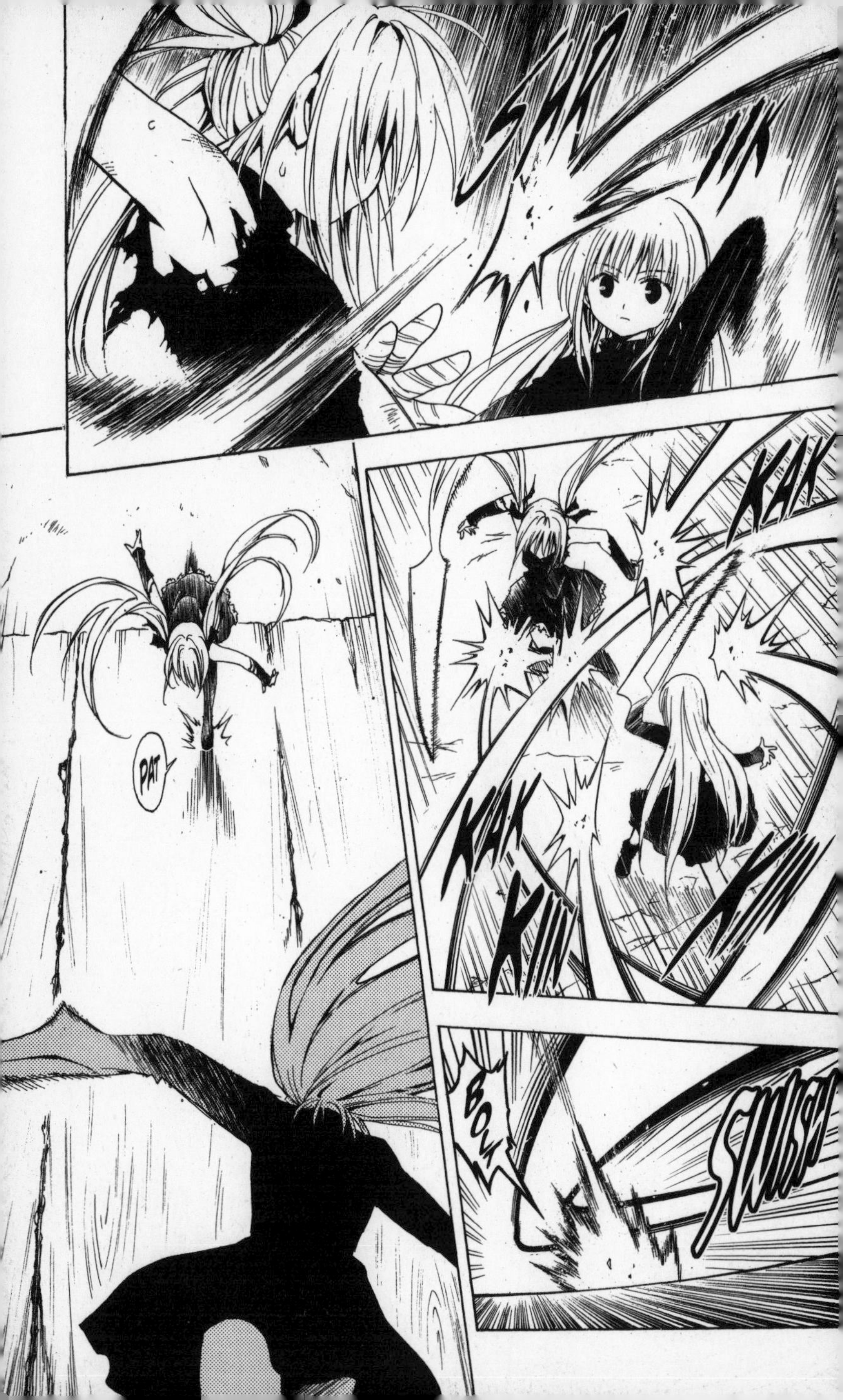
SHAIK
KAK
KAK
KIIIN
KIIIN
PAT
BOW

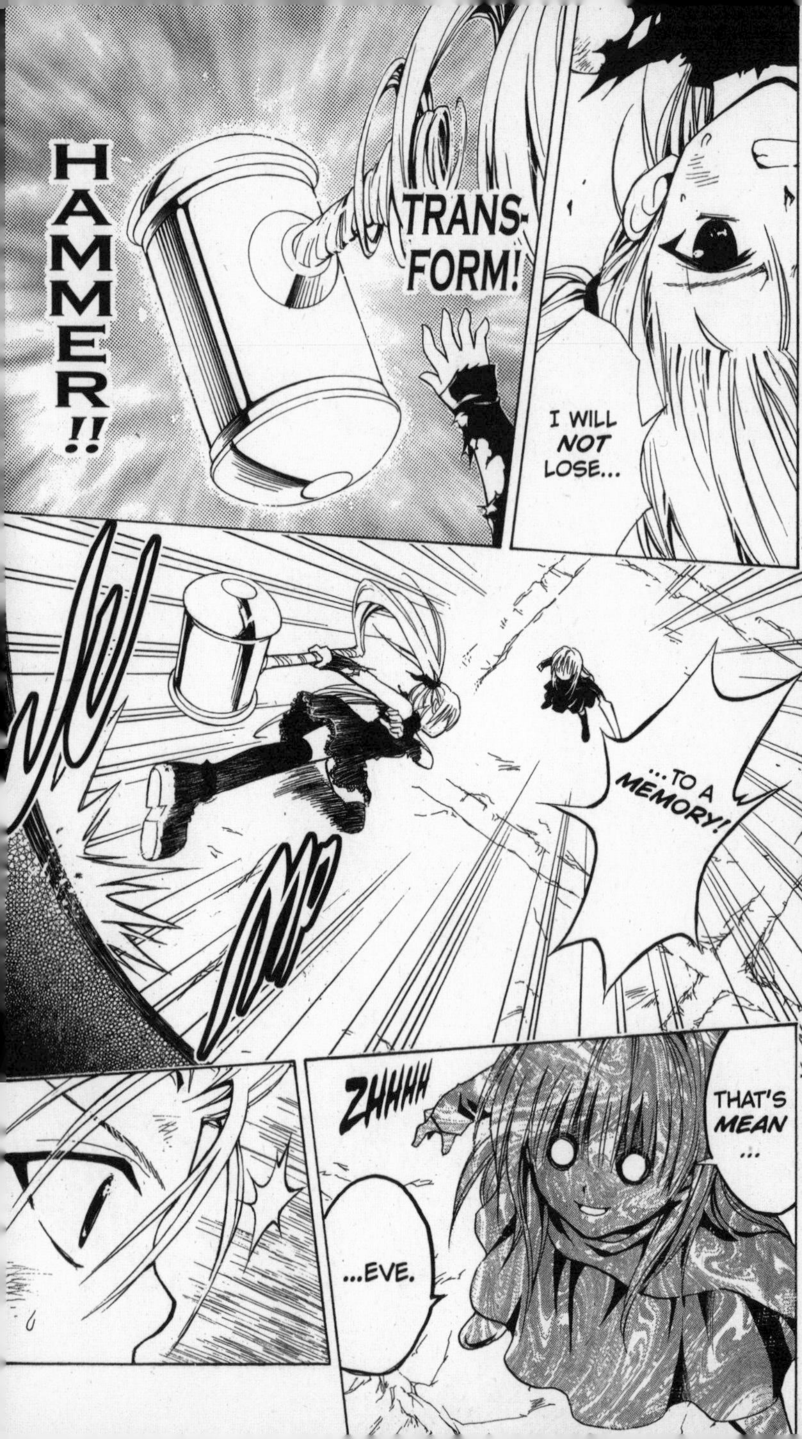
I WILL NOT LOSE...
TRANS-FORM!
HAMMER!!
...TO A MEMORY!!
THAT'S MEAN ...
ZHHHH
...EVE.

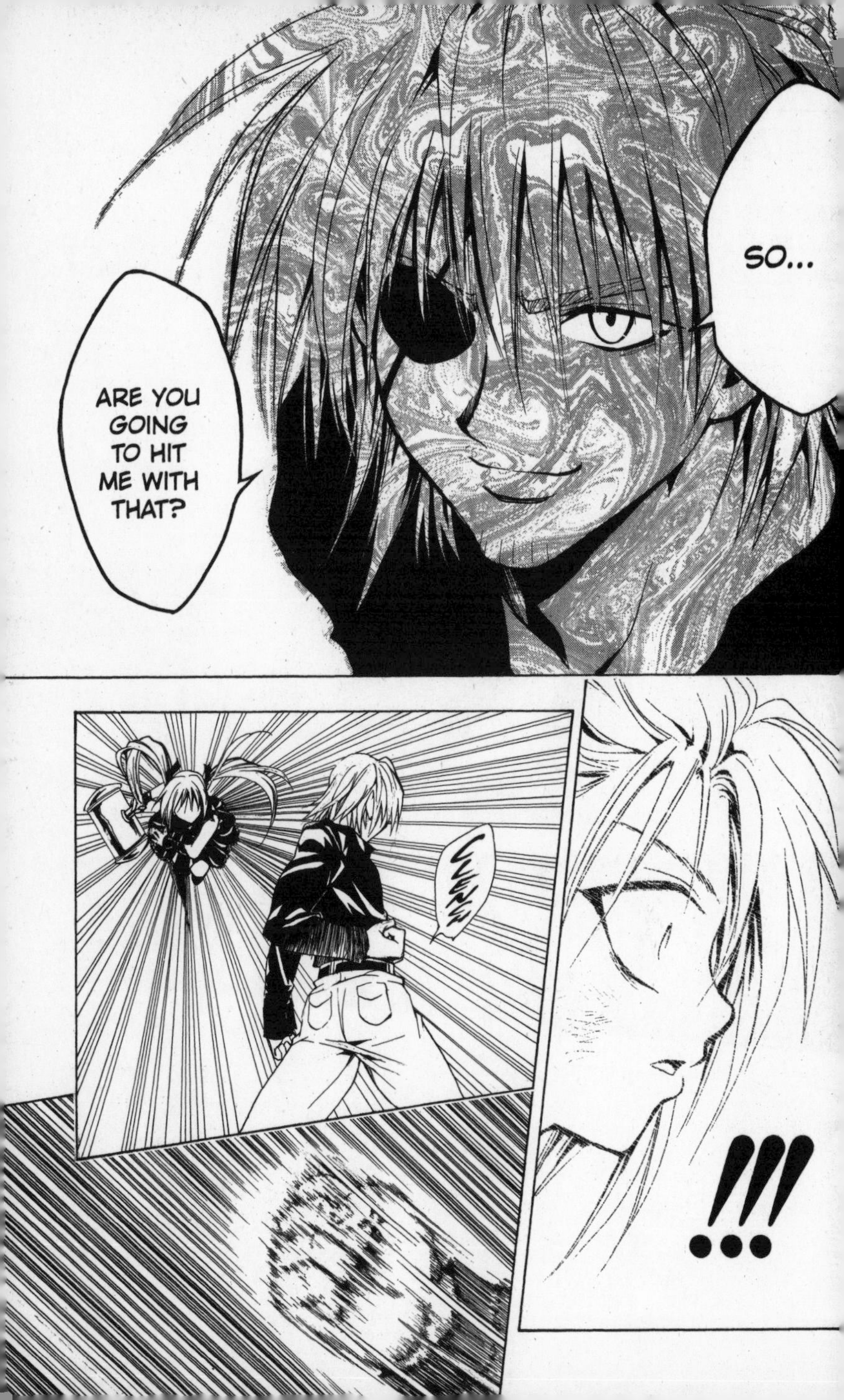
SO...
ARE YOU GOING TO HIT ME WITH THAT?
!!!

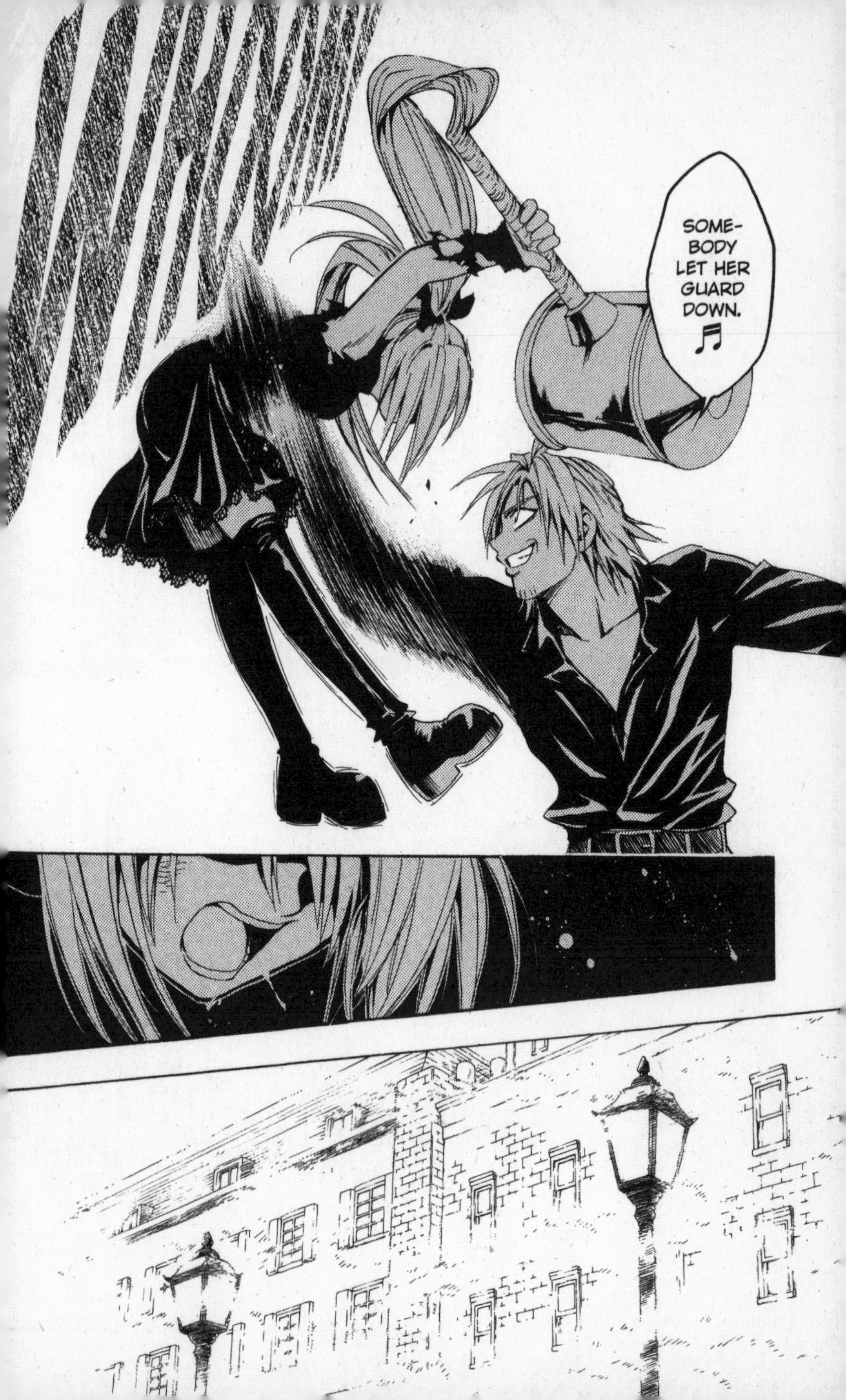
SOME-BODY LET HER GUARD DOWN. ♬

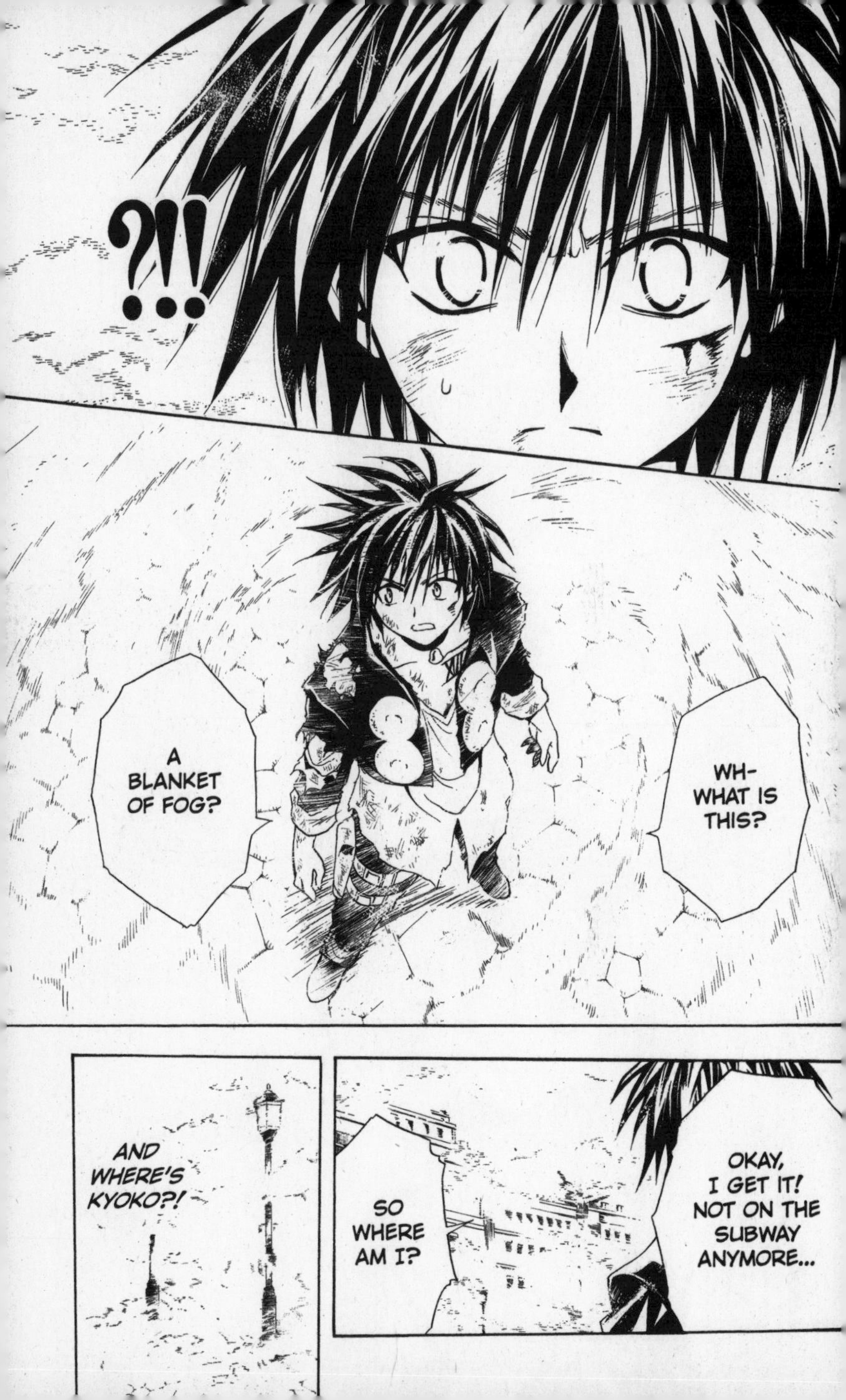
?!!
WH- WHAT IS THIS?
A BLANKET OF FOG?
OKAY, I GET IT! NOT ON THE SUBWAY ANYMORE...
SO WHERE AM I?
AND WHERE'S KYOKO?!

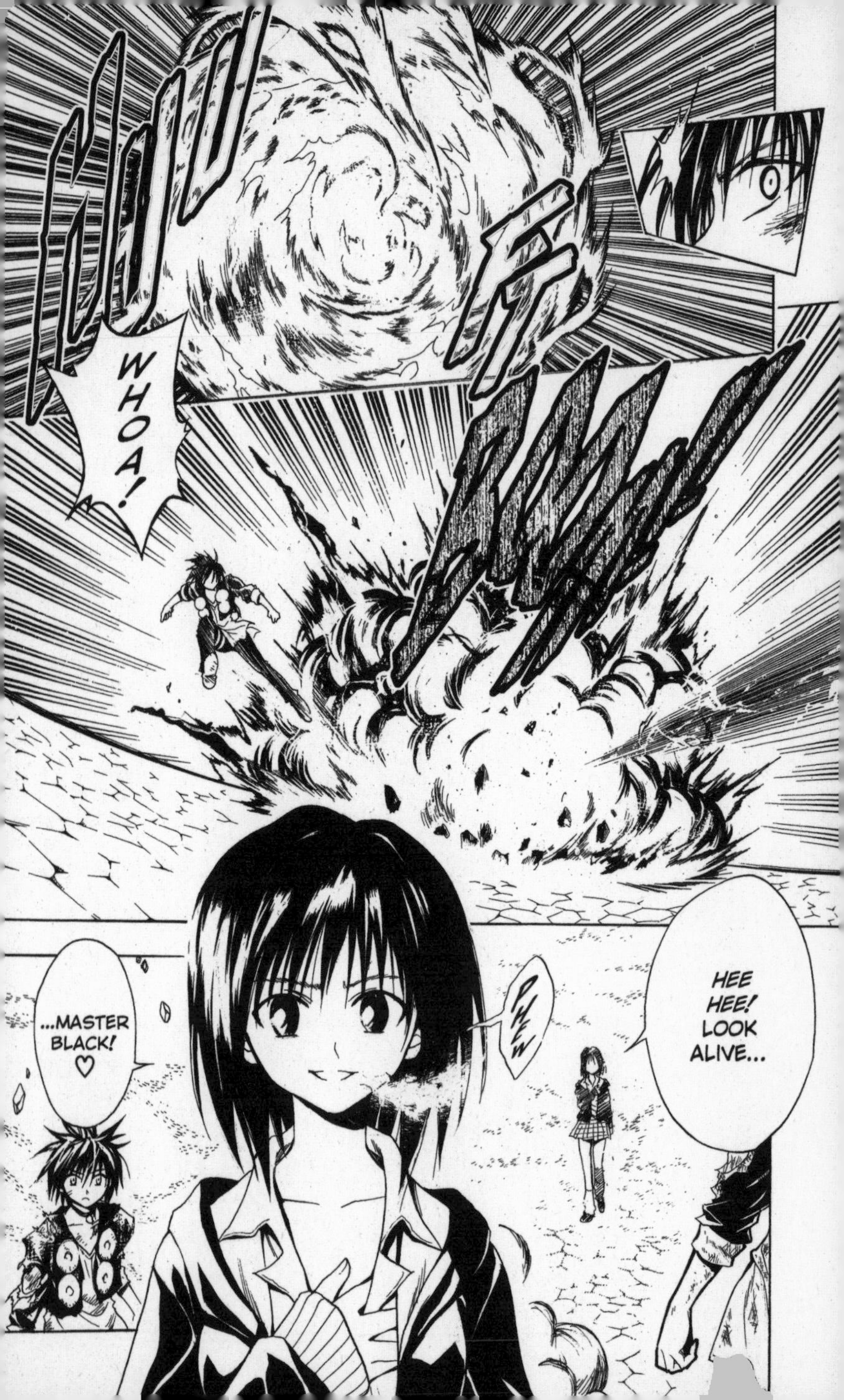
WHOA!
HEE HEE! LOOK ALIVE...
PHEW
...MASTER BLACK! ♡

READ THIS WAY

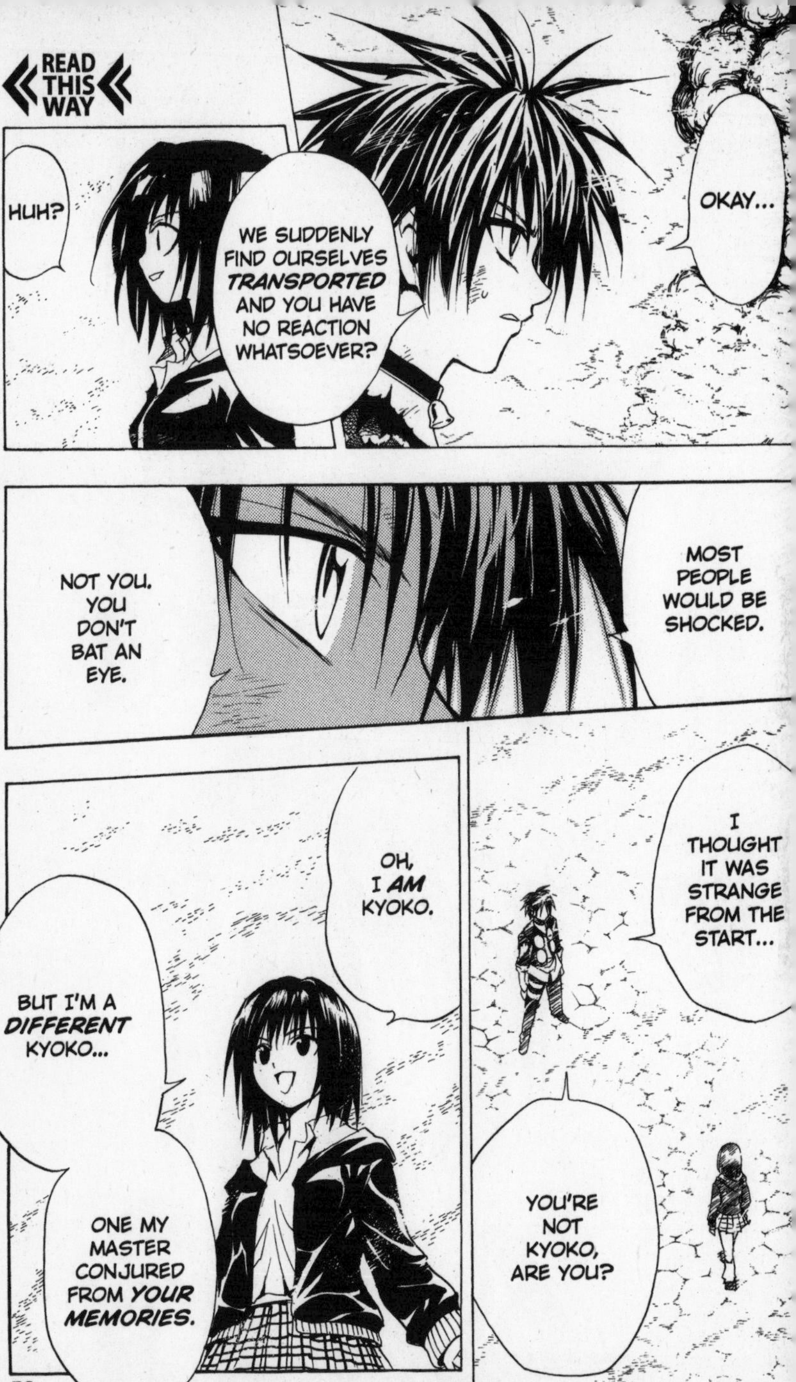

OKAY...
WE SUDDENLY FIND OURSELVES TRANSPORTED AND YOU HAVE NO REACTION WHATSOEVER?
HUH?
MOST PEOPLE WOULD BE SHOCKED.
NOT YOU. YOU DON'T BAT AN EYE.
I THOUGHT IT WAS STRANGE FROM THE START...
YOU'RE NOT KYOKO, ARE YOU?
OH, I AM KYOKO.
BUT I'M A DIFFERENT KYOKO...
ONE MY MASTER CONJURED FROM YOUR MEMORIES.

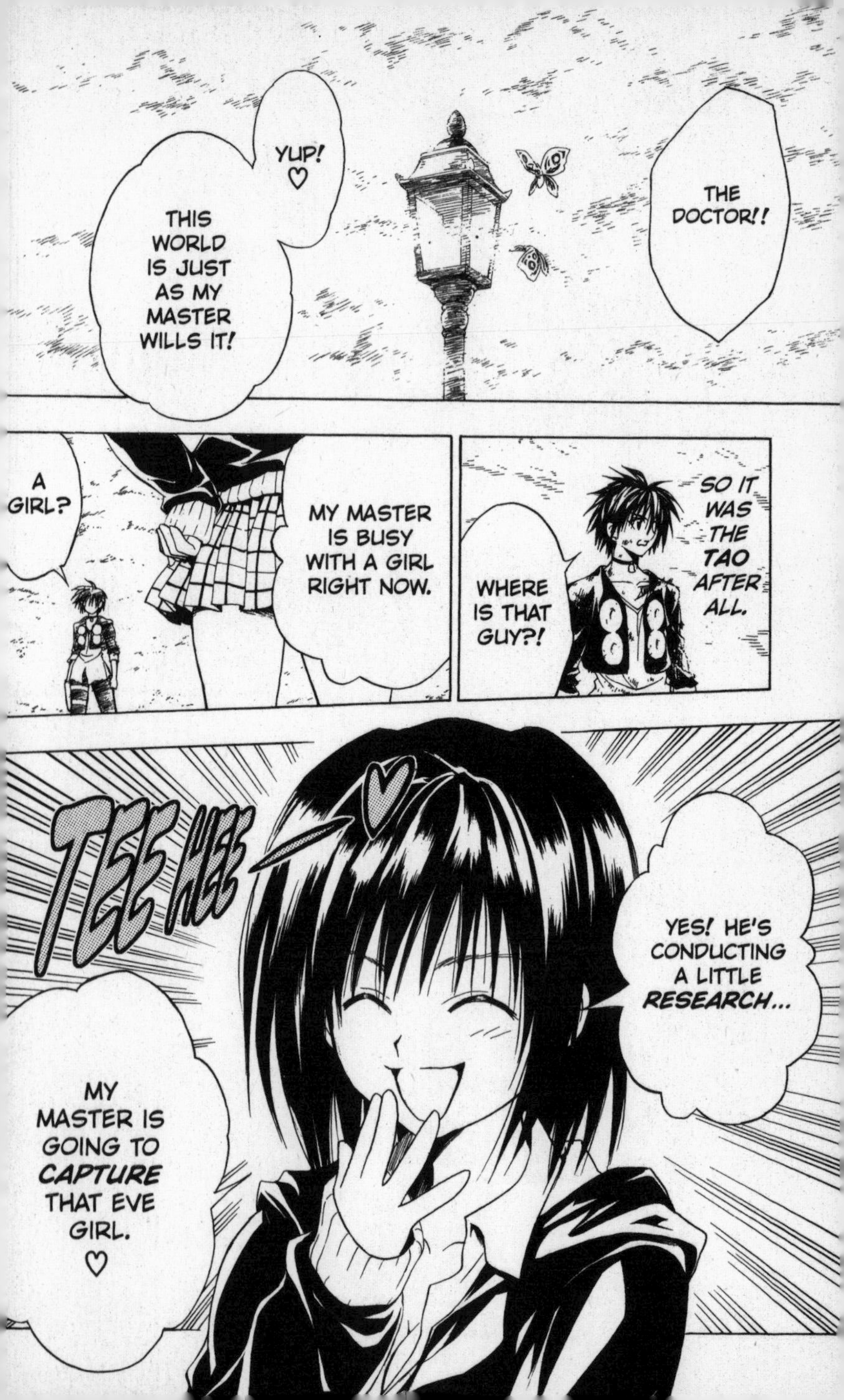
THE DOCTOR!!
YUP! ♡
THIS WORLD IS JUST AS MY MASTER WILLS IT!
SO IT WAS THE TAO AFTER ALL.
WHERE IS THAT GUY?!
MY MASTER IS BUSY WITH A GIRL RIGHT NOW.
A GIRL?
YES! HE'S CONDUCTING A LITTLE *RESEARCH*...
TEE HEE
MY MASTER IS GOING TO *CAPTURE* THAT EVE GIRL. ♡

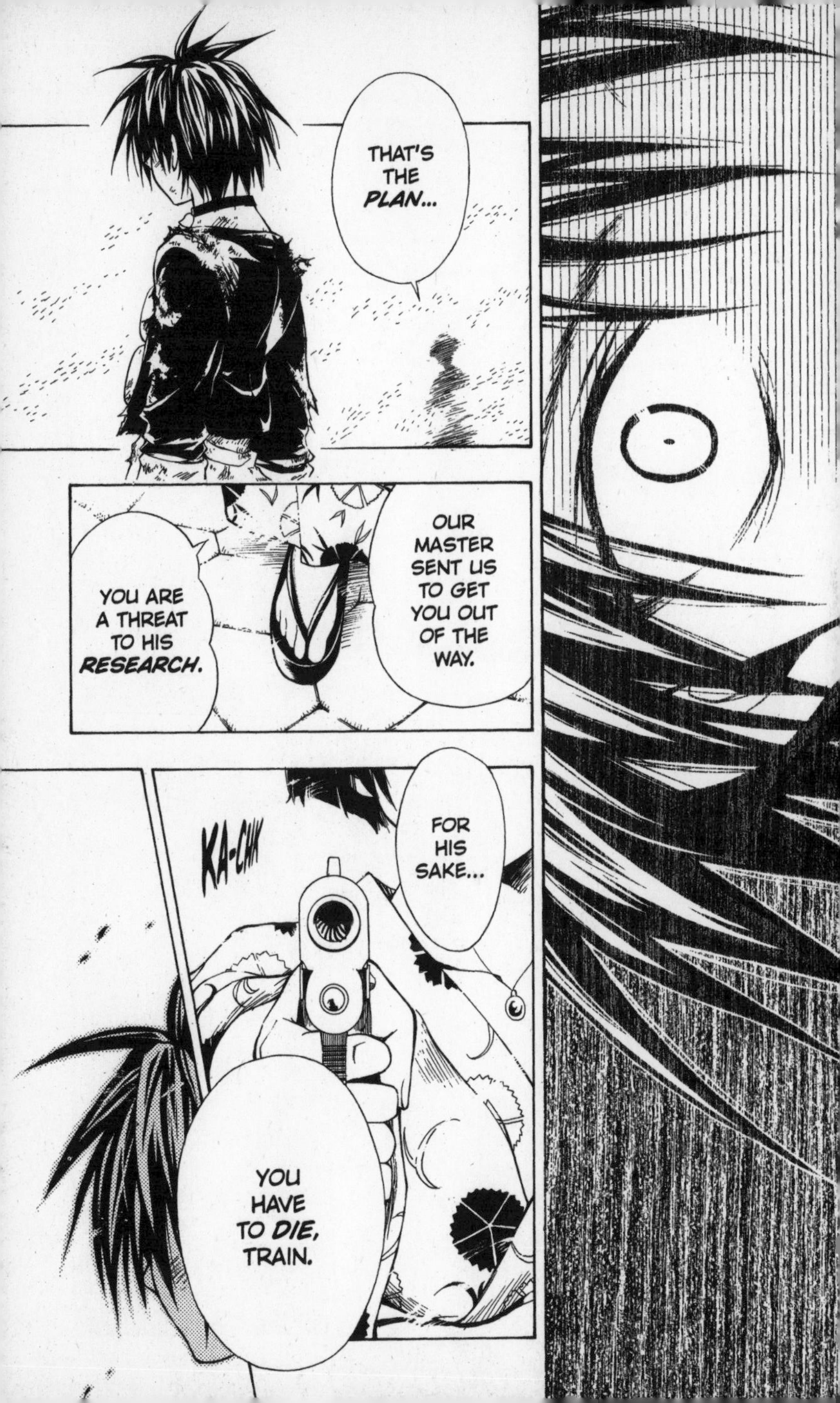
THAT'S THE *PLAN*...
OUR MASTER SENT US TO GET YOU OUT OF THE WAY.
YOU ARE A THREAT TO HIS *RESEARCH*.
FOR HIS SAKE...
KA-CHK
YOU HAVE TO *DIE*, TRAIN.

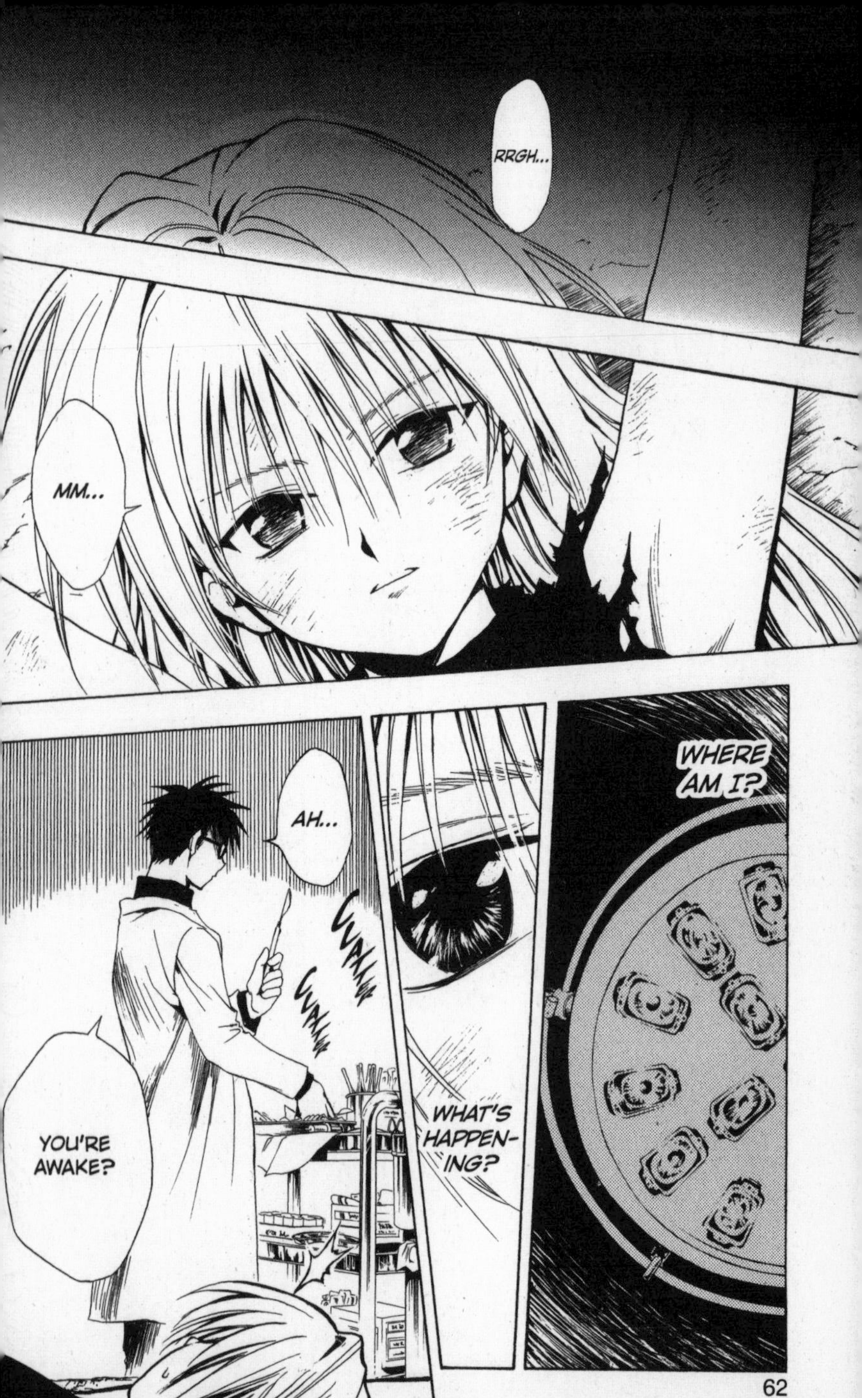
RRGH...
MM...
WHERE AM I?
WHAT'S HAPPEN-ING?
AH...
YOU'RE AWAKE?

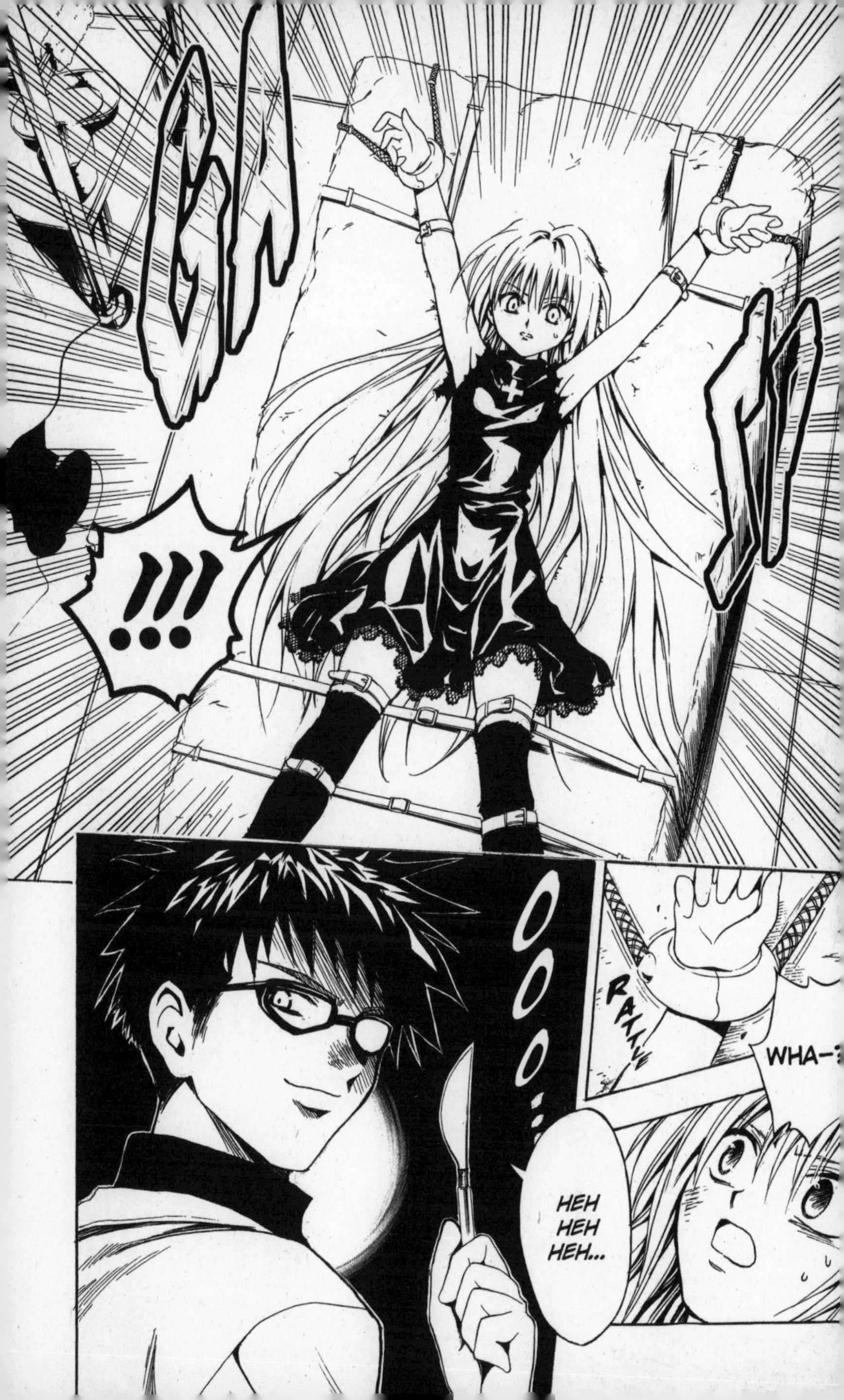
!!!...
WHA-?
OOO...
HEH HEH HEH...

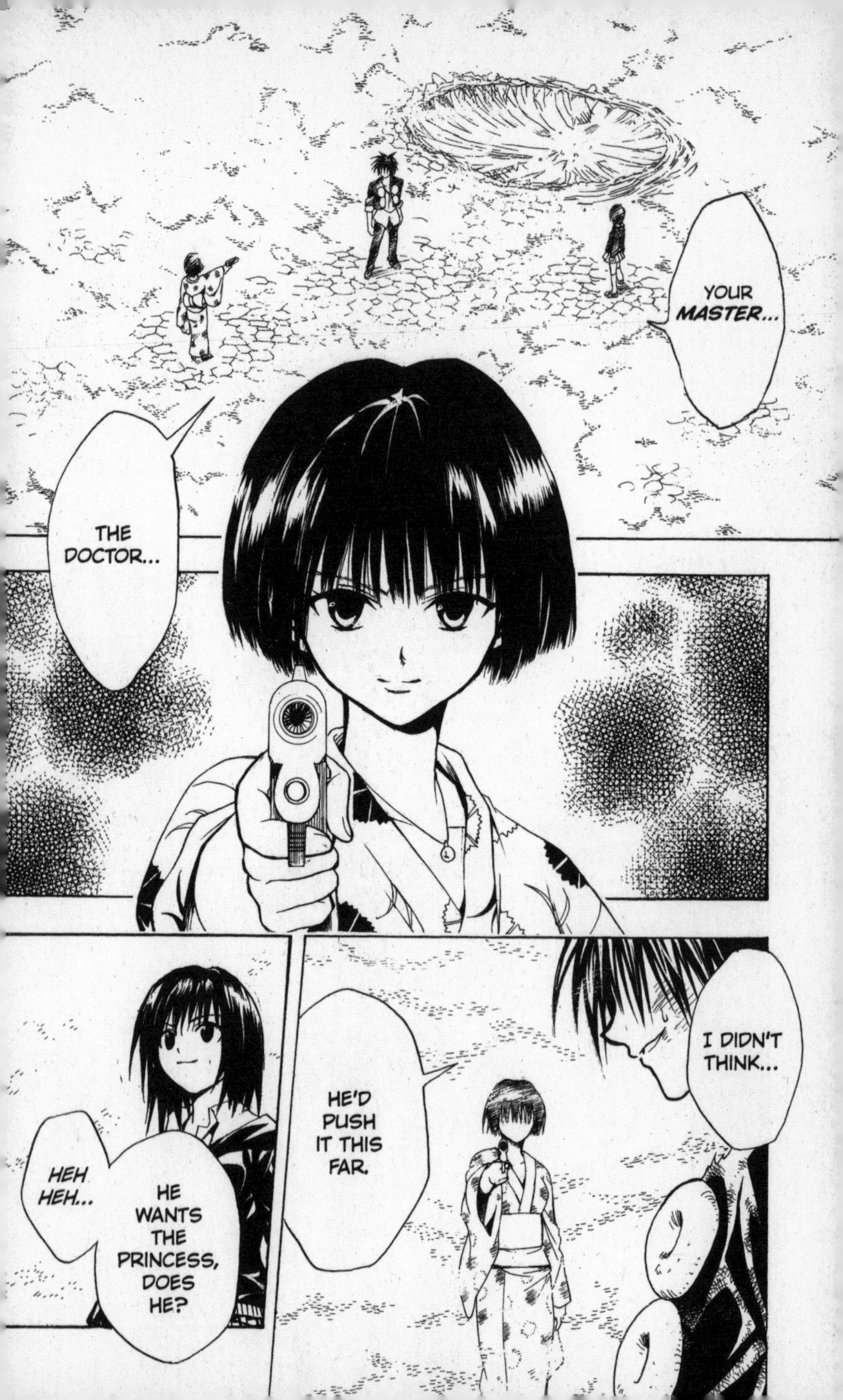
YOUR MASTER...
THE DOCTOR...
I DIDN'T THINK...
HE'D PUSH IT THIS FAR.
HEH HEH...
HE WANTS THE PRINCESS, DOES HE?

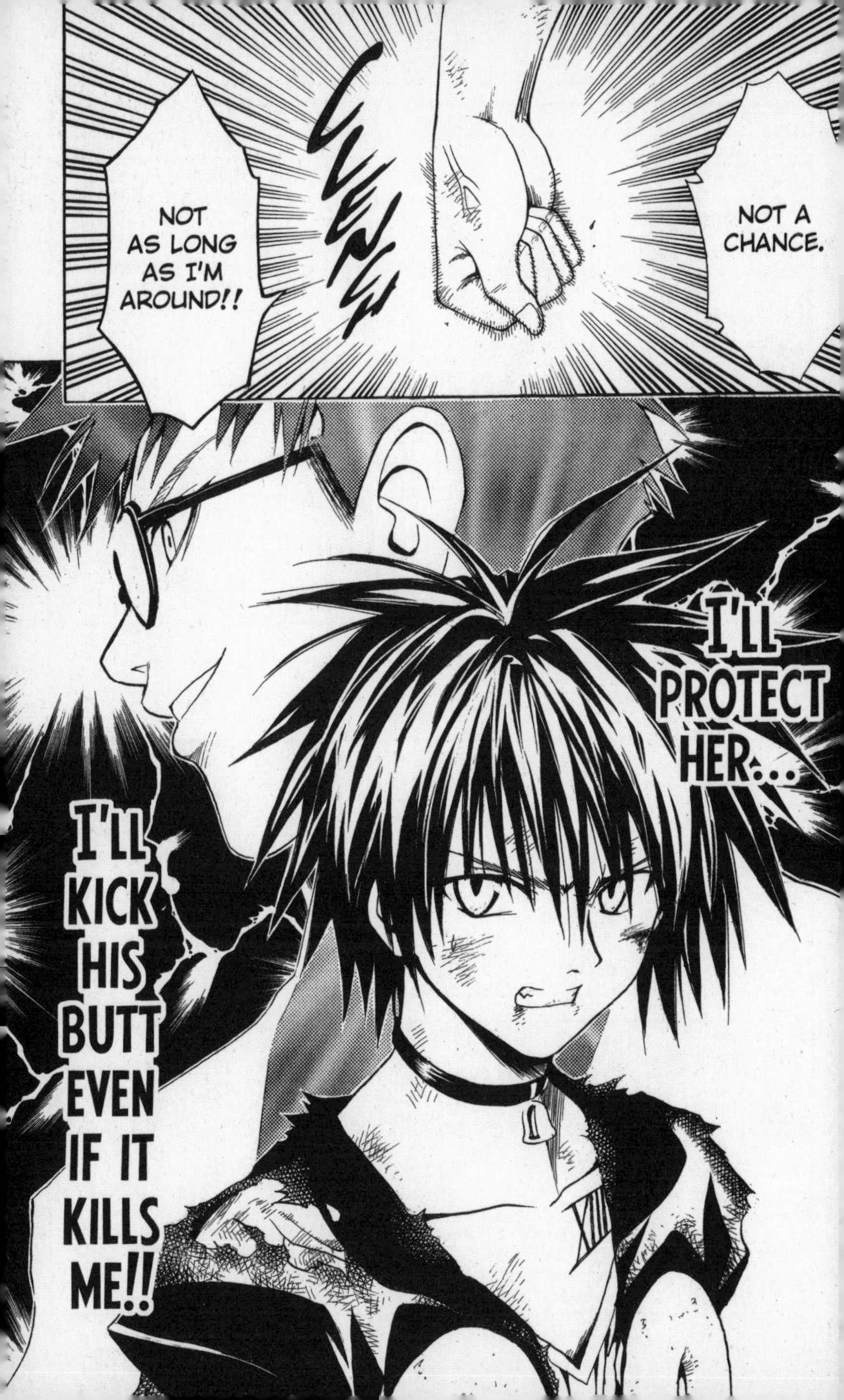
NOT A CHANCE.
NOT AS LONG AS I'M AROUND!!
I'LL PROTECT HER...
I'LL KICK HIS BUTT EVEN IF IT KILLS ME!!

A GROWN MAN WITH AN ACTION FIGURE BY AKIRA MIYAZAKI

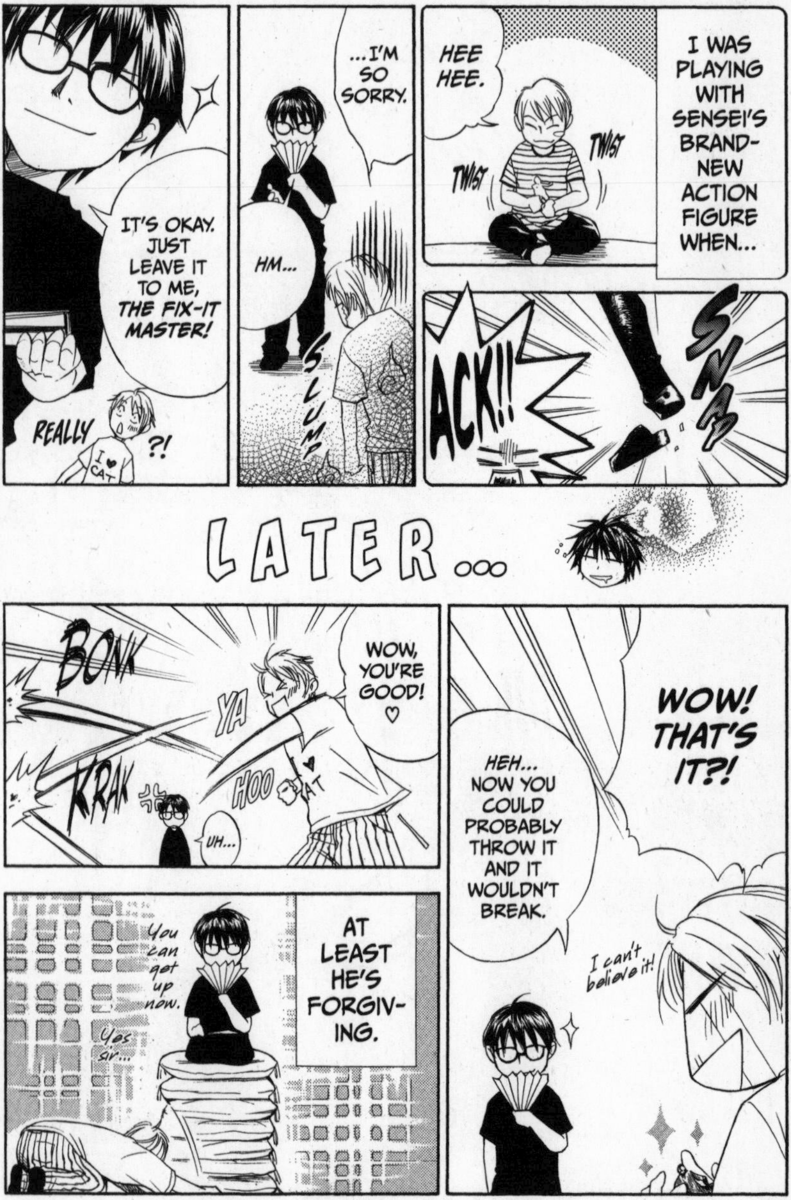
I WAS PLAYING WITH SENSEI'S BRAND-NEW ACTION FIGURE WHEN...
HEE HEE.
TWIST
TWIST
SNAP
ACK!!
...I'M SO SORRY.
HM...
SLUMP
IT'S OKAY. JUST LEAVE IT TO ME, THE FIX-IT MASTER!
REALLY
?!
LATER...
WOW! THAT'S IT?!
HEH... NOW YOU COULD PROBABLY THROW IT AND IT WOULDN'T BREAK.
I can't believe it!
BONK
YA
KRAK
HOO
WOW, YOU'RE GOOD! ♡
UH...
AT LEAST HE'S FORGIV-ING.
You can get up now.
Yes sir...

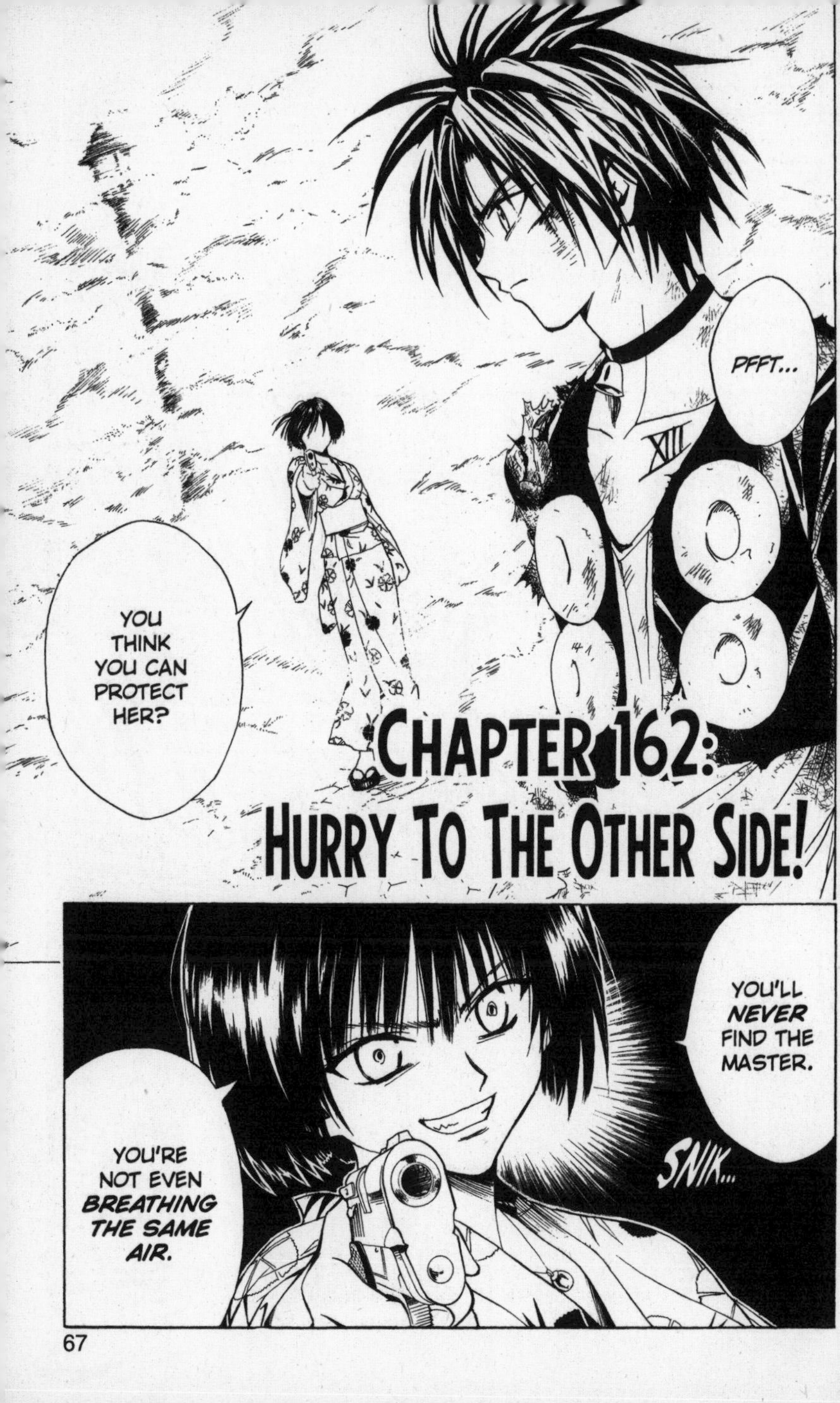
PFFT...
YOU THINK YOU CAN PROTECT HER?
CHAPTER 162: HURRY TO THE OTHER SIDE!
YOU'LL *NEVER* FIND THE MASTER.
SNIK...
YOU'RE NOT EVEN *BREATHING THE SAME AIR*.

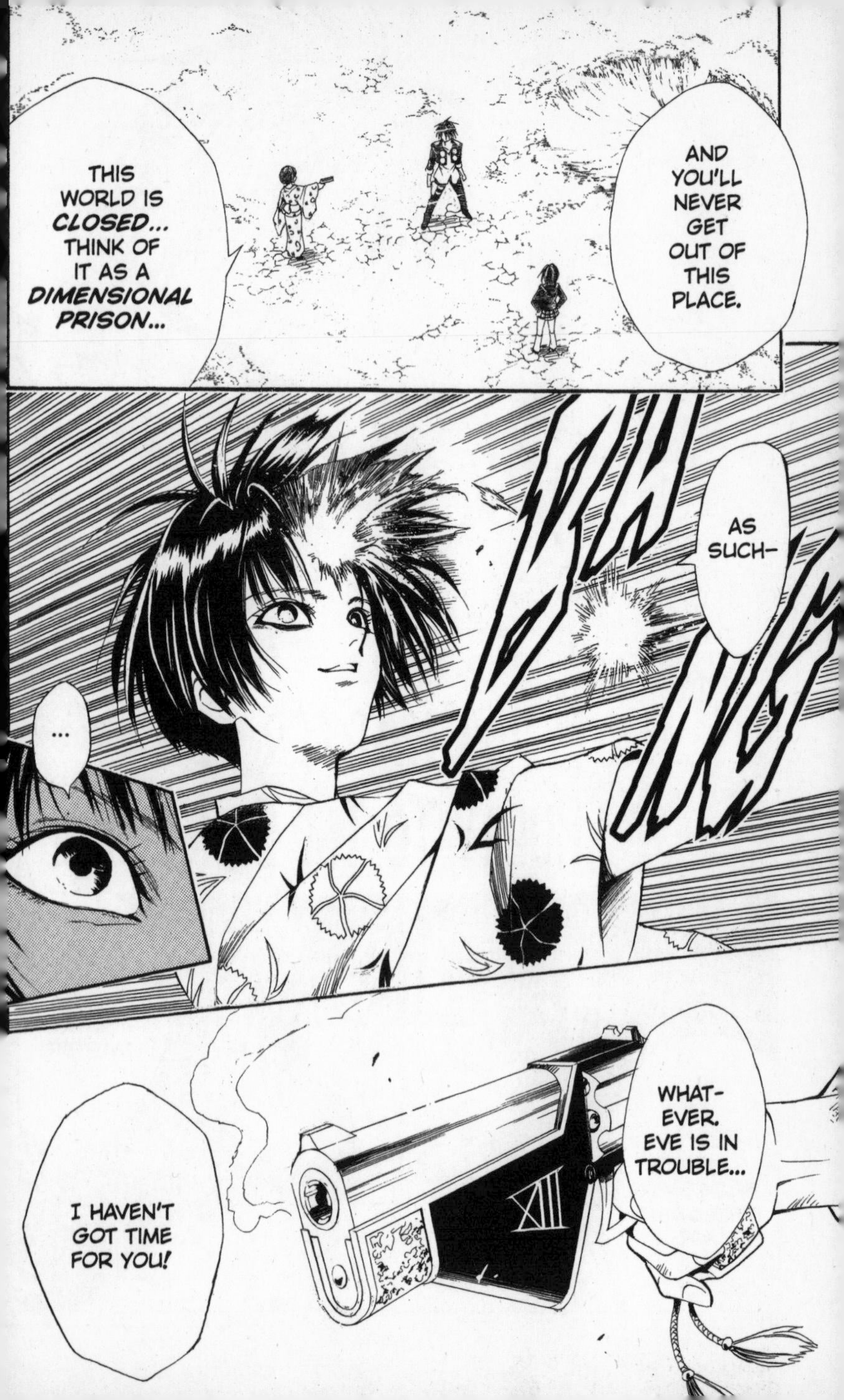
THIS WORLD IS *CLOSED*... THINK OF IT AS A *DIMENSIONAL PRISON*...
AND YOU'LL NEVER GET OUT OF THIS PLACE.
AS SUCH—
...
WHAT-EVER. EVE IS IN TROUBLE...
I HAVEN'T GOT TIME FOR YOU!

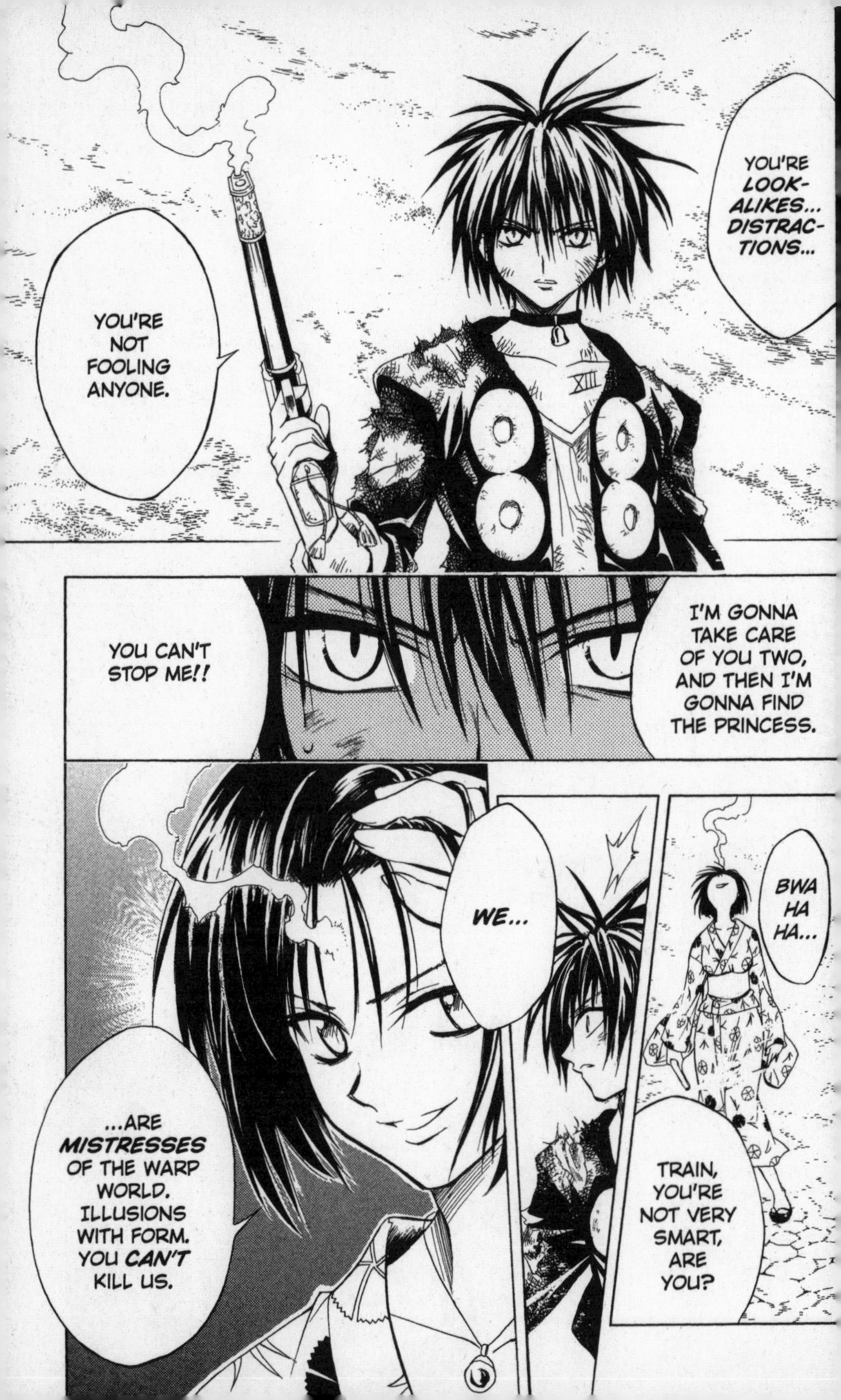
YOU'RE *LOOK-ALIKES... DISTRACTIONS...*
YOU'RE NOT FOOLING ANYONE.
I'M GONNA TAKE CARE OF YOU TWO, AND THEN I'M GONNA FIND THE PRINCESS.
YOU CAN'T STOP ME!!
BWA HA HA...
TRAIN, YOU'RE NOT VERY SMART, ARE YOU?
WE...
...ARE *MISTRESSES* OF THE WARP WORLD. ILLUSIONS WITH FORM. YOU *CAN'T* KILL US.

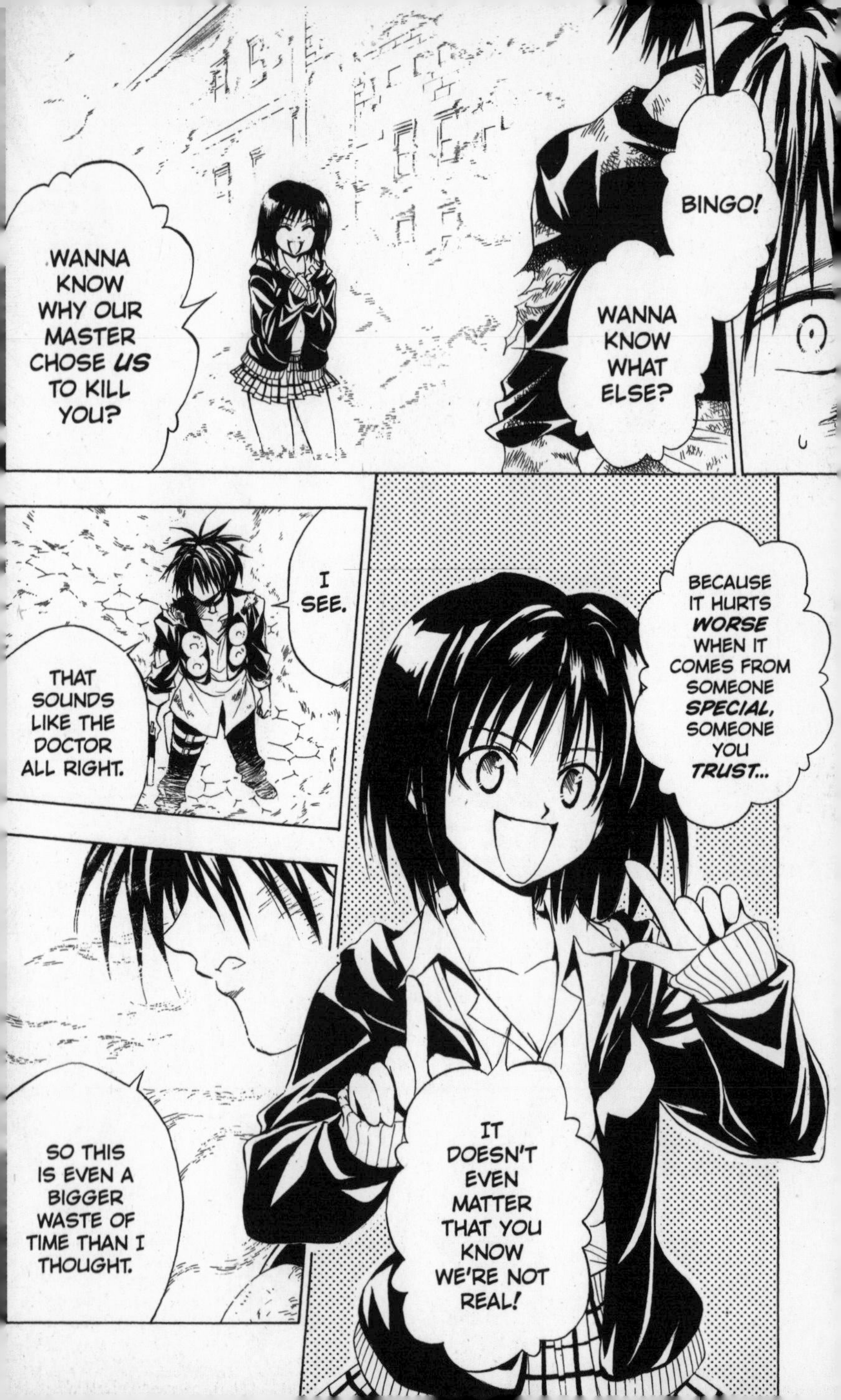

BINGO!
WANNA KNOW WHAT ELSE?
WANNA KNOW WHY OUR MASTER CHOSE *US* TO KILL YOU?
BECAUSE IT HURTS *WORSE* WHEN IT COMES FROM SOMEONE *SPECIAL*, SOMEONE YOU *TRUST*...
IT DOESN'T EVEN MATTER THAT YOU KNOW WE'RE NOT REAL!
I SEE.
THAT SOUNDS LIKE THE DOCTOR ALL RIGHT.
SO THIS IS EVEN A BIGGER WASTE OF TIME THAN I THOUGHT.

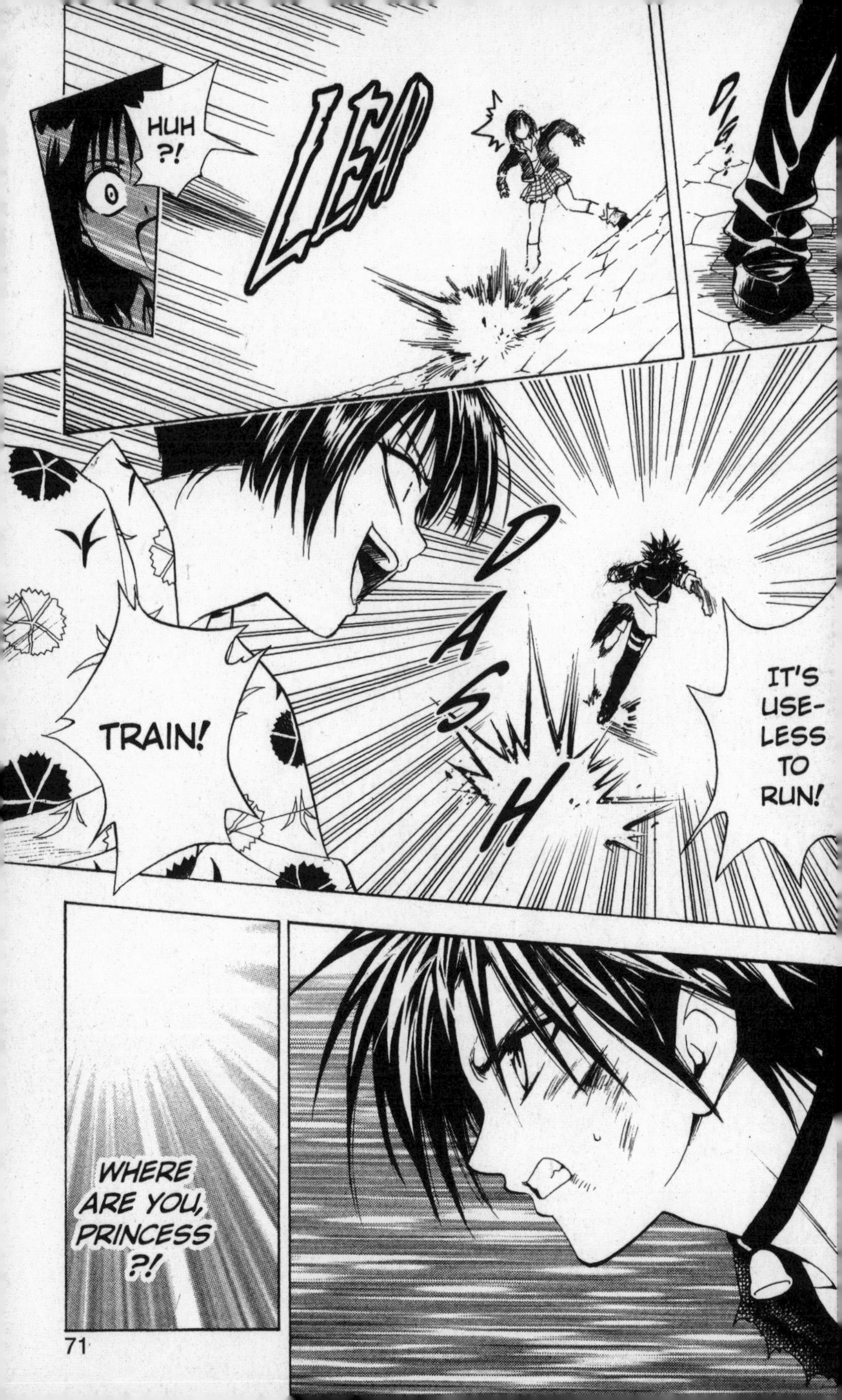
LEAP
HUH ?!
IT'S USE-LESS TO RUN!
DASH
TRAIN!
WHERE ARE YOU, PRINCESS ?!

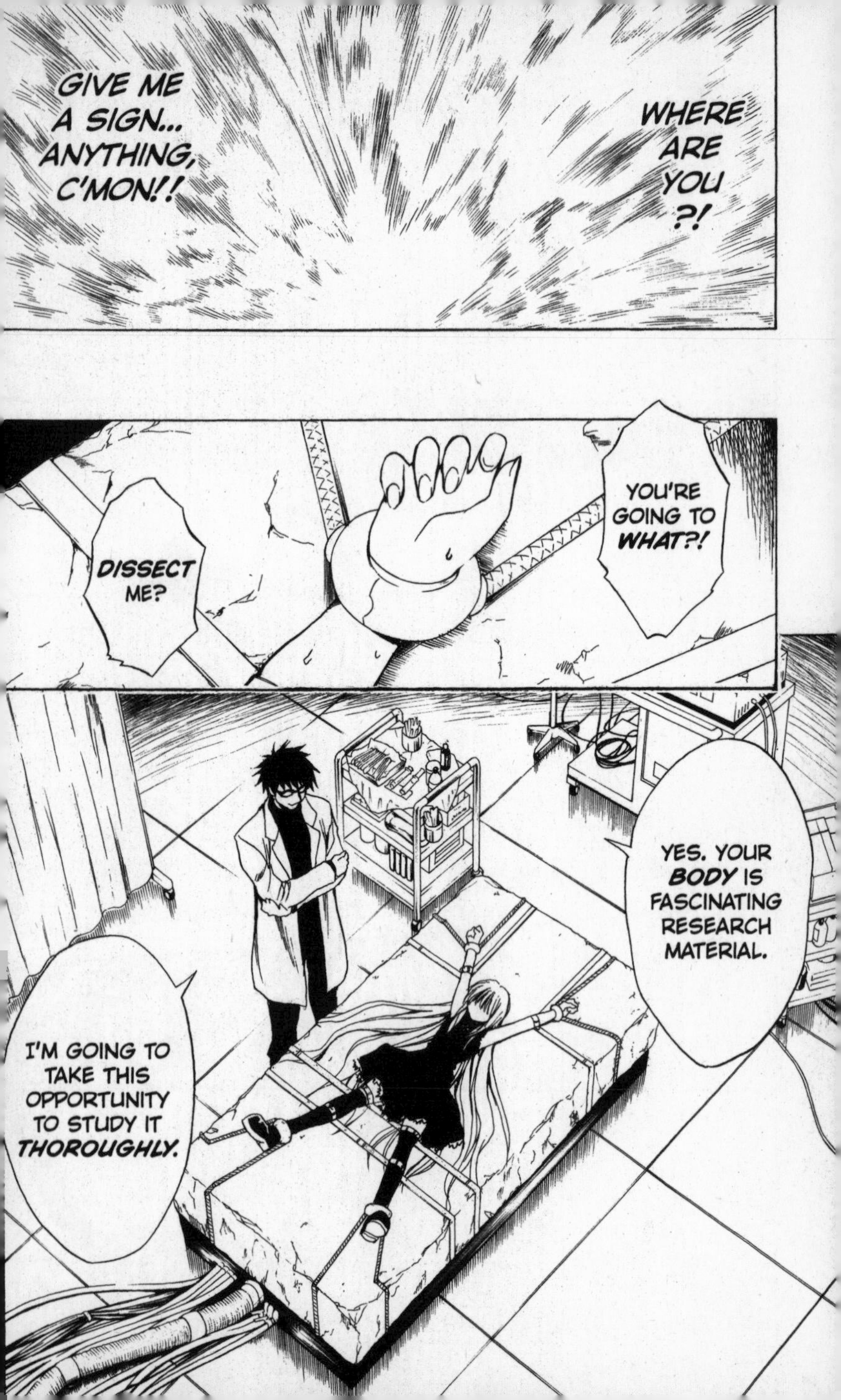
WHERE ARE YOU ?!
GIVE ME A SIGN... ANYTHING, C'MON!!
YOU'RE GOING TO *WHAT?!*
DISSECT ME?
YES. YOUR *BODY* IS FASCINATING RESEARCH MATERIAL.
I'M GOING TO TAKE THIS OPPORTUNITY TO STUDY IT *THOROUGHLY.*

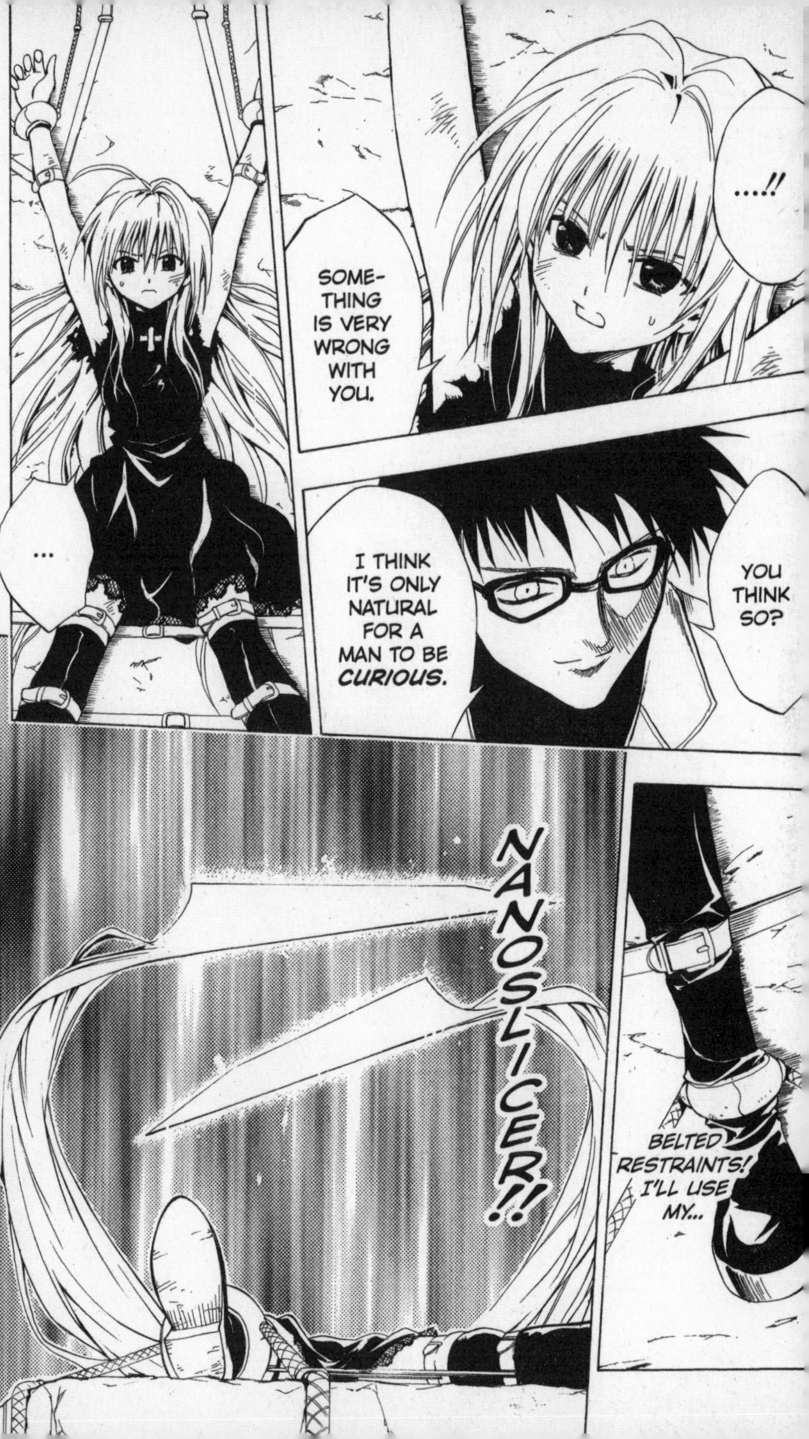

....!!
SOME-THING IS VERY WRONG WITH YOU.
YOU THINK SO?
I THINK IT'S ONLY NATURAL FOR A MAN TO BE *CURIOUS.*
...
BELTED RESTRAINTS! I'LL USE MY...
NANOSLICER!!

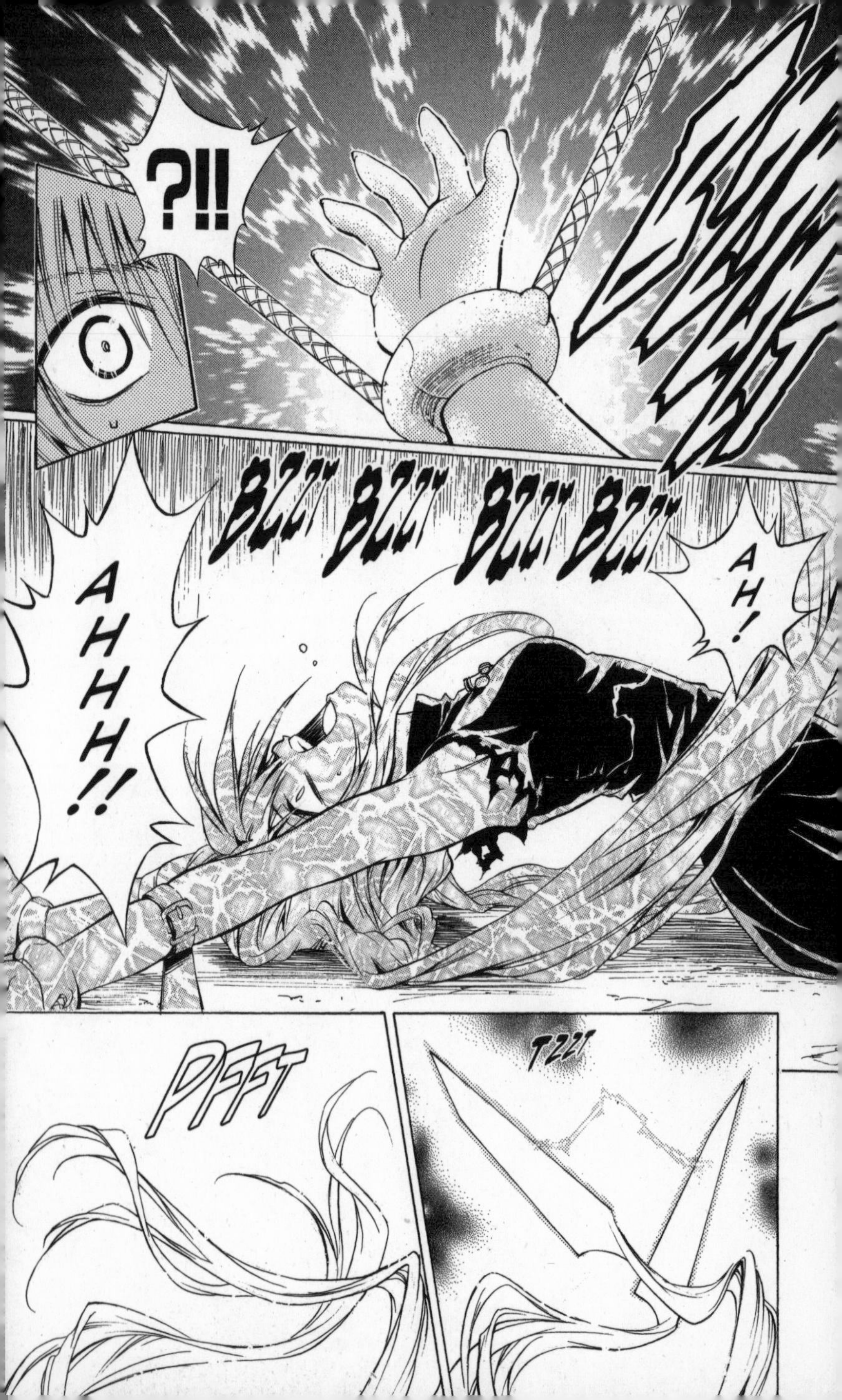
?!!
BZZT BZZT BZZT BZZT
AH!
AHHHH!!
TZZT
PFFT

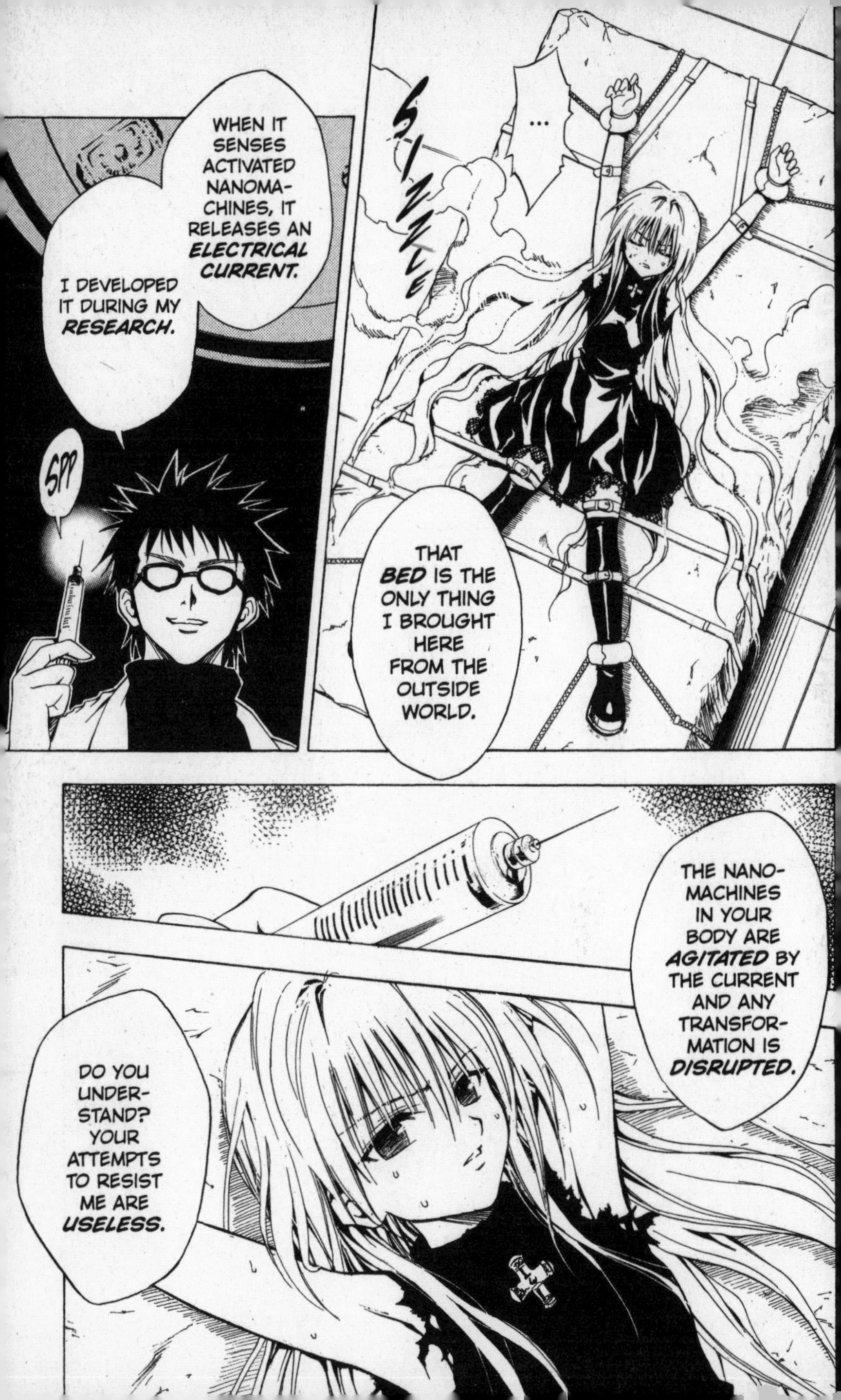
...
SIZZLE
THAT BED IS THE ONLY THING I BROUGHT HERE FROM THE OUTSIDE WORLD.
WHEN IT SENSES ACTIVATED NANOMA-CHINES, IT RELEASES AN ELECTRICAL CURRENT.
I DEVELOPED IT DURING MY RESEARCH.
SPP
THE NANO-MACHINES IN YOUR BODY ARE AGITATED BY THE CURRENT AND ANY TRANSFOR-MATION IS DISRUPTED.
DO YOU UNDER-STAND? YOUR ATTEMPTS TO RESIST ME ARE USELESS.

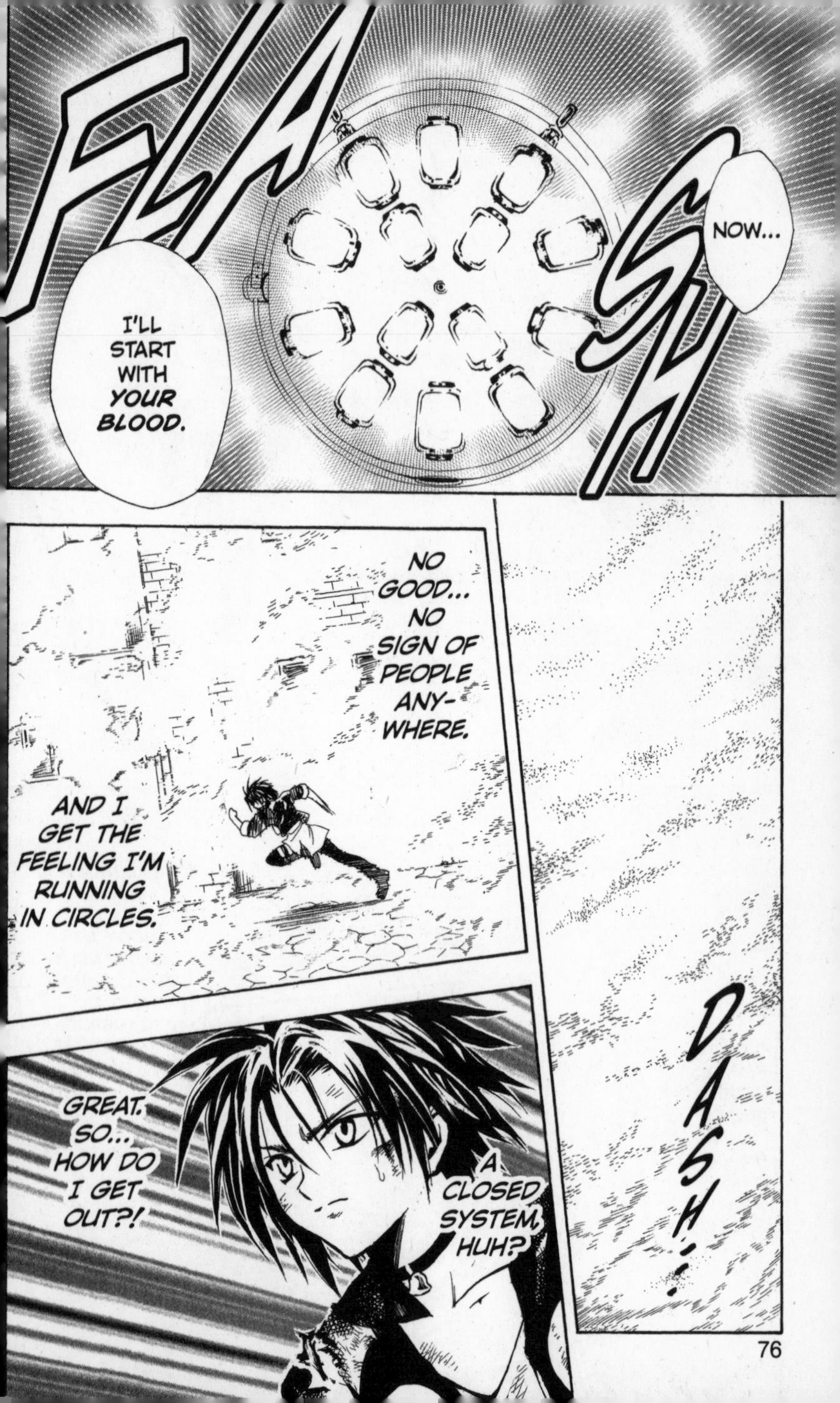
NOW...
I'LL START WITH YOUR BLOOD.
FLASH
DASH!!
NO GOOD... NO SIGN OF PEOPLE ANY-WHERE.
AND I GET THE FEELING I'M RUNNING IN CIRCLES.
A CLOSED SYSTEM, HUH?
GREAT. SO... HOW DO I GET OUT?!

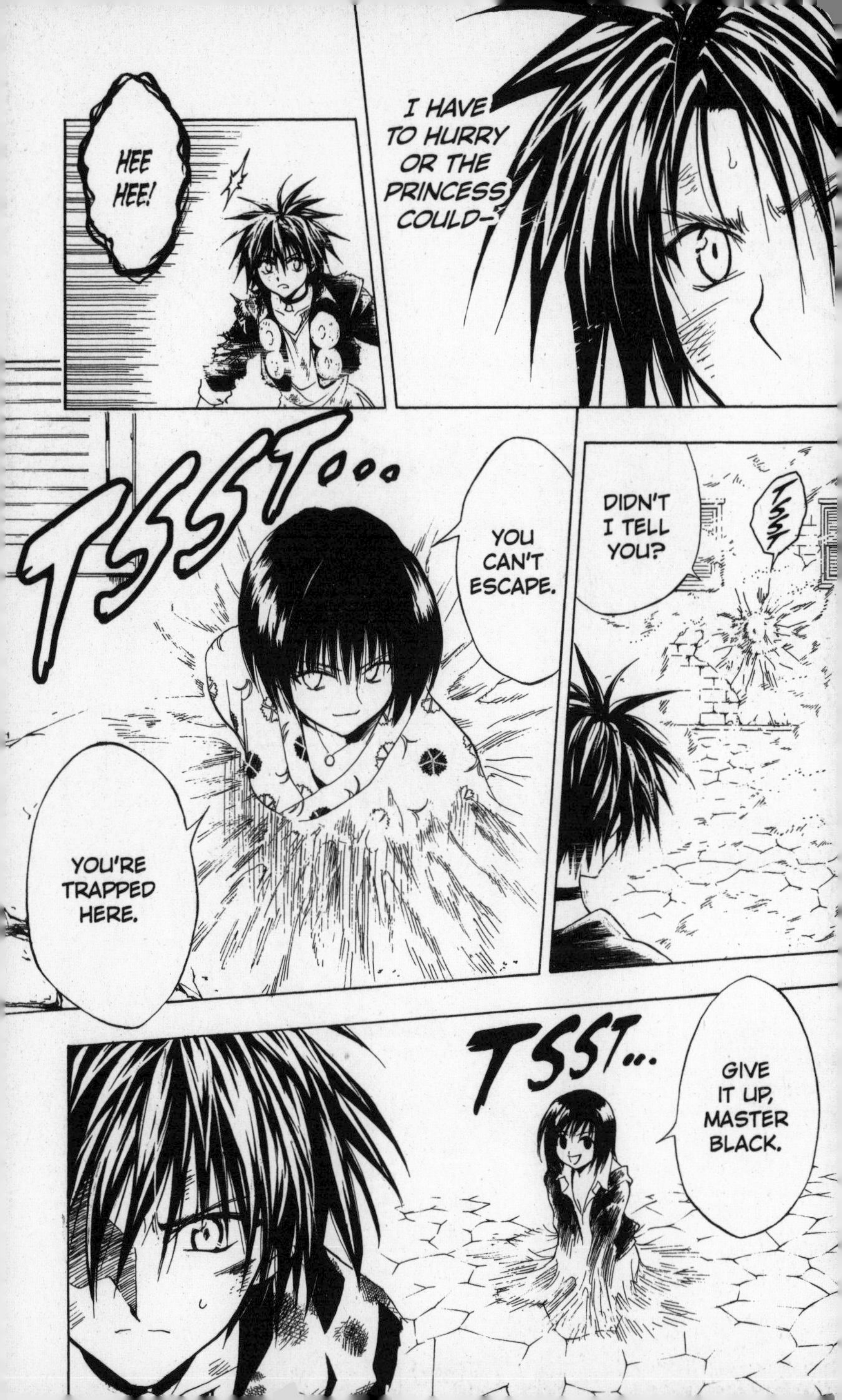
I HAVE TO HURRY OR THE PRINCESS COULD--
HEE HEE!
DIDN'T I TELL YOU?
TSST...
YOU CAN'T ESCAPE.
YOU'RE TRAPPED HERE.
TSST...
GIVE IT UP, MASTER BLACK.

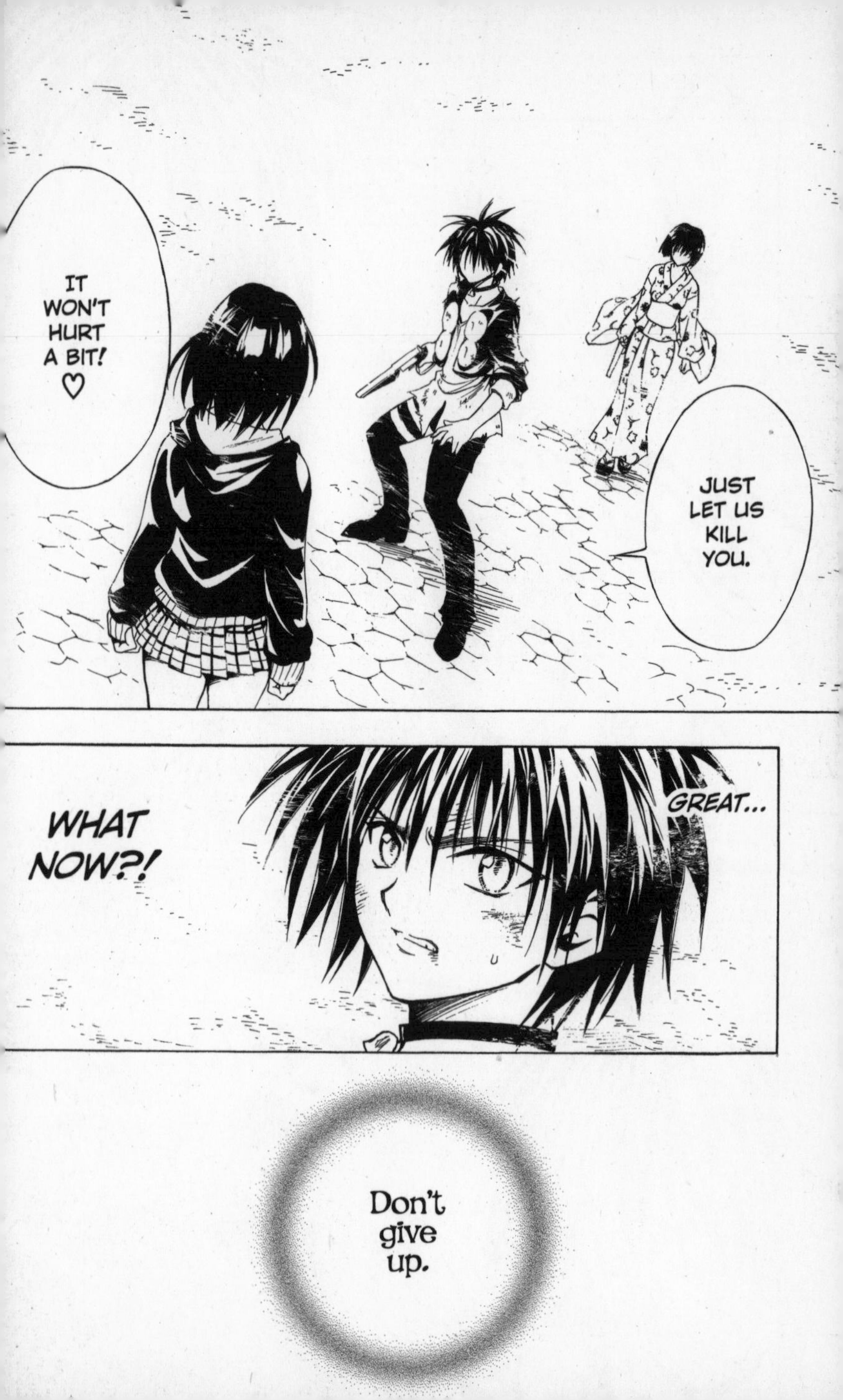
JUST LET US KILL YOU.
IT WON'T HURT A BIT! ♡
GREAT...
WHAT NOW?!
Don't give up.

READ THIS WAY

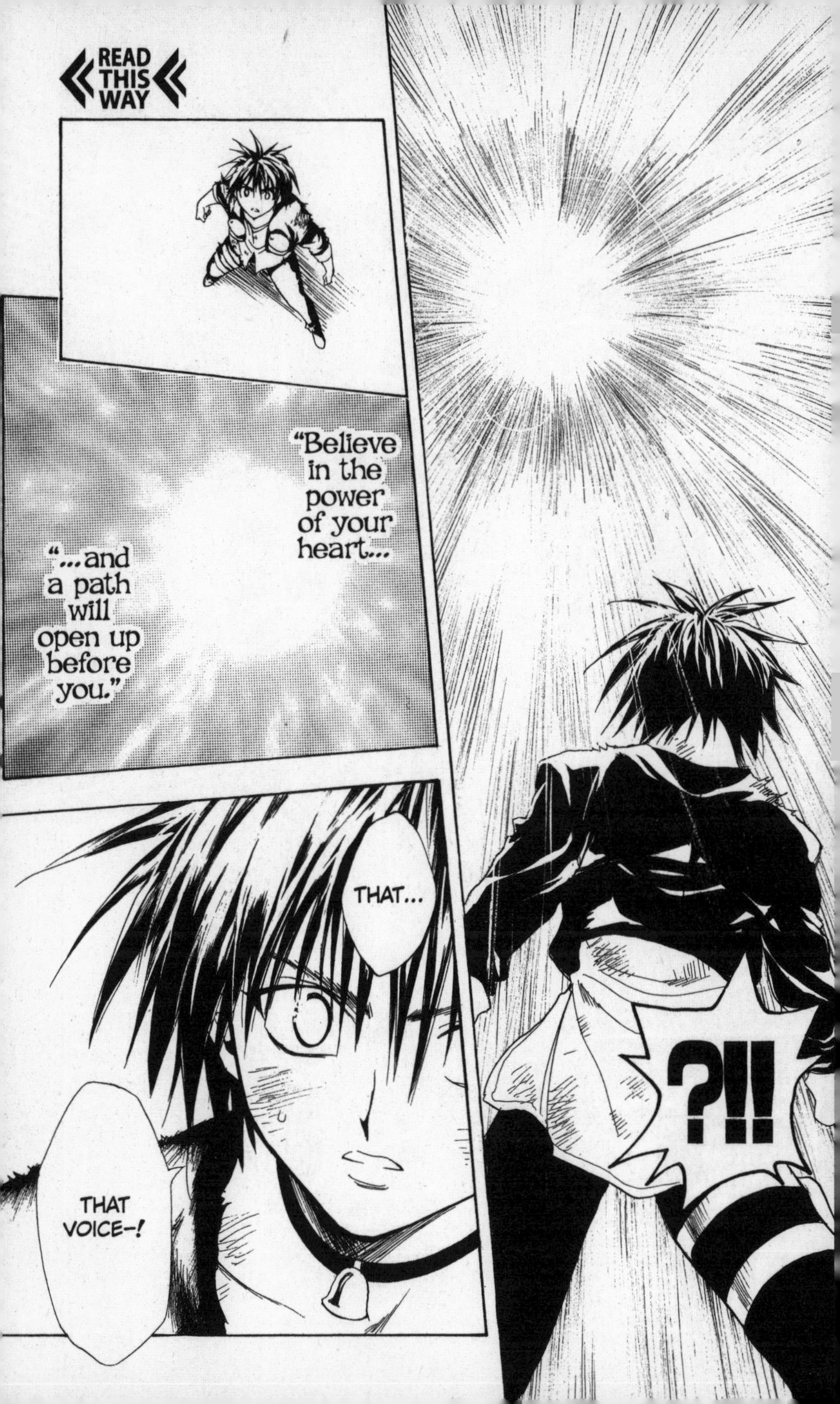
?!!
"Believe in the power of your heart...
"...and a path will open up before you."
THAT...
THAT VOICE-!

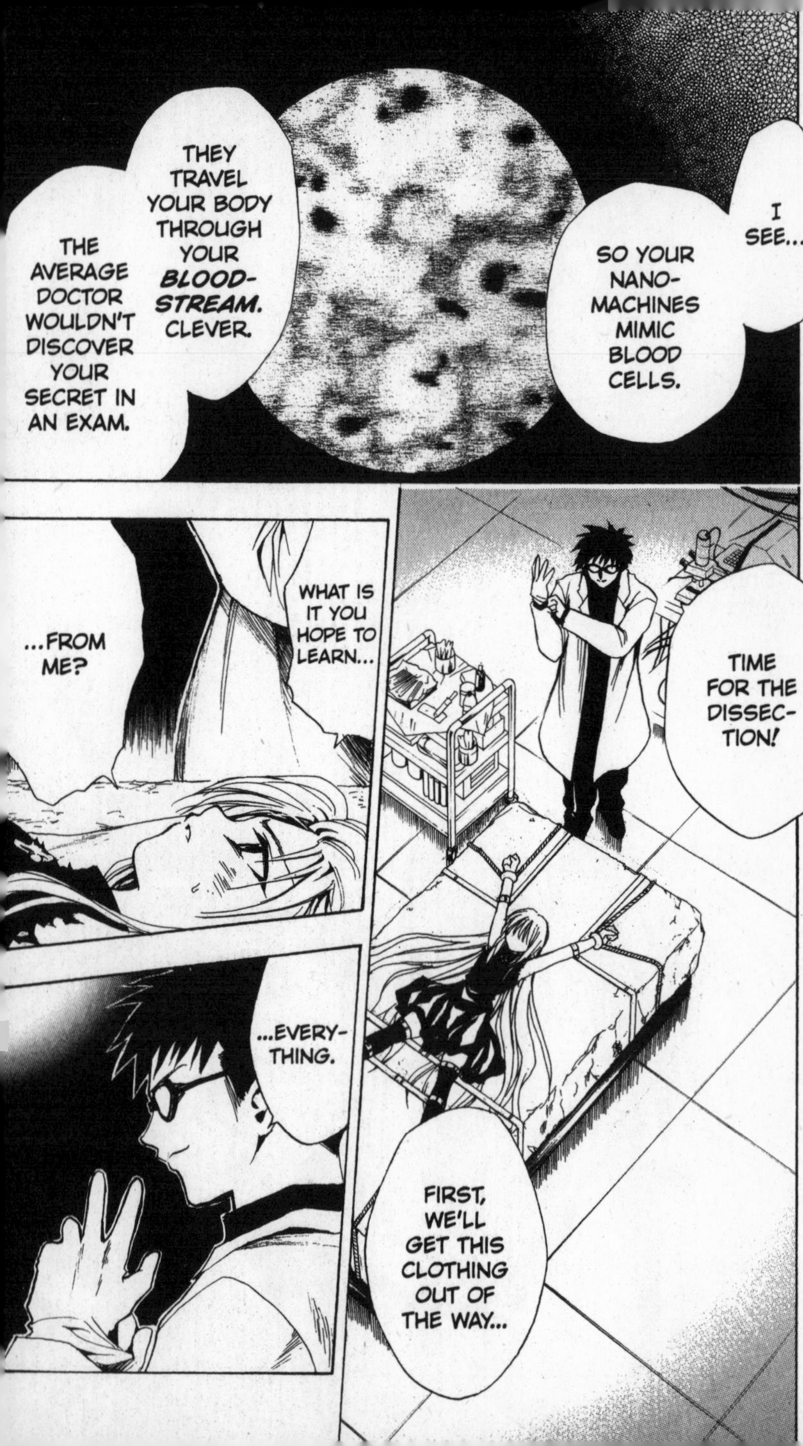
I SEE...
SO YOUR NANO-MACHINES MIMIC BLOOD CELLS.
THEY TRAVEL YOUR BODY THROUGH YOUR *BLOOD-STREAM.* CLEVER.
THE AVERAGE DOCTOR WOULDN'T DISCOVER YOUR SECRET IN AN EXAM.
TIME FOR THE DISSEC-TION!
FIRST, WE'LL GET THIS CLOTHING OUT OF THE WAY...
WHAT IS IT YOU HOPE TO LEARN...
...FROM ME?
...EVERY-THING.

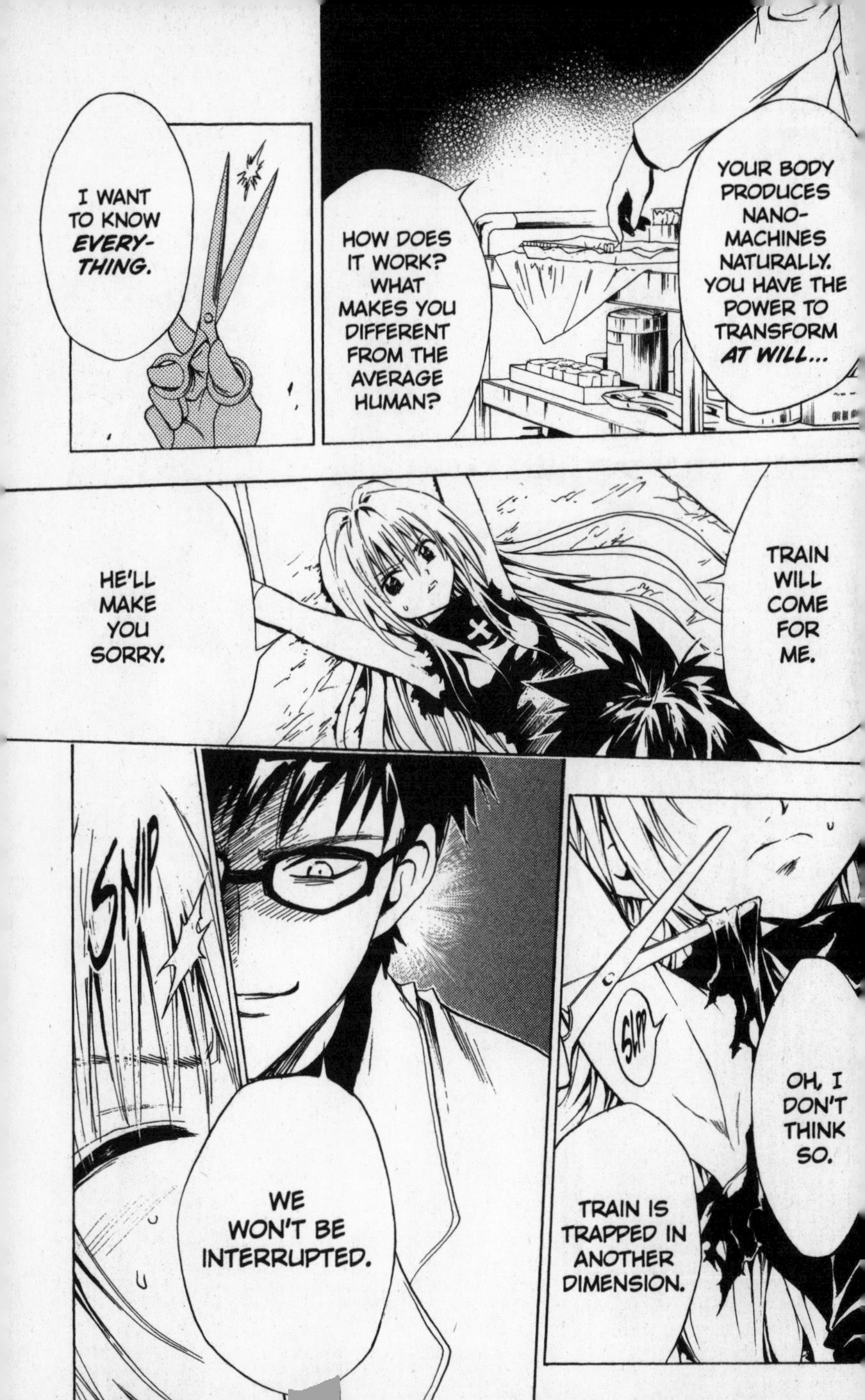
YOUR BODY PRODUCES NANO-MACHINES NATURALLY. YOU HAVE THE POWER TO TRANSFORM *AT WILL...*
HOW DOES IT WORK? WHAT MAKES YOU DIFFERENT FROM THE AVERAGE HUMAN?
I WANT TO KNOW *EVERY-THING.*
TRAIN WILL COME FOR ME.
HE'LL MAKE YOU SORRY.
SLIP
OH, I DON'T THINK SO.
TRAIN IS TRAPPED IN ANOTHER DIMENSION.
SNIP
WE WON'T BE INTERRUPTED.

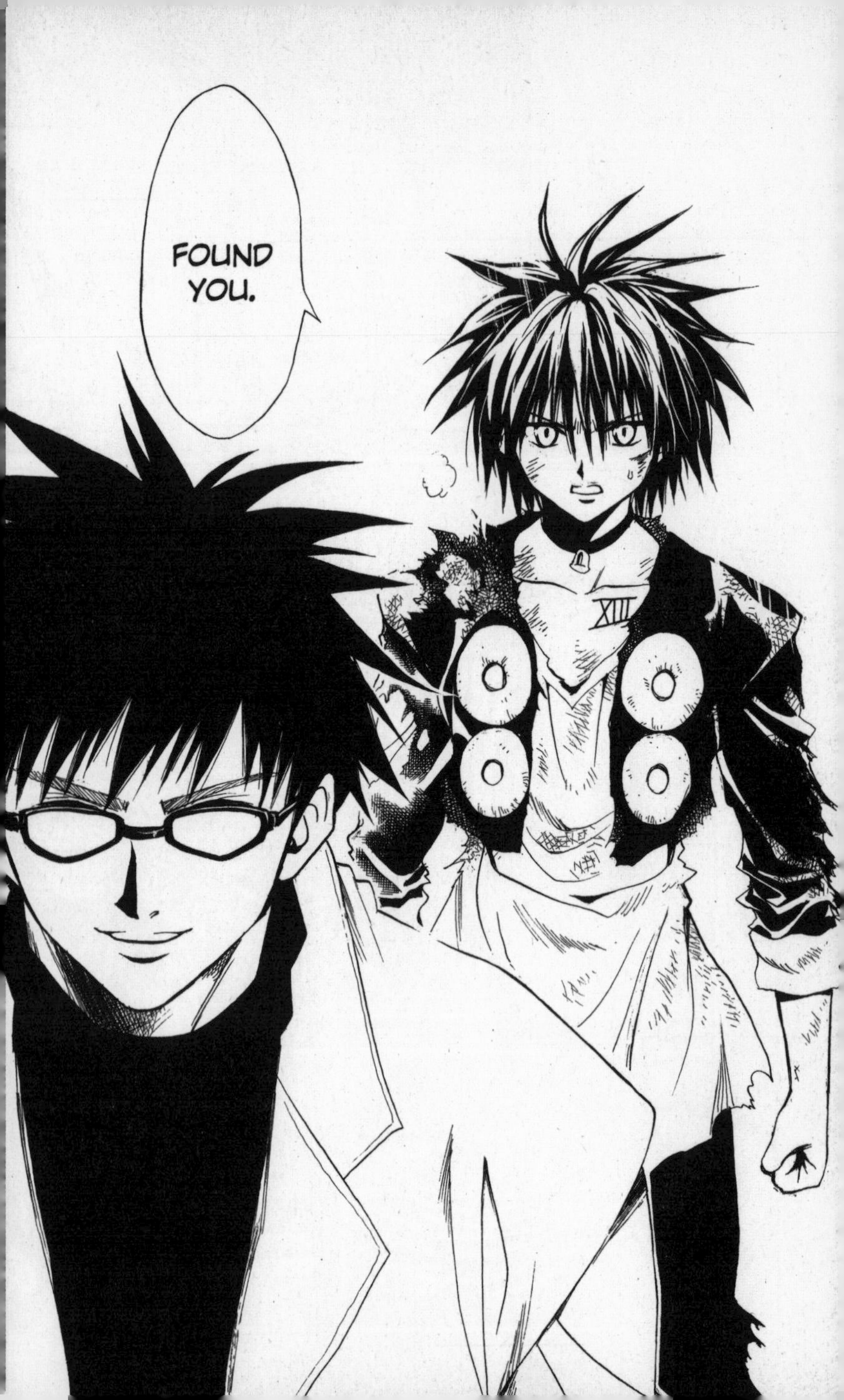
FOUND YOU.

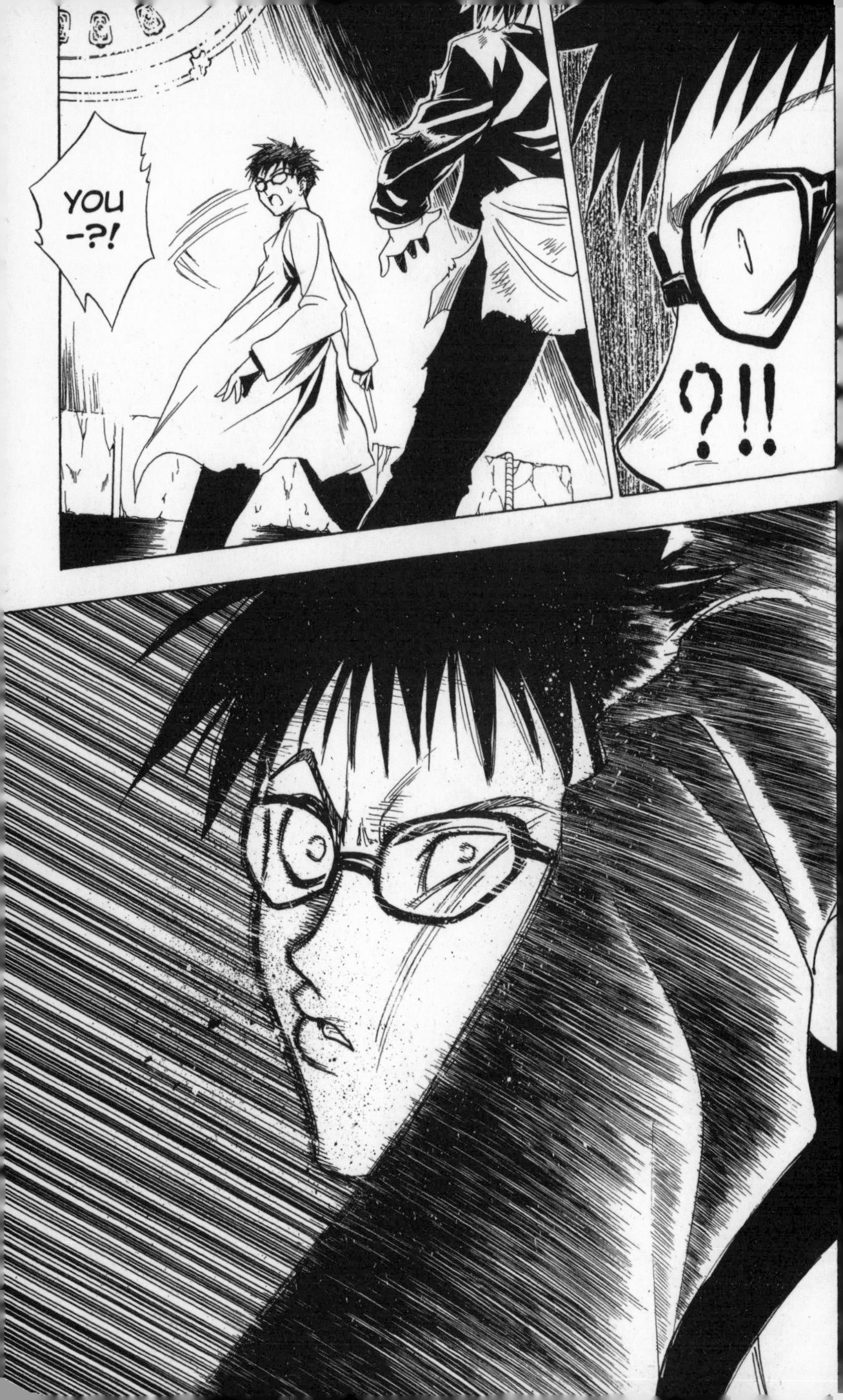
?!!
YOU –?!

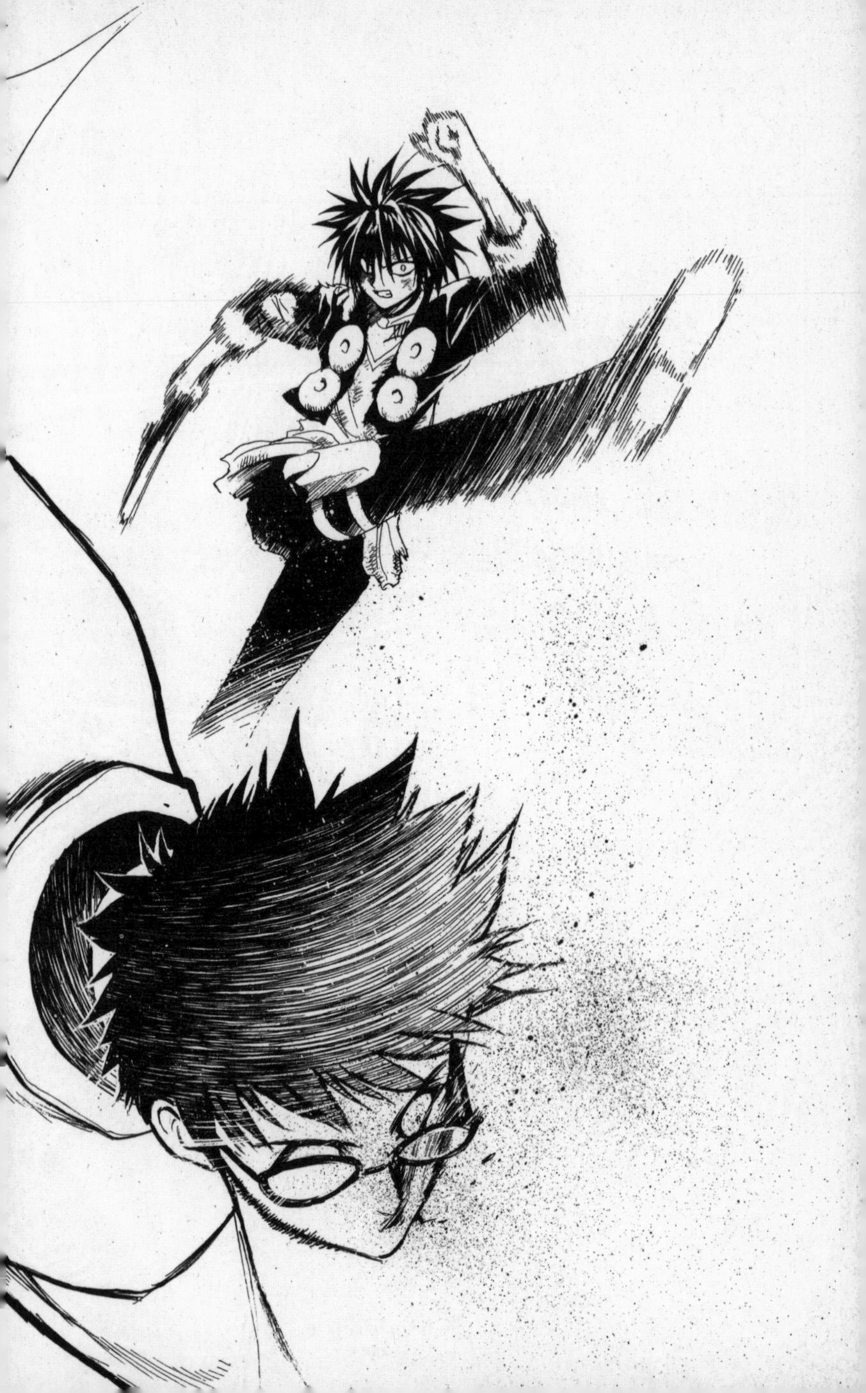

READ THIS WAY

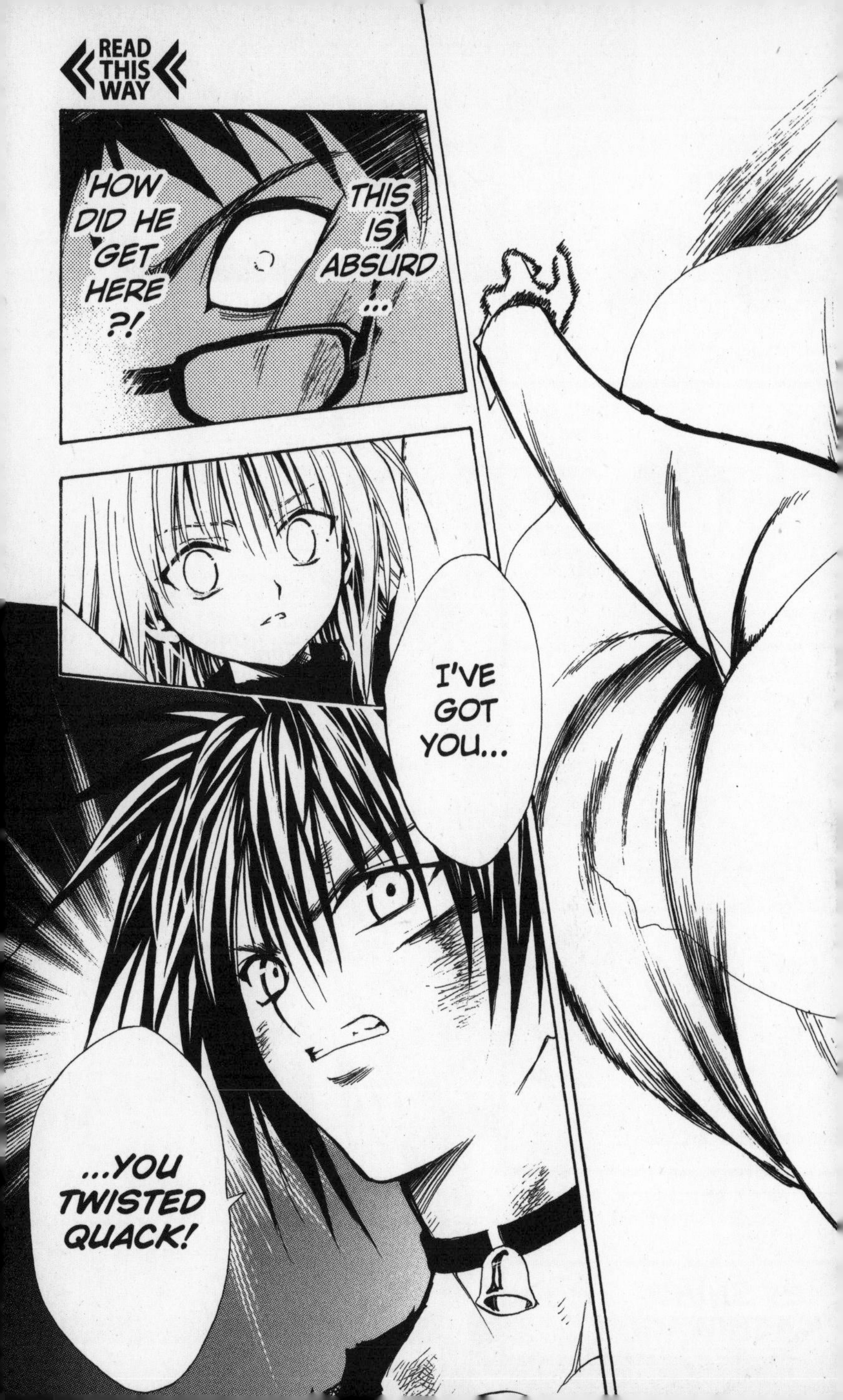
THIS IS ABSURD...
HOW DID HE GET HERE?!
I'VE GOT YOU...
...YOU TWISTED QUACK!

For this volume's inserts,
please enjoy manga drawn by my staff.

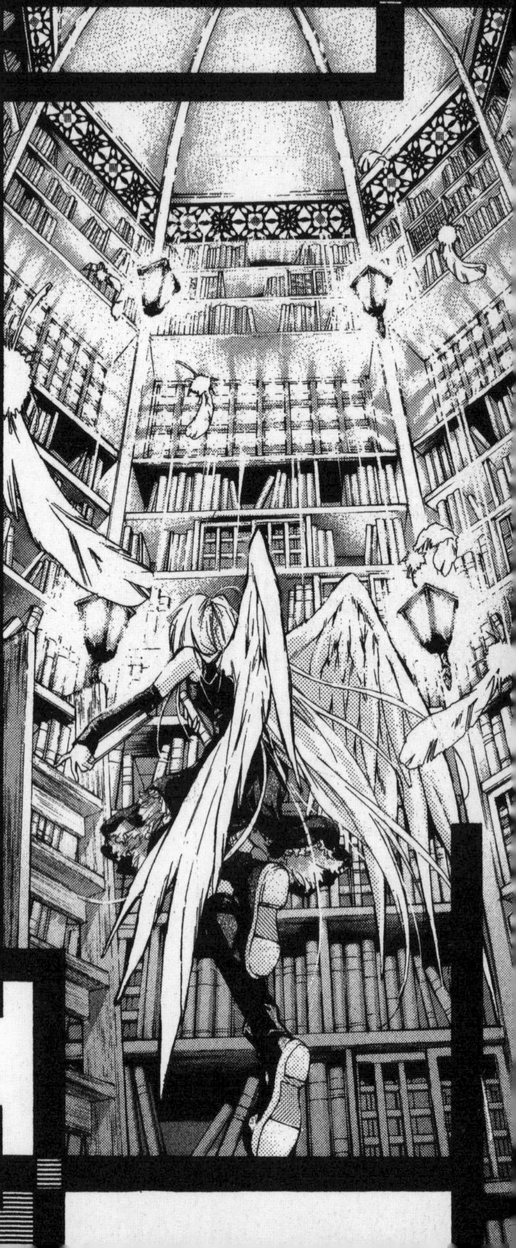

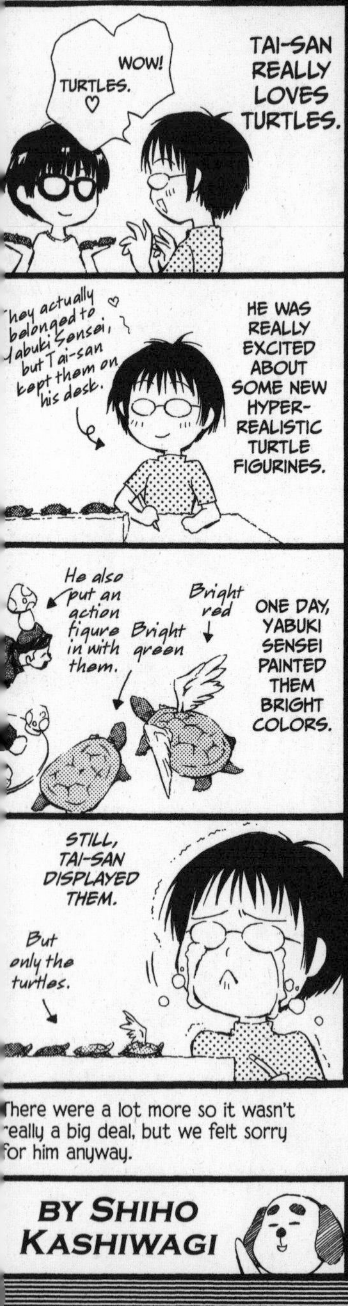

TAI-SAN REALLY LOVES TURTLES.
WOW!
TURTLES. ♡
HE WAS REALLY EXCITED ABOUT SOME NEW HYPER-REALISTIC TURTLE FIGURINES.
They actually belonged to Yabuki Sensei, but Tai-san kept them on his desk.
ONE DAY, YABUKI SENSEI PAINTED THEM BRIGHT COLORS.
Bright red
Bright green
He also put an action figure in with them.
STILL, TAI-SAN DISPLAYED THEM.
But only the turtles.
There were a lot more so it wasn't really a big deal, but we felt sorry for him anyway.
BY SHIHO KASHIWAGI

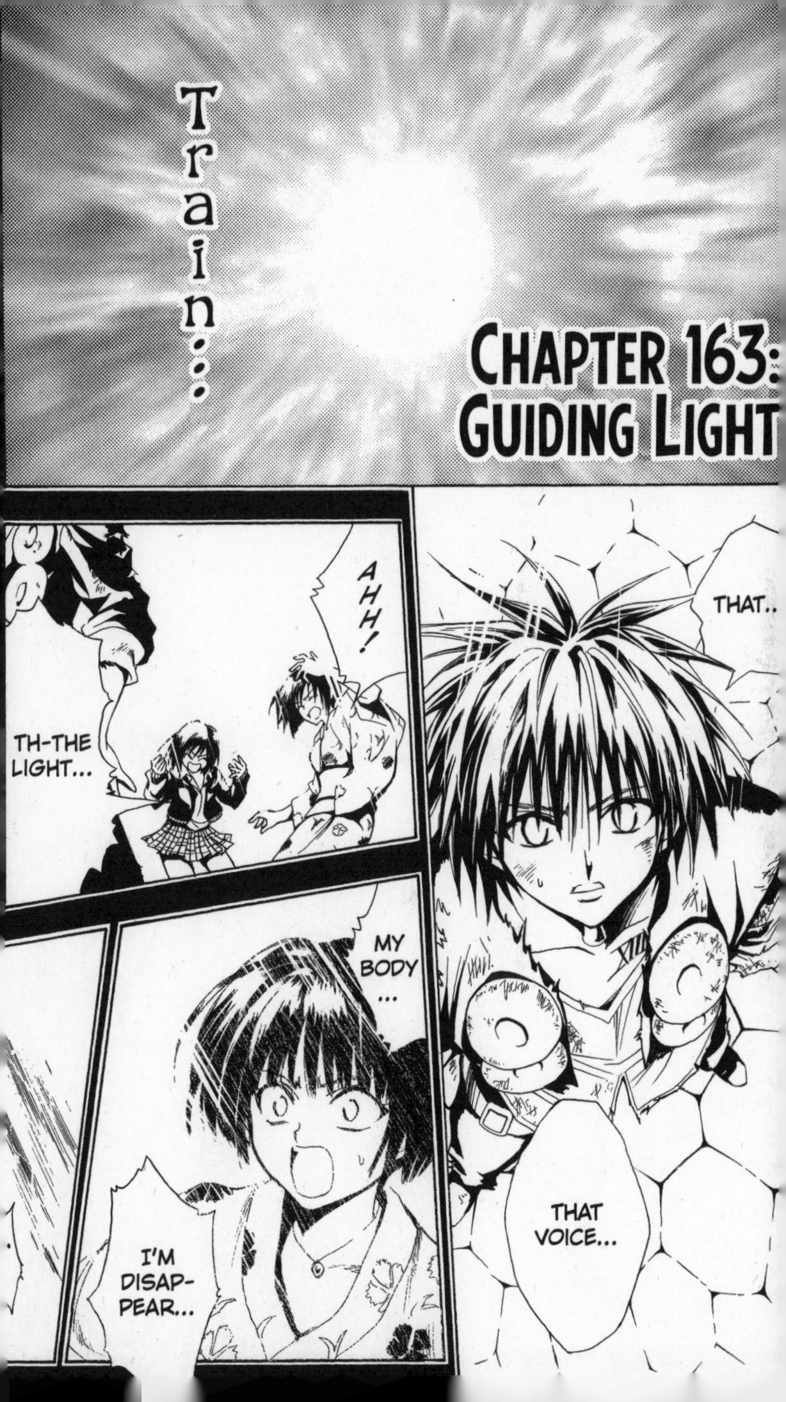
CHAPTER 163: GUIDING LIGHT
Train...
THAT...
THAT VOICE...
AHH!
TH-THE LIGHT...
MY BODY ...
I'M DISAP-PEAR...

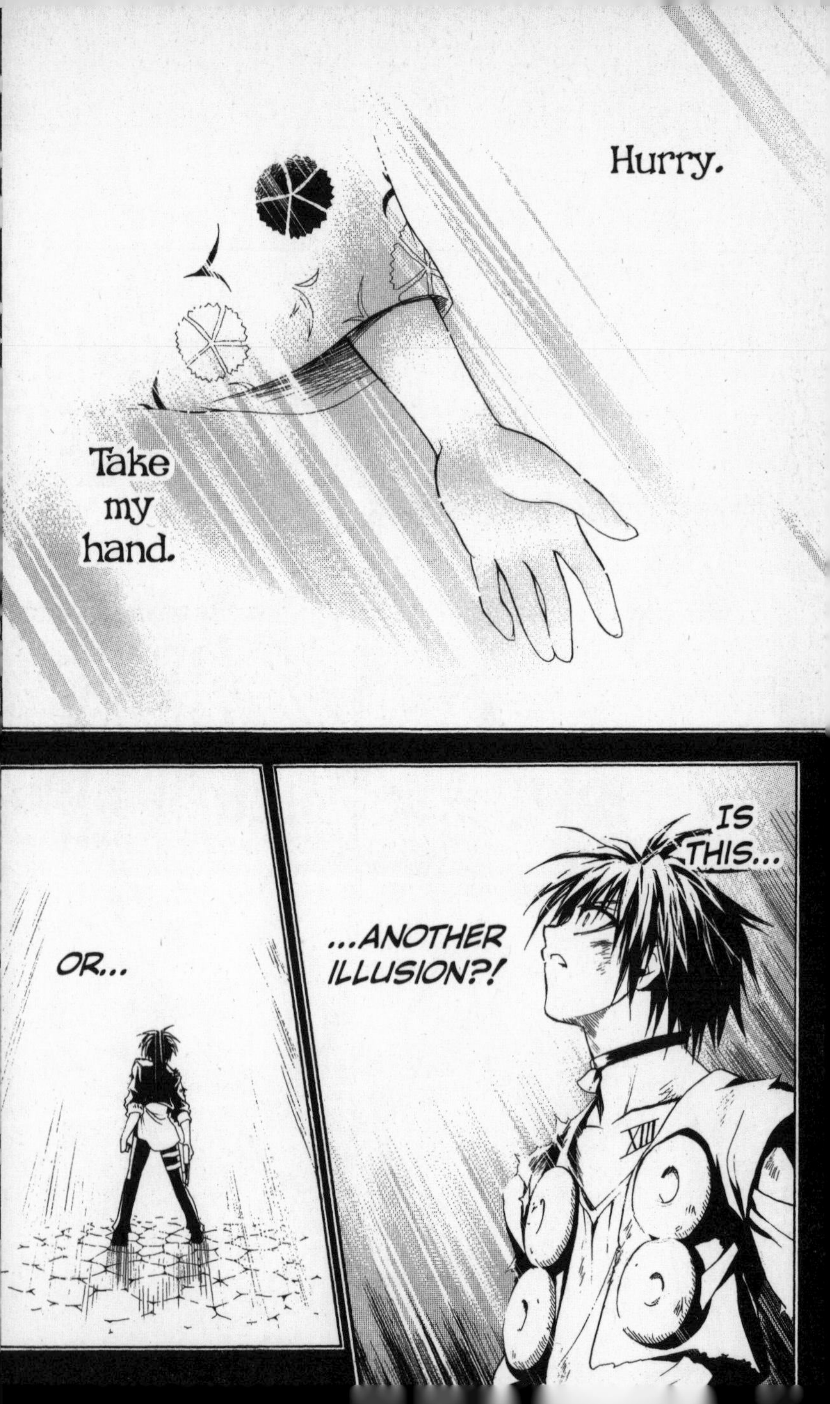
Hurry.
Take my hand.
IS THIS...
...ANOTHER ILLUSION?!
OR...

READ THIS WAY

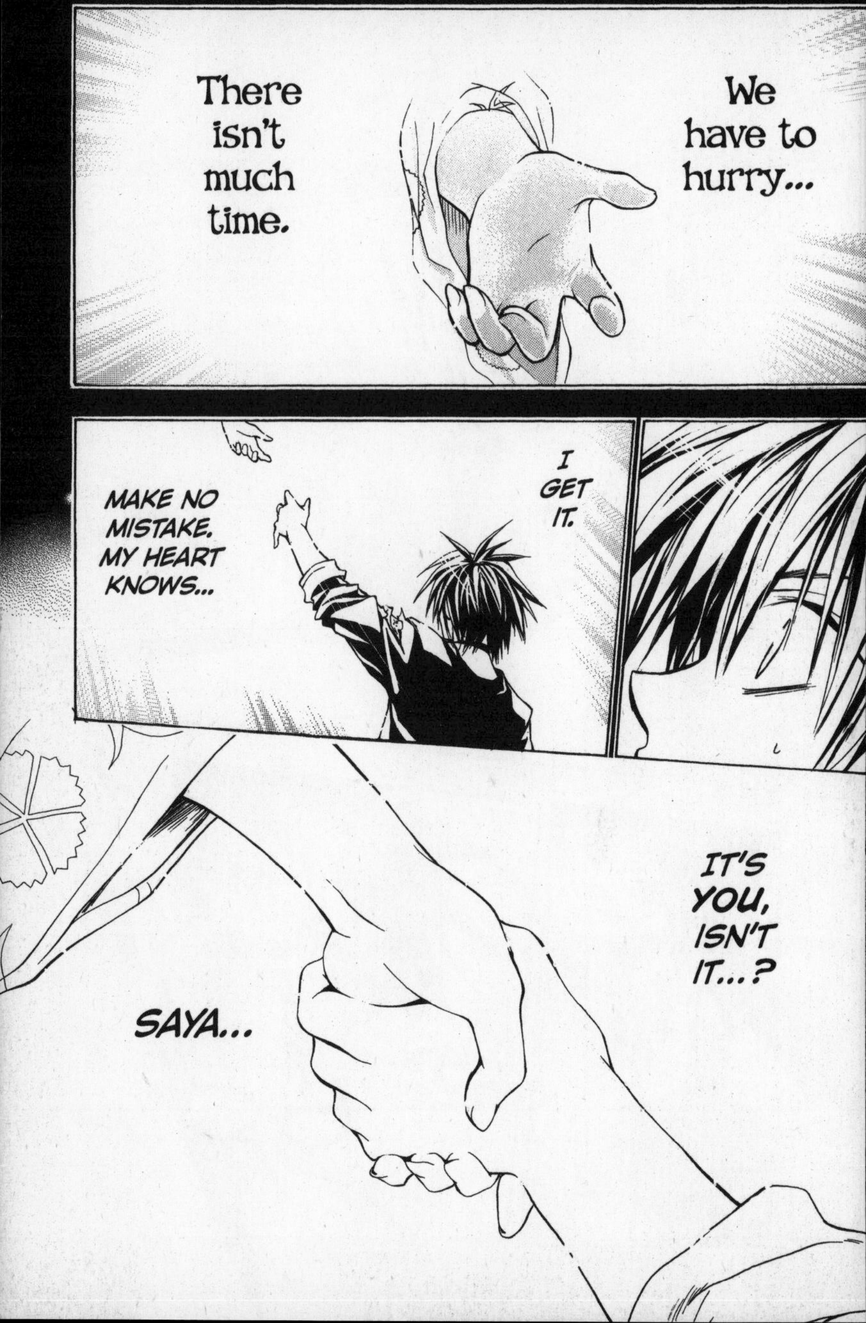

We have to hurry...
There isn't much time.
I GET IT.
MAKE NO MISTAKE. MY HEART KNOWS...
IT'S YOU, ISN'T IT...?
SAYA...

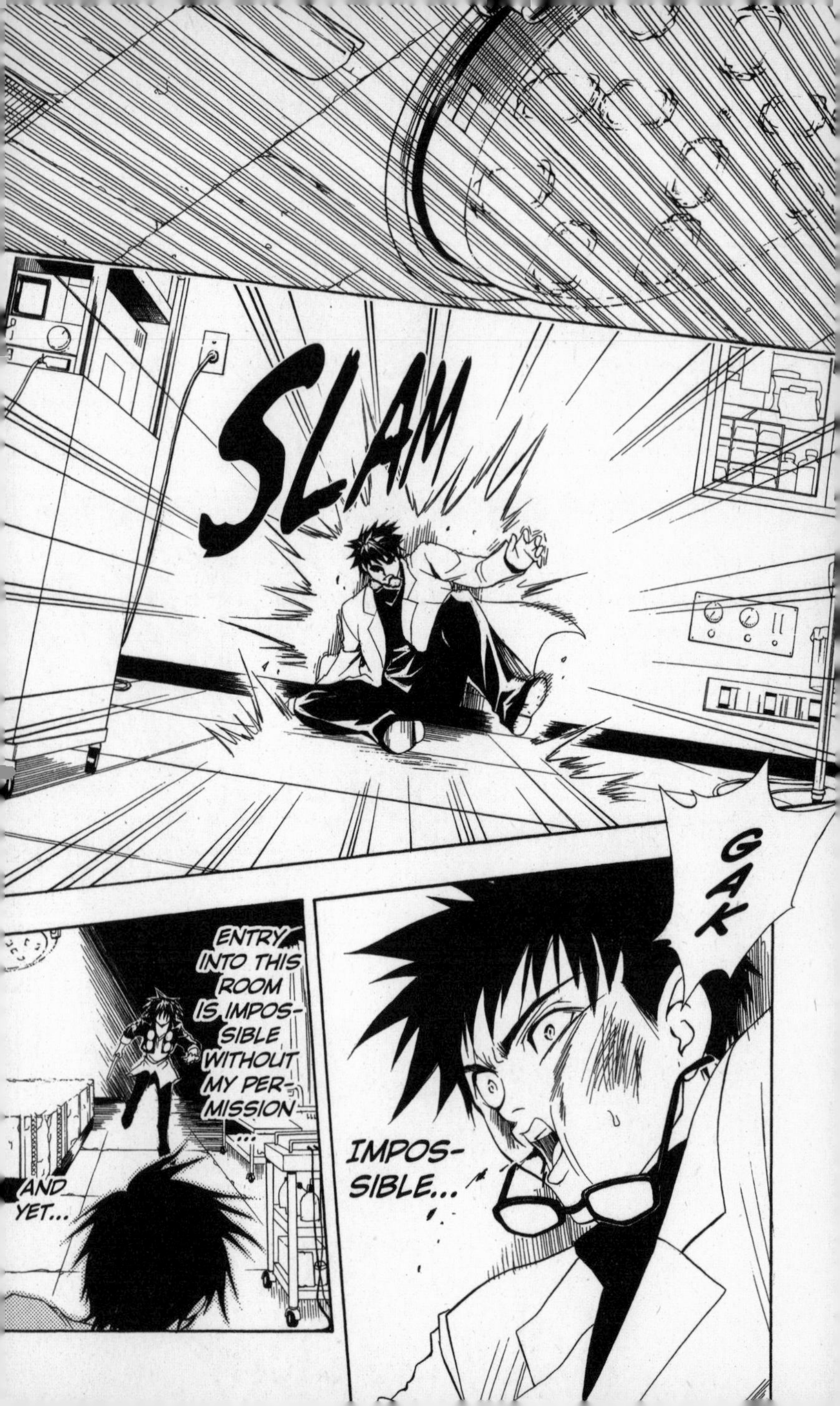
SLAM
GAK
IMPOSSIBLE...
ENTRY INTO THIS ROOM IS IMPOSSIBLE WITHOUT MY PERMISSION...
AND YET...

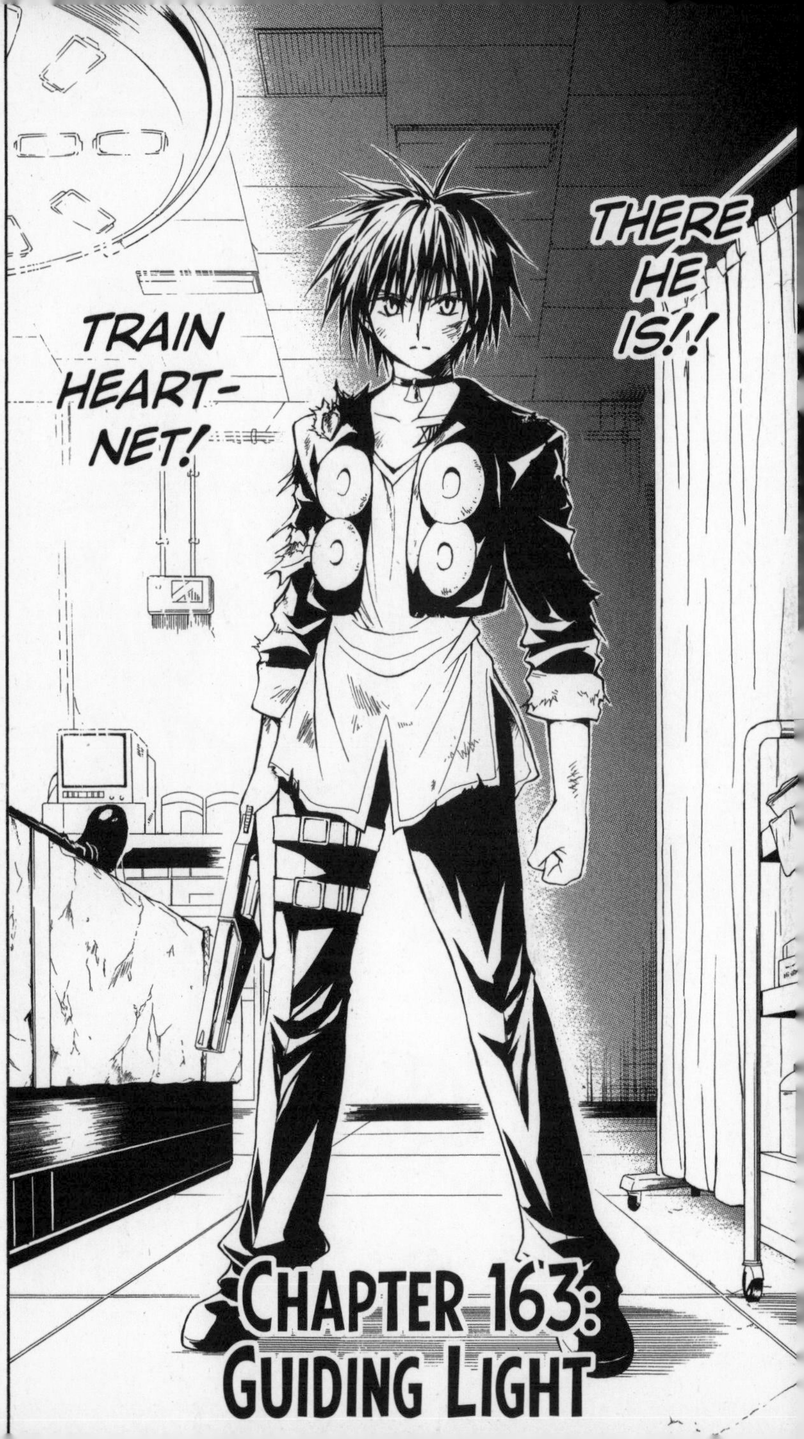
THERE HE IS!!
TRAIN HEART-NET!
CHAPTER 163: GUIDING LIGHT

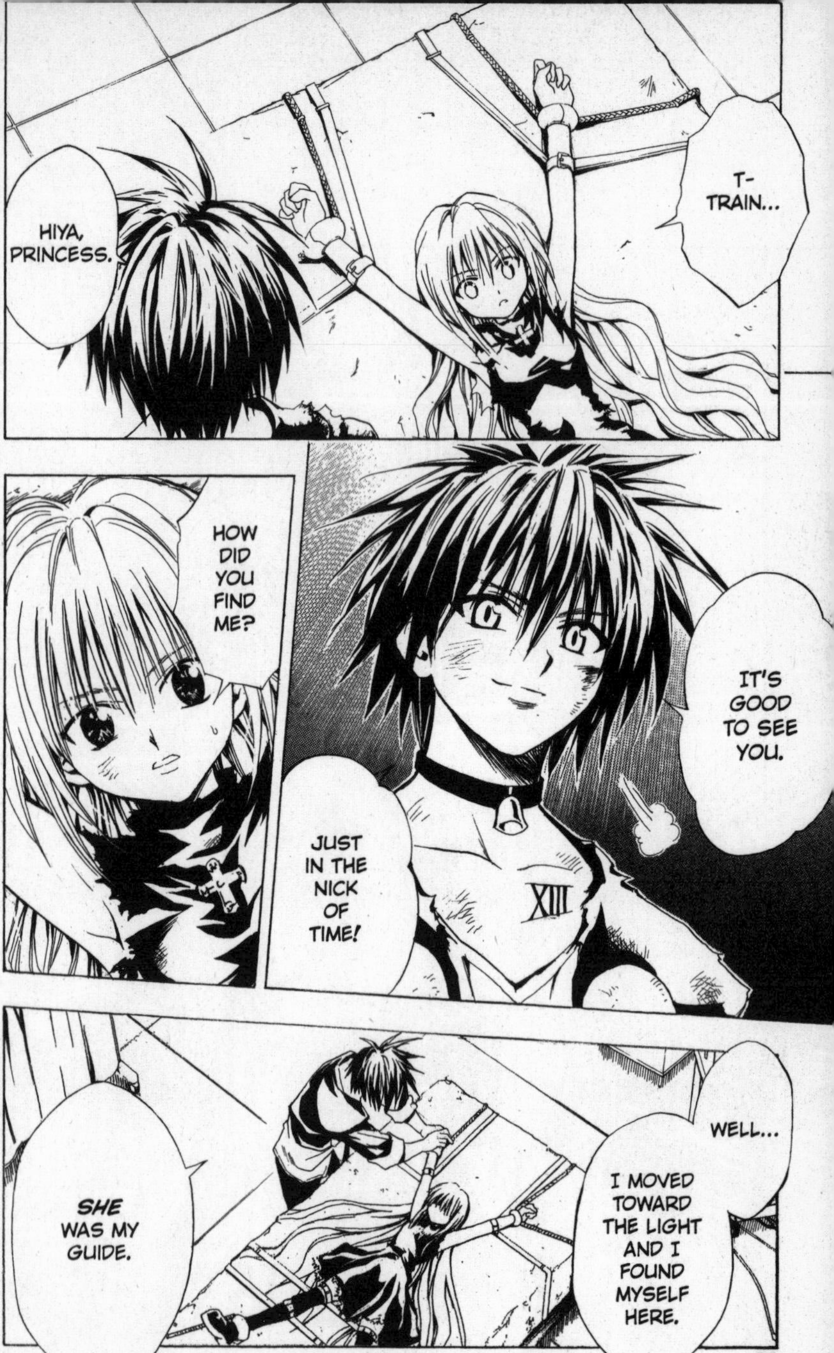
T-TRAIN...
HIYA, PRINCESS.
IT'S GOOD TO SEE YOU.
JUST IN THE NICK OF TIME!
HOW DID YOU FIND ME?
WELL...
I MOVED TOWARD THE LIGHT AND I FOUND MYSELF HERE.
SHE WAS MY GUIDE.

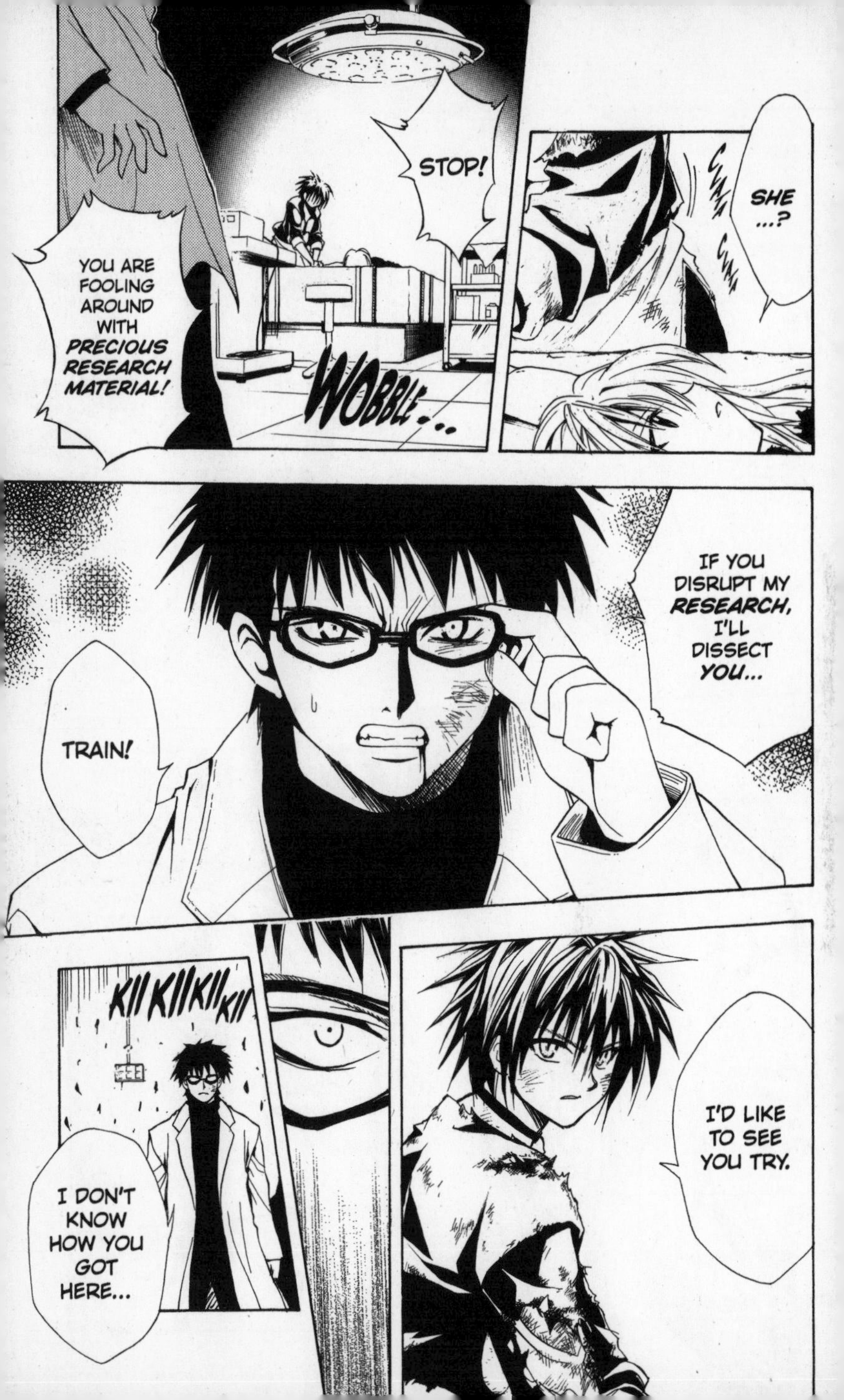
SHE ...?
STOP!
YOU ARE FOOLING AROUND WITH *PRECIOUS RESEARCH MATERIAL!*
WOBBLE...
IF YOU DISRUPT MY *RESEARCH,* I'LL DISSECT *YOU...*
TRAIN!
I'D LIKE TO SEE YOU TRY.
KII KII KII KII
I DON'T KNOW HOW YOU GOT HERE...

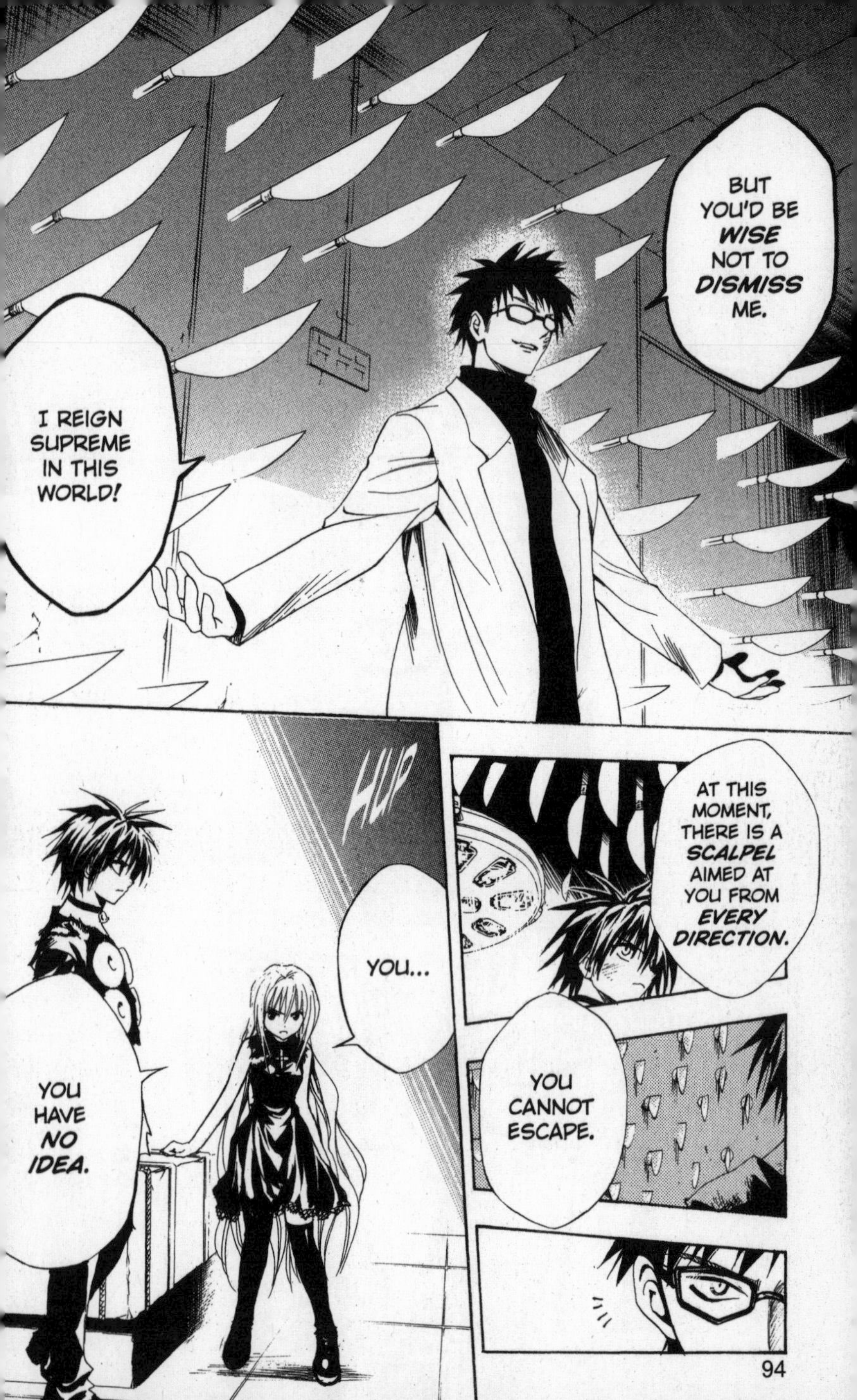
BUT YOU'D BE WISE NOT TO DISMISS ME.
I REIGN SUPREME IN THIS WORLD!
AT THIS MOMENT, THERE IS A SCALPEL AIMED AT YOU FROM EVERY DIRECTION.
YOU CANNOT ESCAPE.
HUP
YOU...
YOU HAVE NO IDEA.

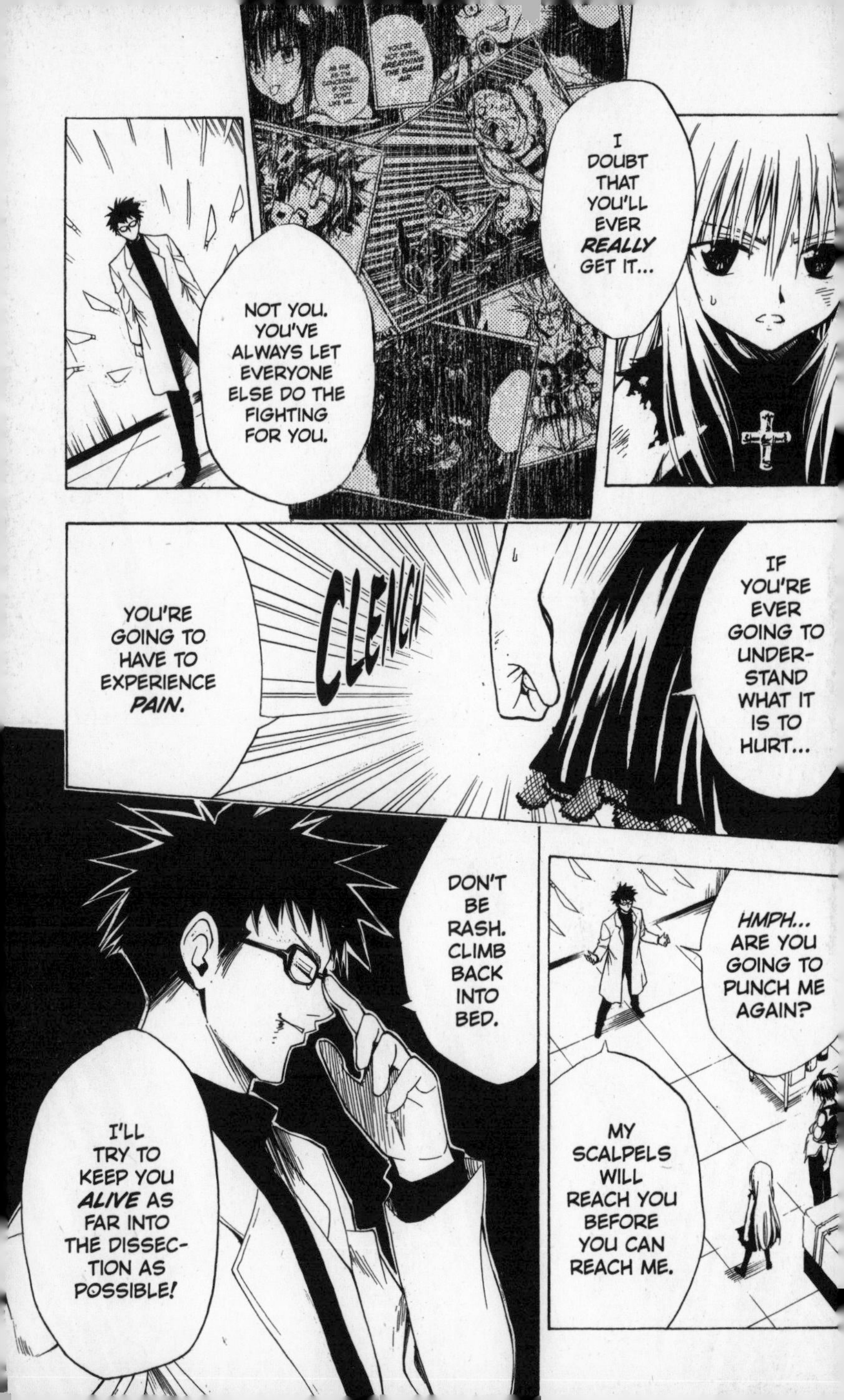
I DOUBT THAT YOU'LL EVER REALLY GET IT...
YOU'RE NOT EVEN BREATHING THE SAME AIR.
AS FAR AS I'M CONCERNED, IF YOU DON'T LIKE ME...
NOT YOU. YOU'VE ALWAYS LET EVERYONE ELSE DO THE FIGHTING FOR YOU.
IF YOU'RE EVER GOING TO UNDER-STAND WHAT IT IS TO HURT...
CLENCH
YOU'RE GOING TO HAVE TO EXPERIENCE PAIN.
HMPH... ARE YOU GOING TO PUNCH ME AGAIN?
MY SCALPELS WILL REACH YOU BEFORE YOU CAN REACH ME.
DON'T BE RASH. CLIMB BACK INTO BED.
I'LL TRY TO KEEP YOU ALIVE AS FAR INTO THE DISSEC-TION AS POSSIBLE!

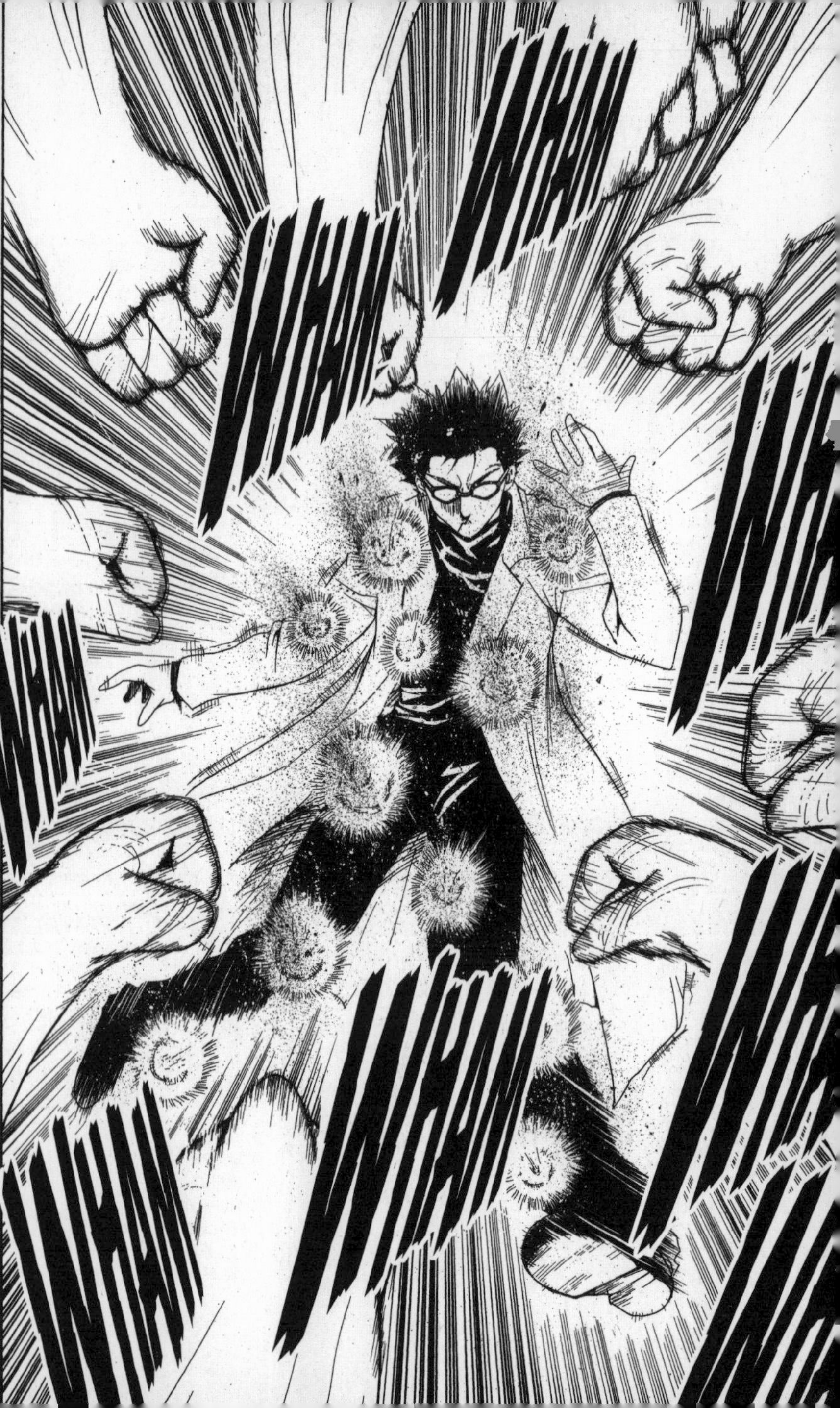
WHAM
WHAM
WHAM
WHAM
WHAM

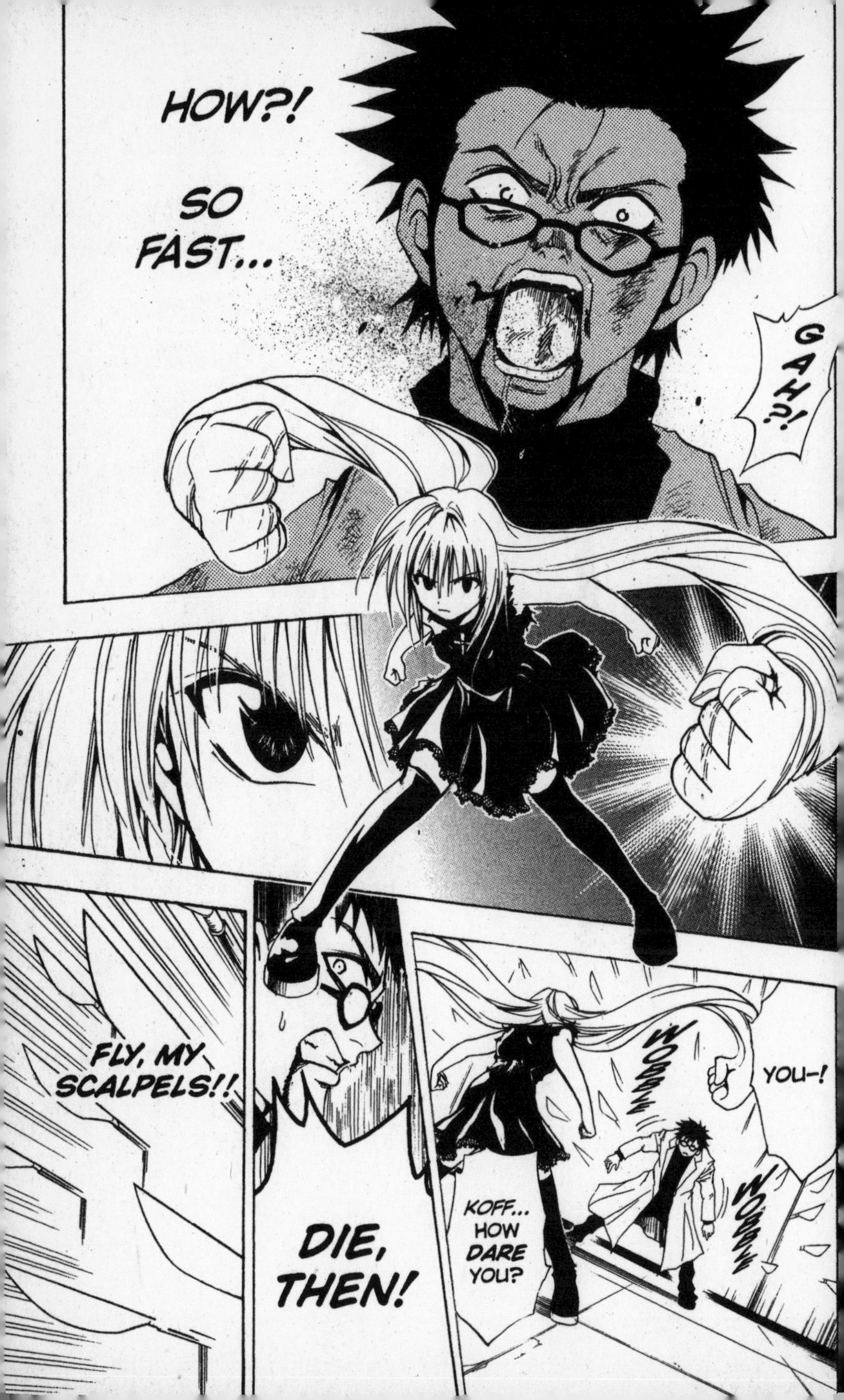
GAH?!
HOW?!
SO FAST...
YOU-!
KOFF... HOW DARE YOU?
DIE, THEN!
FLY, MY SCALPELS!!

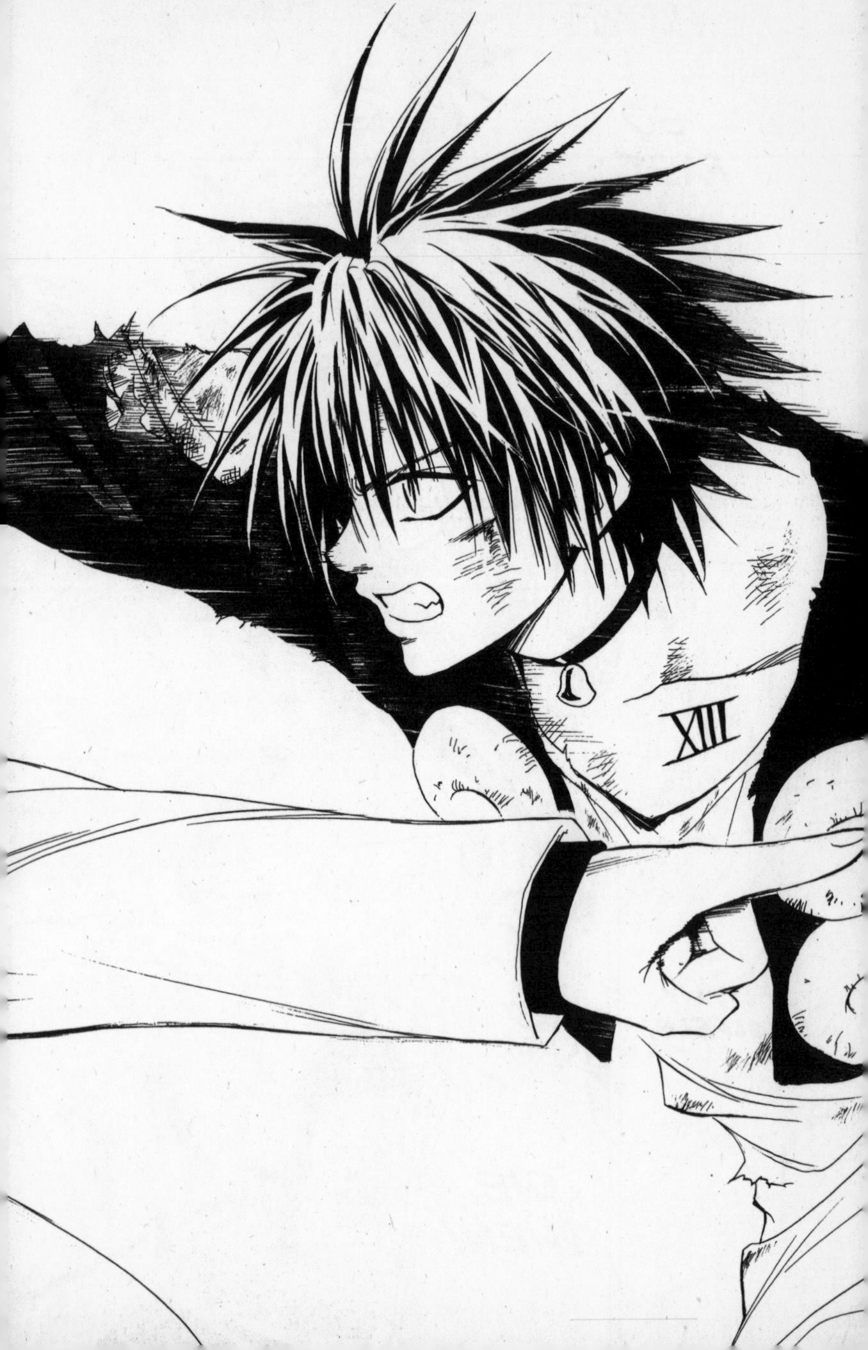
XIII

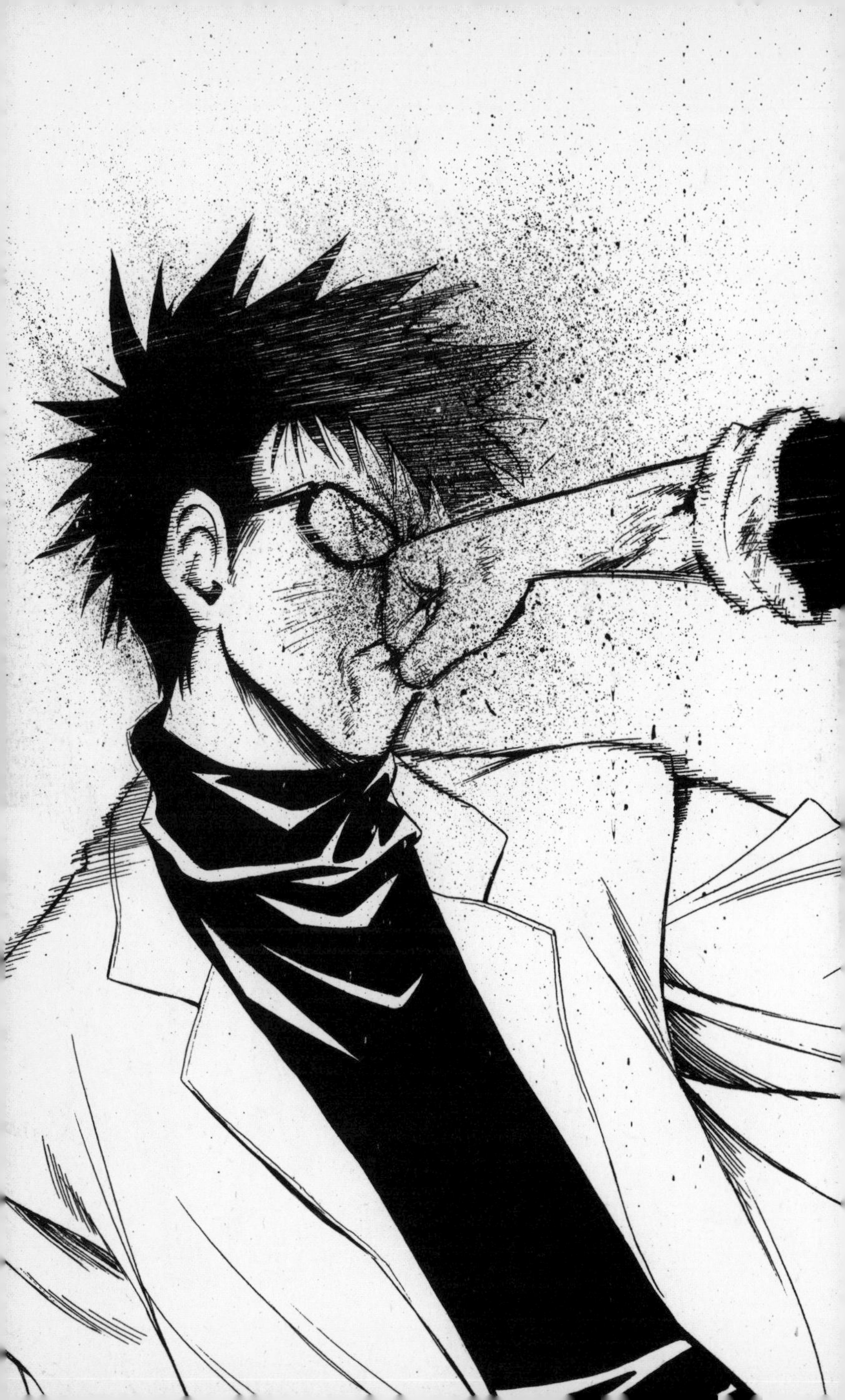

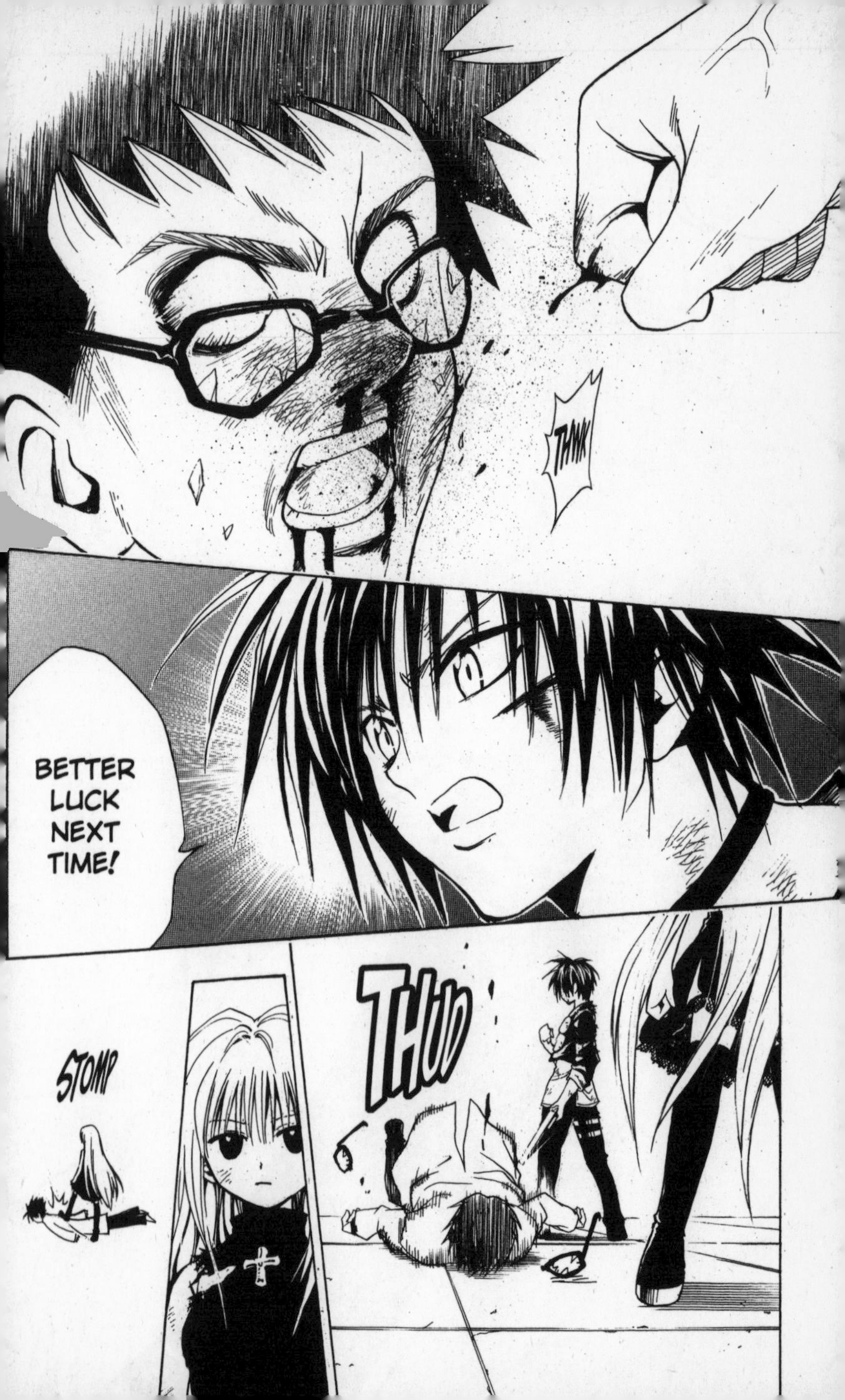
THNK
BETTER LUCK NEXT TIME!
THUD
STOMP

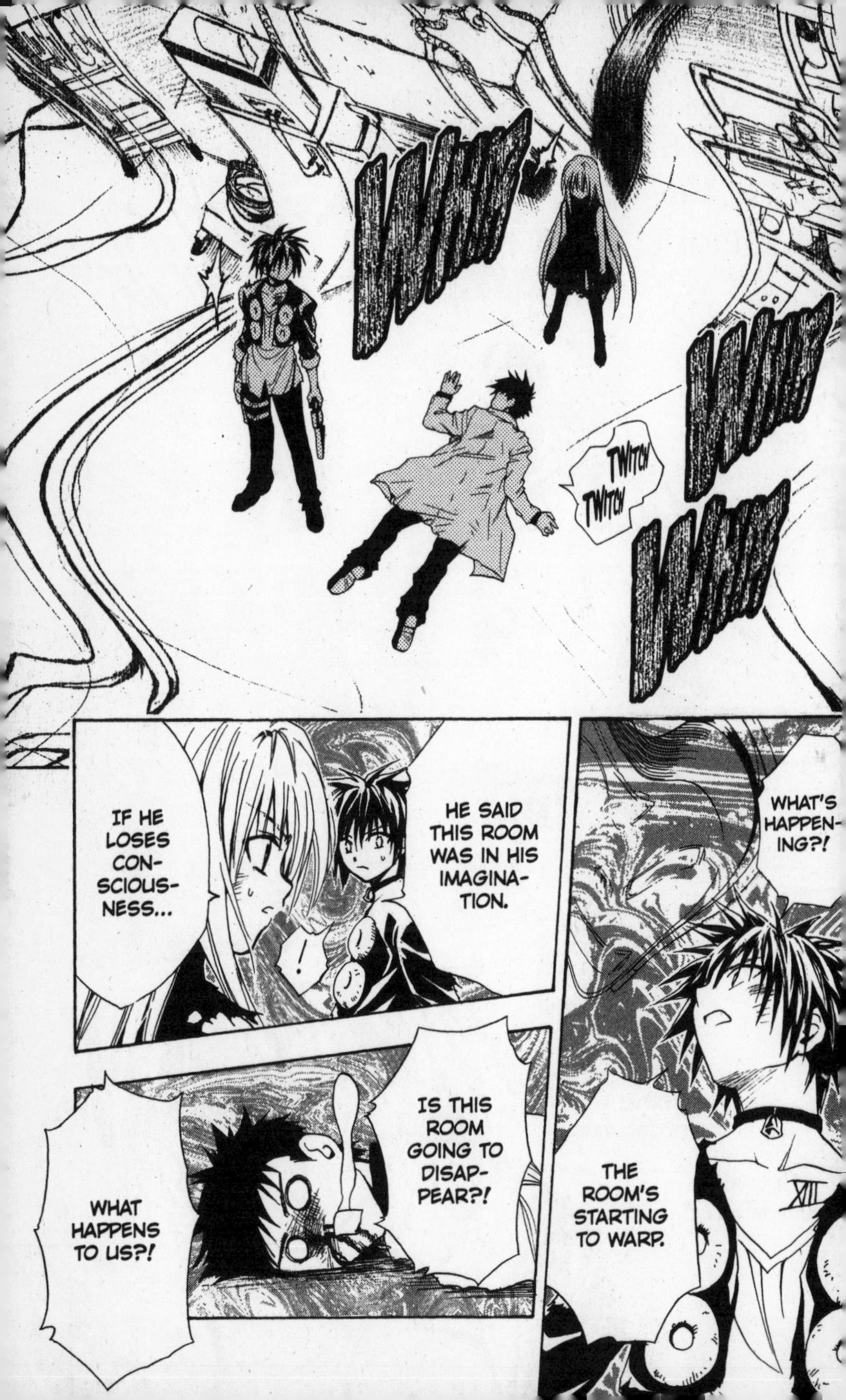
TWITCH
TWITCH
WHAT'S HAPPEN-ING?!
THE ROOM'S STARTING TO WARP.
HE SAID THIS ROOM WAS IN HIS IMAGINA-TION.
IF HE LOSES CON-SCIOUS-NESS...
!
IS THIS ROOM GOING TO DISAP-PEAR?!
WHAT HAPPENS TO US?!

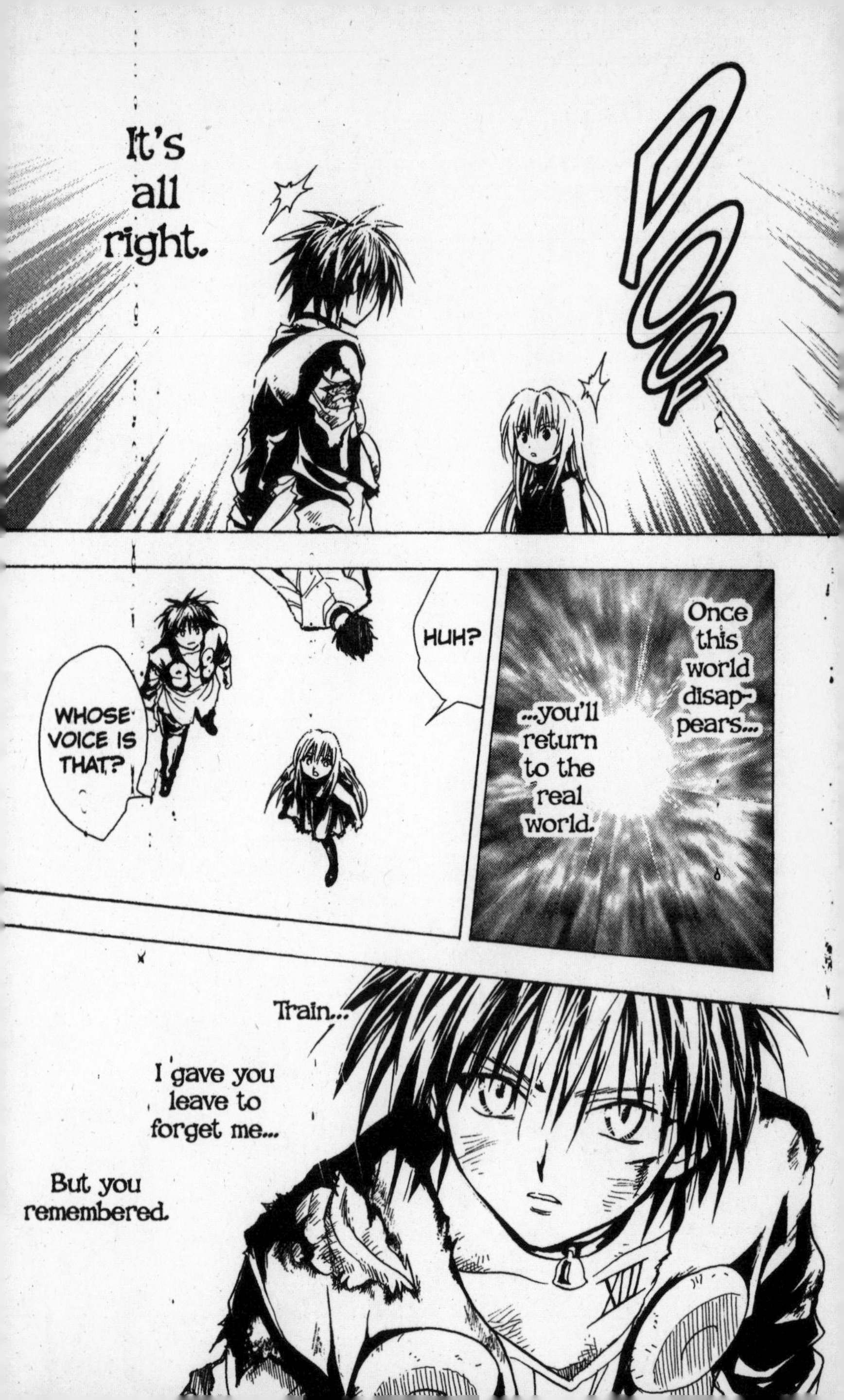
It's all right.
Once this world disappears...
...you'll return to the real world.
HUH?
WHOSE VOICE IS THAT?
Train...
I gave you leave to forget me...
But you remembered.

READ THIS WAY

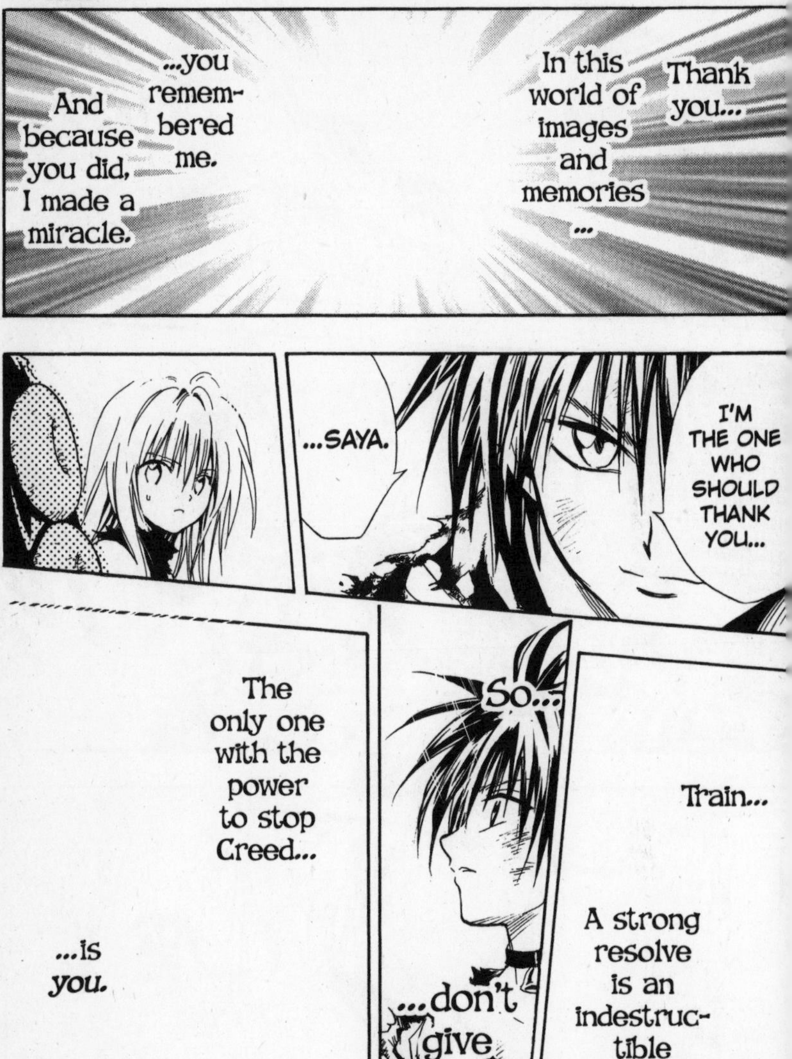

Thank you...
In this world of images and memories...
...you remembered me.
And because you did, I made a miracle.
I'M THE ONE WHO SHOULD THANK YOU...
...SAYA.
Train...
A strong resolve is an indestructible weapon.
So...
...don't give up.
The only one with the power to stop Creed...
...is *you.*

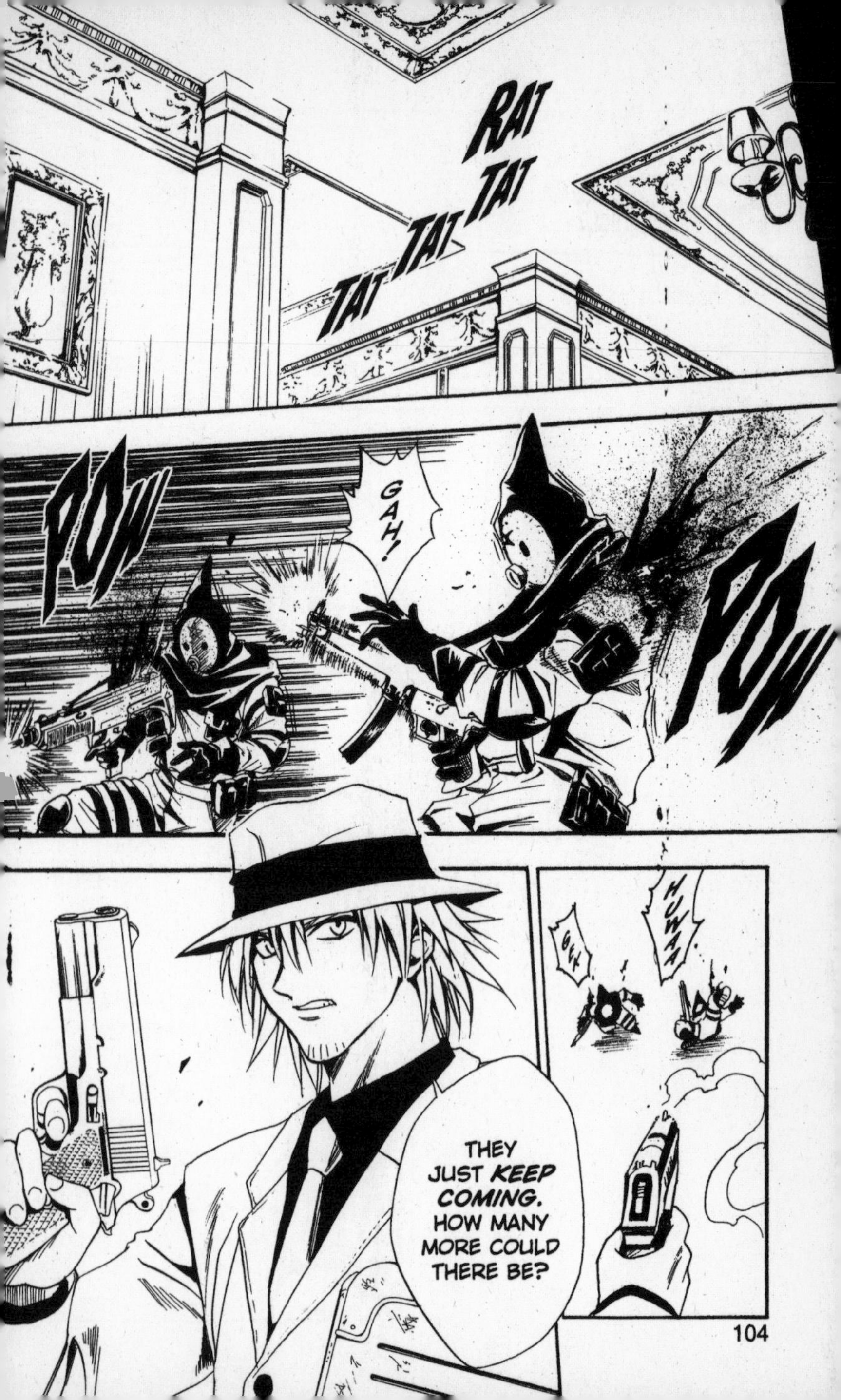
RAT TAT TAT TAT
POW
GAH!
POW
HUWAA
GEK
THEY JUST KEEP COMING. HOW MANY MORE COULD THERE BE?

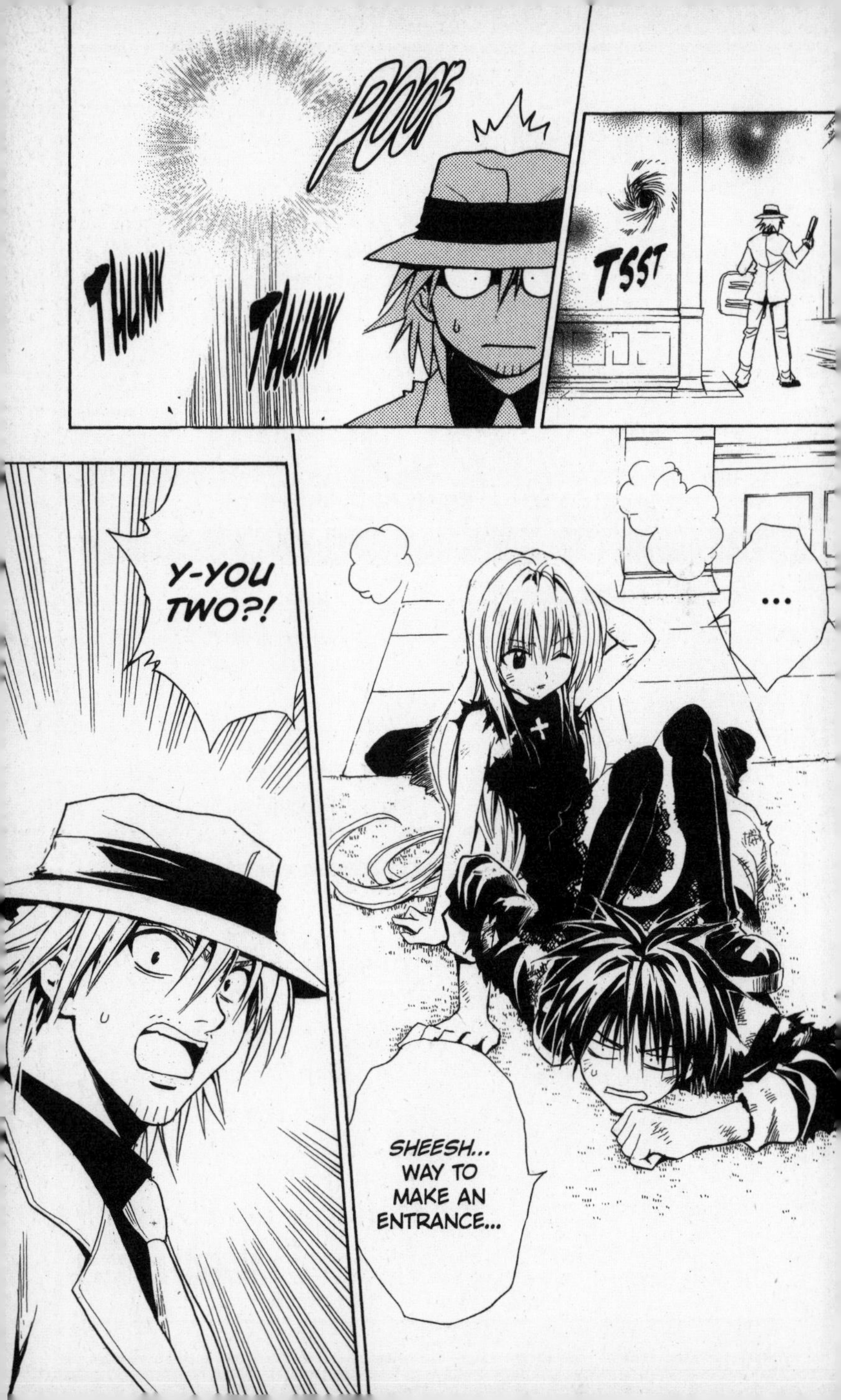
TSST
POOF
THUNK
THUNK
...
SHEESH... WAY TO MAKE AN ENTRANCE...
Y-YOU TWO?!

profile

THE DOCTOR

DATA	
BIRTHDATE:	JULY 7
AGE:	26
BLOOD TYPE:	B
HEIGHT:	173 CM
WEIGHT:	63 KG
POWER:	WARP WORLD, SPIRITUAL CHI KUNG
INTERESTS:	THE GAME OF GO, EXPERIMENTAL RESEARCH ON LIVING SUBJECTS
LIKES:	THE THRILL OF DISCOVERY, MONSTER MOVIES
DISLIKES:	BAD TELEVISION
COMMENTS:	THE DOCTOR WAS AMONG THE FIRST APOSTLES RECRUITED BY CREED DURING HIS TRAVELS, AFTER SHIKI AND MARO. HE HAILS FROM JIPANGU, LIKE KYOKO.

Chapter 164: The Tao Copy

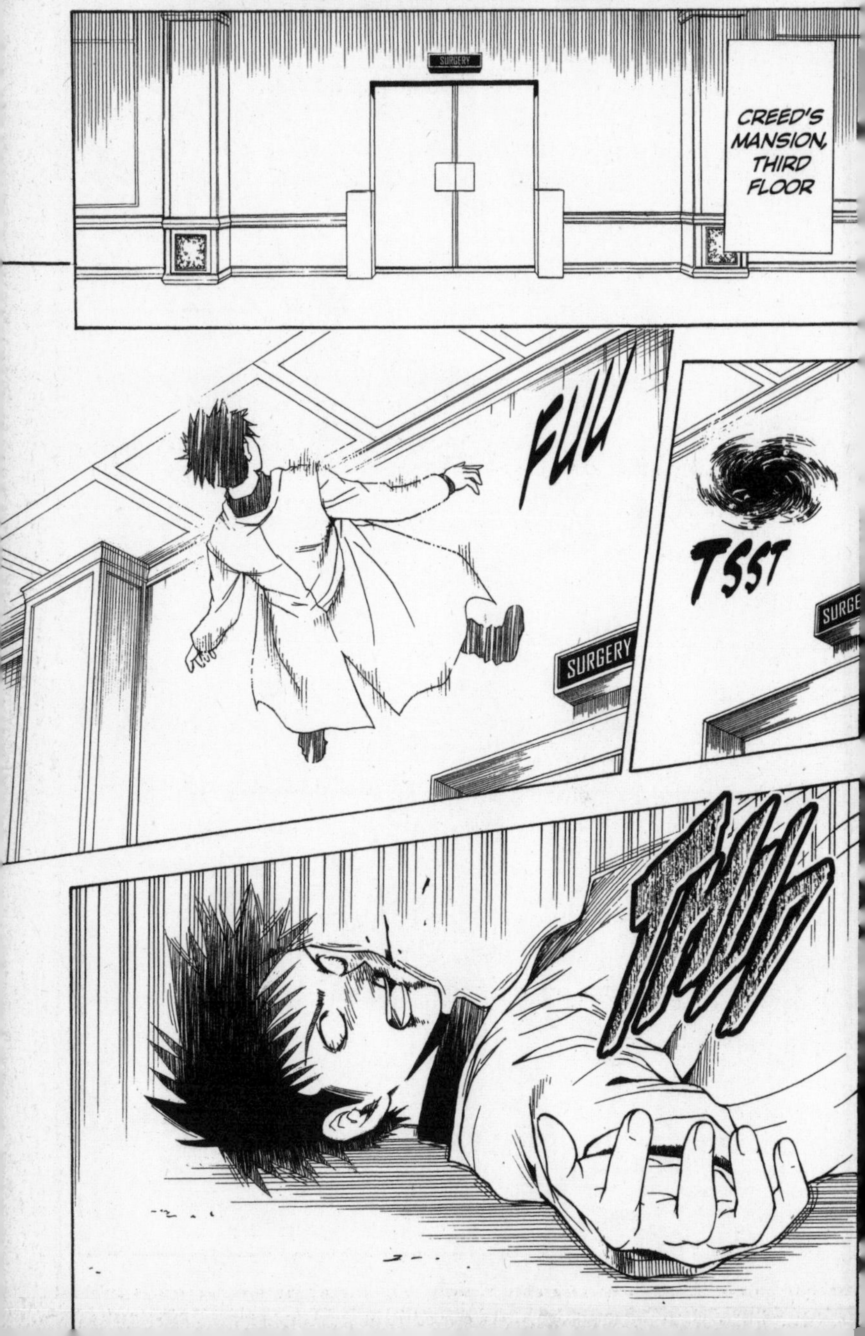
SURGERY
CREED'S MANSION, THIRD FLOOR
TSST
FUU
SURGERY

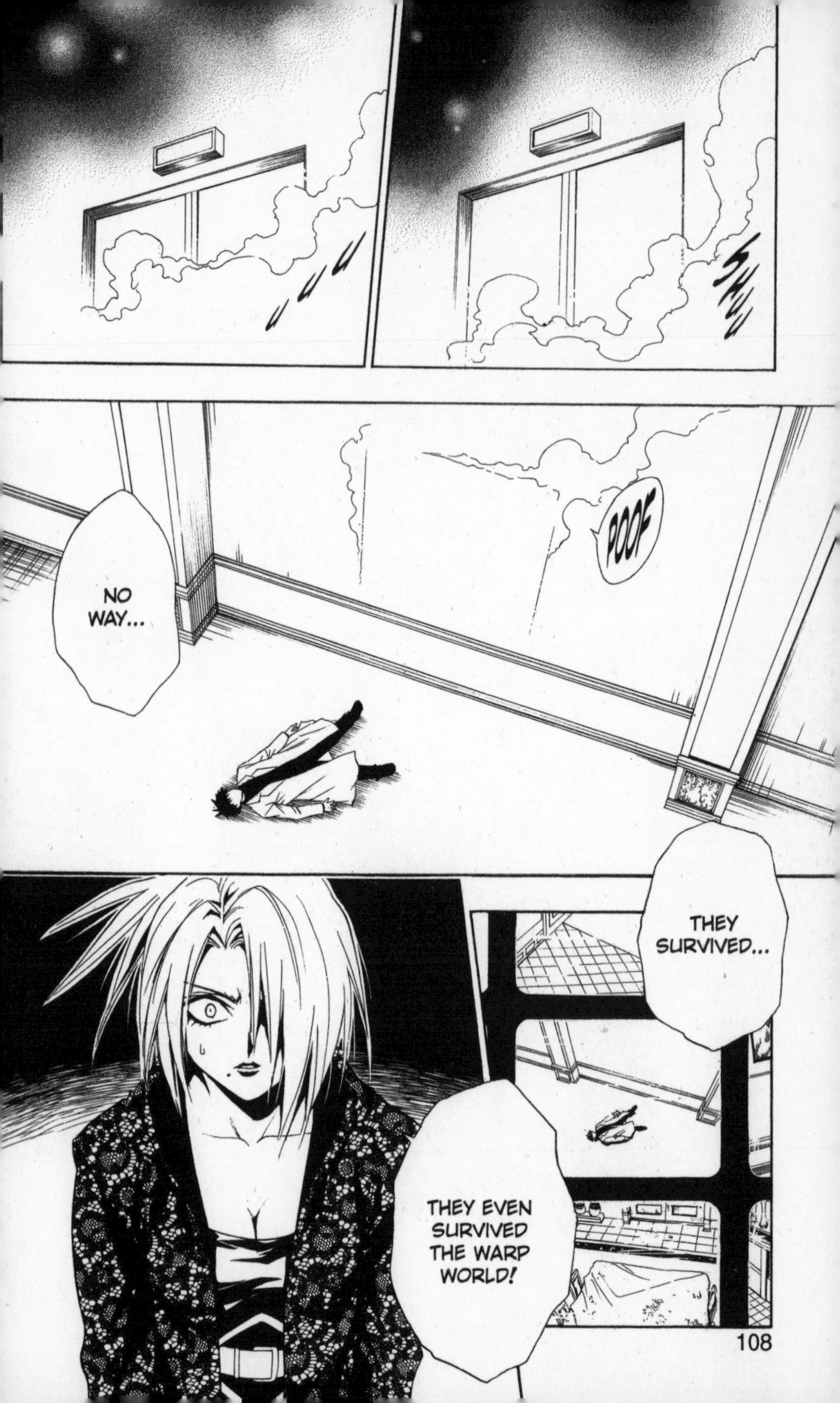
SHUU
POOF
NO WAY...
THEY SURVIVED...
THEY EVEN SURVIVED THE WARP WORLD!

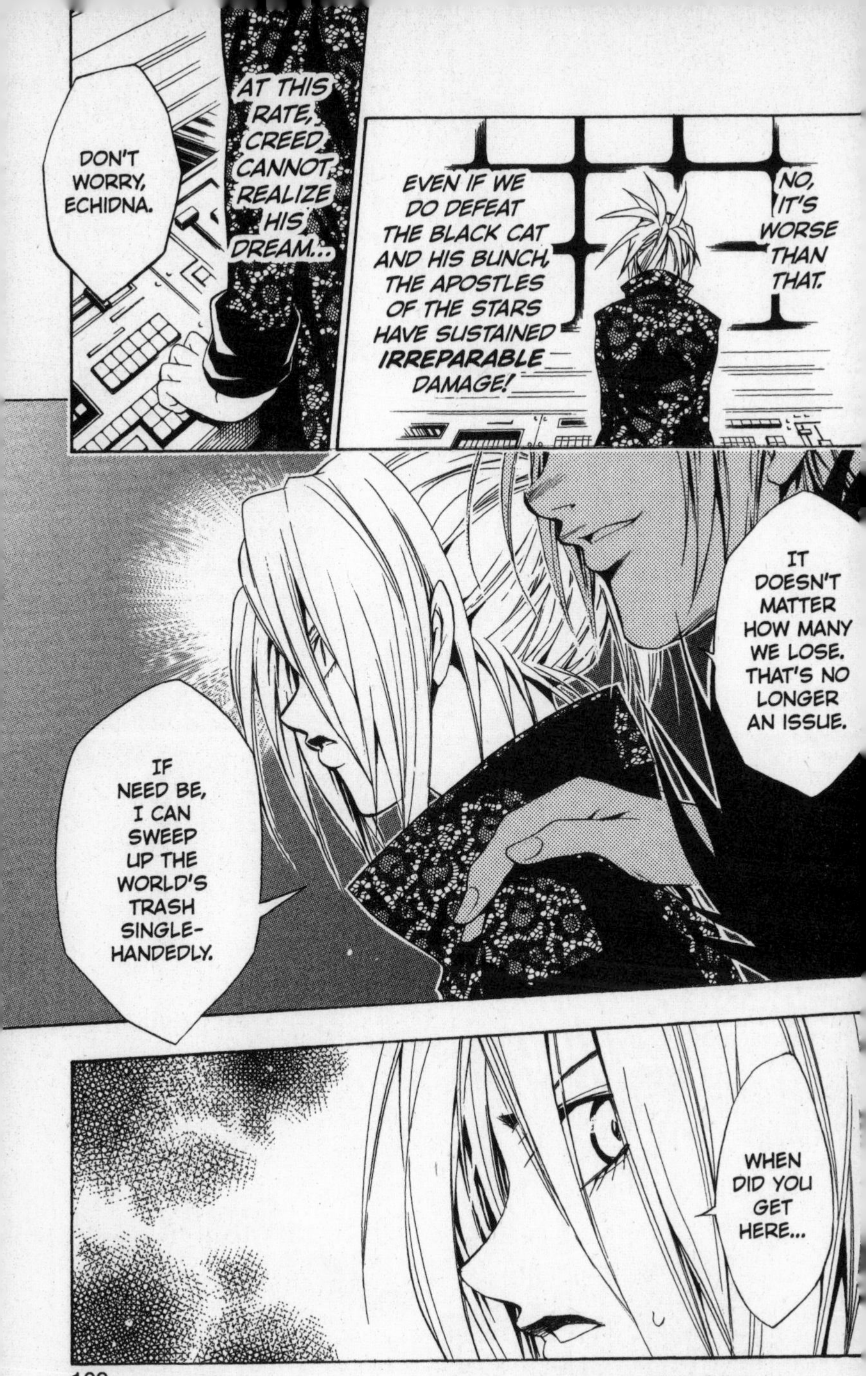
NO, IT'S WORSE THAN THAT.
EVEN IF WE DO DEFEAT THE BLACK CAT AND HIS BUNCH, THE APOSTLES OF THE STARS HAVE SUSTAINED IRREPARABLE DAMAGE!
AT THIS RATE, CREED CANNOT REALIZE HIS DREAM...
DON'T WORRY, ECHIDNA.
IT DOESN'T MATTER HOW MANY WE LOSE. THAT'S NO LONGER AN ISSUE.
IF NEED BE, I CAN SWEEP UP THE WORLD'S TRASH SINGLE-HANDEDLY.
WHEN DID YOU GET HERE...

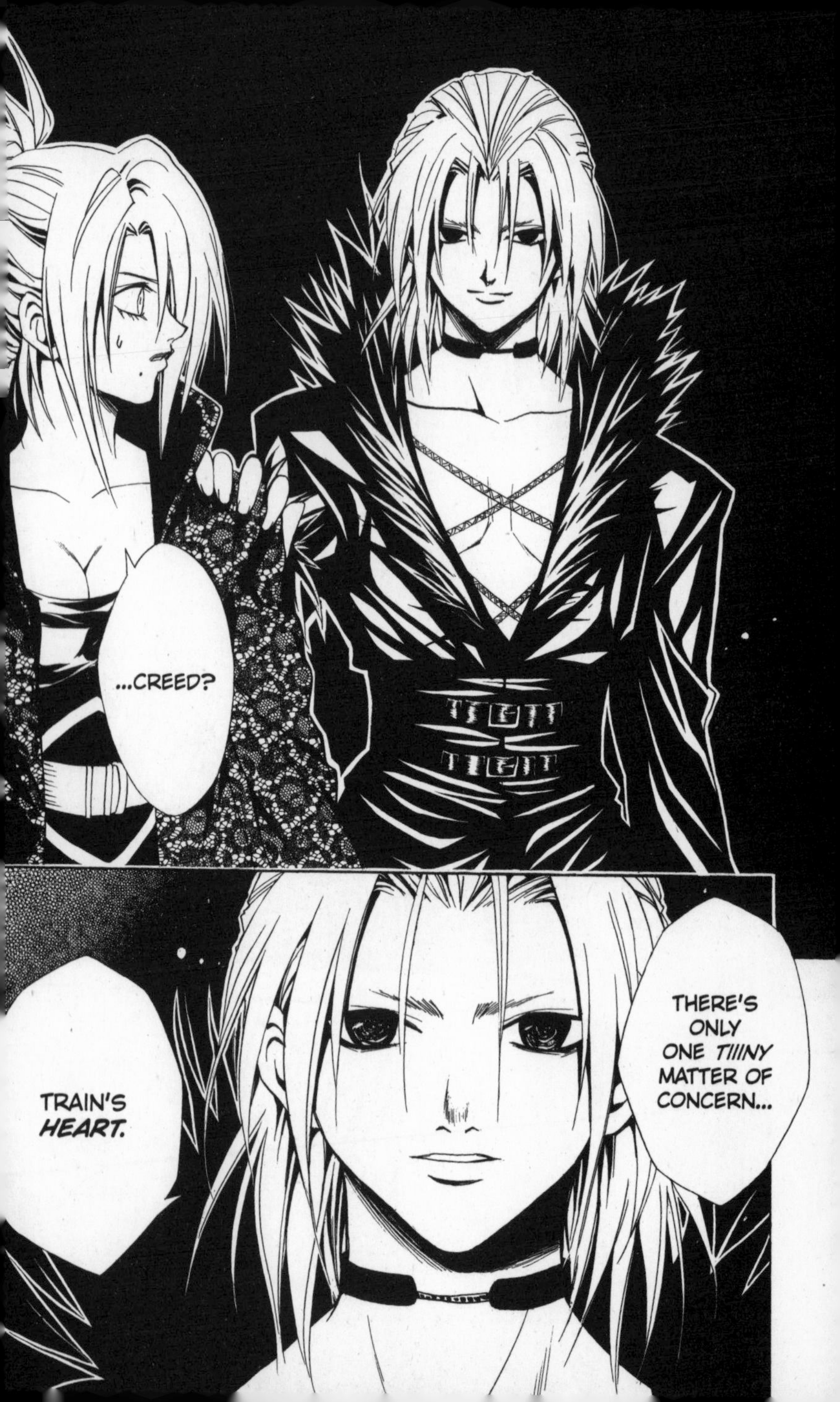
...CREED?
THERE'S ONLY ONE *TIIINY* MATTER OF CONCERN...
TRAIN'S *HEART.*

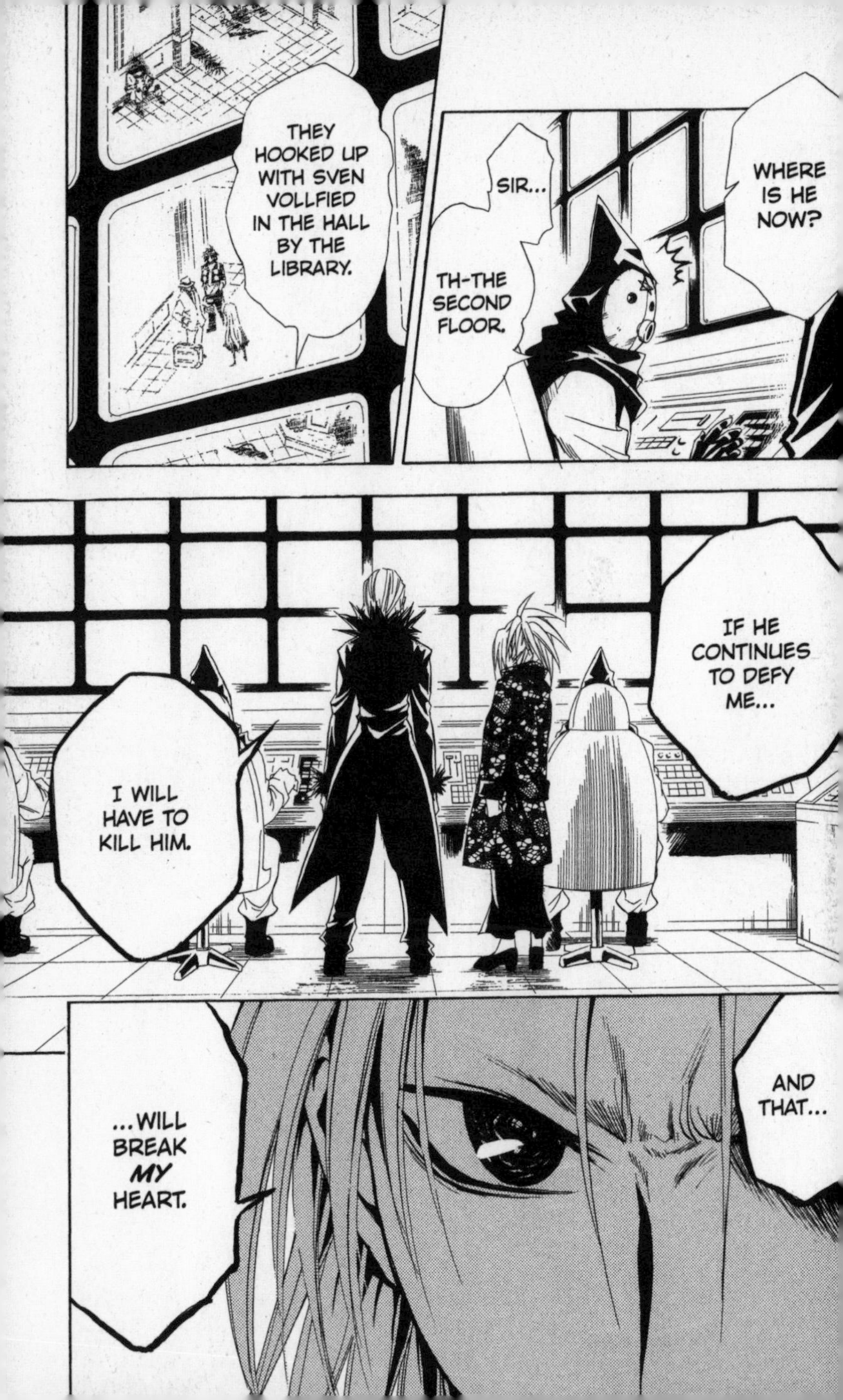
WHERE IS HE NOW?
SIR...
TH-THE SECOND FLOOR.
THEY HOOKED UP WITH SVEN VOLLFIED IN THE HALL BY THE LIBRARY.
IF HE CONTINUES TO DEFY ME...
I WILL HAVE TO KILL HIM.
AND THAT...
...WILL BREAK *MY* HEART.

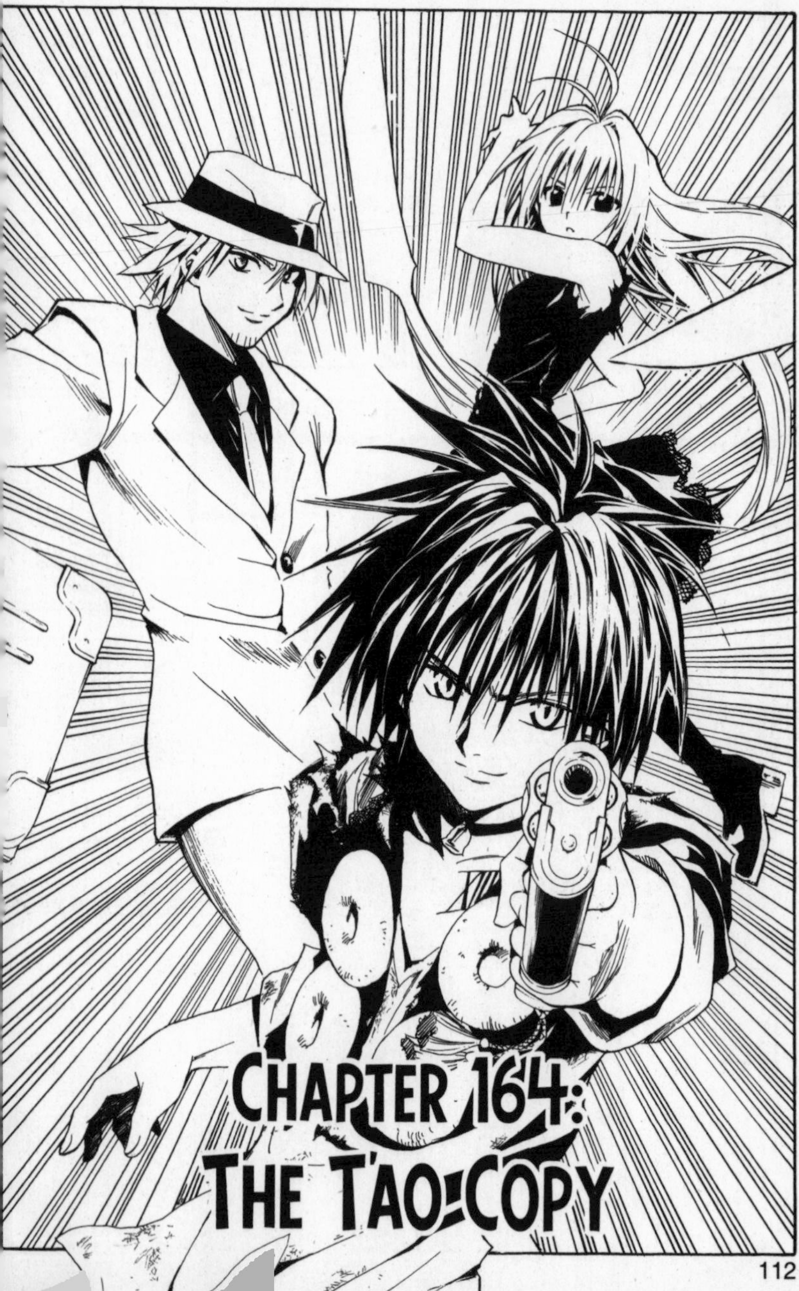
CHAPTER 164:
THE TAO-COPY

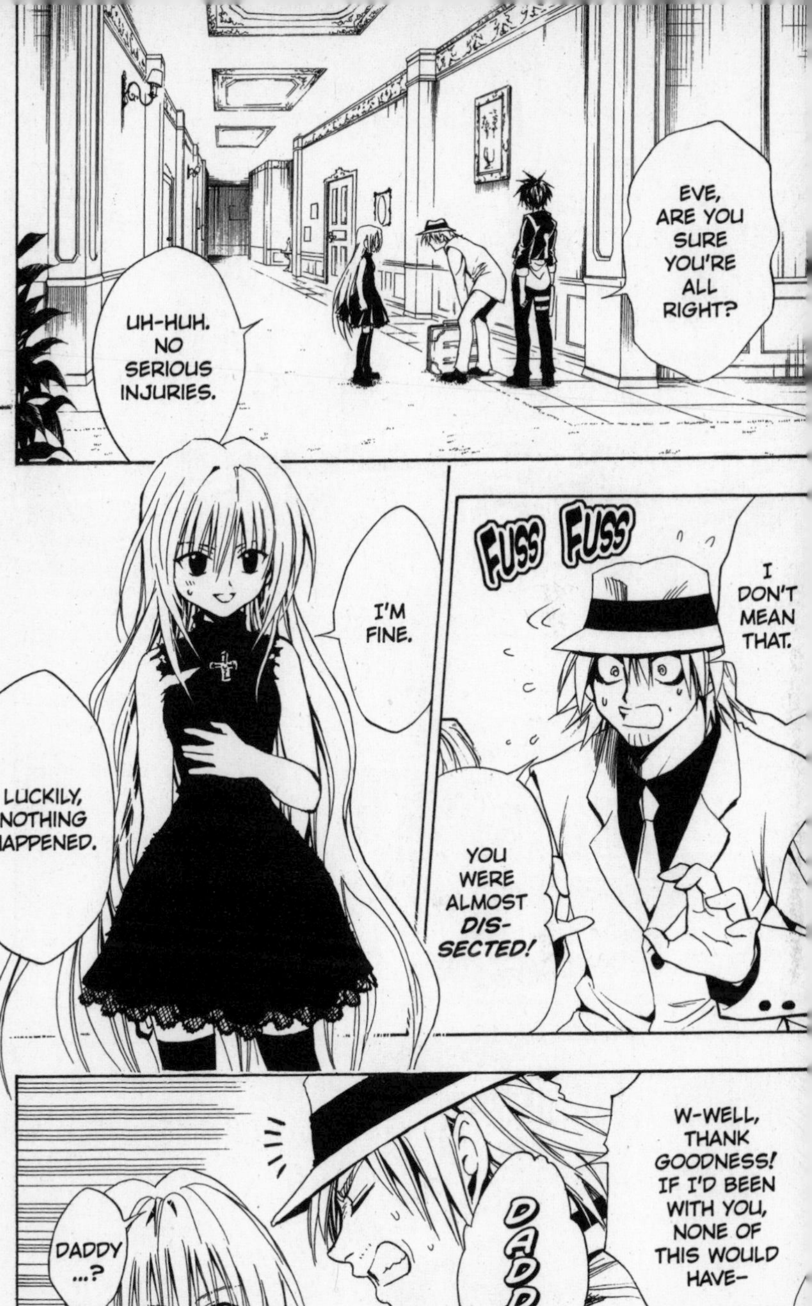

EVE, ARE YOU SURE YOU'RE ALL RIGHT?
UH-HUH. NO SERIOUS INJURIES.
I'M FINE.
LUCKILY, NOTHING HAPPENED.
FUSS FUSS
I DON'T MEAN THAT.
YOU WERE ALMOST DIS-SECTED!
W-WELL, THANK GOODNESS! IF I'D BEEN WITH YOU, NONE OF THIS WOULD HAVE-
DADDY!
DADDY ...?

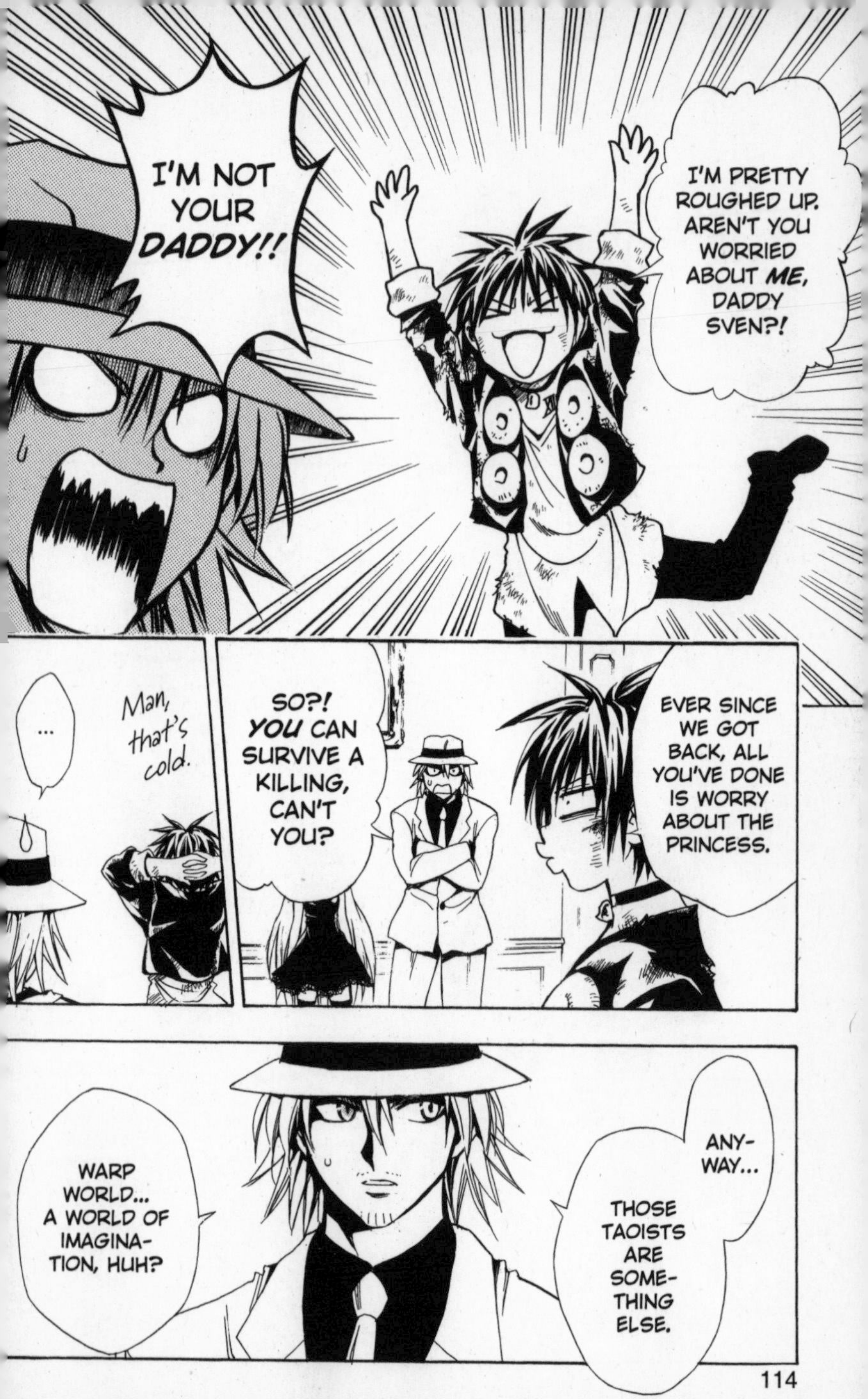
I'M PRETTY ROUGHED UP. AREN'T YOU WORRIED ABOUT *ME*, DADDY SVEN?!
I'M NOT YOUR *DADDY!!*
EVER SINCE WE GOT BACK, ALL YOU'VE DONE IS WORRY ABOUT THE PRINCESS.
SO?! *YOU* CAN SURVIVE A KILLING, CAN'T YOU?
Man, that's cold.
...
ANY-WAY...
THOSE TAOISTS ARE SOME-THING ELSE.
WARP WORLD... A WORLD OF IMAGINA-TION, HUH?

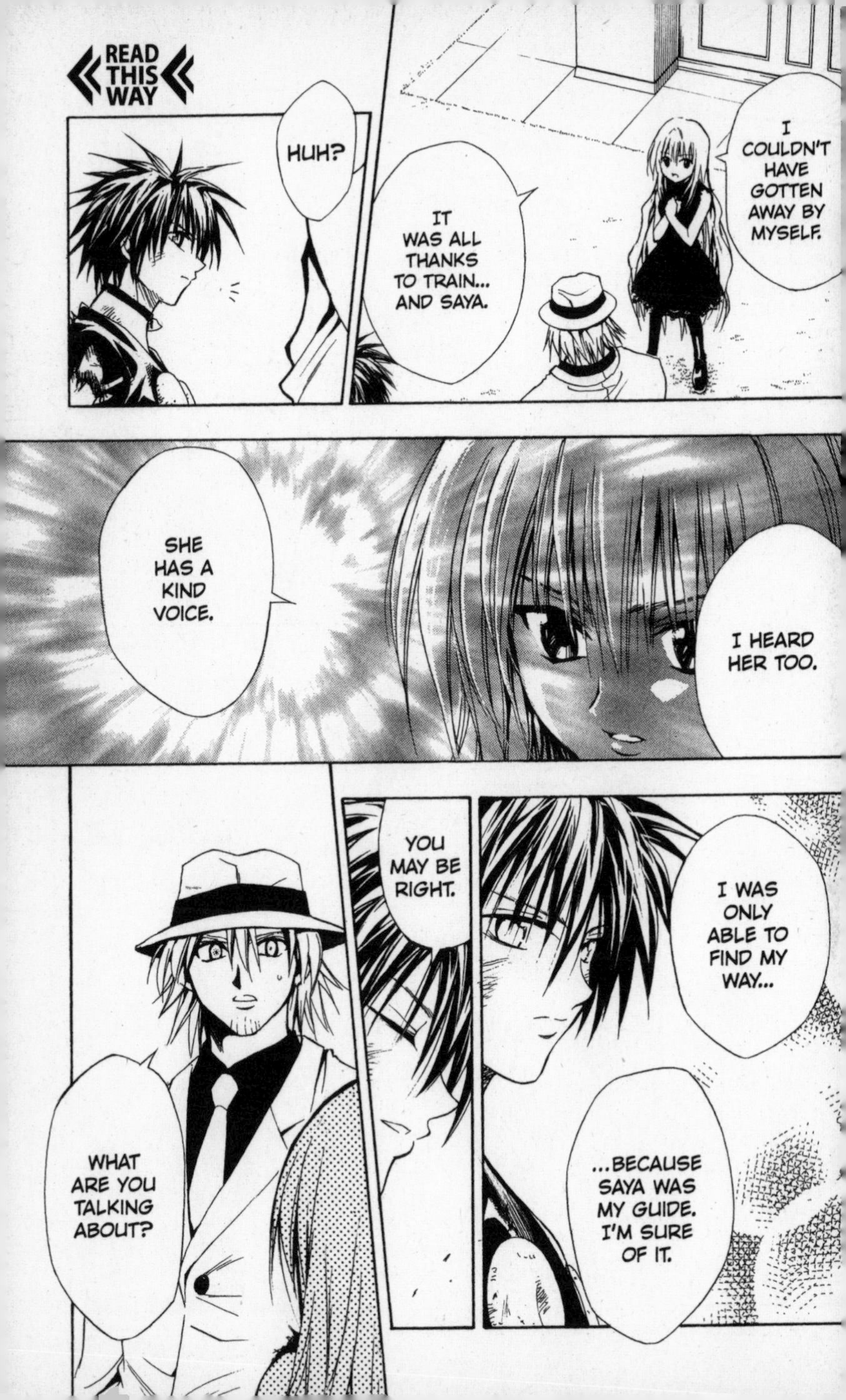
READ THIS WAY
I COULDN'T HAVE GOTTEN AWAY BY MYSELF.
IT WAS ALL THANKS TO TRAIN... AND SAYA.
HUH?
I HEARD HER TOO.
SHE HAS A KIND VOICE.
I WAS ONLY ABLE TO FIND MY WAY...
...BECAUSE SAYA WAS MY GUIDE. I'M SURE OF IT.
YOU MAY BE RIGHT.
WHAT ARE YOU TALKING ABOUT?

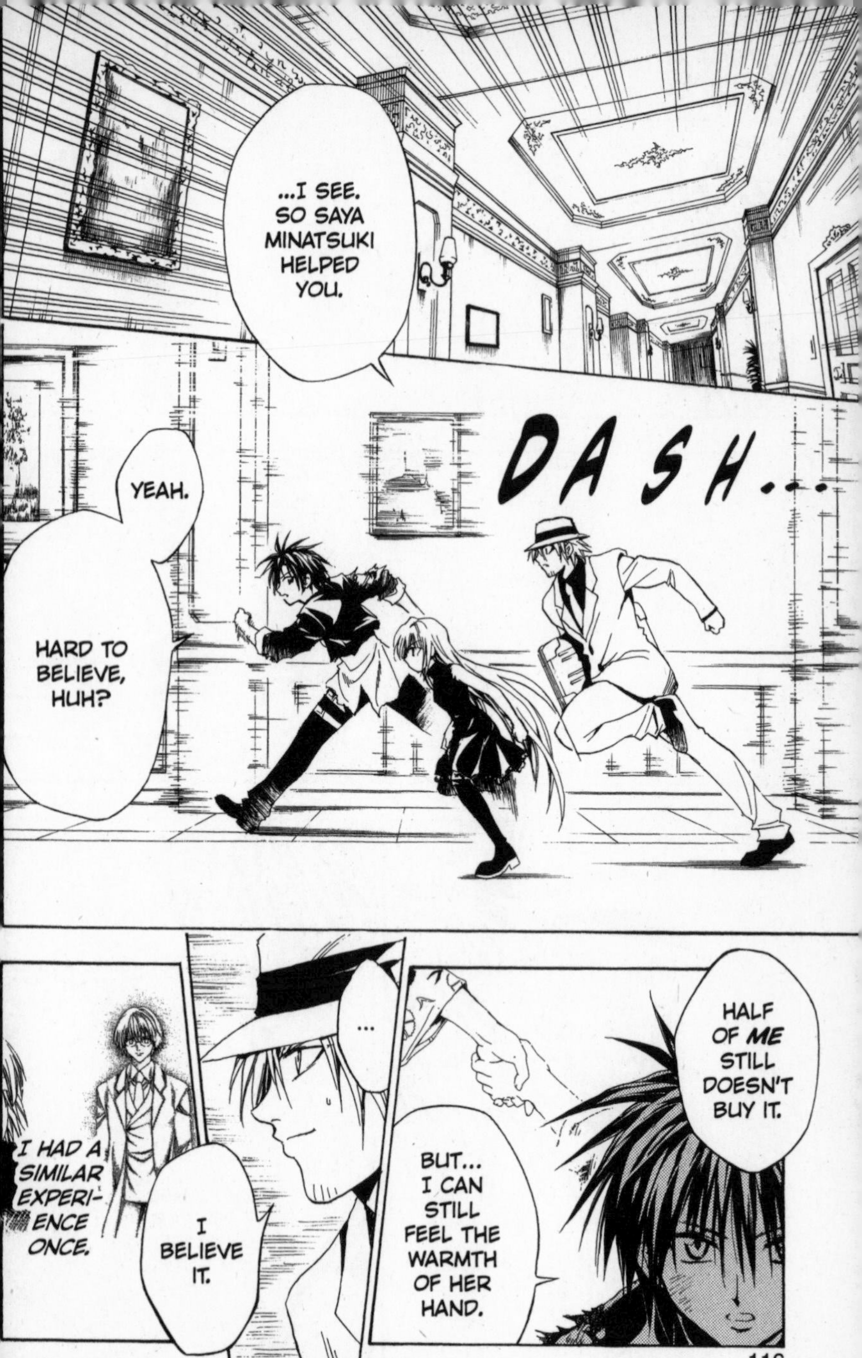
...I SEE. SO SAYA MINATSUKI HELPED YOU.
DASH...
YEAH.
HARD TO BELIEVE, HUH?
HALF OF *ME* STILL DOESN'T BUY IT.
BUT... I CAN STILL FEEL THE WARMTH OF HER HAND.
...
I BELIEVE IT.
I HAD A SIMILAR EXPERI-ENCE ONCE.

READ THIS WAY

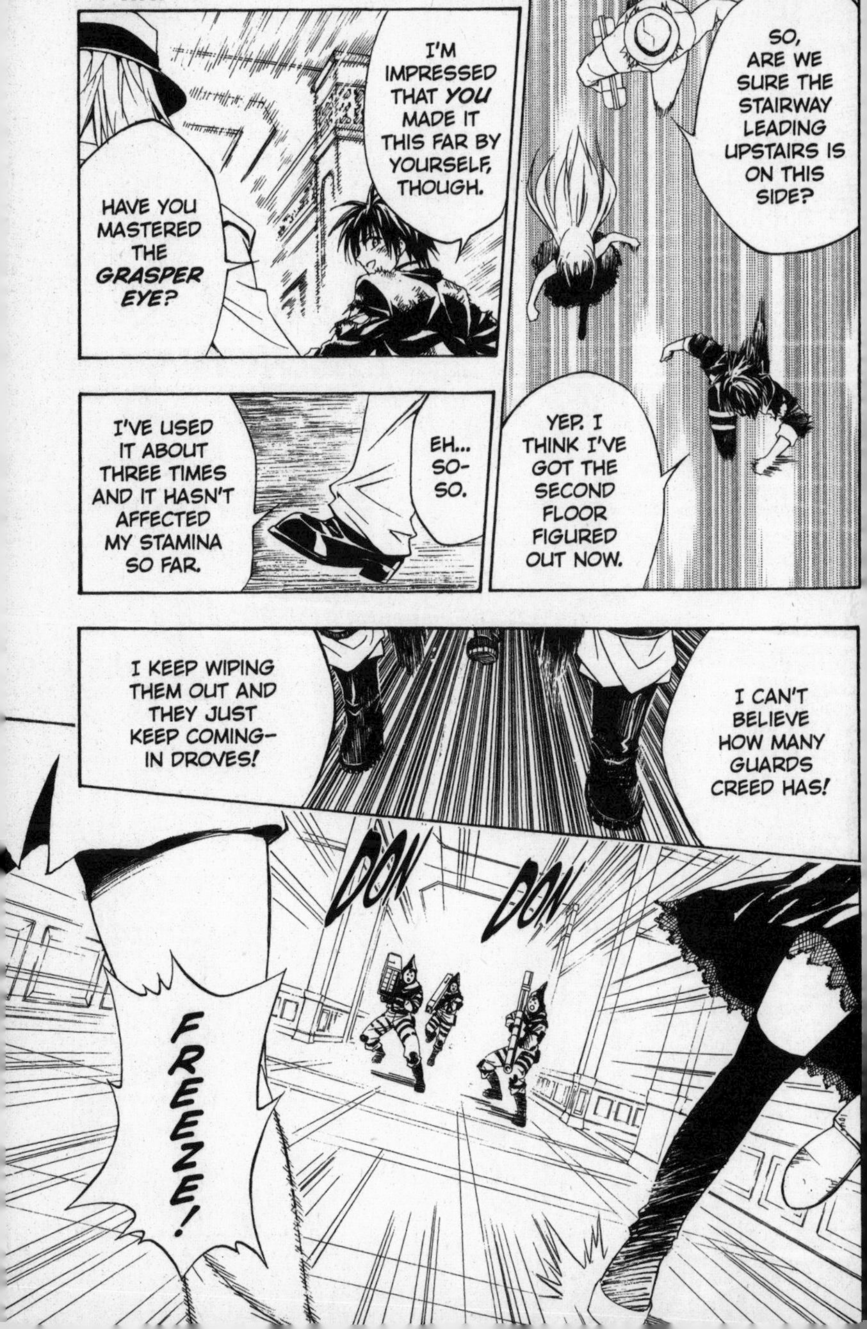

SO, ARE WE SURE THE STAIRWAY LEADING UPSTAIRS IS ON THIS SIDE?
YEP. I THINK I'VE GOT THE SECOND FLOOR FIGURED OUT NOW.
I'M IMPRESSED THAT *YOU* MADE IT THIS FAR BY YOURSELF, THOUGH.
HAVE YOU MASTERED THE *GRASPER EYE?*
EH... SO-SO.
I'VE USED IT ABOUT THREE TIMES AND IT HASN'T AFFECTED MY STAMINA SO FAR.
I CAN'T BELIEVE HOW MANY GUARDS CREED HAS!
I KEEP WIPING THEM OUT AND THEY JUST KEEP COMING-IN DROVES!
DON
DON
FREEZE!

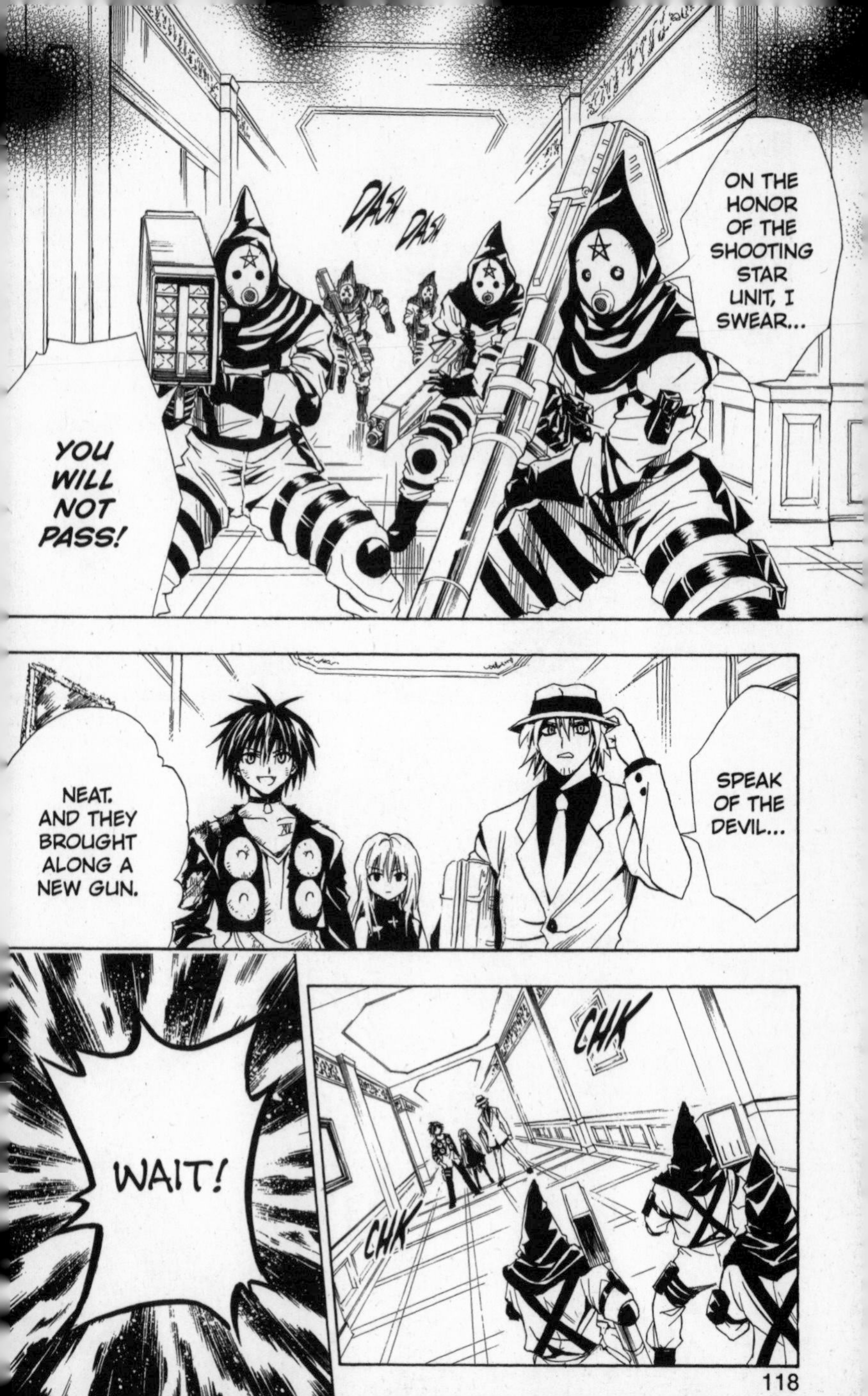
ON THE HONOR OF THE SHOOTING STAR UNIT, I SWEAR...
DASH
DASH
YOU WILL NOT PASS!
SPEAK OF THE DEVIL...
NEAT. AND THEY BROUGHT ALONG A NEW GUN.
CHK
CHK
WAIT!

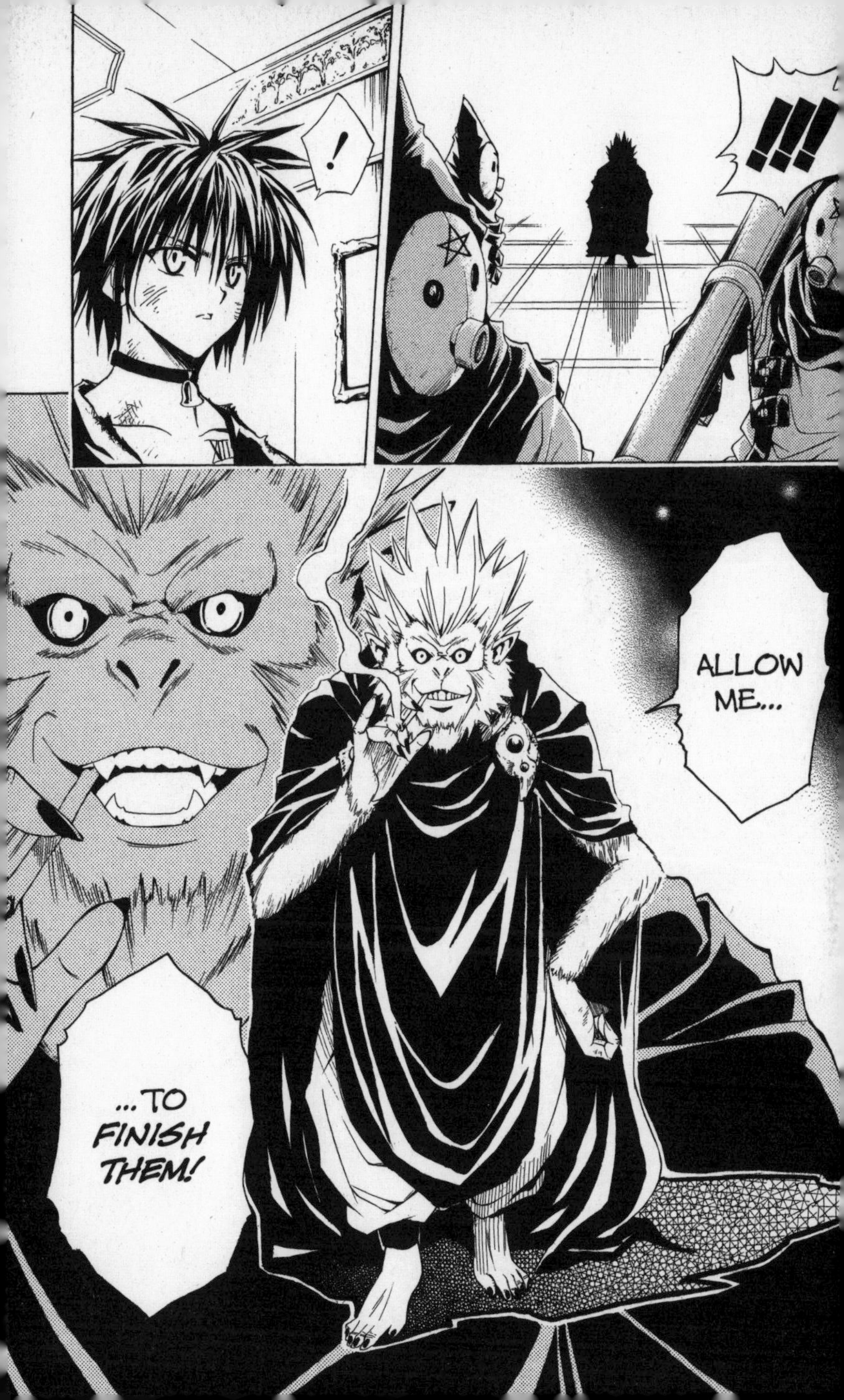
!!!
!
ALLOW ME...
...TO FINISH THEM!

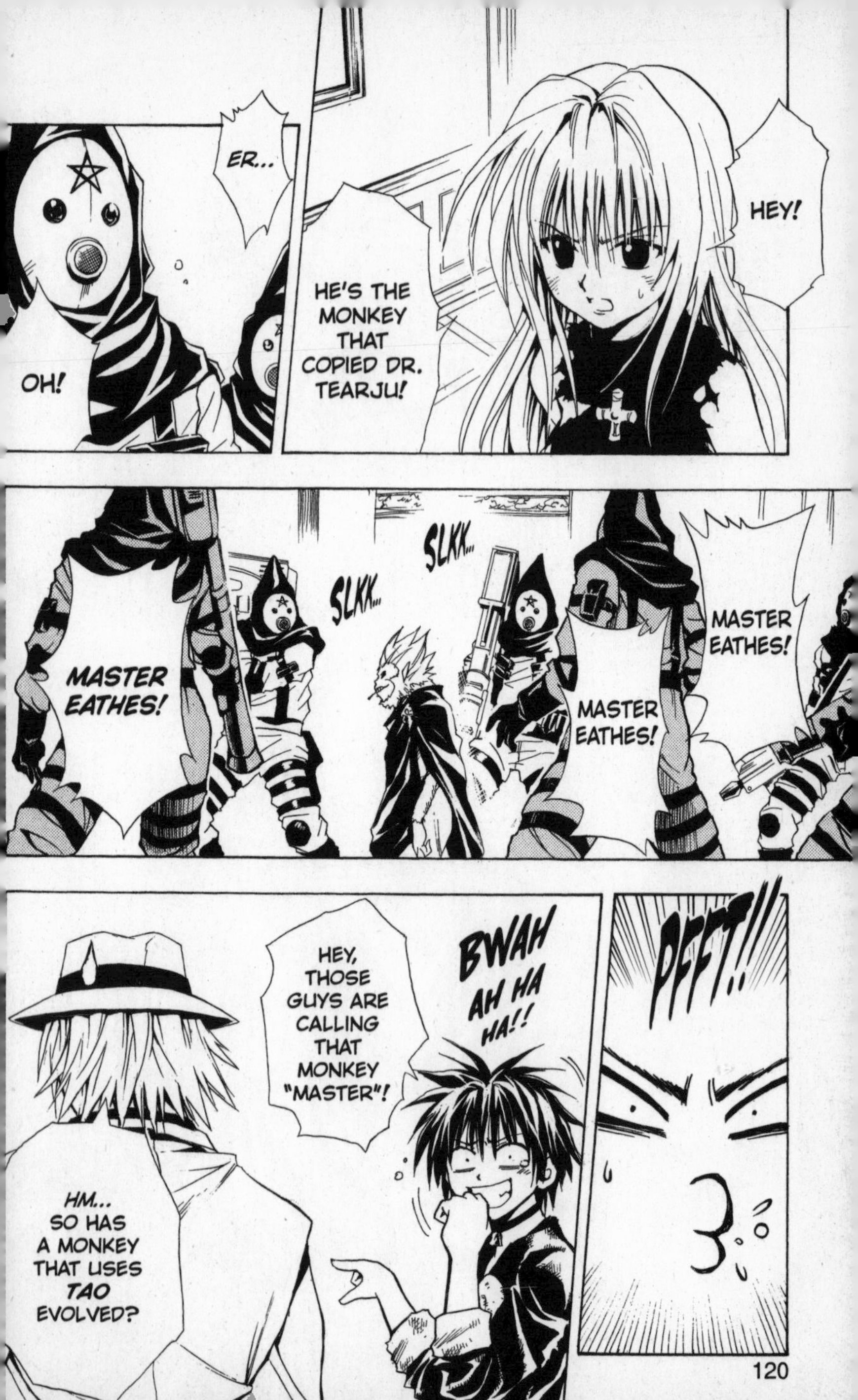
HEY!
HE'S THE MONKEY THAT COPIED DR. TEARJU!
ER...
OH!
MASTER EATHES!
MASTER EATHES!
SLKK...
SLKK...
MASTER EATHES!
PFFT!!
BWAH AH HA HA!!
HEY, THOSE GUYS ARE CALLING THAT MONKEY "MASTER"!
HM... SO HAS A MONKEY THAT USES *TAO* EVOLVED?

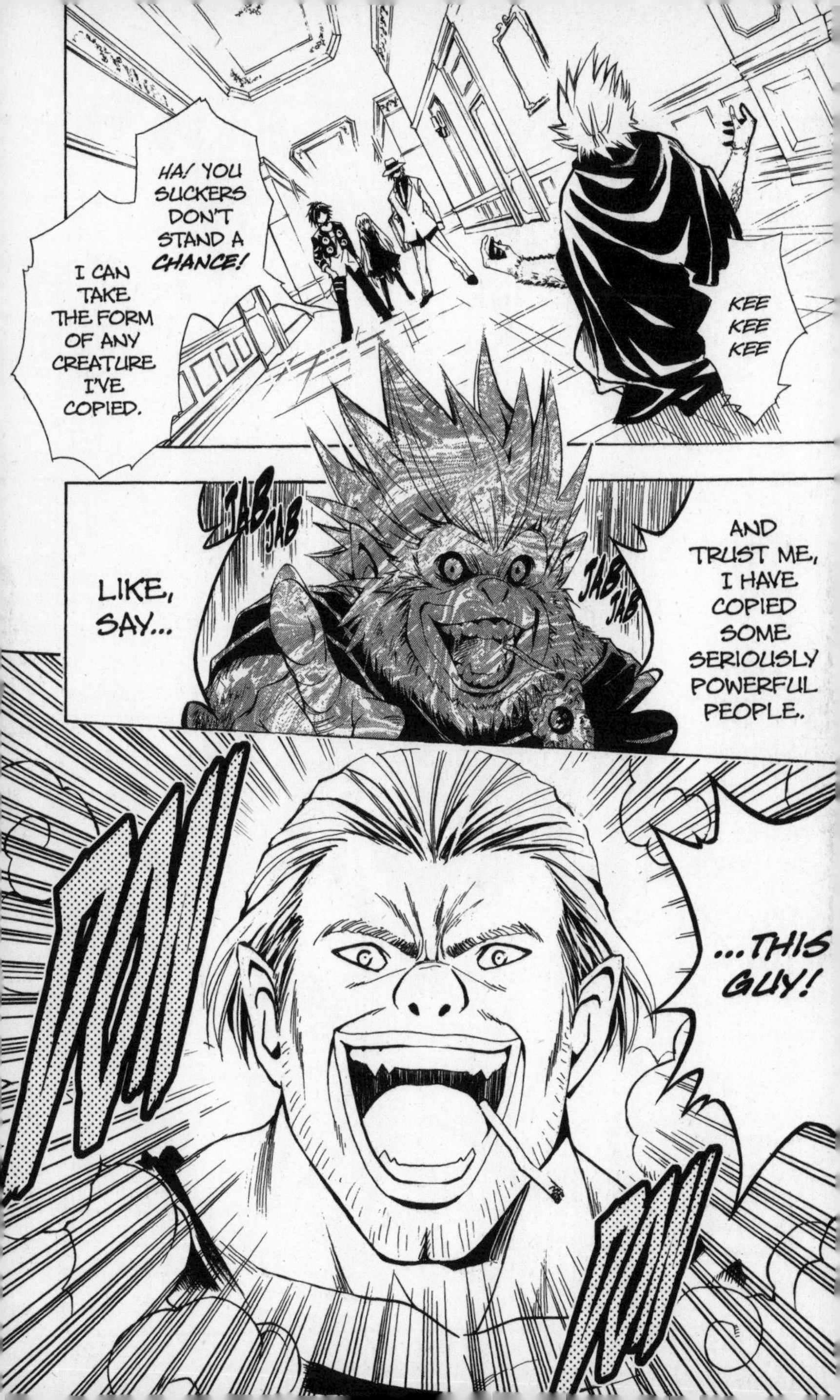
KEE KEE KEE
HA! YOU SUCKERS DON'T STAND A CHANCE!
I CAN TAKE THE FORM OF ANY CREATURE I'VE COPIED.
AND TRUST ME, I HAVE COPIED SOME SERIOUSLY POWERFUL PEOPLE.
JAB JAB
JAB JAB
LIKE, SAY...
...THIS GUY!

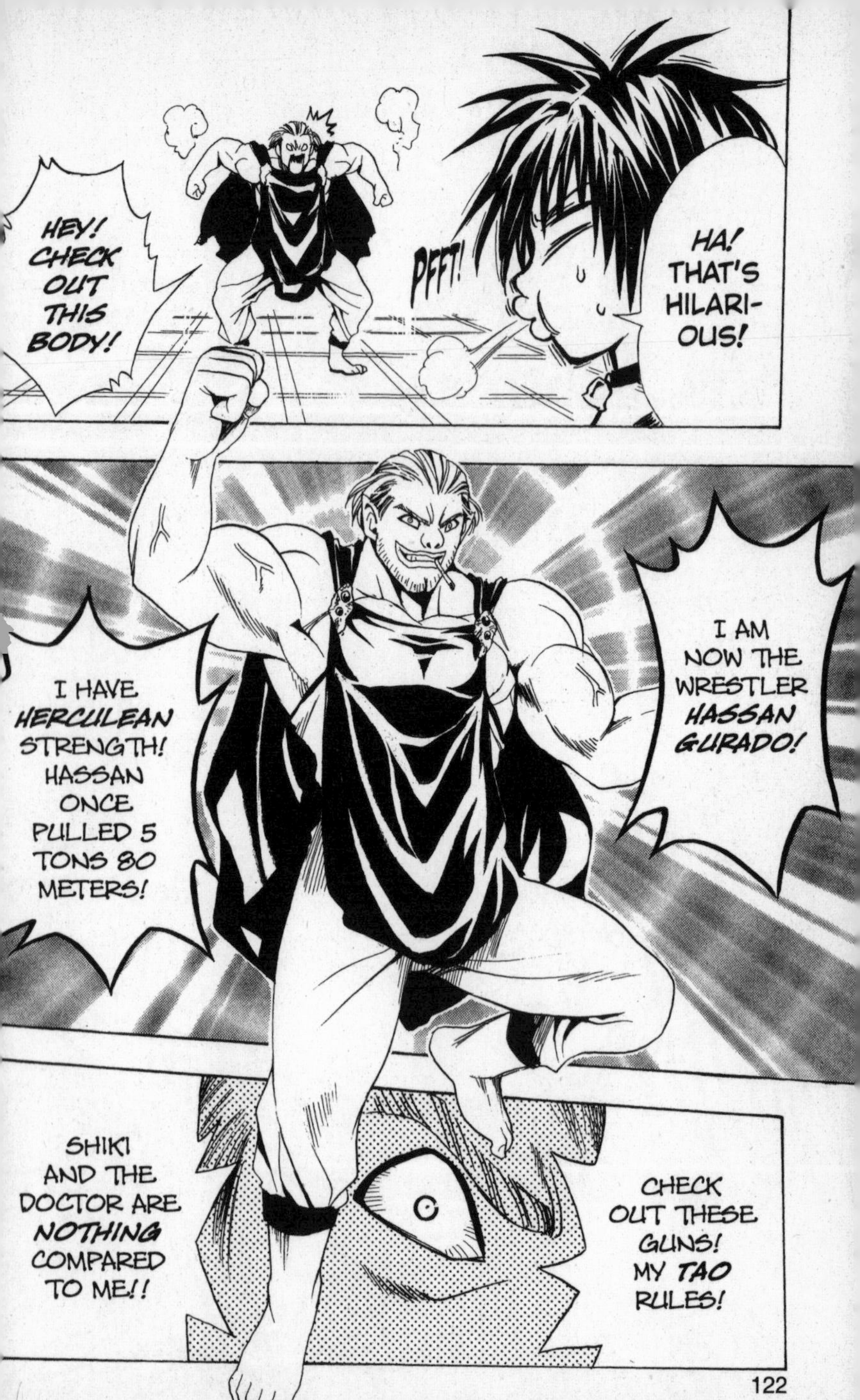
HA! THAT'S HILARI-OUS!
PFFT!
HEY! CHECK OUT THIS BODY!
I AM NOW THE WRESTLER HASSAN GURADO!
I HAVE HERCULEAN STRENGTH! HASSAN ONCE PULLED 5 TONS 80 METERS!
CHECK OUT THESE GUNS! MY TAO RULES!
SHIKI AND THE DOCTOR ARE NOTHING COMPARED TO ME!!

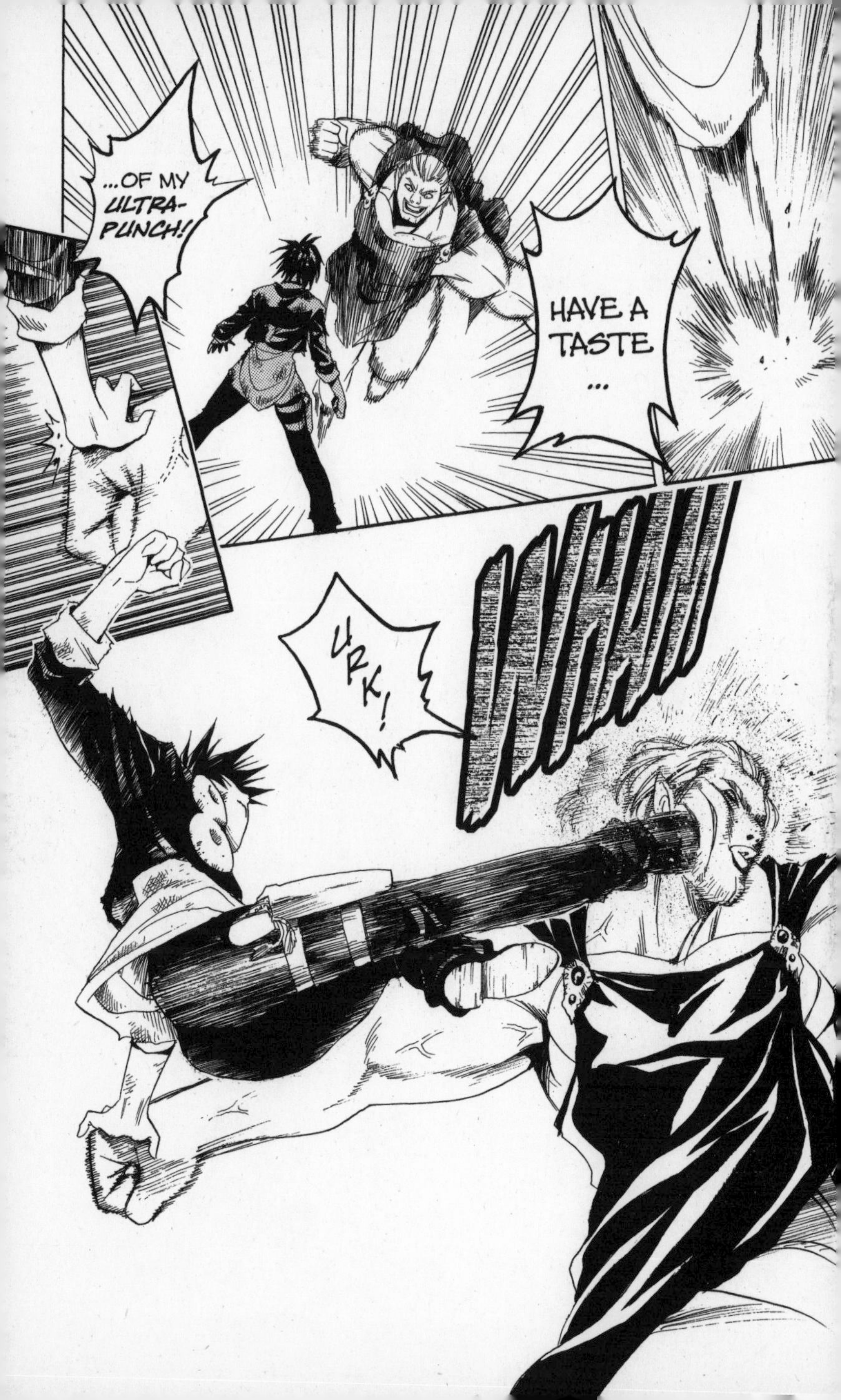
HAVE A TASTE ...
...OF MY ULTRA-PUNCH!!
WHAM
URK!

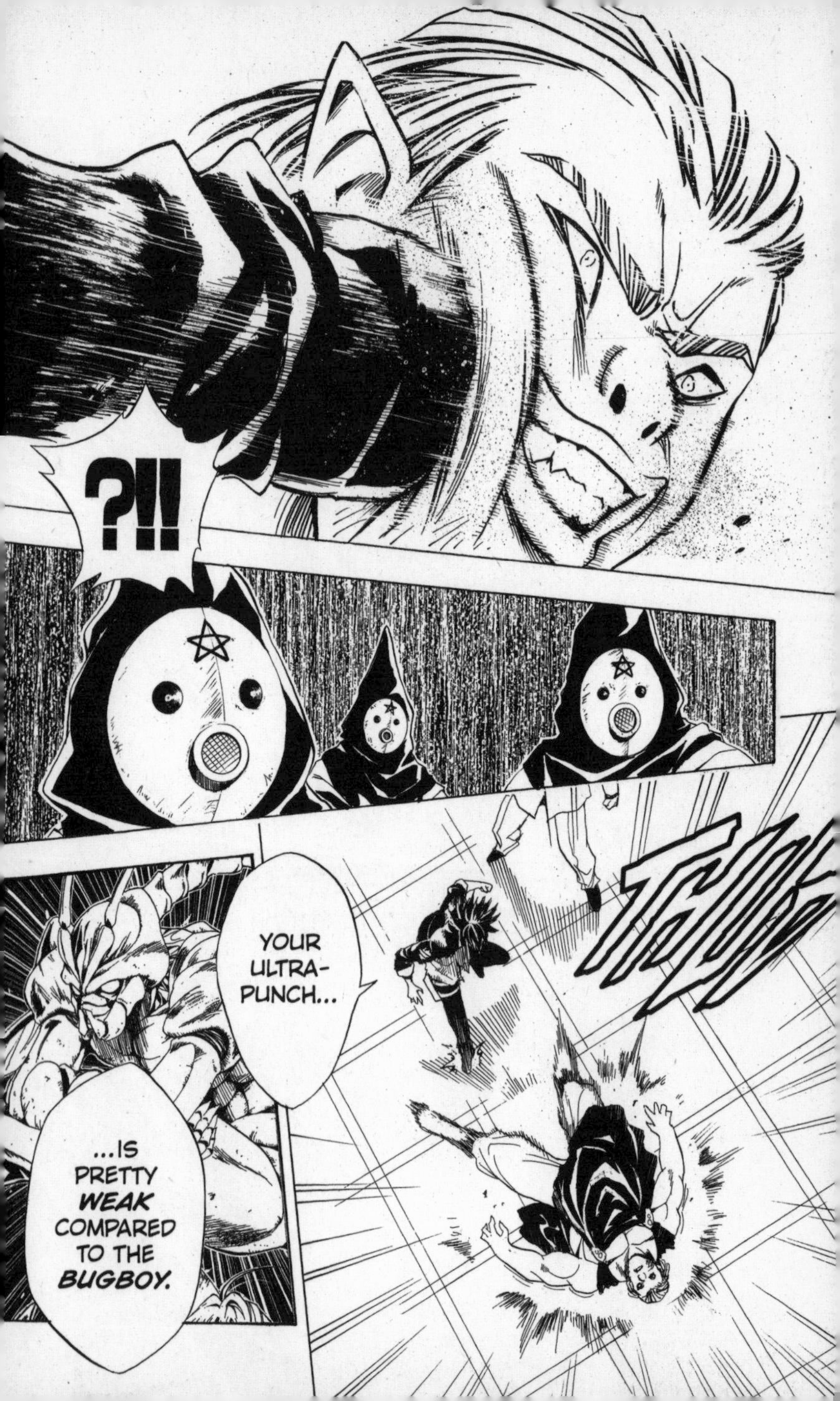
?!!
YOUR ULTRA-PUNCH...
...IS PRETTY *WEAK* COMPARED TO THE *BUGBOY.*

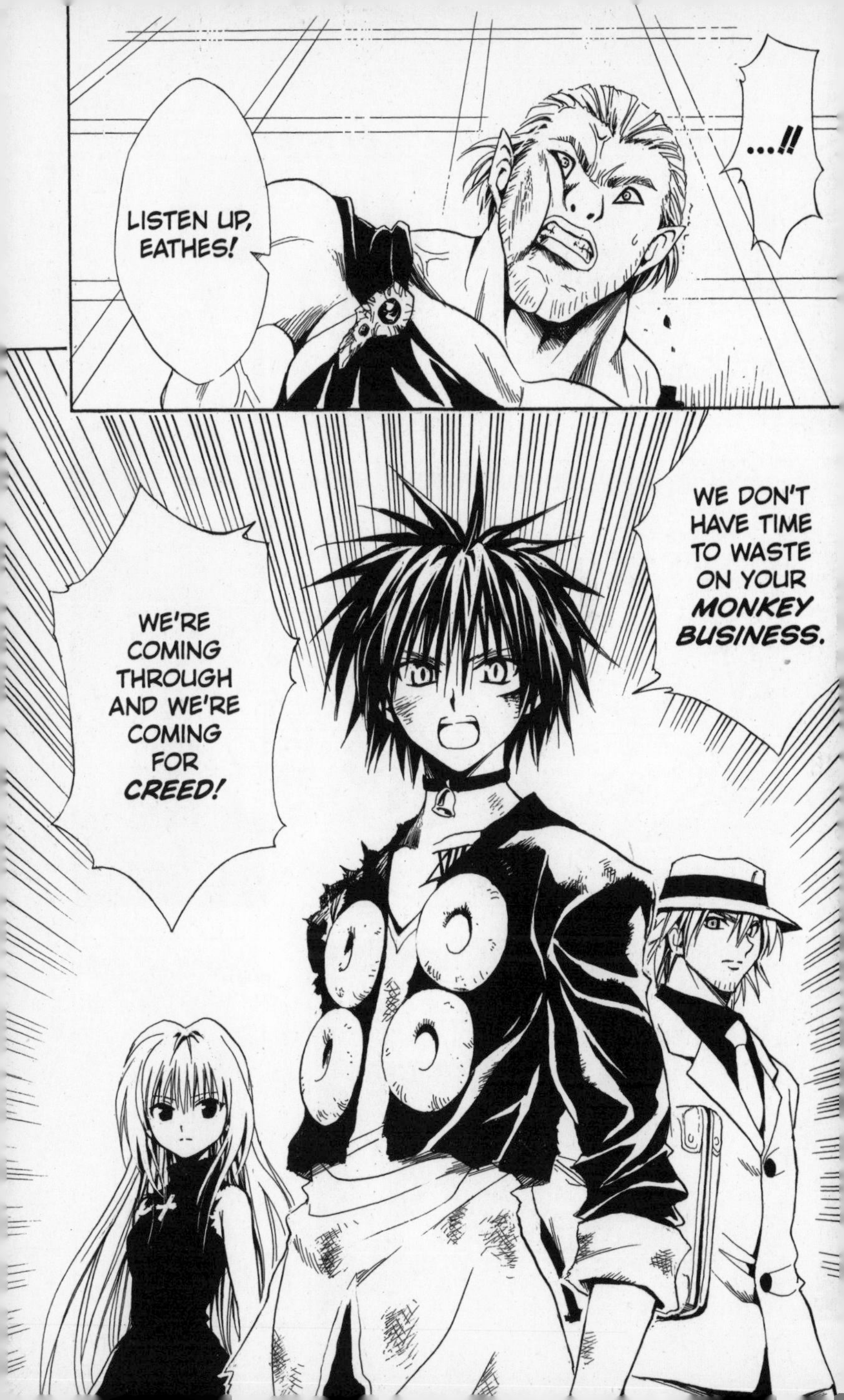
...!!
LISTEN UP, EATHES!
WE DON'T HAVE TIME TO WASTE ON YOUR *MONKEY BUSINESS.*
WE'RE COMING THROUGH AND WE'RE COMING FOR *CREED!*

THE FLYING WORKPLACE BY KOZATO TAI

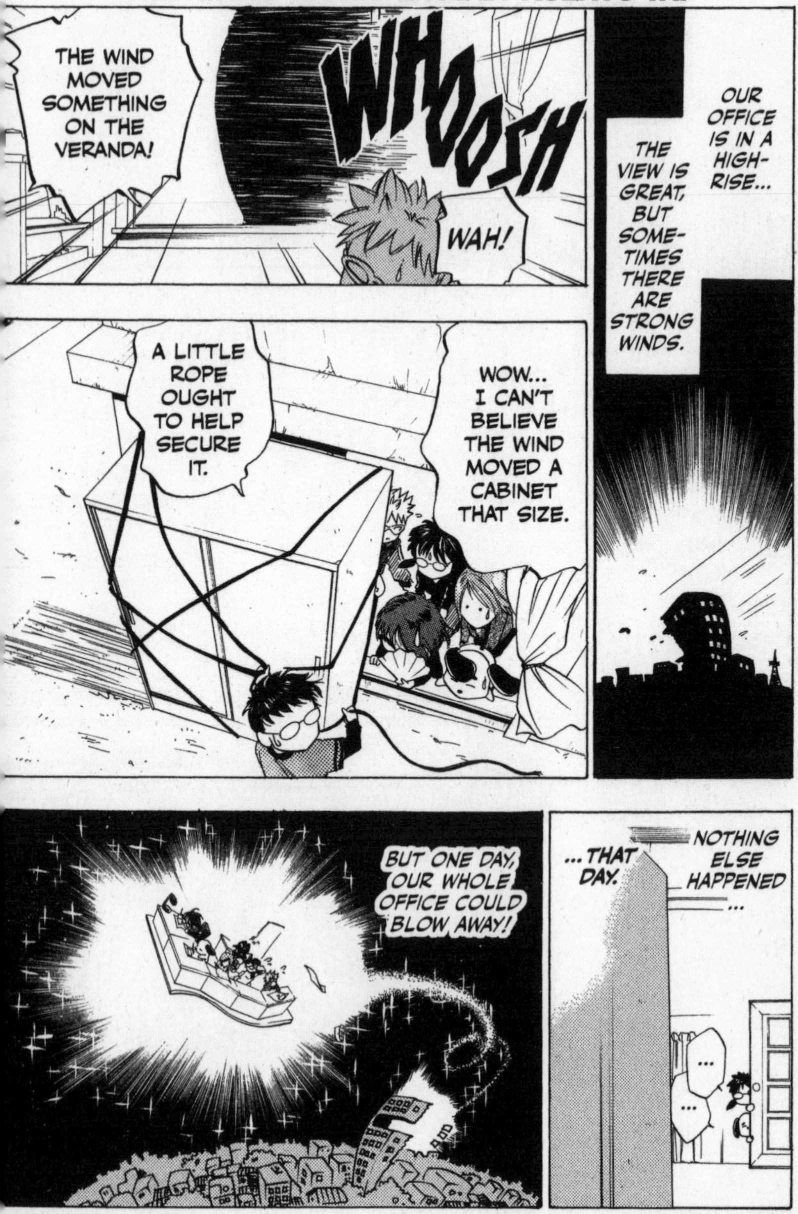

OUR OFFICE IS IN A HIGH-RISE...
THE VIEW IS GREAT, BUT SOMETIMES THERE ARE STRONG WINDS.
WHOOSH
THE WIND MOVED SOMETHING ON THE VERANDA!
WAH!
WOW... I CAN'T BELIEVE THE WIND MOVED A CABINET THAT SIZE.
A LITTLE ROPE OUGHT TO HELP SECURE IT.
NOTHING ELSE HAPPENED...
...THAT DAY.
...
...
BUT ONE DAY, OUR WHOLE OFFICE COULD BLOW AWAY!

Chapter 165: Shaolee's Technique

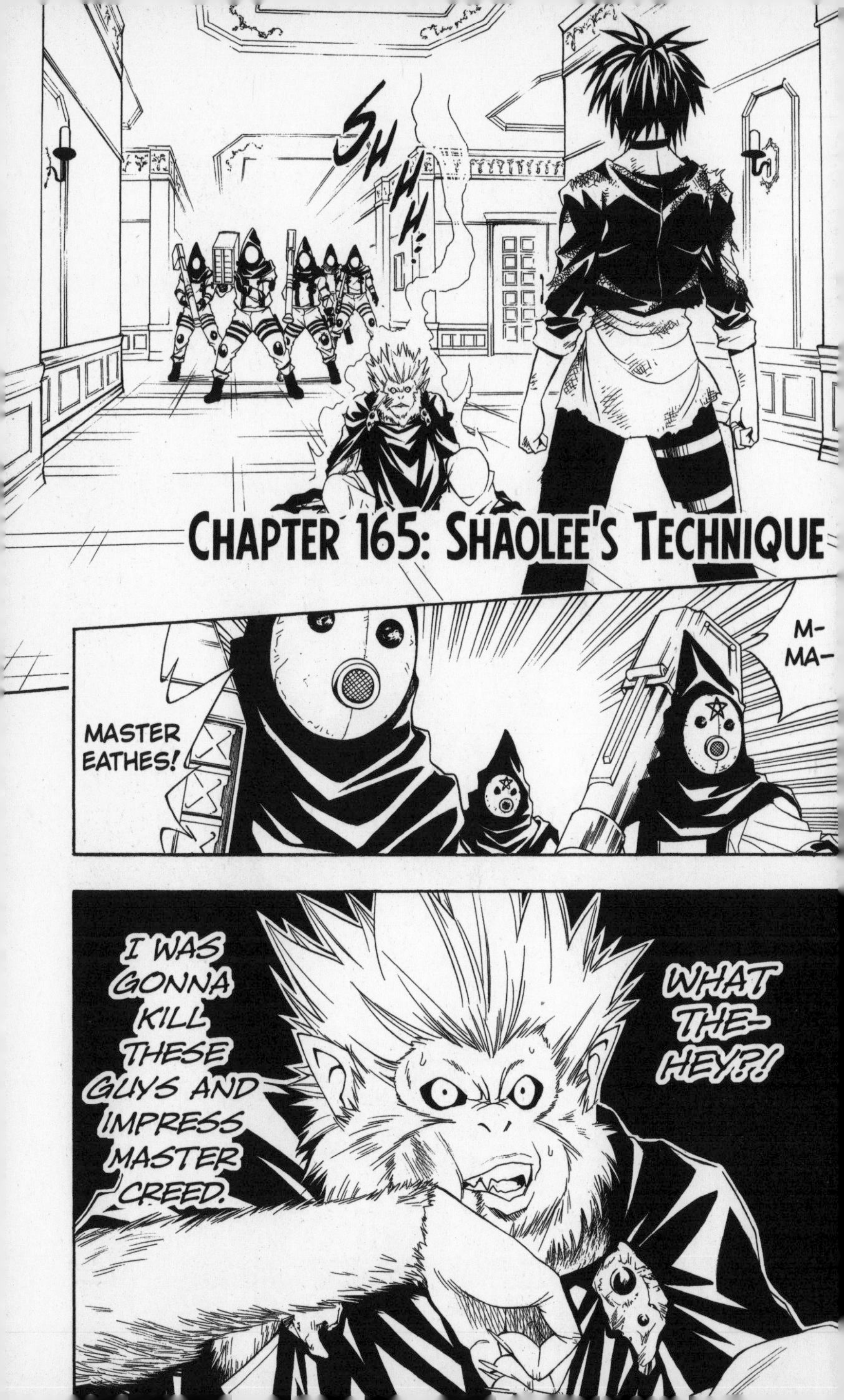
SHHH
M- MA-
MASTER EATHES!
WHAT THE- HEY?!
I WAS GONNA KILL THESE GUYS AND IMPRESS MASTER CREED.

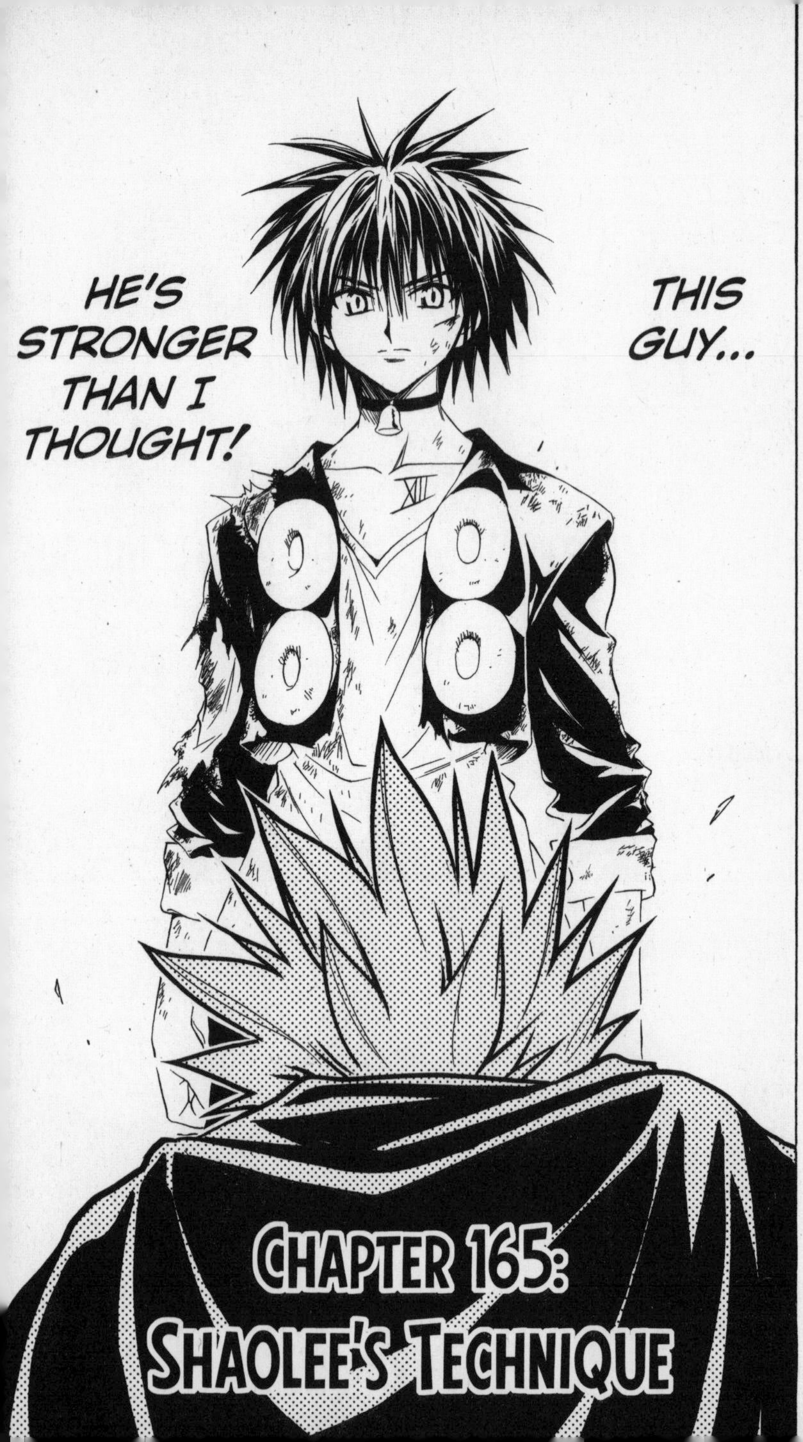
THIS GUY...
HE'S STRONGER THAN I THOUGHT!
CHAPTER 165:
SHAOLEE'S TECHNIQUE

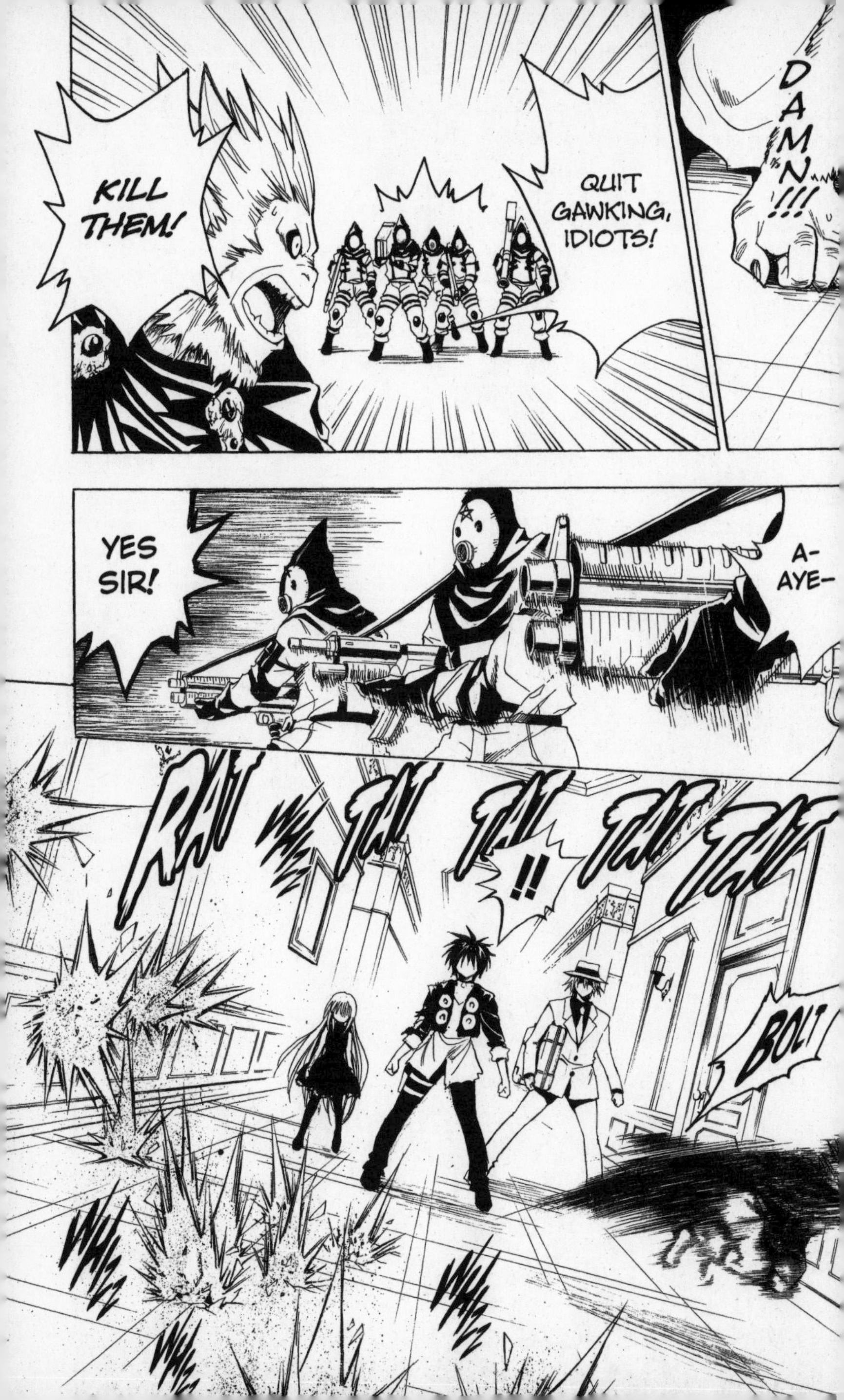
DAMN!!!
QUIT GAWKING, IDIOTS!
KILL THEM!
A- AYE-
YES SIR!
BOLT
!!

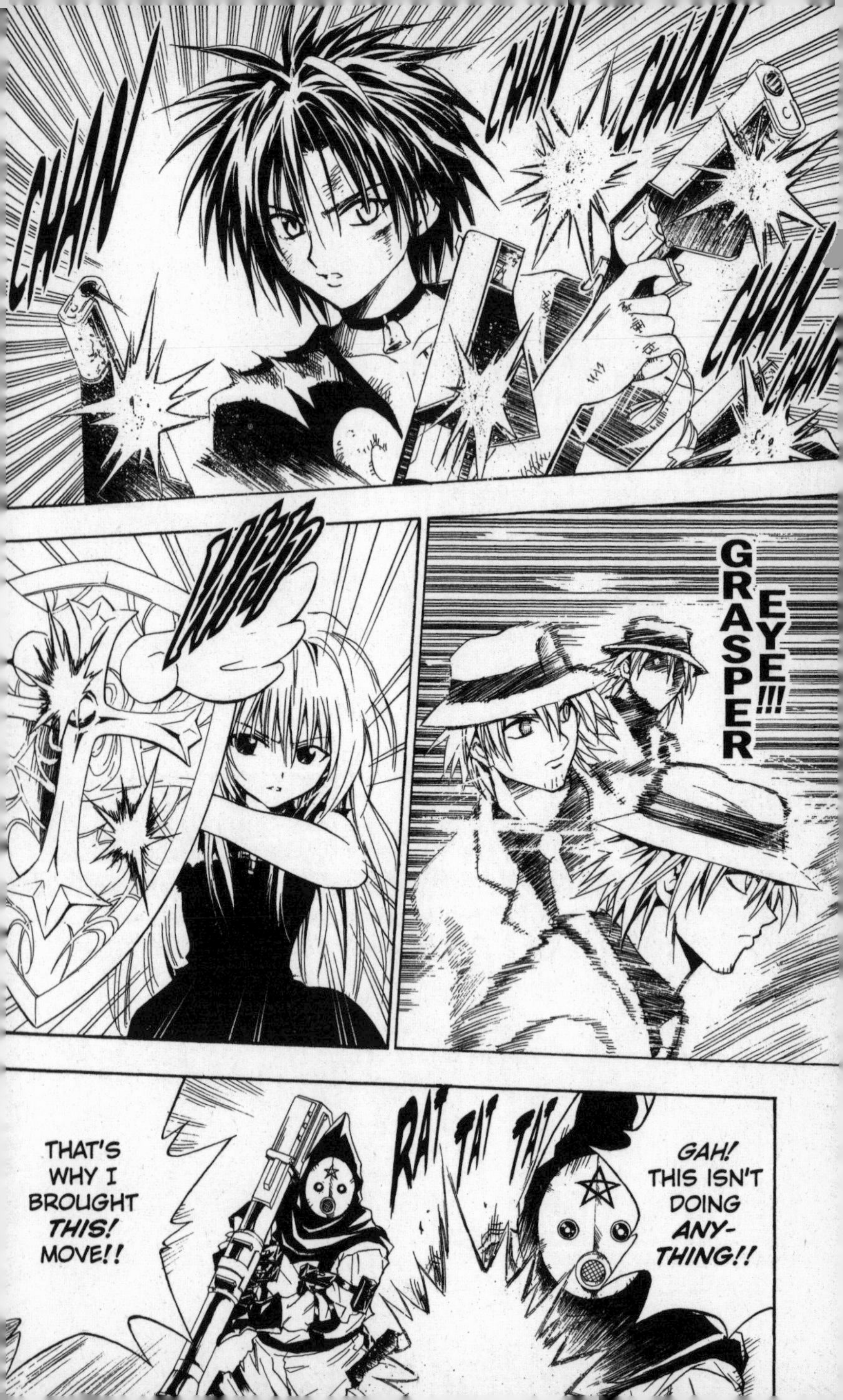
CHAN CHAN
CHAN CHAN CHAN
CHAN
GRASPER EYE!!!
GAH! THIS ISN'T DOING *ANY-THING!!*
RAT TAT TAT
THAT'S WHY I BROUGHT *THIS!* MOVE!!

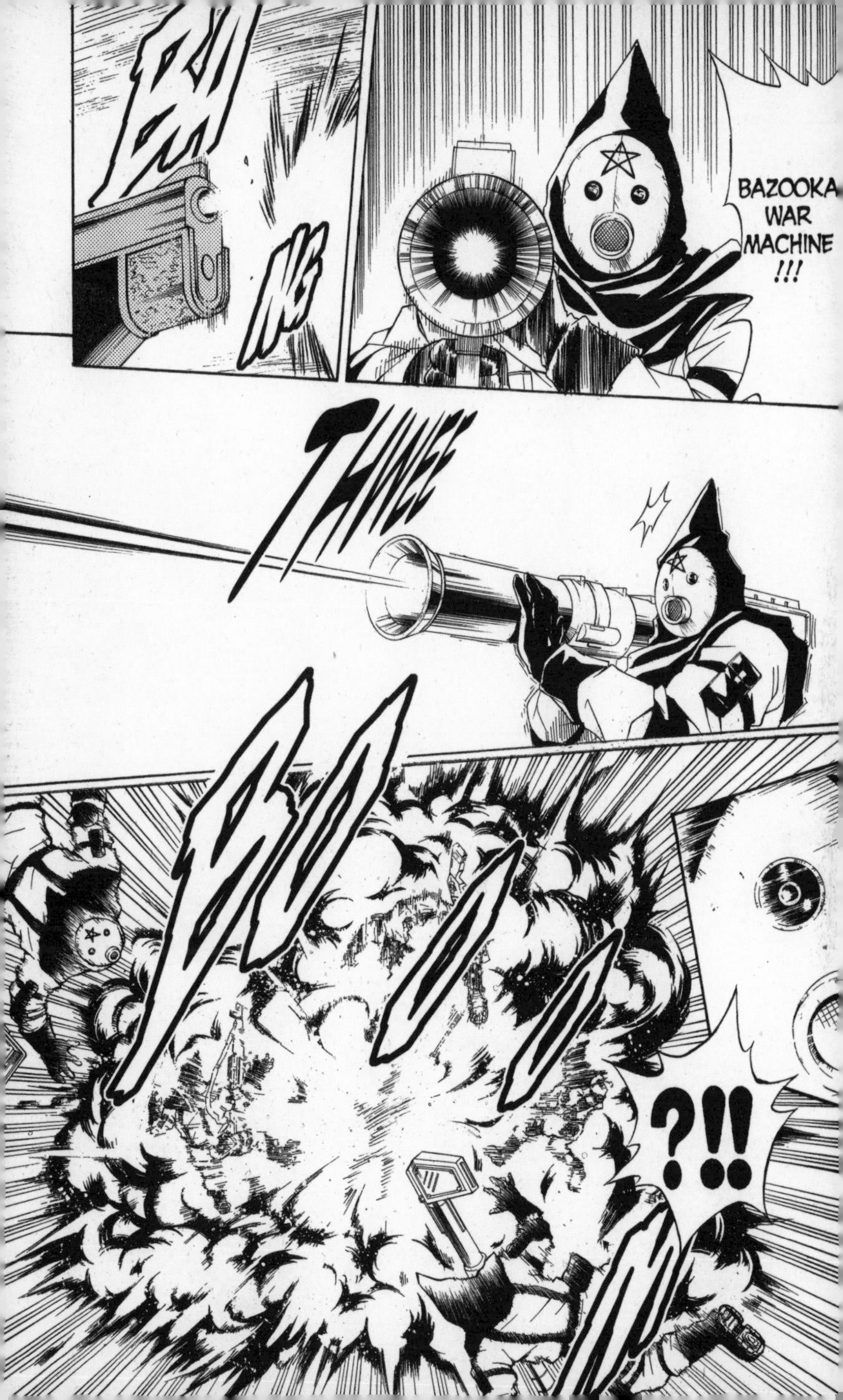
BAZOOKA WAR MACHINE !!!
?!!

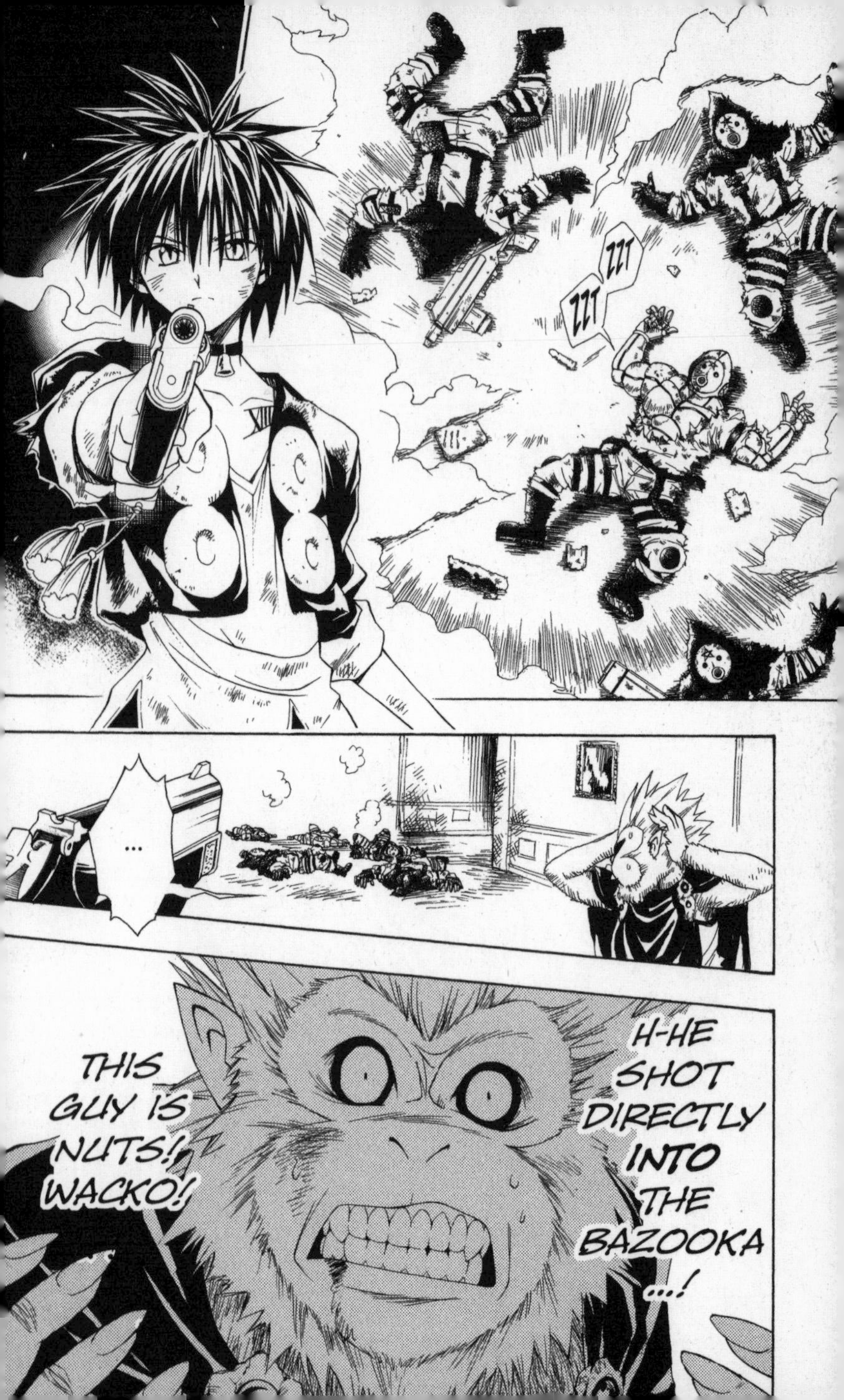
ZZT
ZZT
...
H-HE SHOT DIRECTLY INTO THE BAZOOKA ...!
THIS GUY IS NUTS! WACKO!

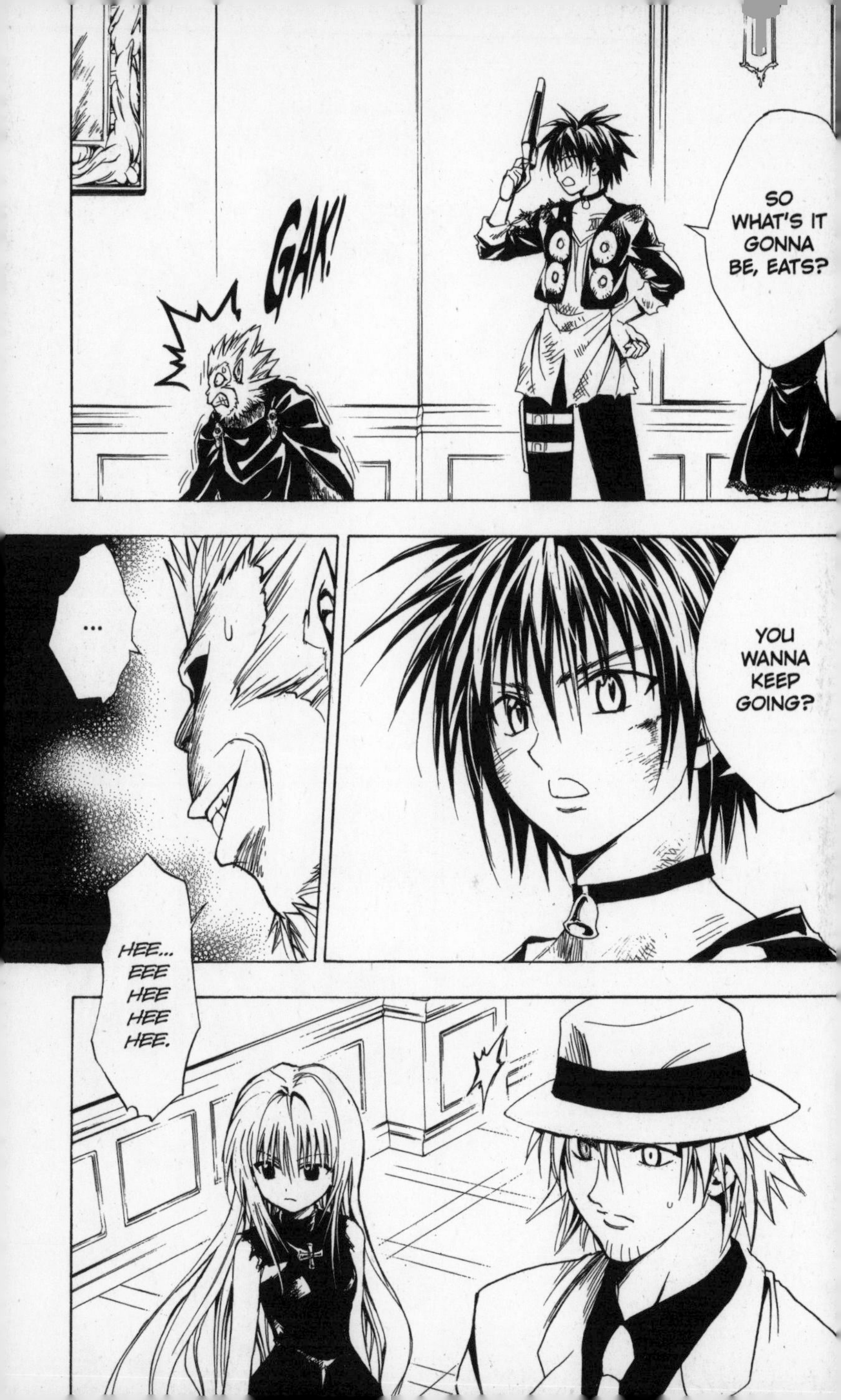
SO WHAT'S IT GONNA BE, EATS?
GAK!
YOU WANNA KEEP GOING?
...
HEE... EEE HEE HEE HEE.

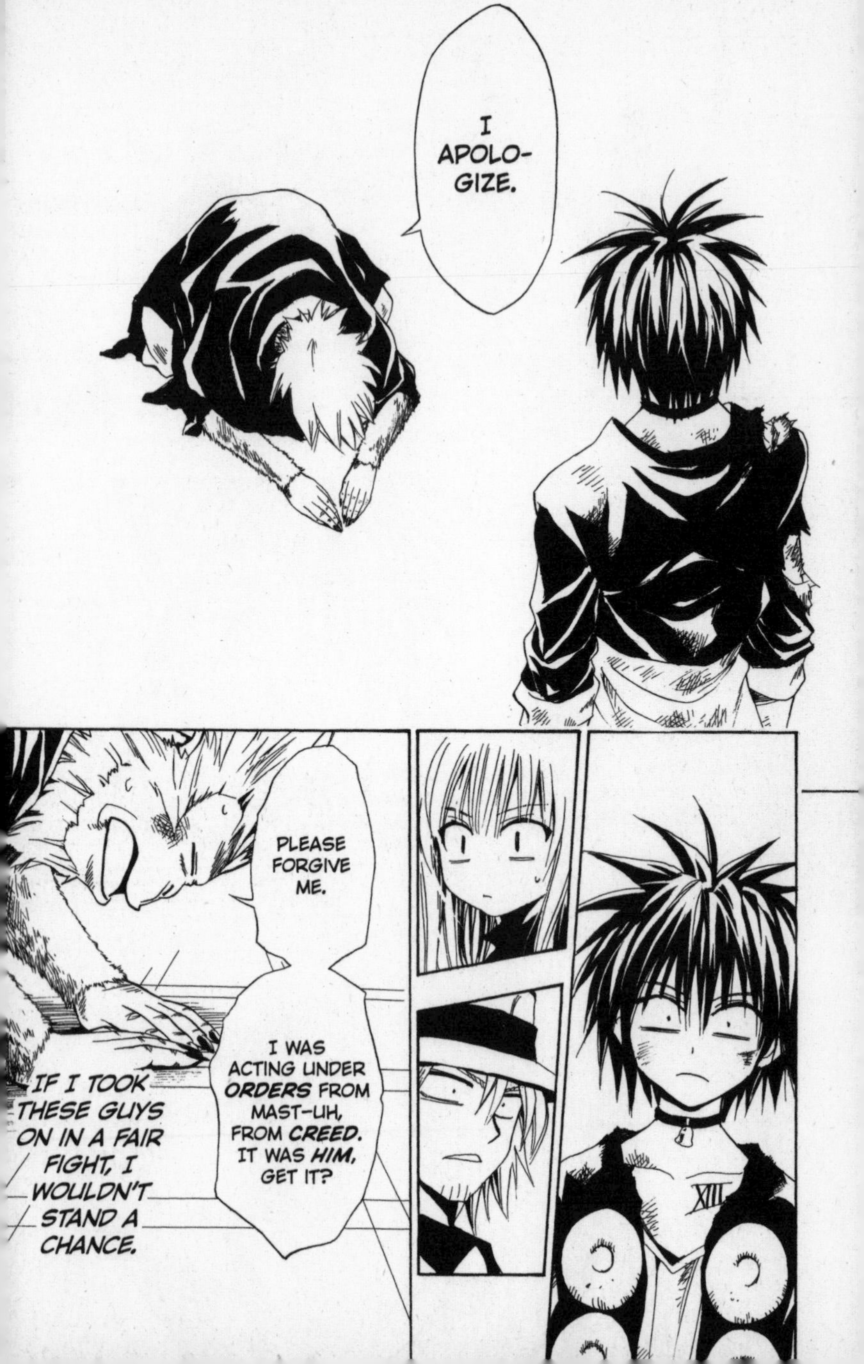
I APOLOGIZE.
PLEASE FORGIVE ME.
I WAS ACTING UNDER ORDERS FROM MAST-UH, FROM CREED. IT WAS HIM, GET IT?
IF I TOOK THESE GUYS ON IN A FAIR FIGHT, I WOULDN'T STAND A CHANCE.

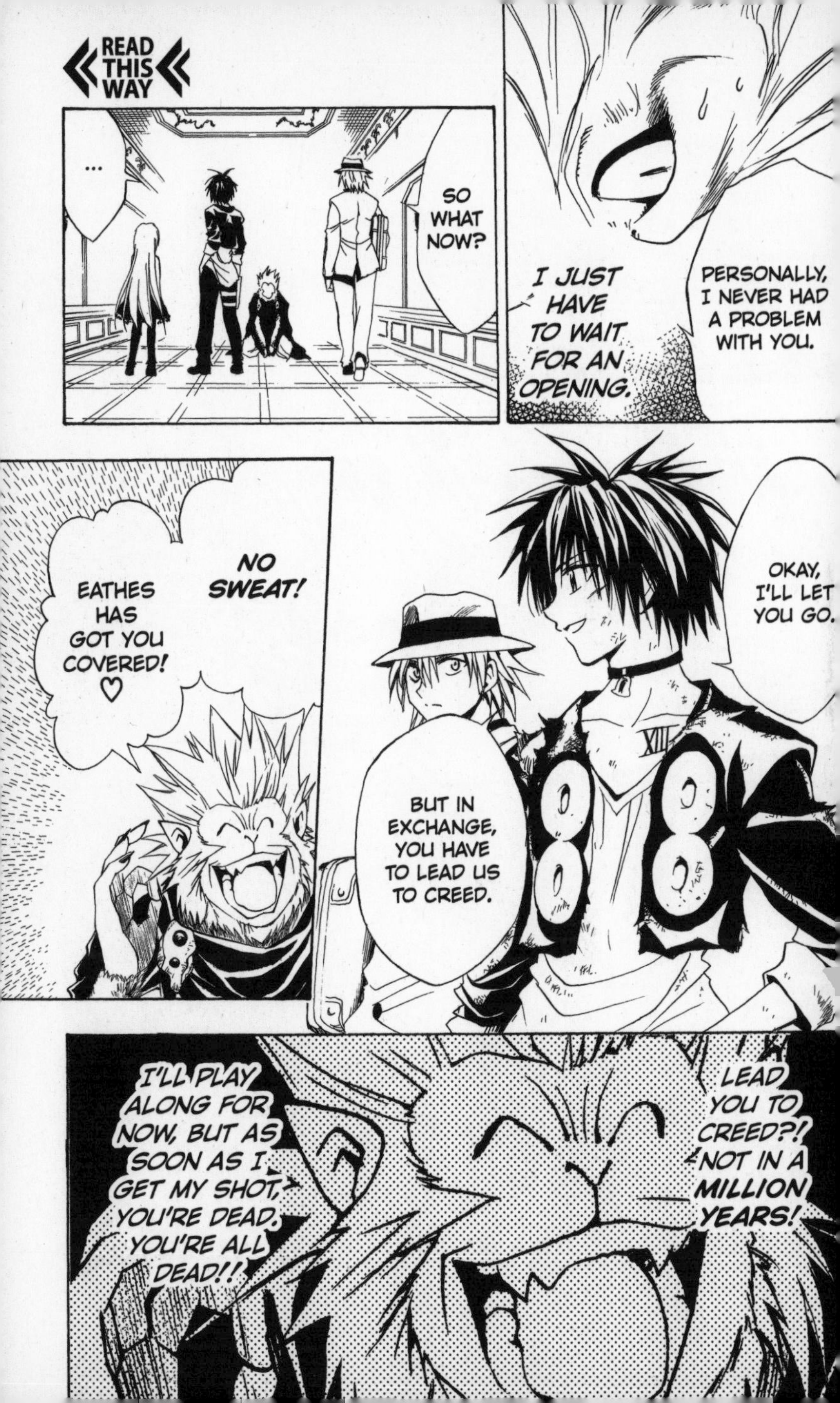
READ THIS WAY
PERSONALLY, I NEVER HAD A PROBLEM WITH YOU.
I JUST HAVE TO WAIT FOR AN OPENING.
SO WHAT NOW?
...
OKAY, I'LL LET YOU GO.
BUT IN EXCHANGE, YOU HAVE TO LEAD US TO CREED.
NO SWEAT!
EATHES HAS GOT YOU COVERED! ♡
LEAD YOU TO CREED?! NOT IN A MILLION YEARS!
I'LL PLAY ALONG FOR NOW, BUT AS SOON AS I GET MY SHOT, YOU'RE DEAD. YOU'RE ALL DEAD!!

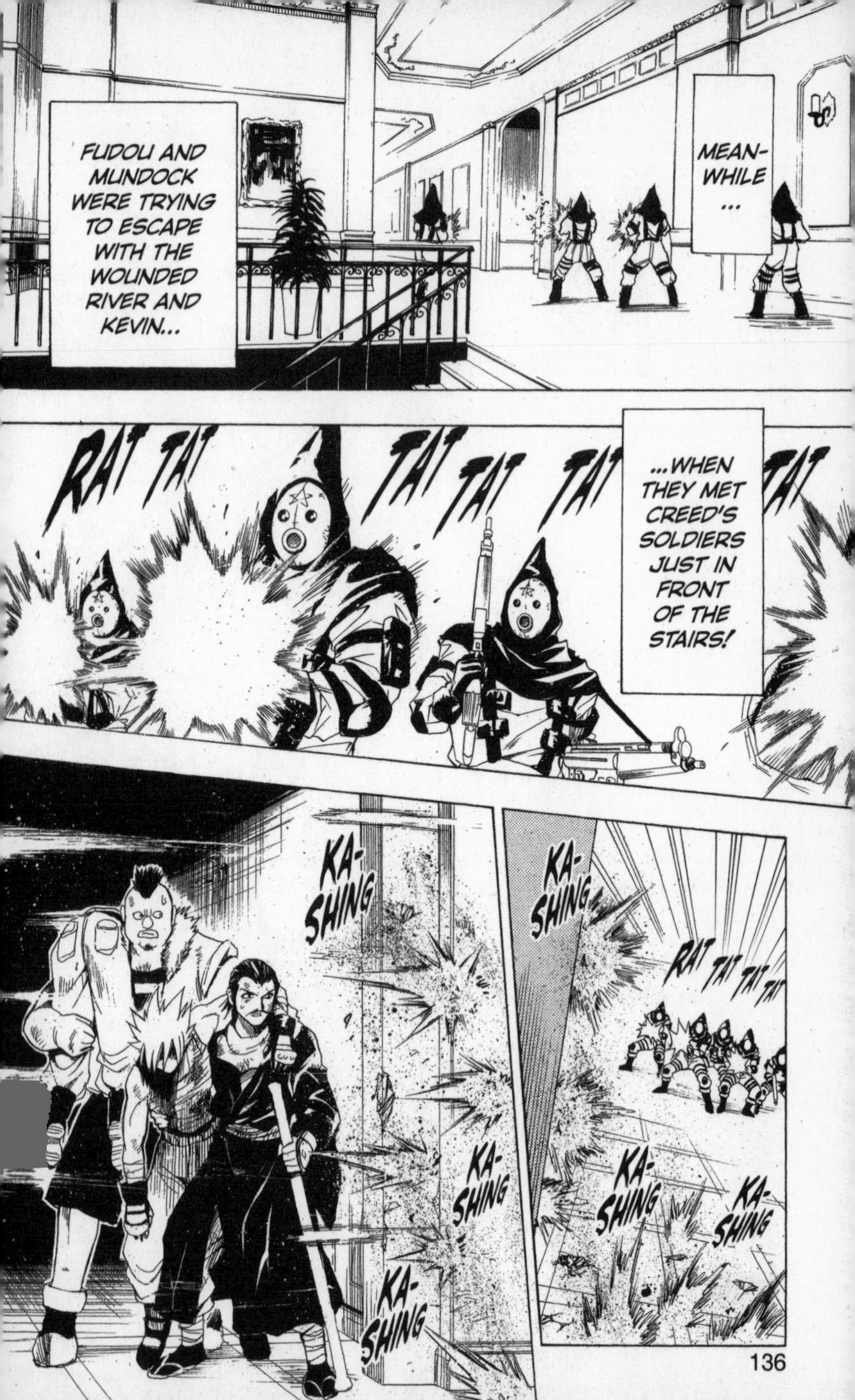
MEAN-WHILE...
FUDOU AND MUNDOCK WERE TRYING TO ESCAPE WITH THE WOUNDED RIVER AND KEVIN...
...WHEN THEY MET CREED'S SOLDIERS JUST IN FRONT OF THE STAIRS!
TAT
TAT
TAT
TAT
RAT TAT
KA-SHING
RAT TAT TAT TAT
KA-SHING
KA-SHING
KA-SHING
KA-SHING
KA-SHING

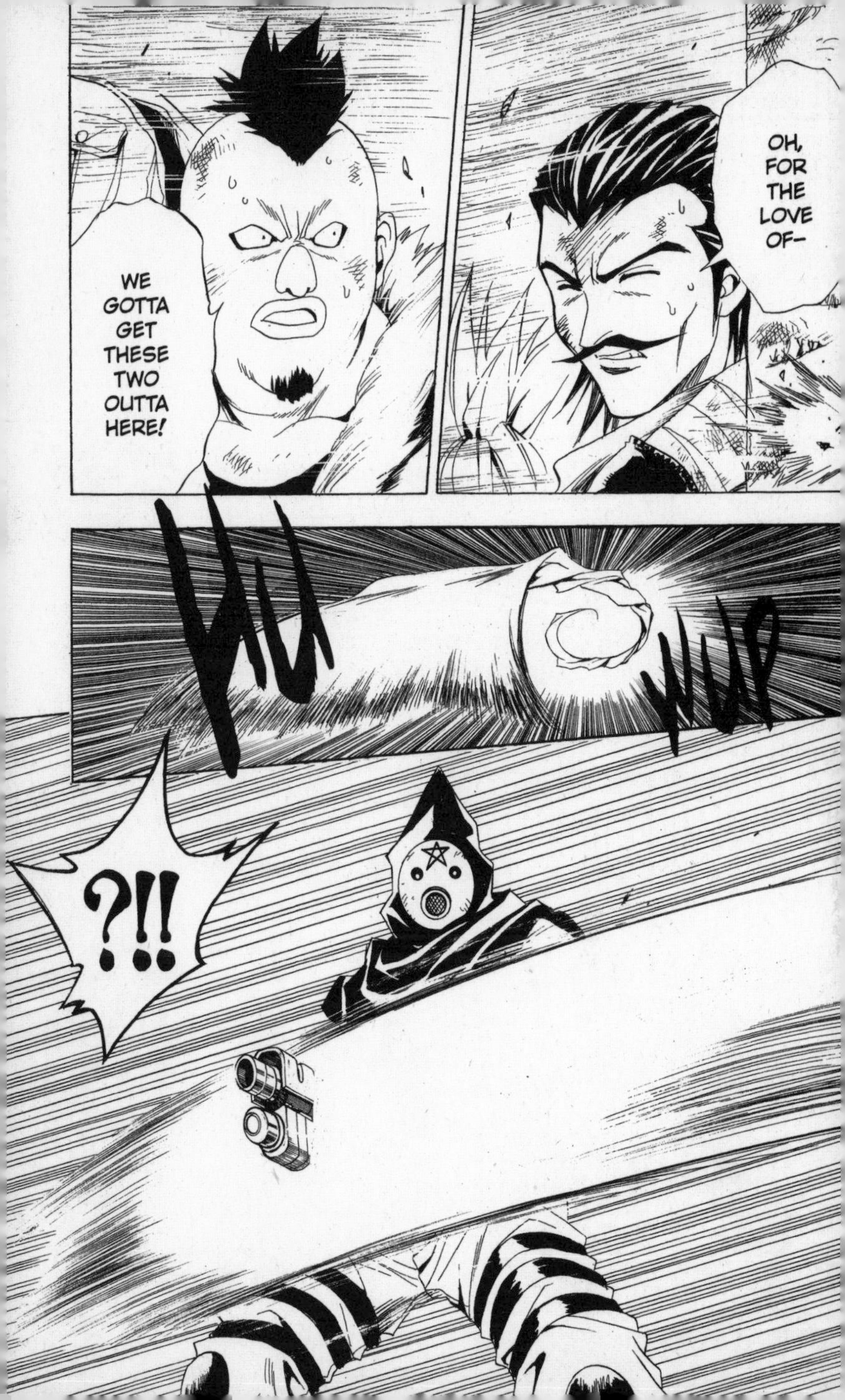
OH, FOR THE LOVE OF-
WE GOTTA GET THESE TWO OUTTA HERE!
WHUP
?!!

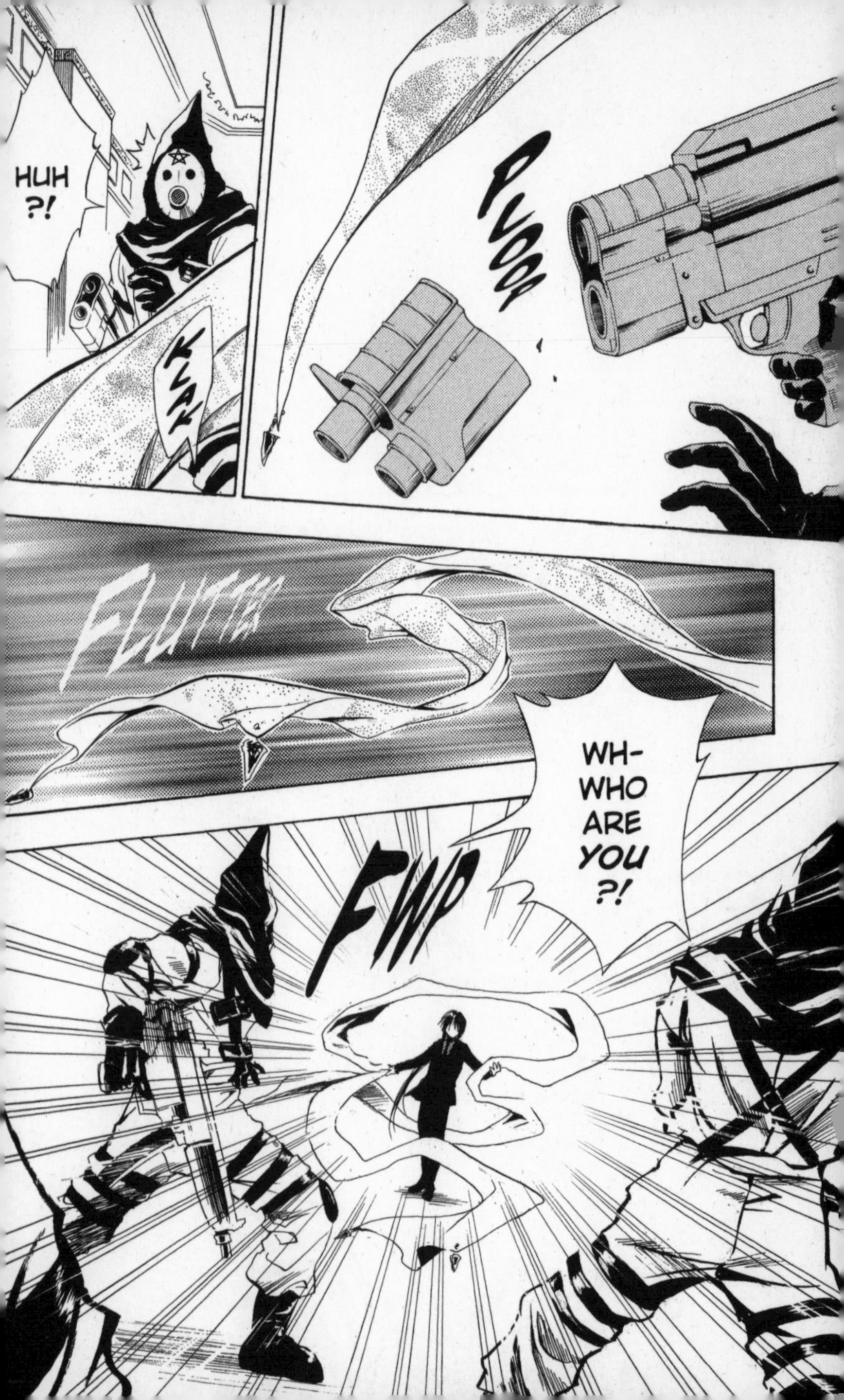

PLOOP
HUH ?!
KLAK
FLUTTER
WH- WHO ARE YOU ?!
FWP

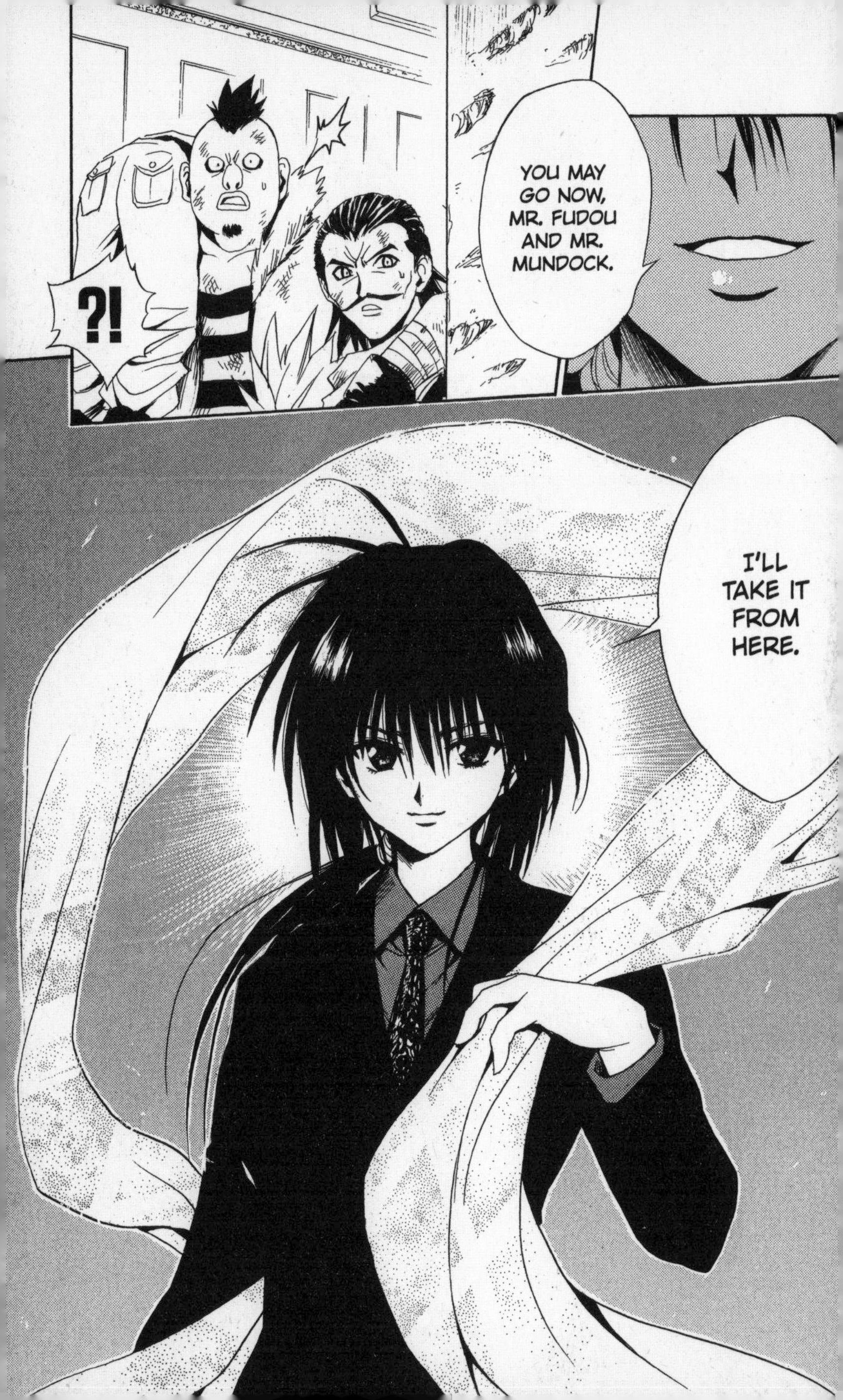
YOU MAY GO NOW, MR. FUDOU AND MR. MUNDOCK.
?!
I'LL TAKE IT FROM HERE.

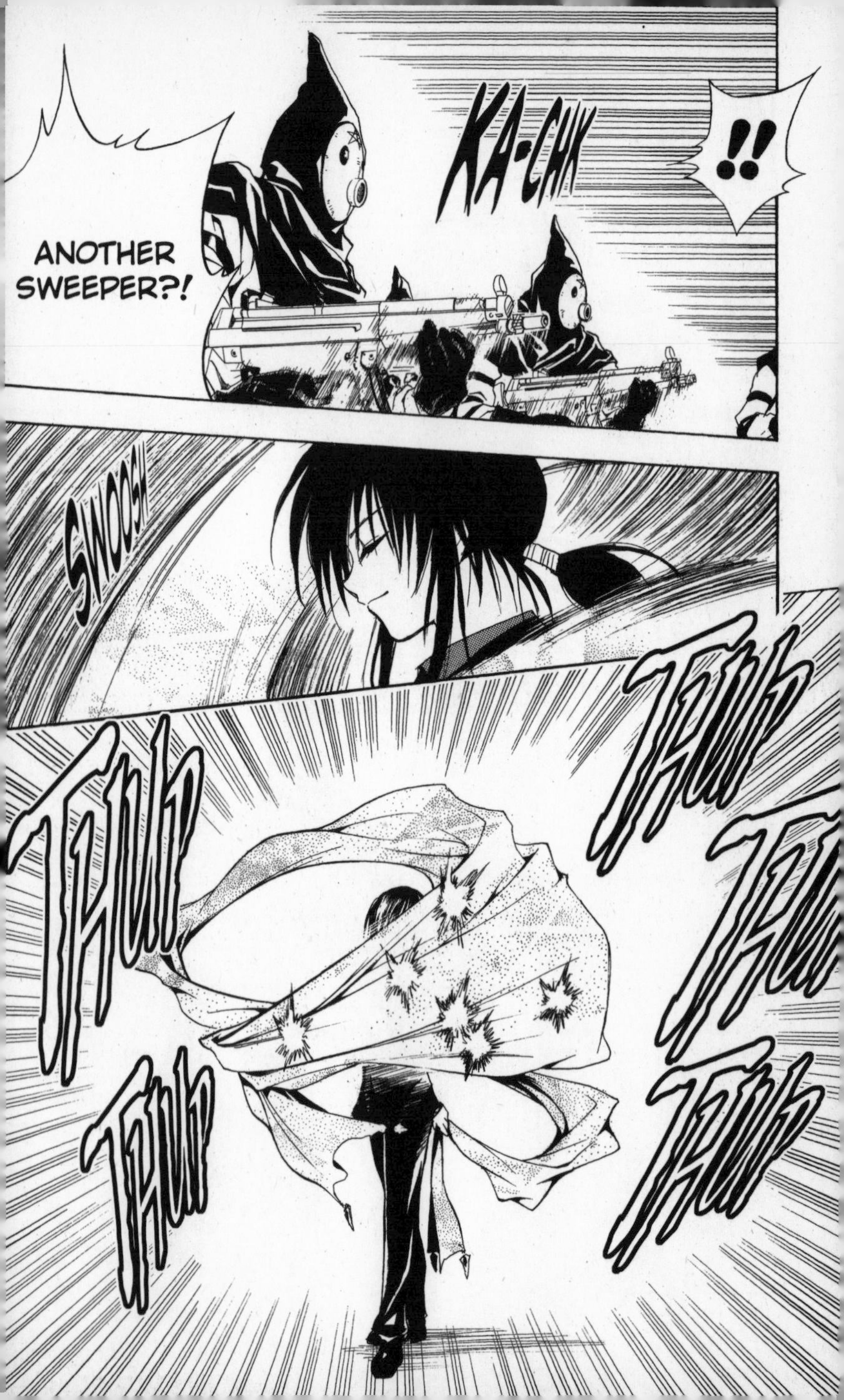
!!
KA-CHK
ANOTHER SWEEPER?!
SWOOSH
TFUH
TFUH
TFUH
TFUH
TFUH
TFUH

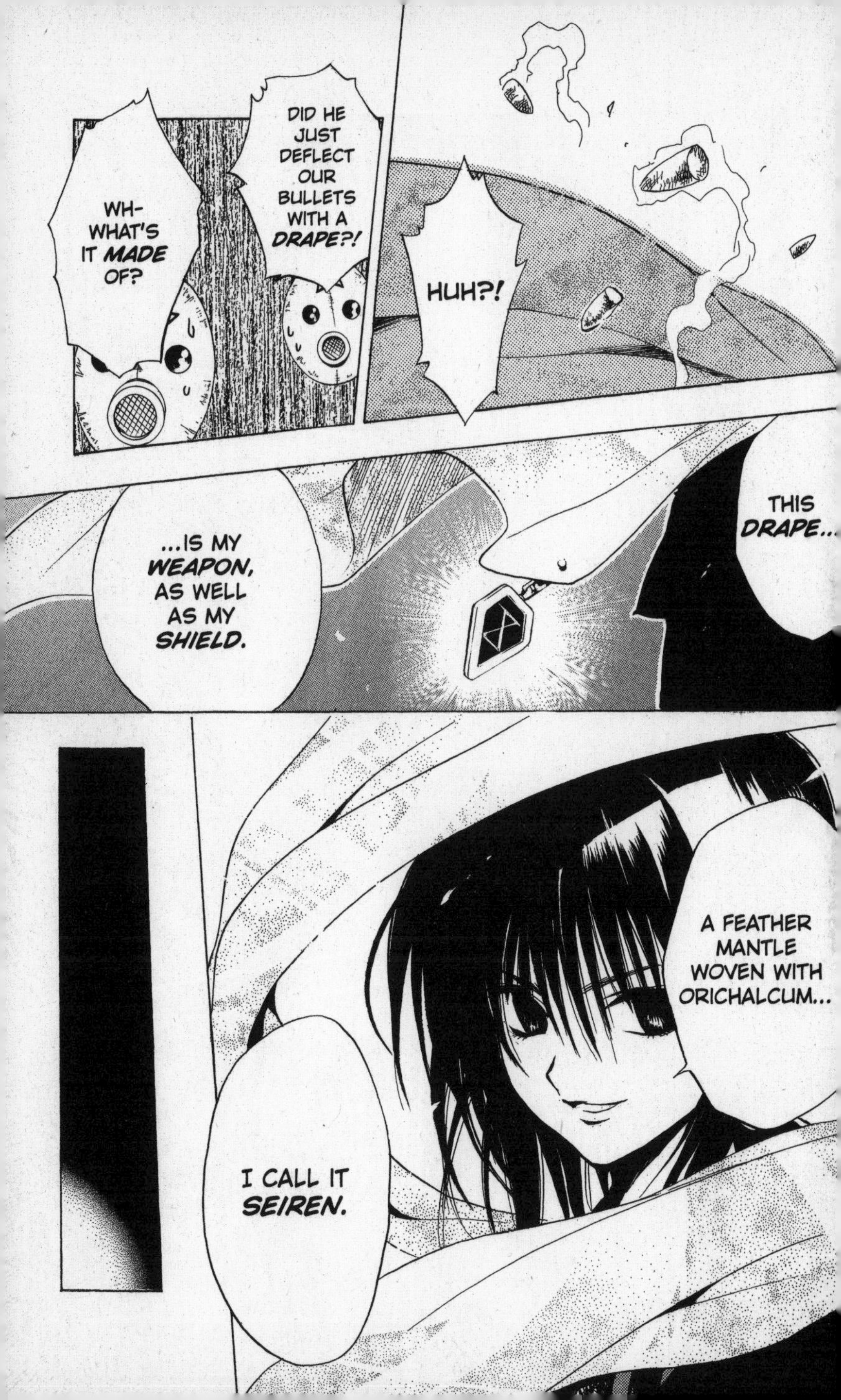
HUH?!
DID HE JUST DEFLECT OUR BULLETS WITH A DRAPE?!
WH- WHAT'S IT MADE OF?
THIS DRAPE...
...IS MY WEAPON, AS WELL AS MY SHIELD.
A FEATHER MANTLE WOVEN WITH ORICHALCUM...
I CALL IT SEIREN.

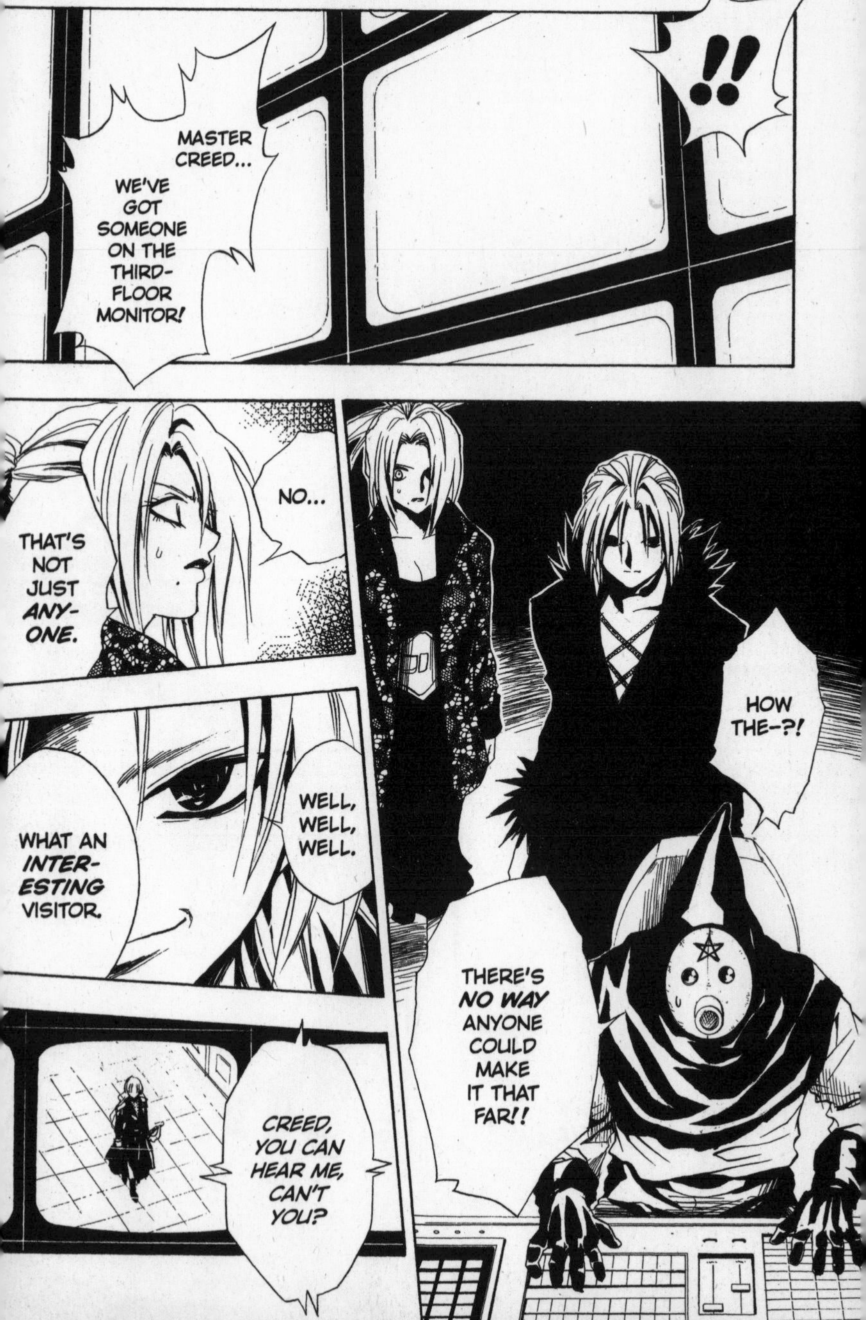
!!
MASTER CREED...
WE'VE GOT SOMEONE ON THE THIRD-FLOOR MONITOR!
HOW THE-?!
THERE'S NO WAY ANYONE COULD MAKE IT THAT FAR!!
NO...
THAT'S NOT JUST ANYONE.
WELL, WELL, WELL.
WHAT AN INTERESTING VISITOR.
CREED, YOU CAN HEAR ME, CAN'T YOU?

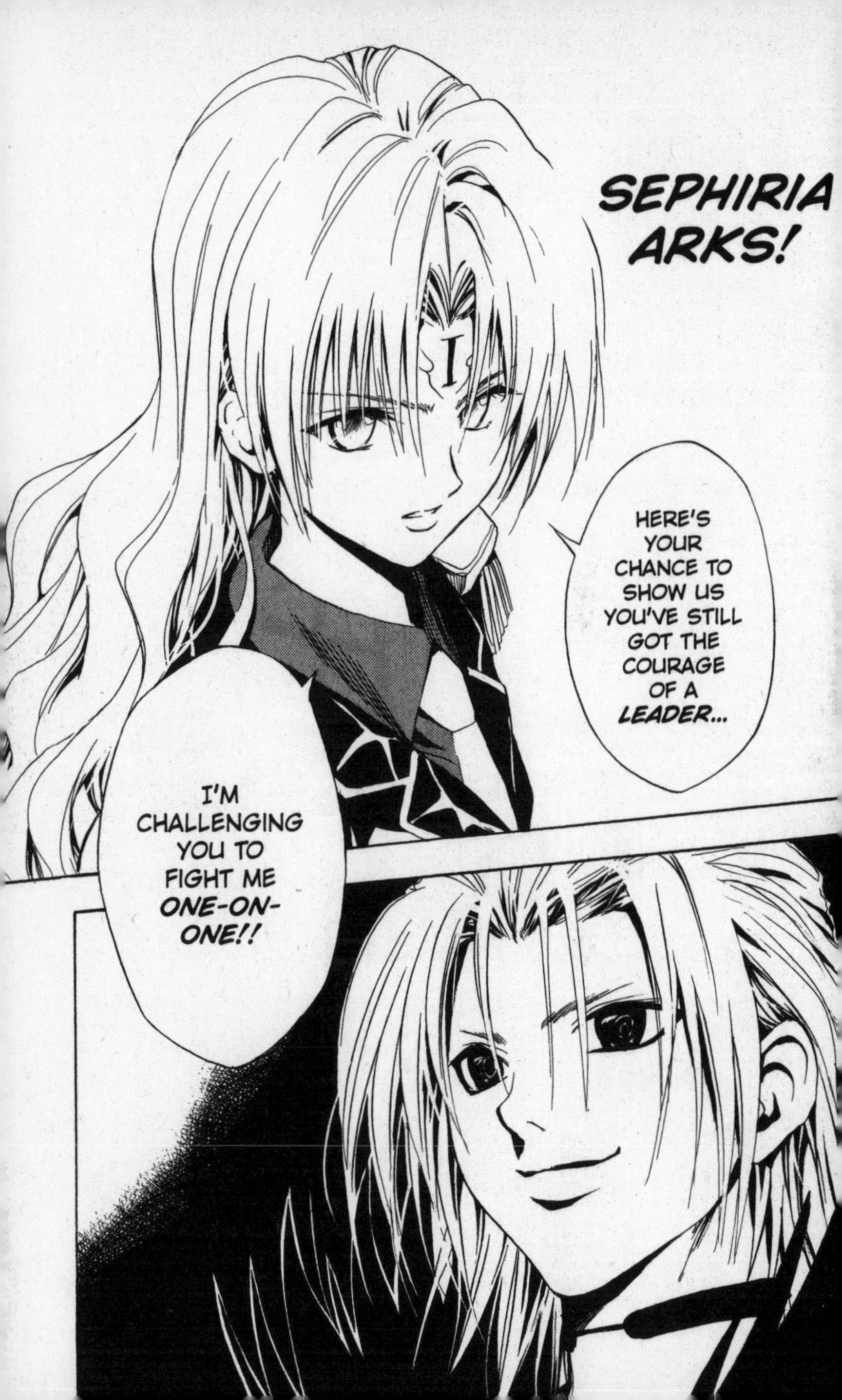
SEPHIRIA ARKS!
HERE'S YOUR CHANCE TO SHOW US YOU'VE STILL GOT THE COURAGE OF A *LEADER*...
I'M CHALLENGING YOU TO FIGHT ME *ONE-ON-ONE!!*

THE WORKPLACE IS A BATTLEFIELD! BY TATSUNORI HIDA

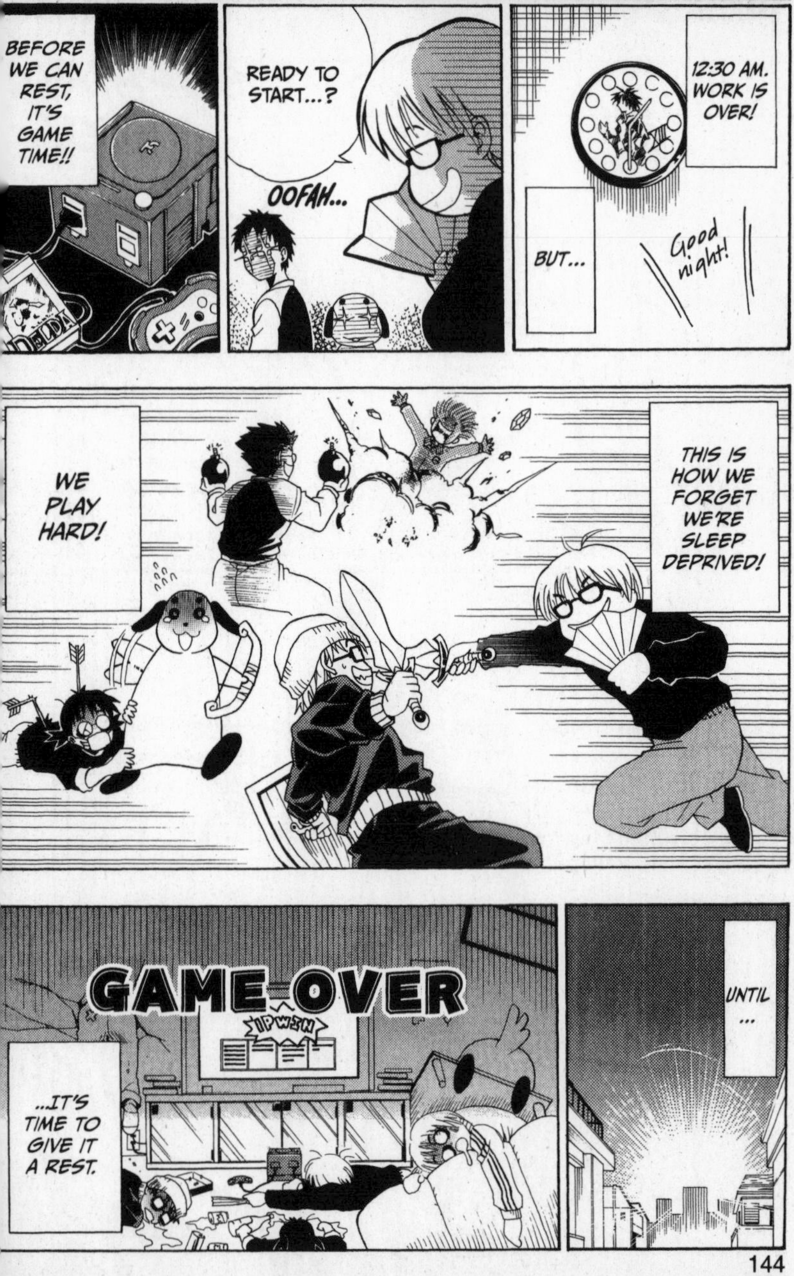

12:30 AM. WORK IS OVER!
Good night!
BUT...
READY TO START...?
OOFAH...
BEFORE WE CAN REST, IT'S GAME TIME!!
THIS IS HOW WE FORGET WE'RE SLEEP DEPRIVED!
WE PLAY HARD!
UNTIL ...
GAME OVER
1P WIN
...IT'S TIME TO GIVE IT A REST.

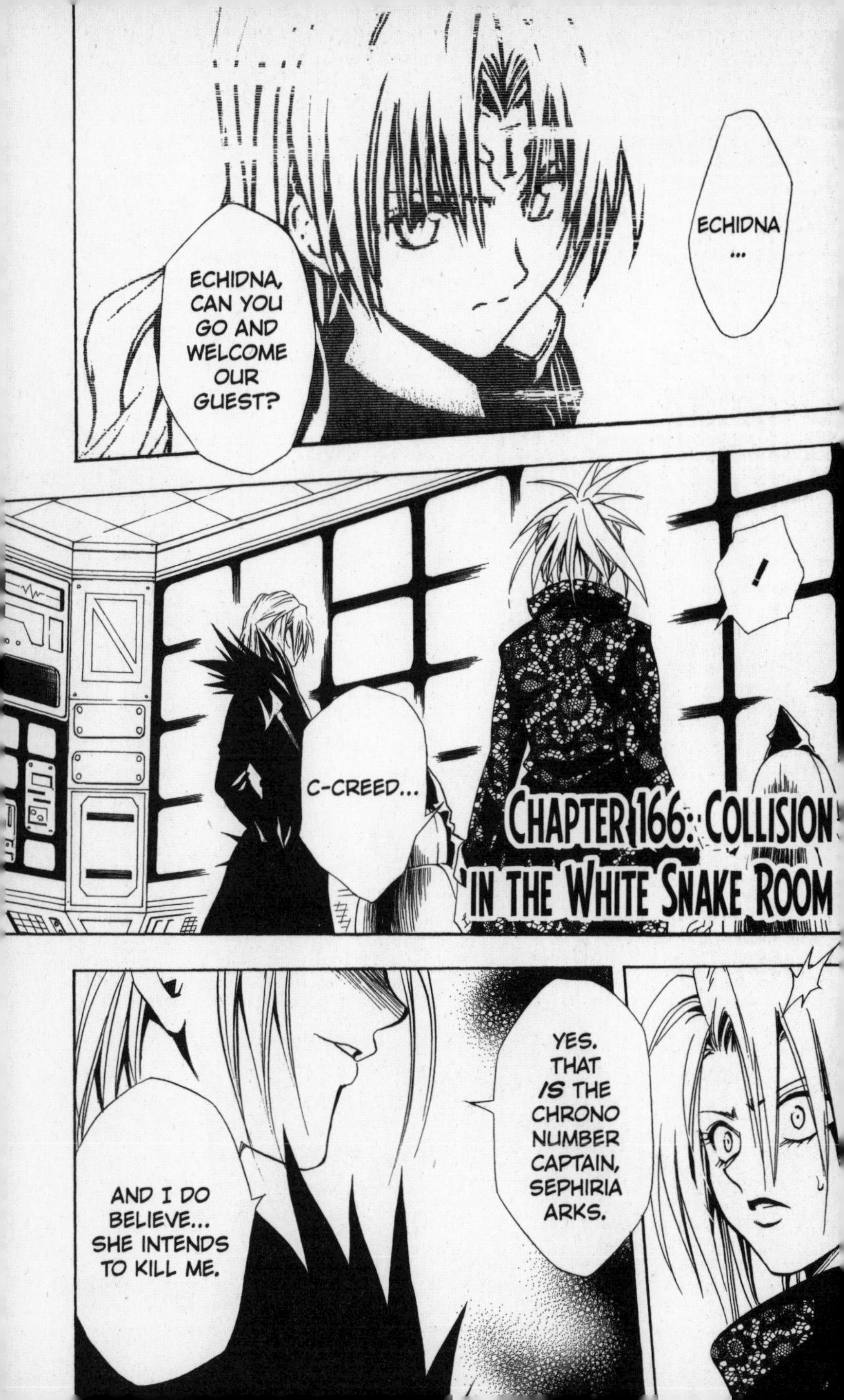
ECHIDNA...
ECHIDNA, CAN YOU GO AND WELCOME OUR GUEST?
!
C-CREED...
CHAPTER 166: COLLISION IN THE WHITE SNAKE ROOM
YES. THAT IS THE CHRONO NUMBER CAPTAIN, SEPHIRIA ARKS.
AND I DO BELIEVE... SHE INTENDS TO KILL ME.

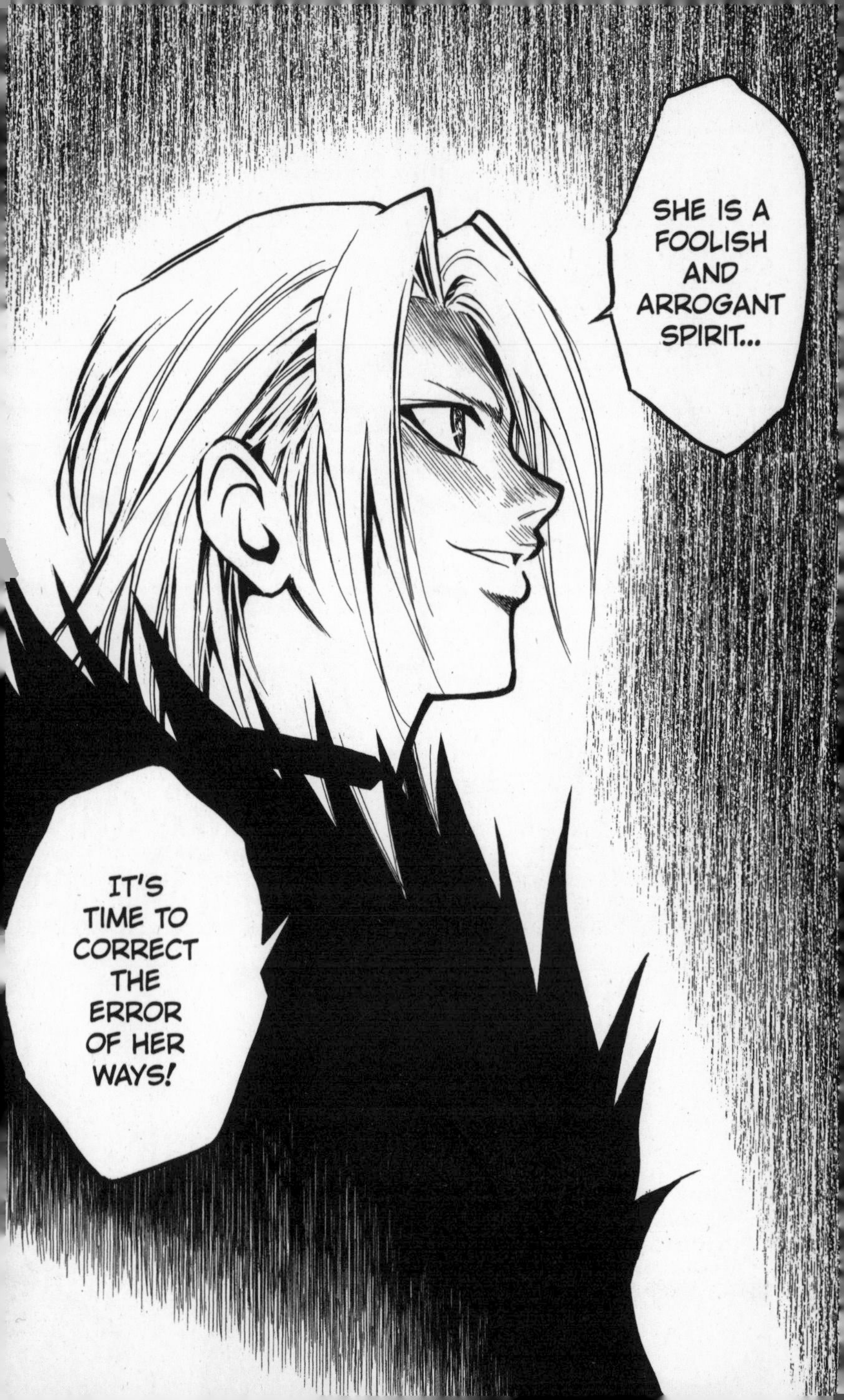
SHE IS A FOOLISH AND ARROGANT SPIRIT...
IT'S TIME TO CORRECT THE ERROR OF HER WAYS!

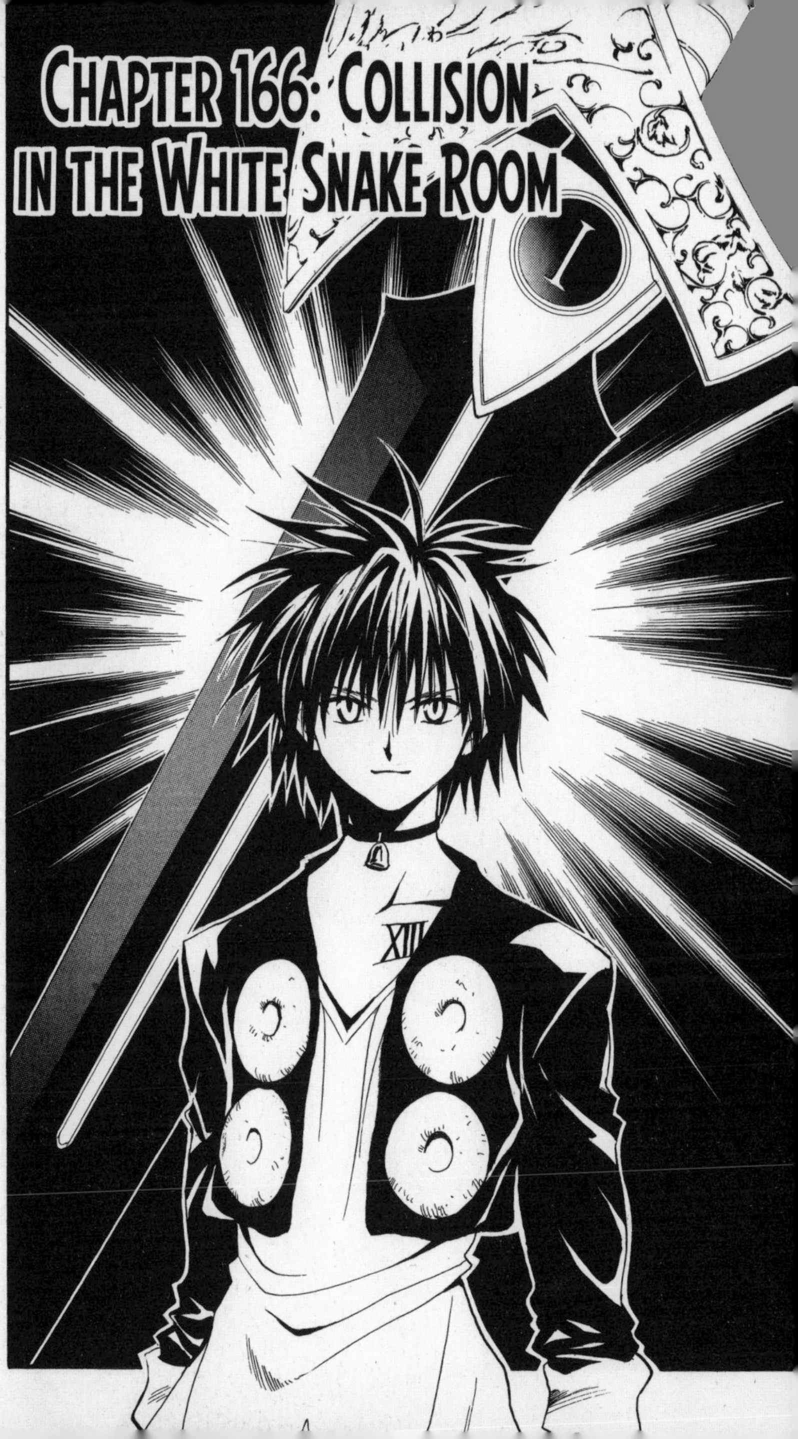
Chapter 166: Collision in the White Snake Room

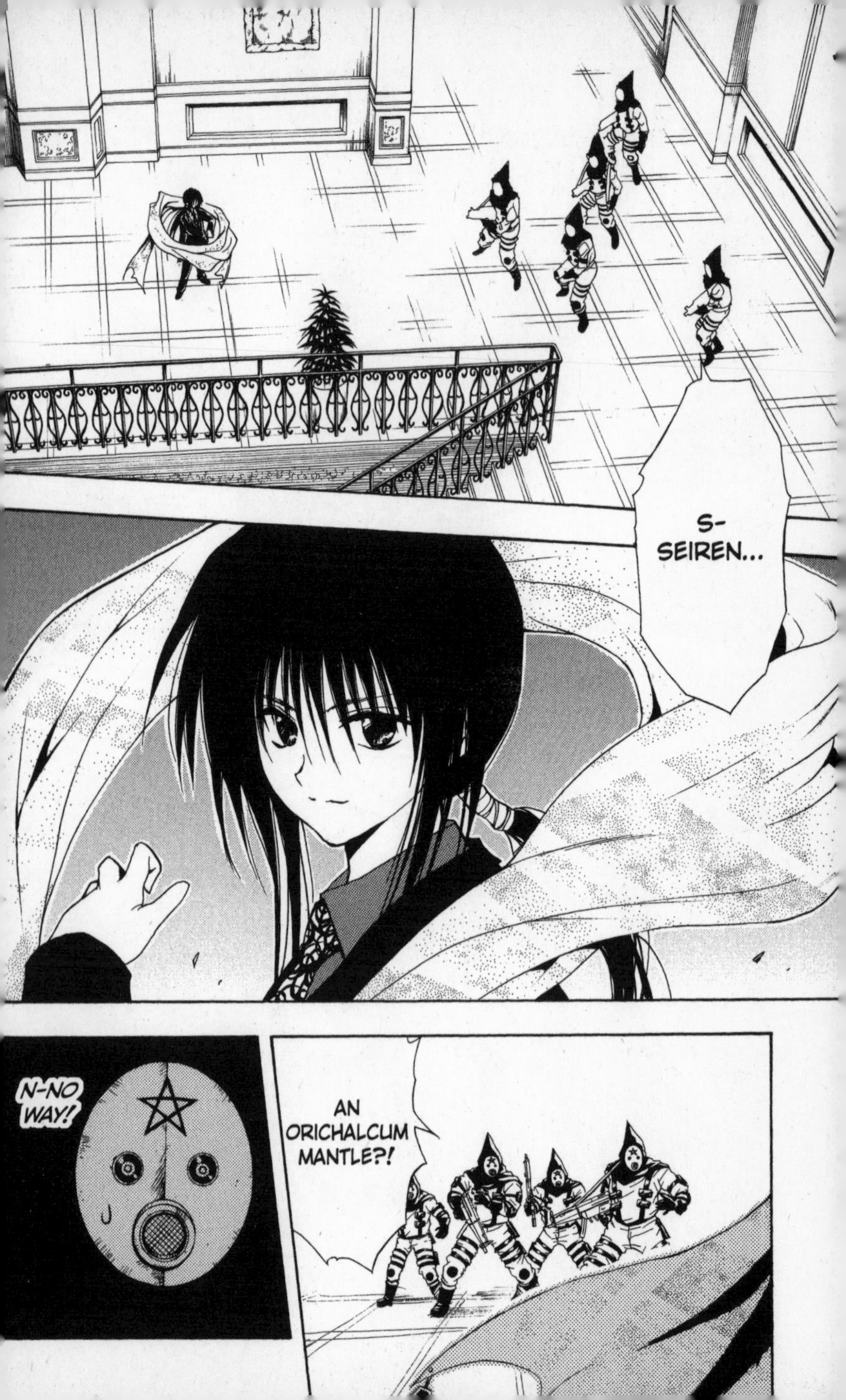
S-SEIREN...
AN ORICHALCUM MANTLE?!
N-NO WAY!

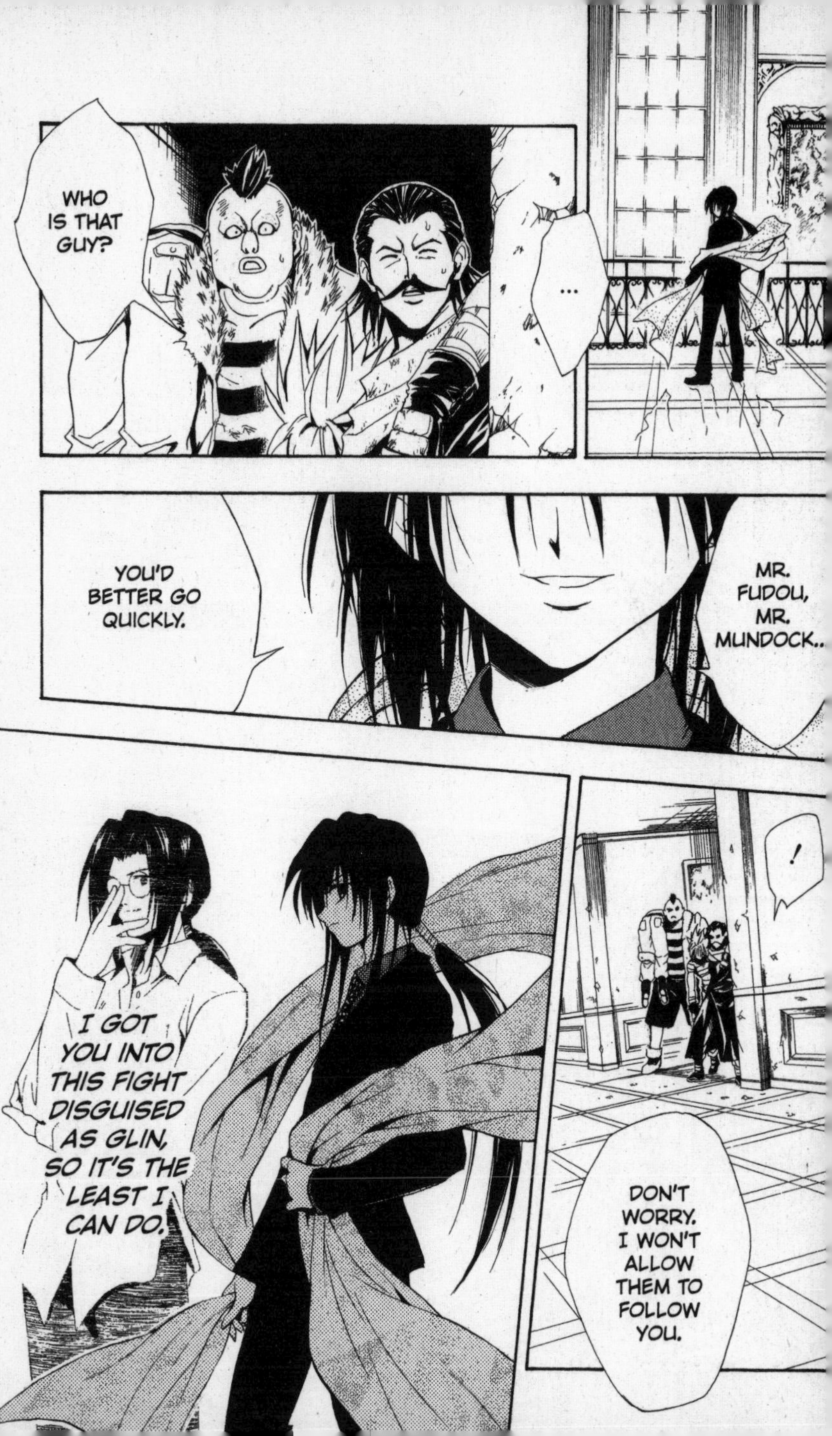
...
WHO IS THAT GUY?
MR. FUDOU, MR. MUNDOCK..
YOU'D BETTER GO QUICKLY.
!
DON'T WORRY. I WON'T ALLOW THEM TO FOLLOW YOU.
I GOT YOU INTO THIS FIGHT DISGUISED AS GLIN, SO IT'S THE LEAST I CAN DO.

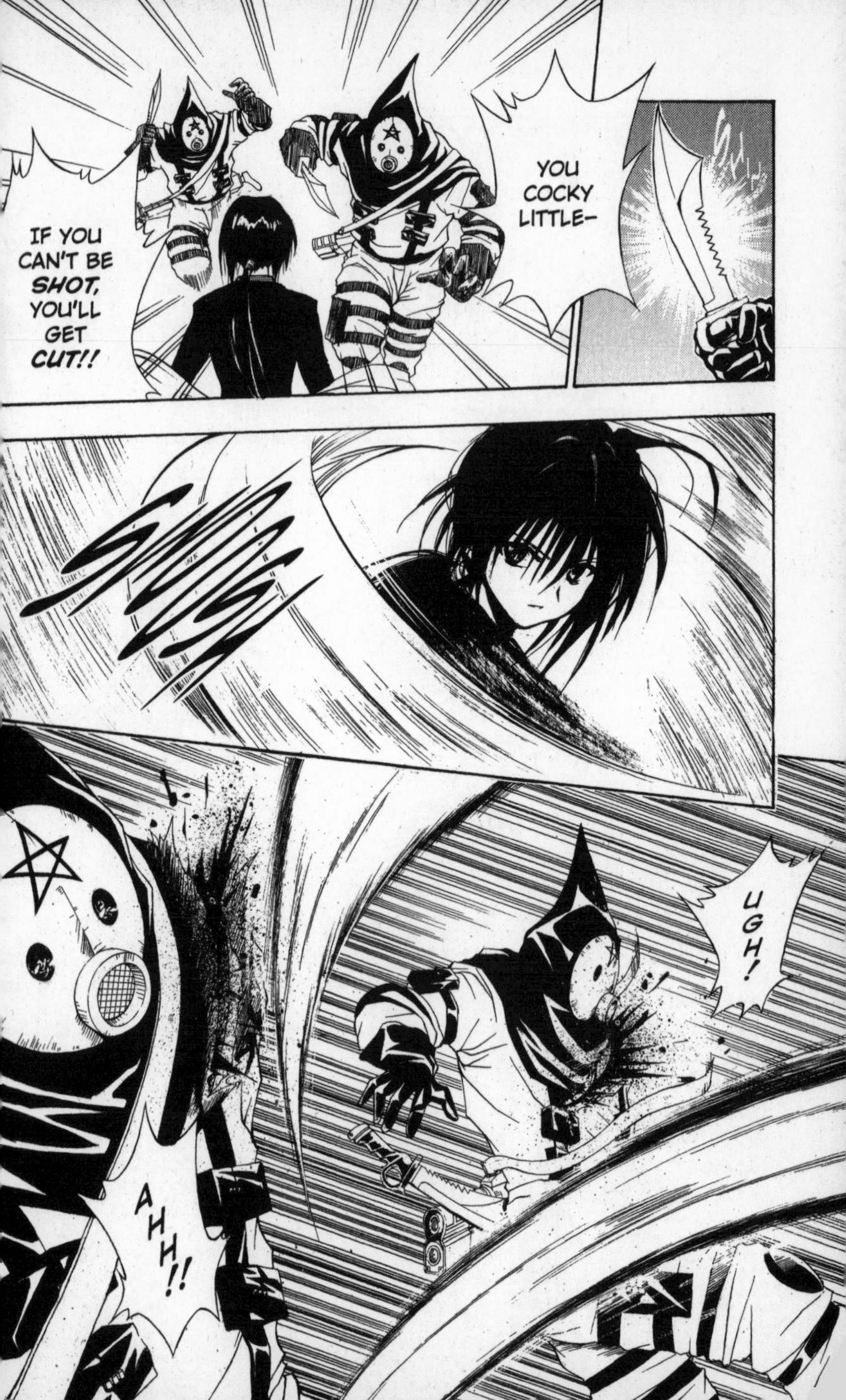
YOU COCKY LITTLE—
IF YOU CAN'T BE *SHOT*, YOU'LL GET *CUT!!*
SWISH
UGH!
AHH!!

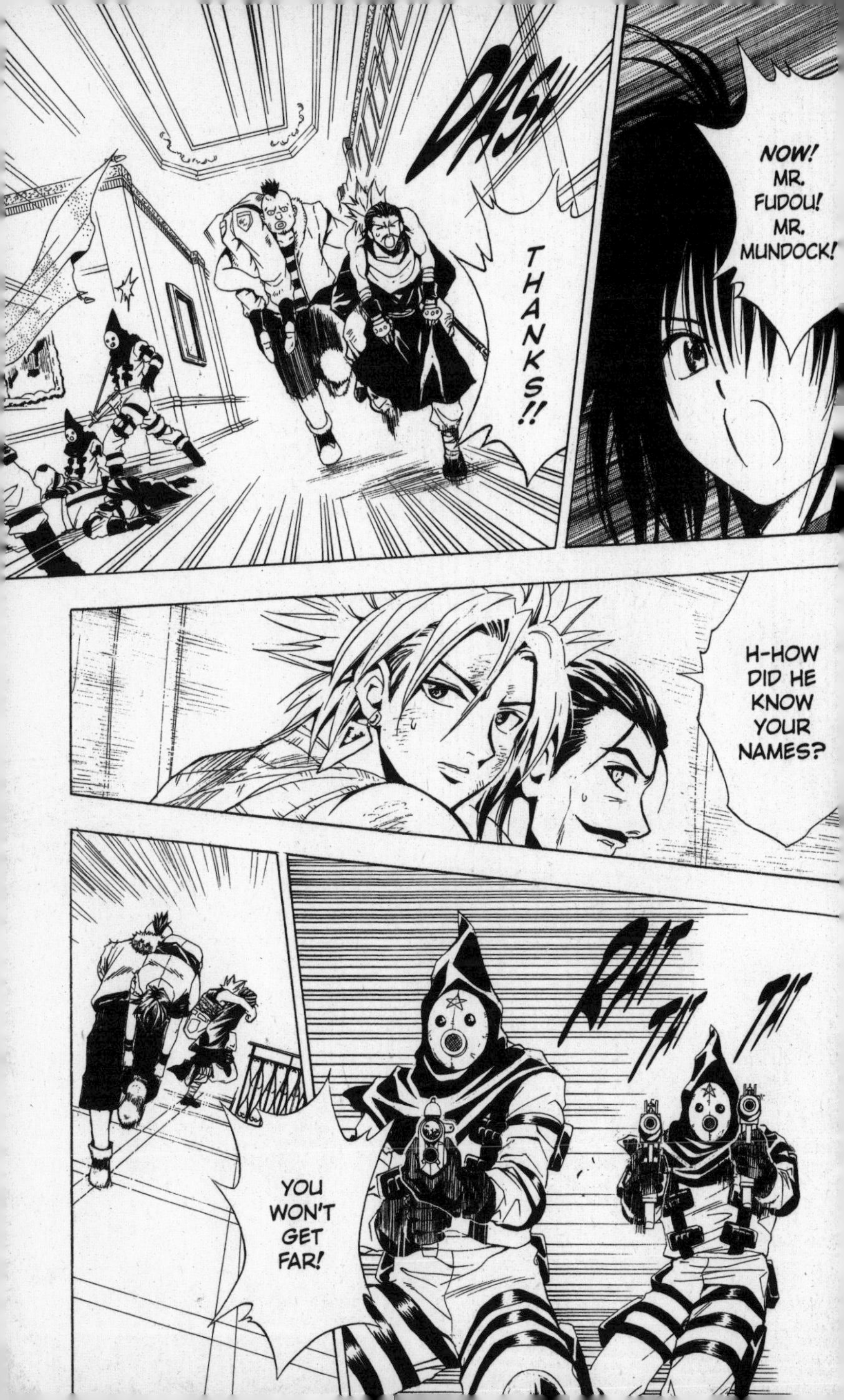
NOW! MR. FUDOU! MR. MUNDOCK!
DASH
THANKS!!
H-HOW DID HE KNOW YOUR NAMES?
RAT TAT TAT
YOU WON'T GET FAR!

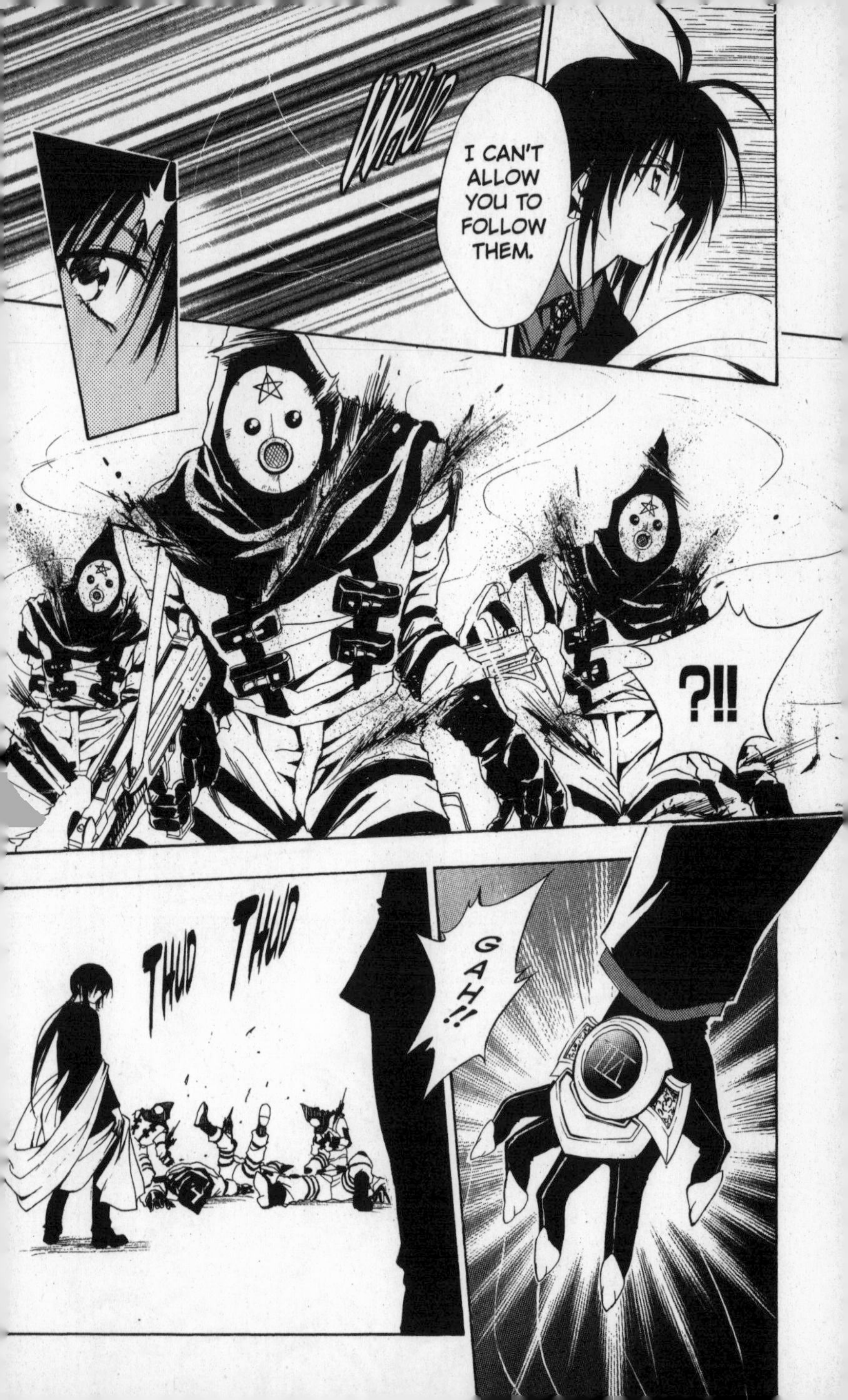
I CAN'T ALLOW YOU TO FOLLOW THEM.
?!!
GAH!!
THUD THUD

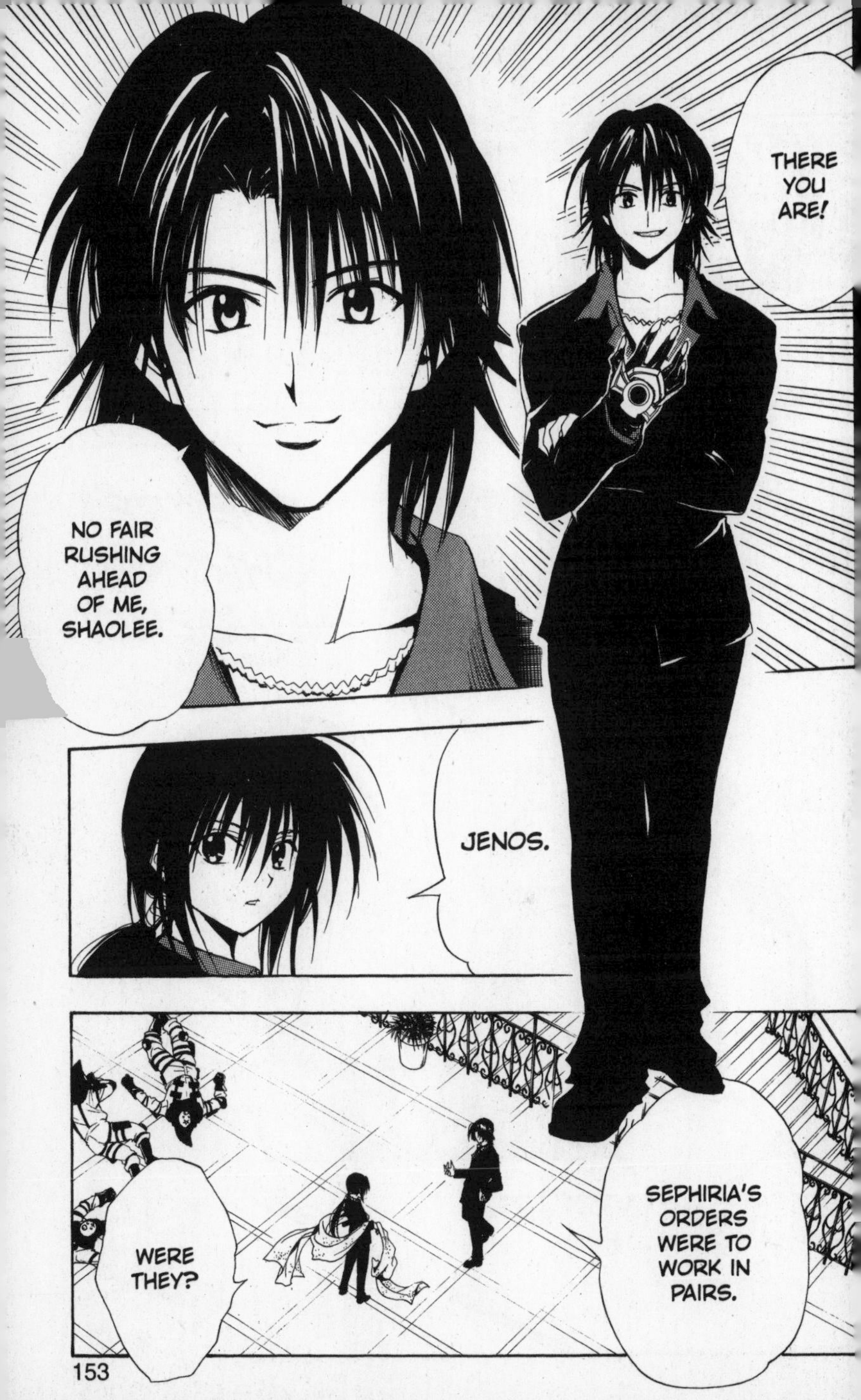
THERE YOU ARE!
NO FAIR RUSHING AHEAD OF ME, SHAOLEE.
JENOS.
SEPHIRIA'S ORDERS WERE TO WORK IN PAIRS.
WERE THEY?

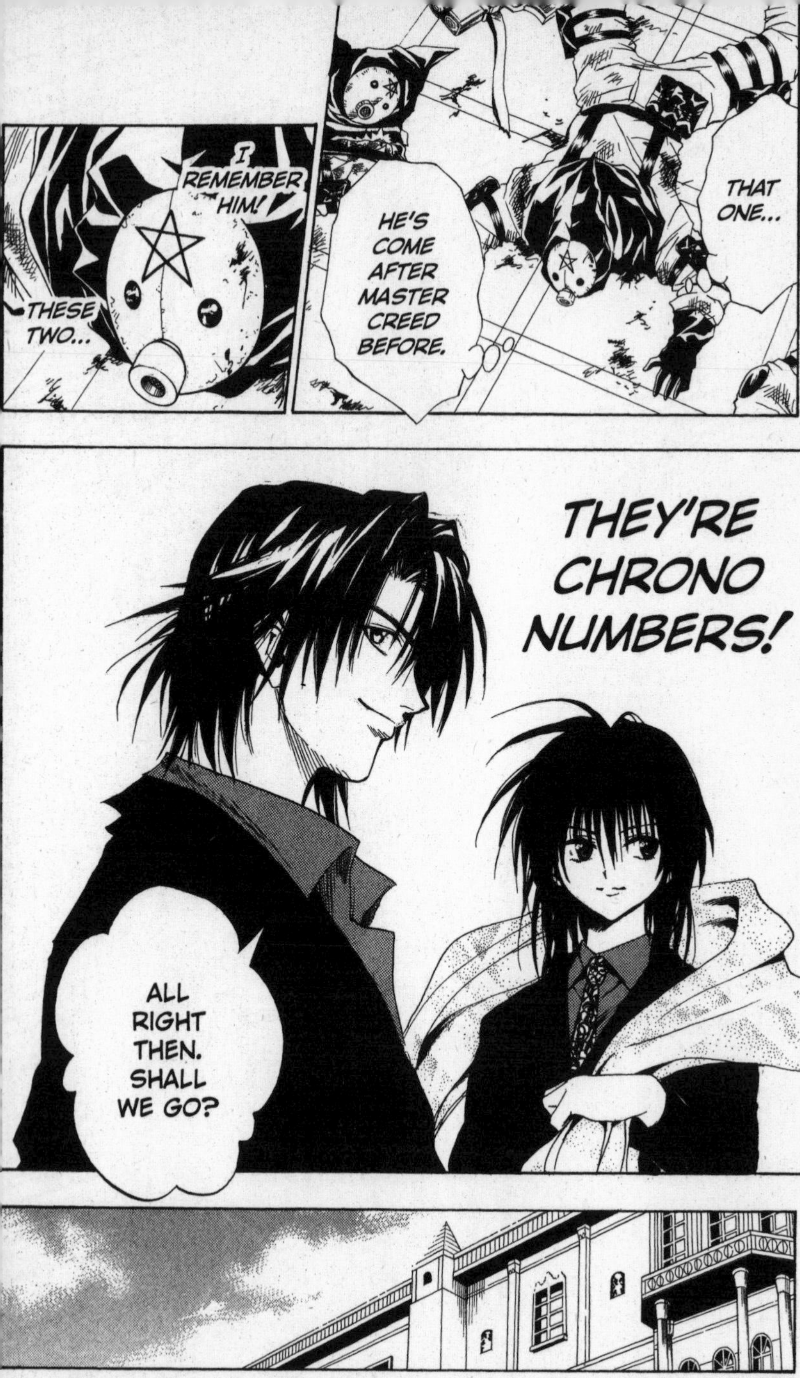
THAT ONE...
HE'S COME AFTER MASTER CREED BEFORE.
I REMEMBER HIM!
THESE TWO...
THEY'RE CHRONO NUMBERS!
ALL RIGHT THEN. SHALL WE GO?

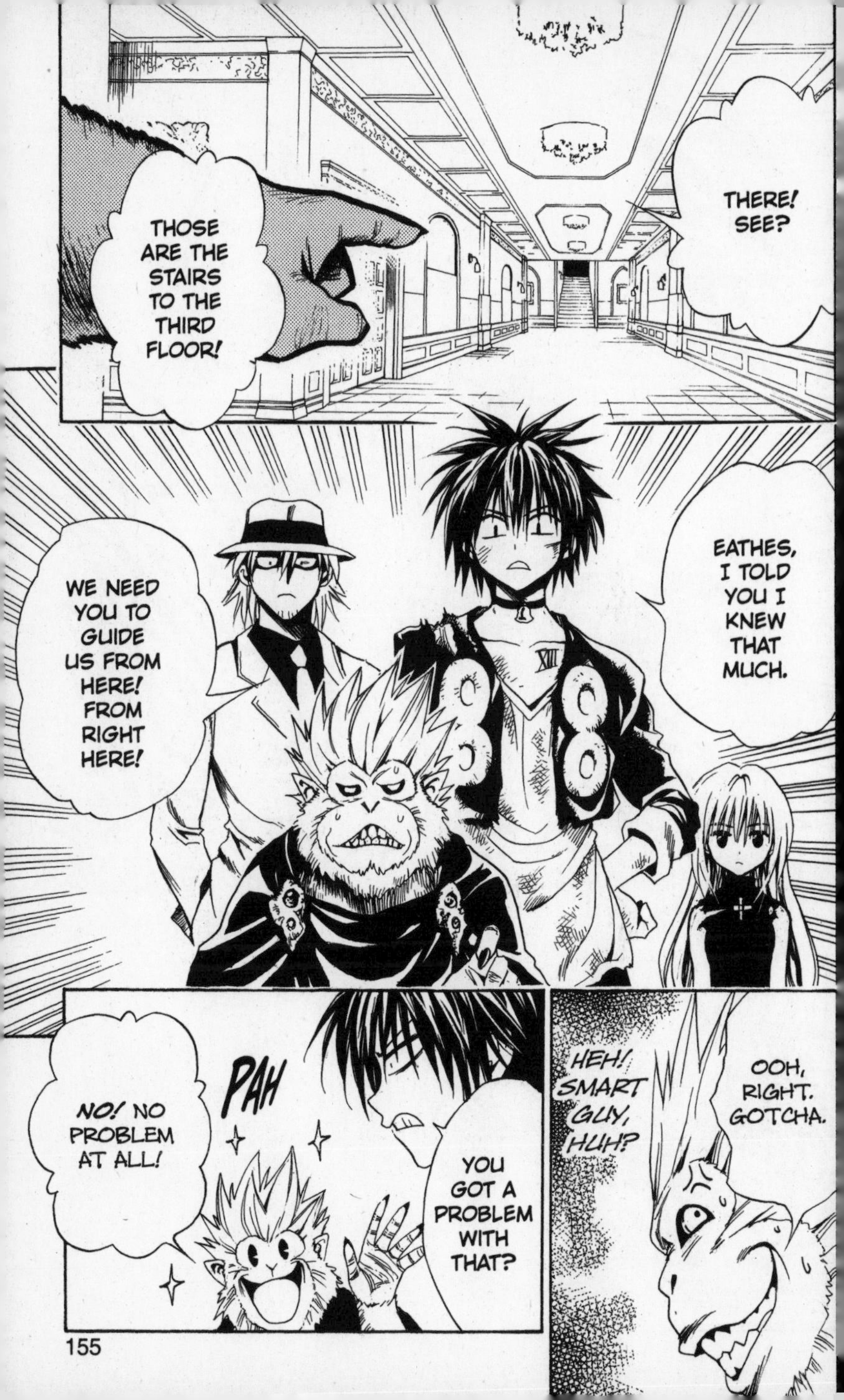
THERE! SEE?
THOSE ARE THE STAIRS TO THE THIRD FLOOR!
EATHES, I TOLD YOU I KNEW THAT MUCH.
WE NEED YOU TO GUIDE US FROM HERE! FROM RIGHT HERE!
OOH, RIGHT. GOTCHA.
HEH! SMART GUY, HUH?
YOU GOT A PROBLEM WITH THAT?
PAH
NO! NO PROBLEM AT ALL!

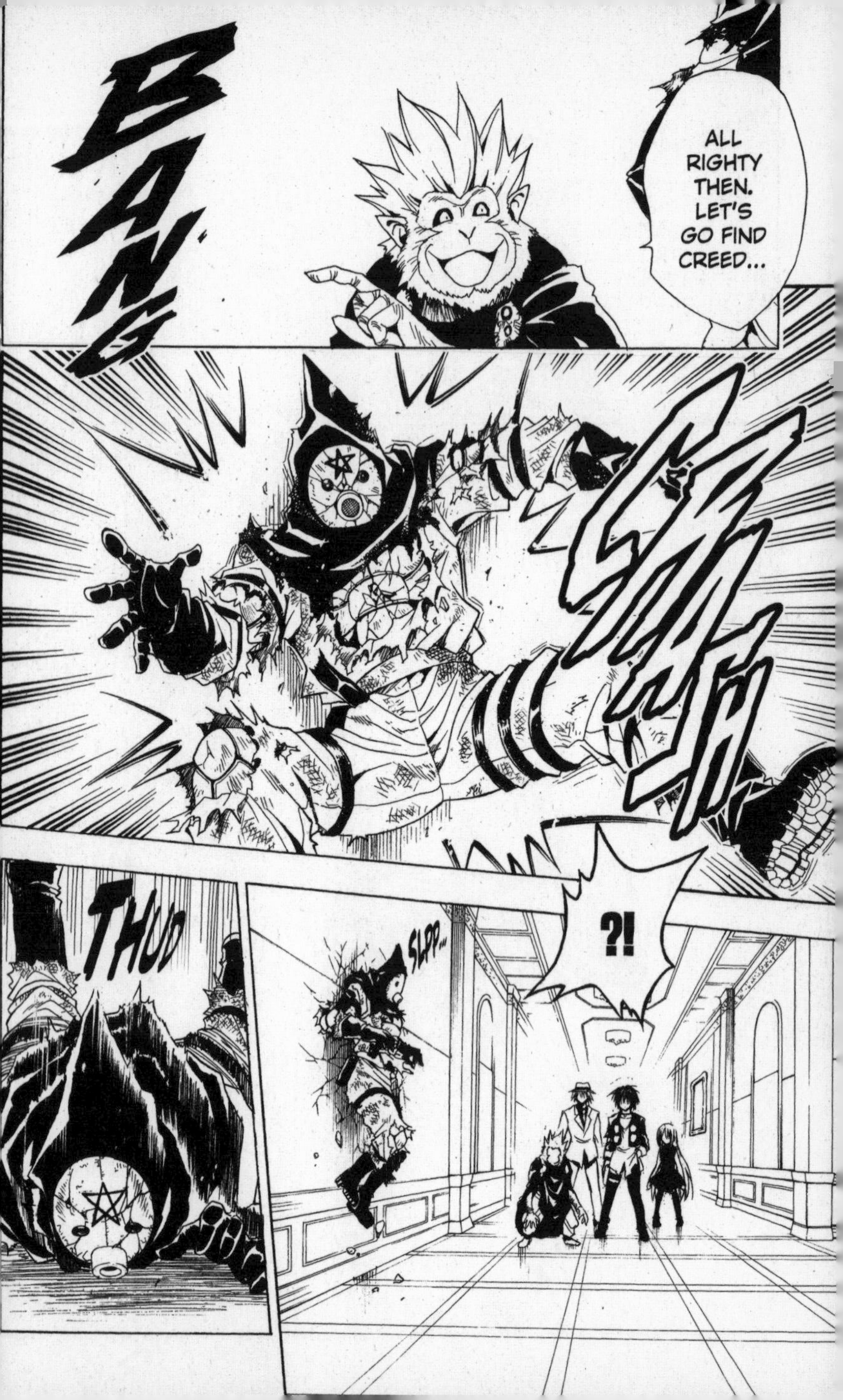
ALL RIGHTY THEN. LET'S GO FIND CREED...
BANG
?!
SLPP...
THUD

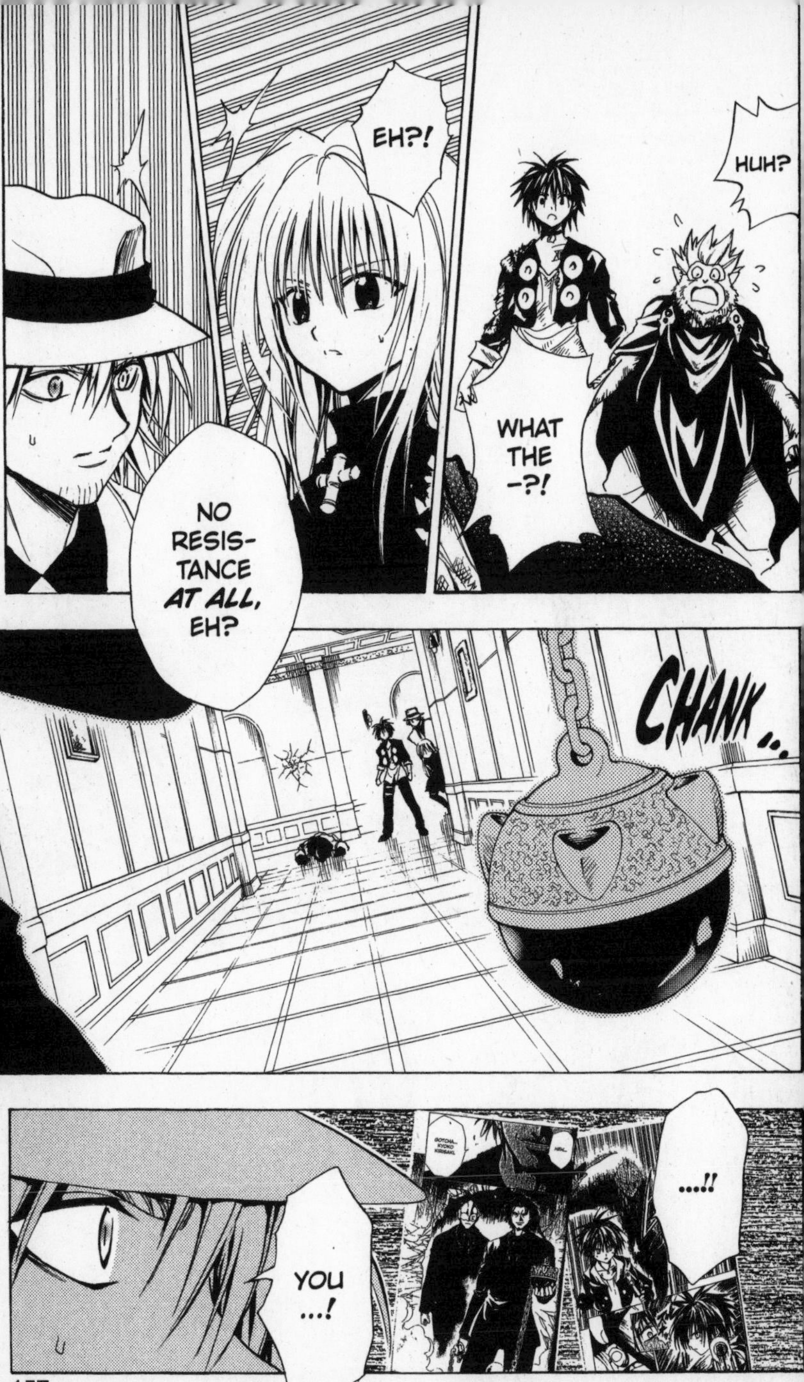
HUH?
WHAT THE -?!
EH?!
NO RESISTANCE AT ALL, EH?
CHANK...
...!!
GOTCHA... KYOKO KIRISAKI.
YOU ...!

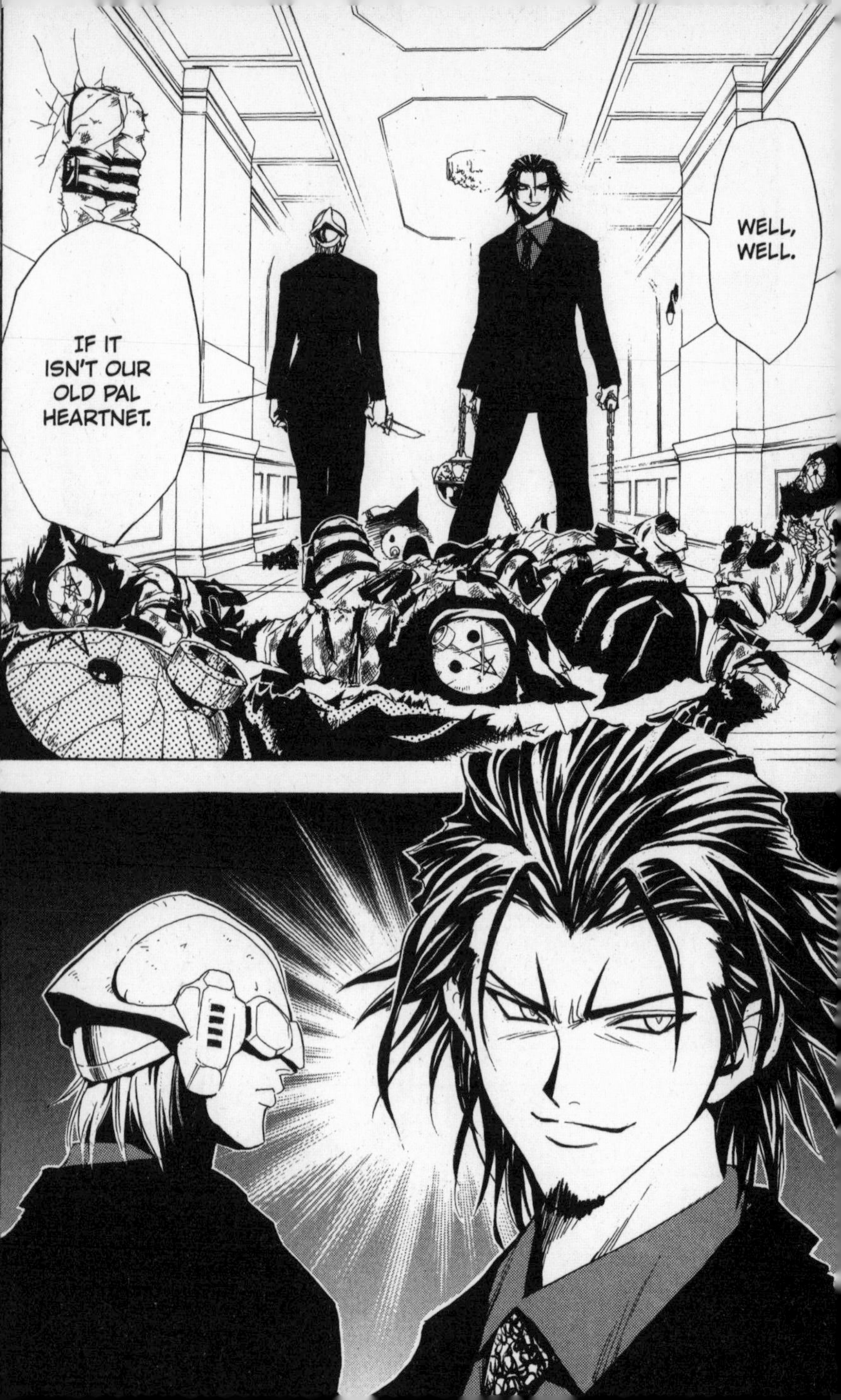
WELL, WELL.
IF IT ISN'T OUR OLD PAL HEARTNET.

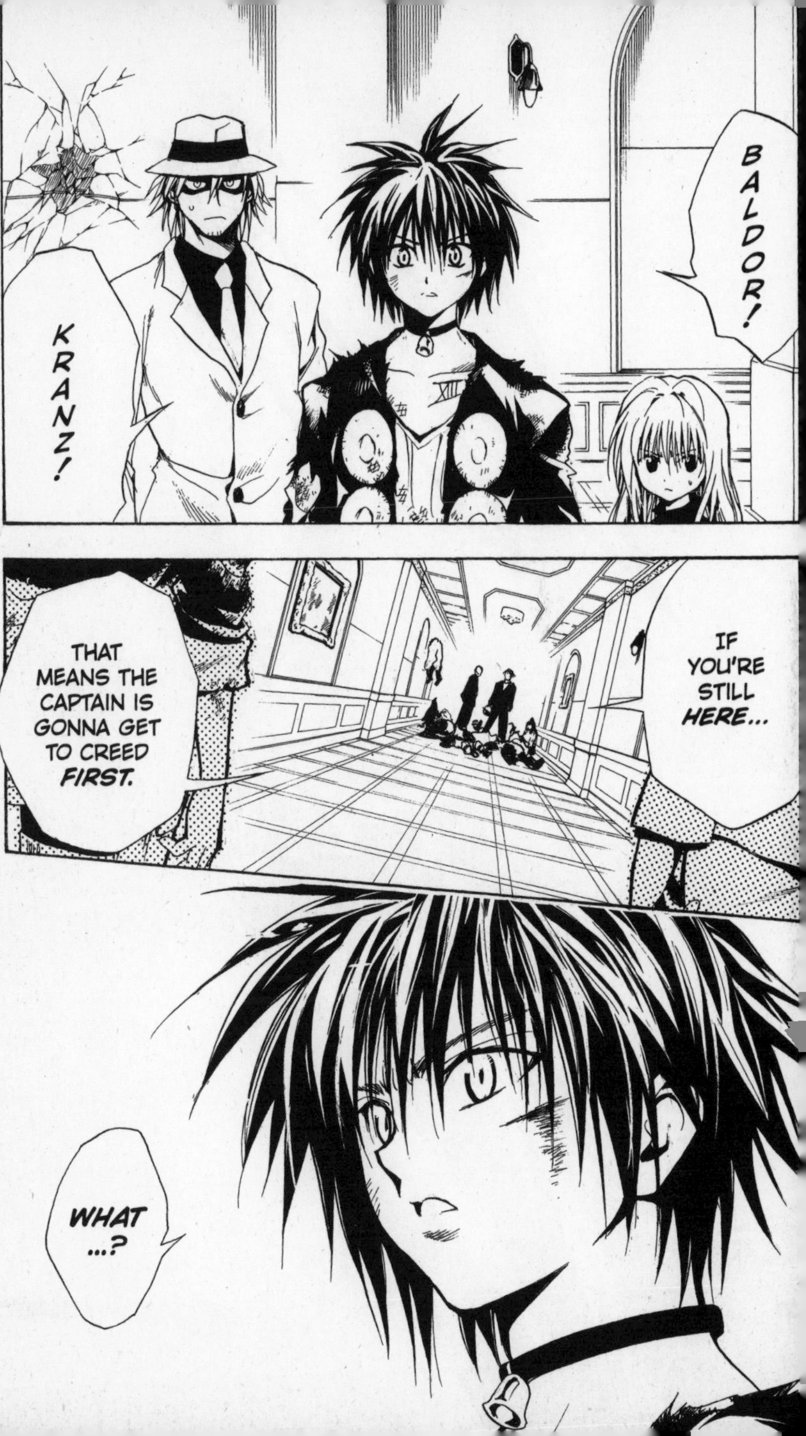
BALDOR!
KRANZ!
IF YOU'RE STILL HERE...
THAT MEANS THE CAPTAIN IS GONNA GET TO CREED FIRST.
WHAT ...?

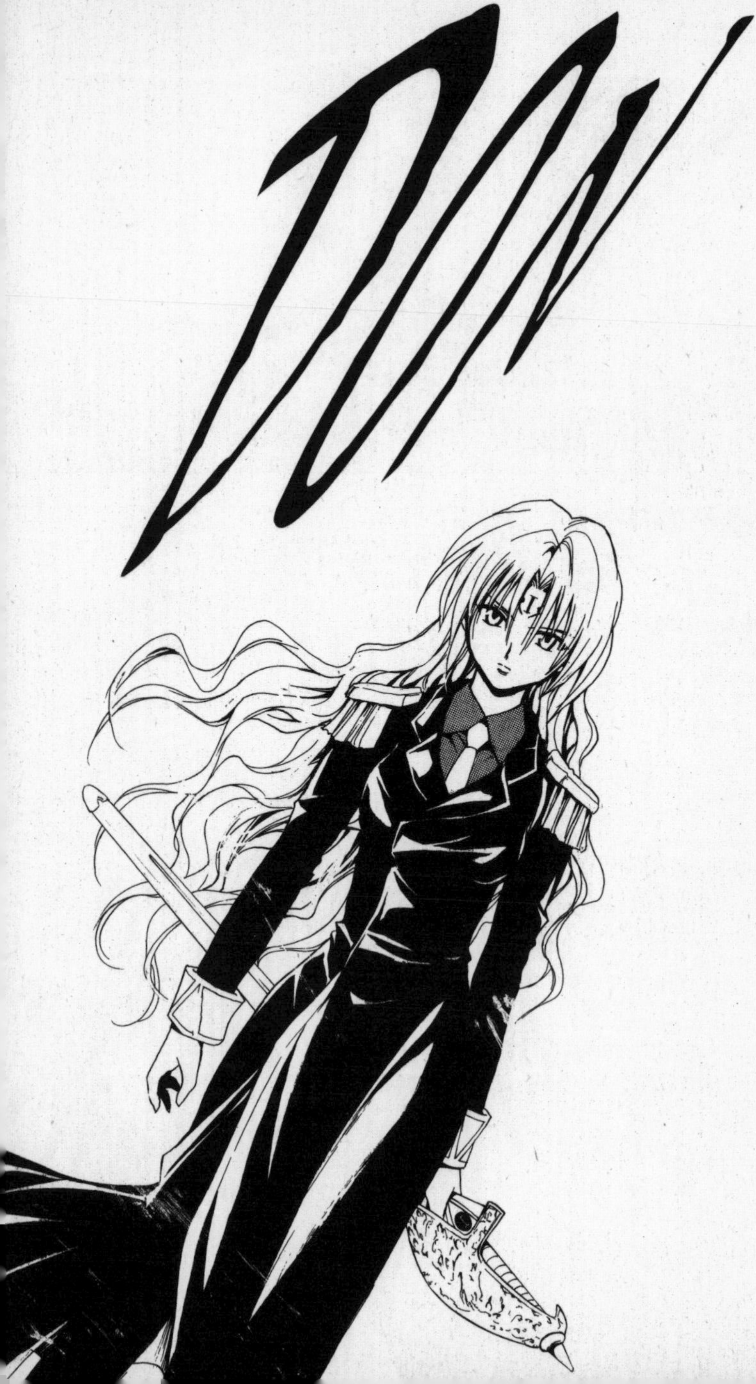

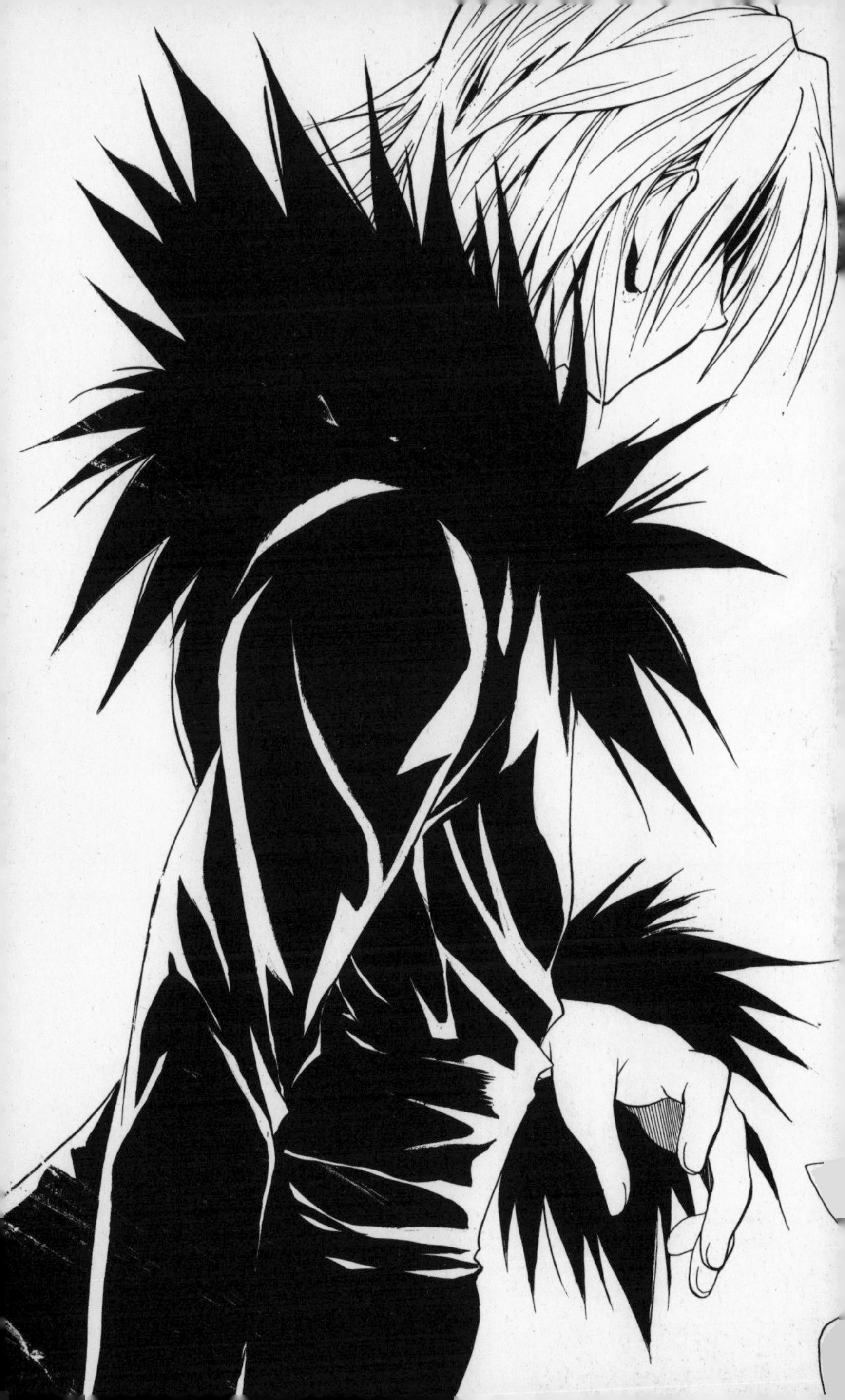

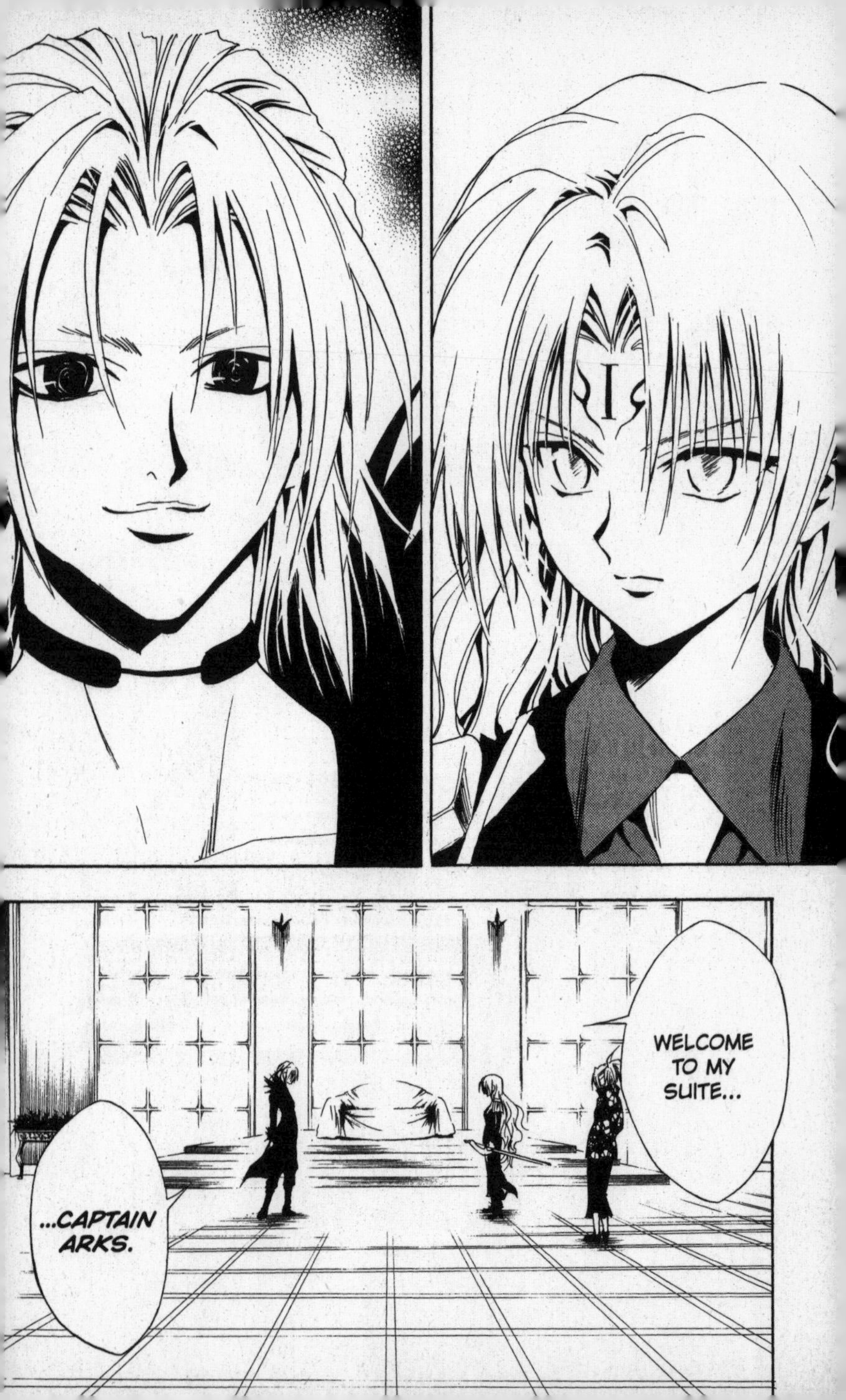
WELCOME TO MY SUITE...
...CAPTAIN ARKS.

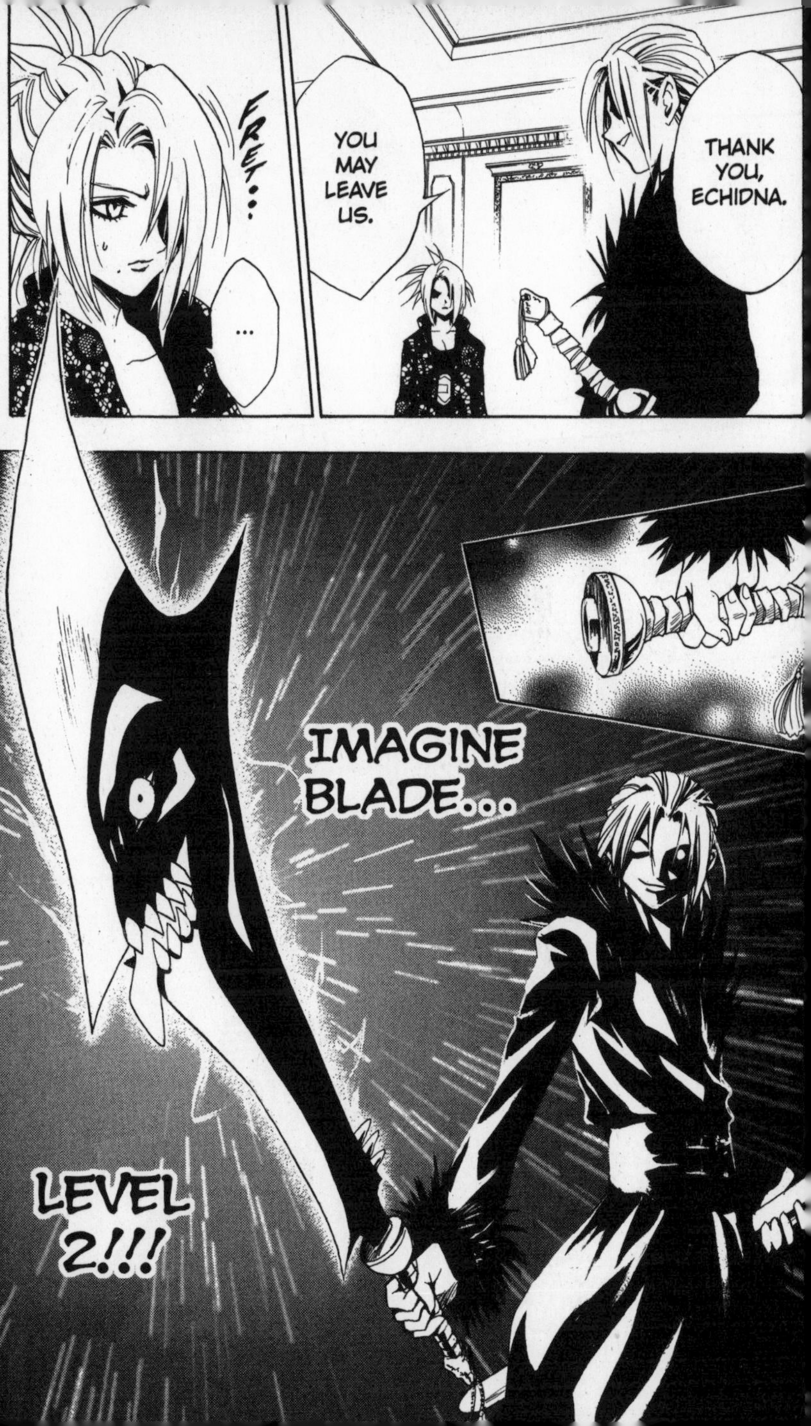
THANK YOU, ECHIDNA.
YOU MAY LEAVE US.
FRET...
...
IMAGINE BLADE...
LEVEL 2!!!

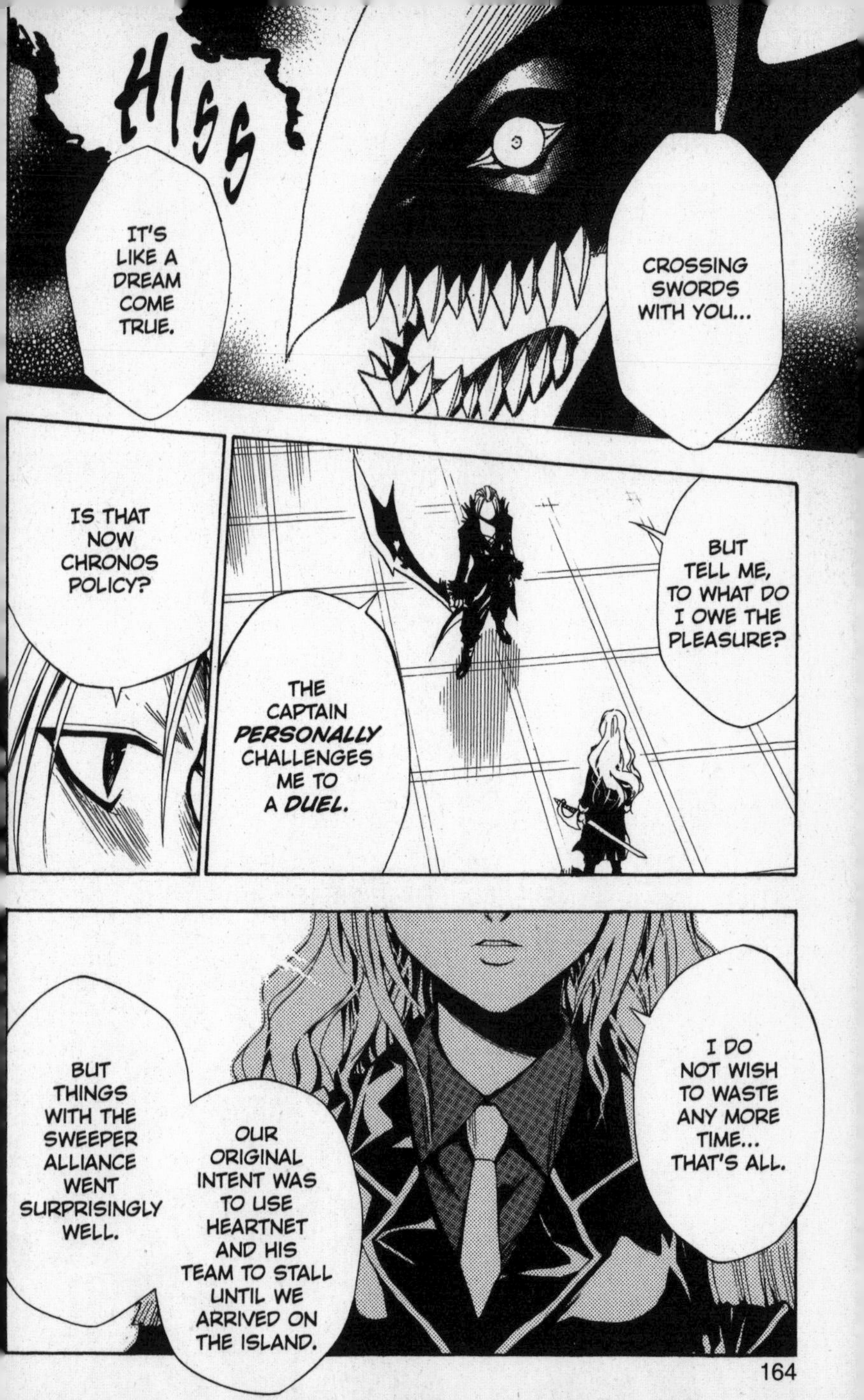
CROSSING SWORDS WITH YOU...
HISS
IT'S LIKE A DREAM COME TRUE.
BUT TELL ME, TO WHAT DO I OWE THE PLEASURE?
THE CAPTAIN *PERSONALLY* CHALLENGES ME TO A *DUEL*.
IS THAT NOW CHRONOS POLICY?
I DO NOT WISH TO WASTE ANY MORE TIME... THAT'S ALL.
OUR ORIGINAL INTENT WAS TO USE HEARTNET AND HIS TEAM TO STALL UNTIL WE ARRIVED ON THE ISLAND.
BUT THINGS WITH THE SWEEPER ALLIANCE WENT SURPRISINGLY WELL.

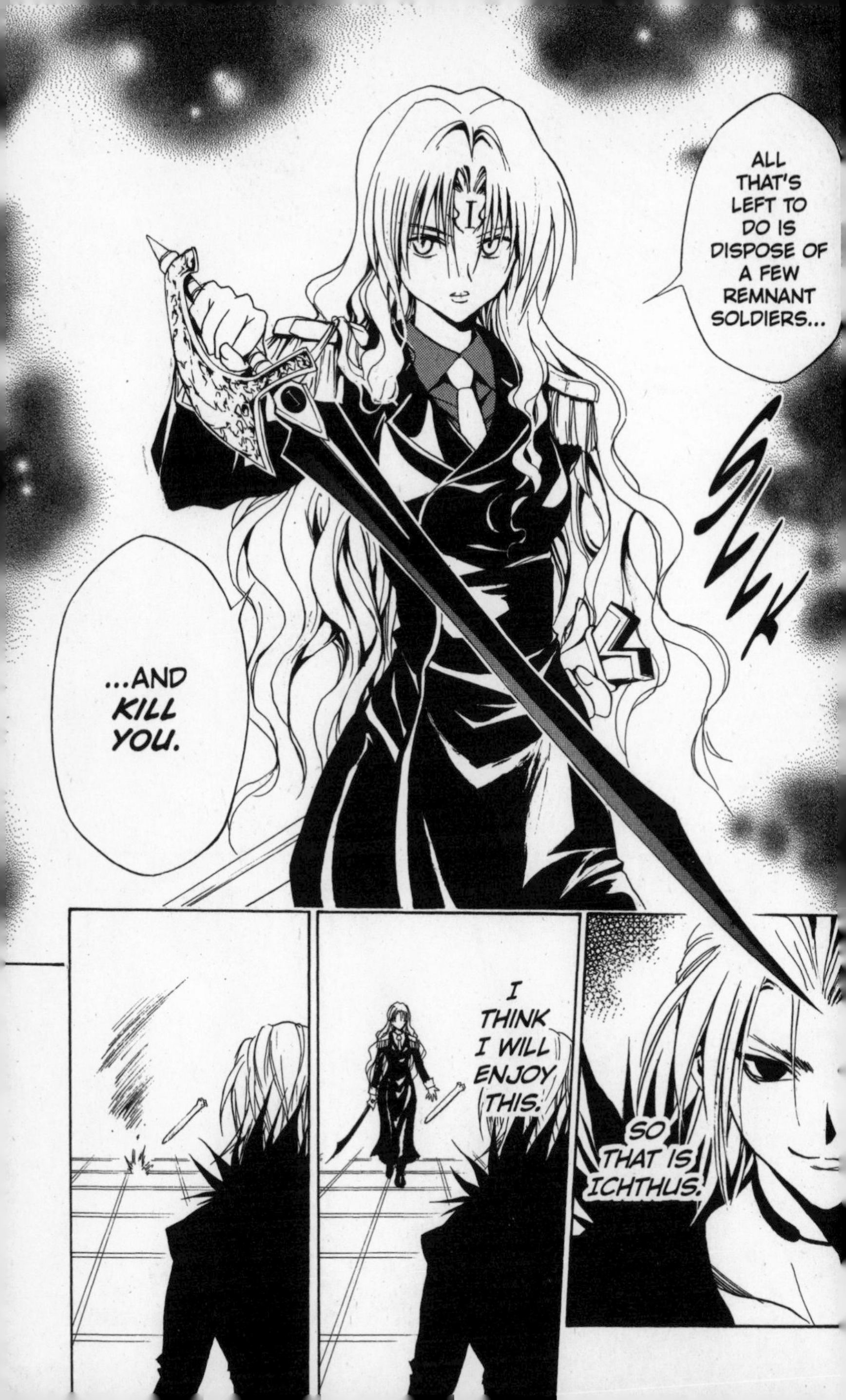
ALL THAT'S LEFT TO DO IS DISPOSE OF A FEW REMNANT SOLDIERS...
...AND KILL YOU.
SO THAT IS ICHTHUS.
I THINK I WILL ENJOY THIS.

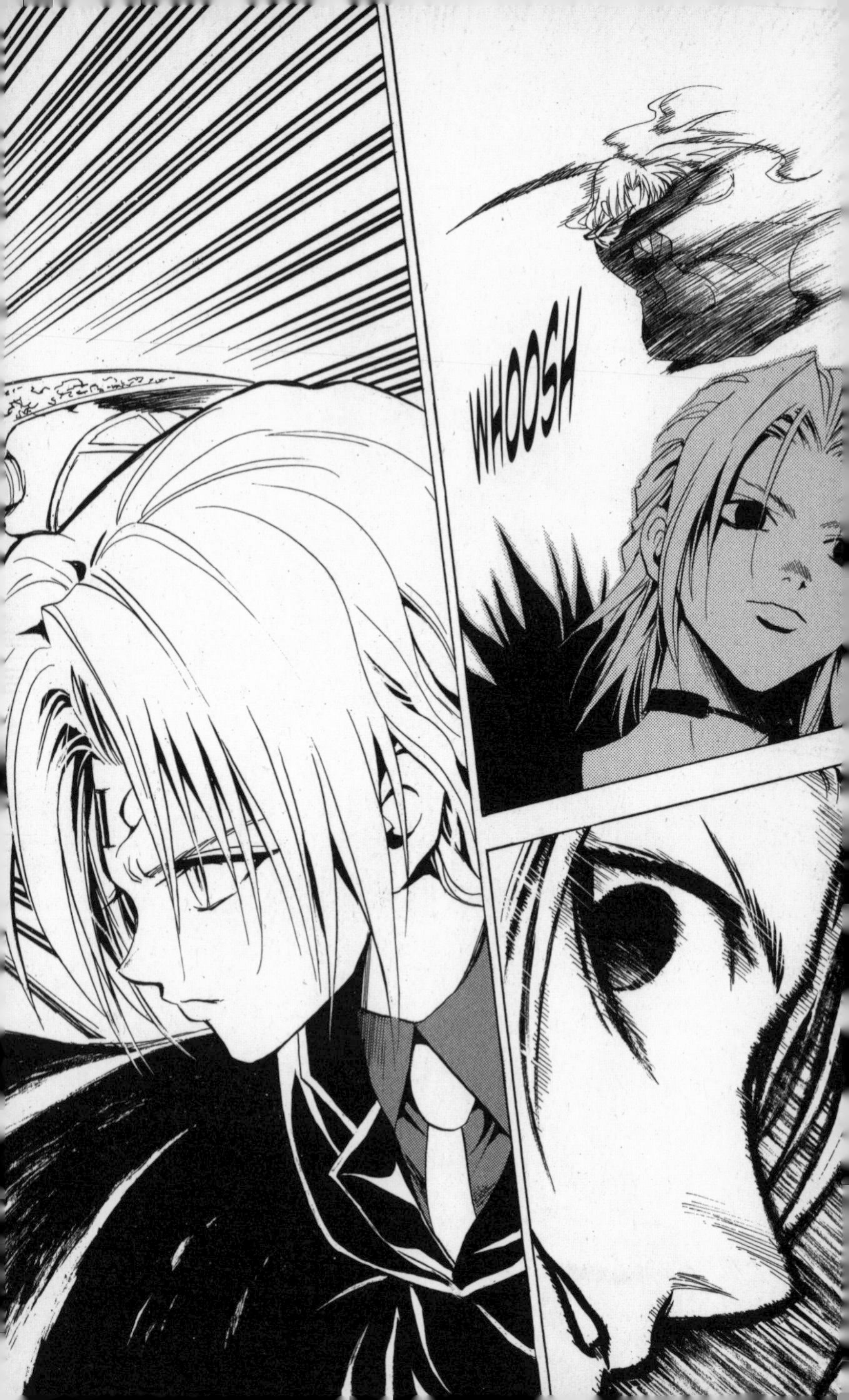
WHOOSH

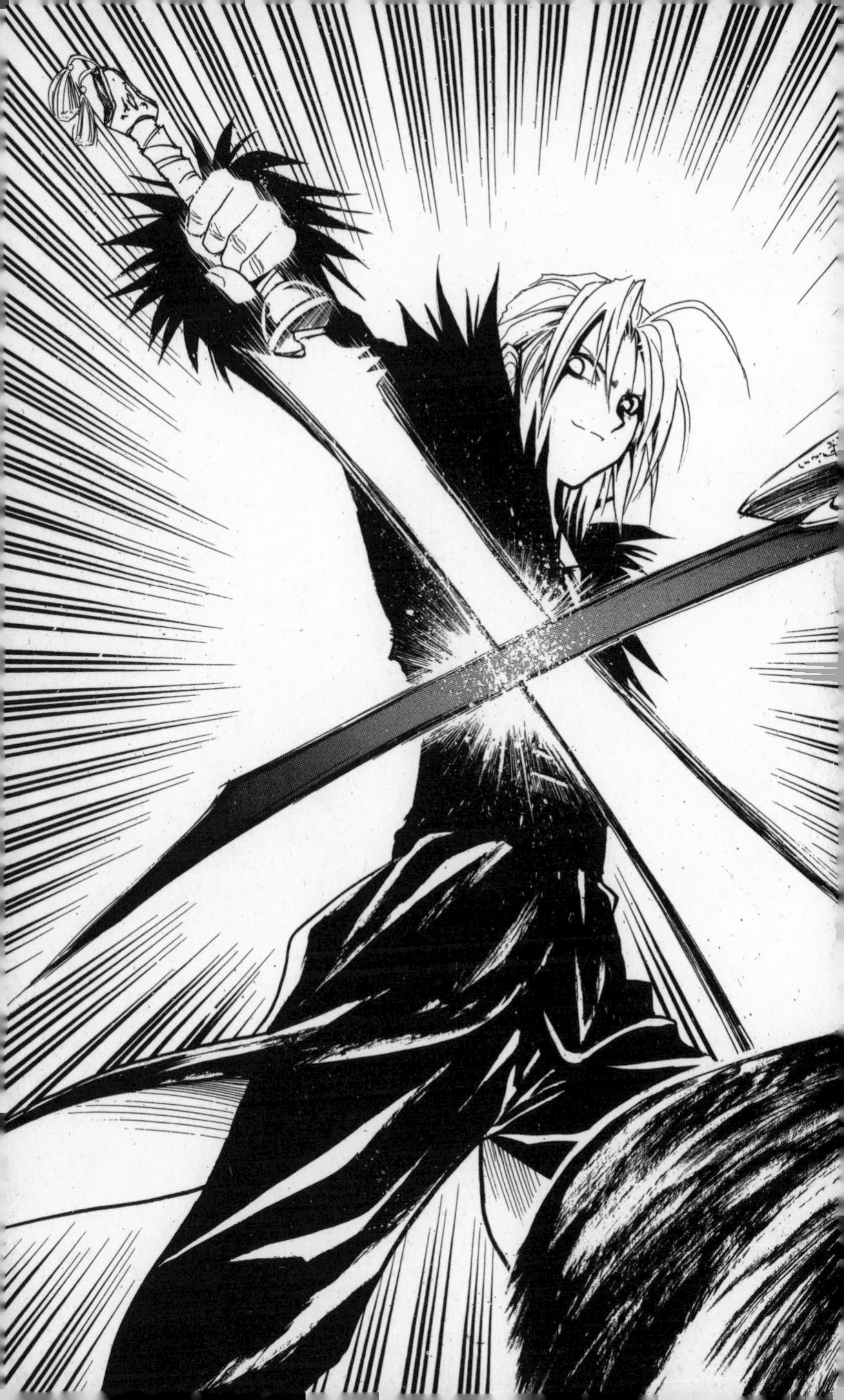

SKETCHES: NUMBER 2

© SEPHIRIA

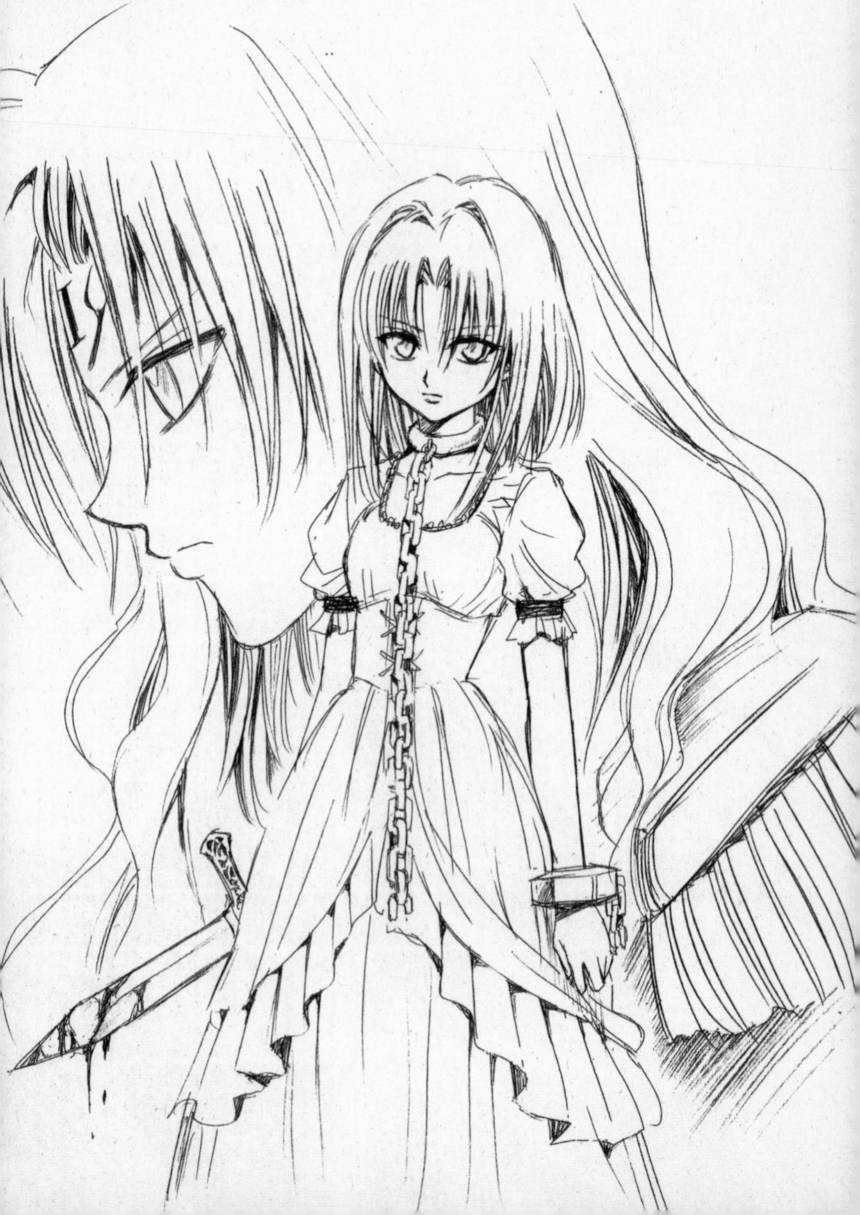

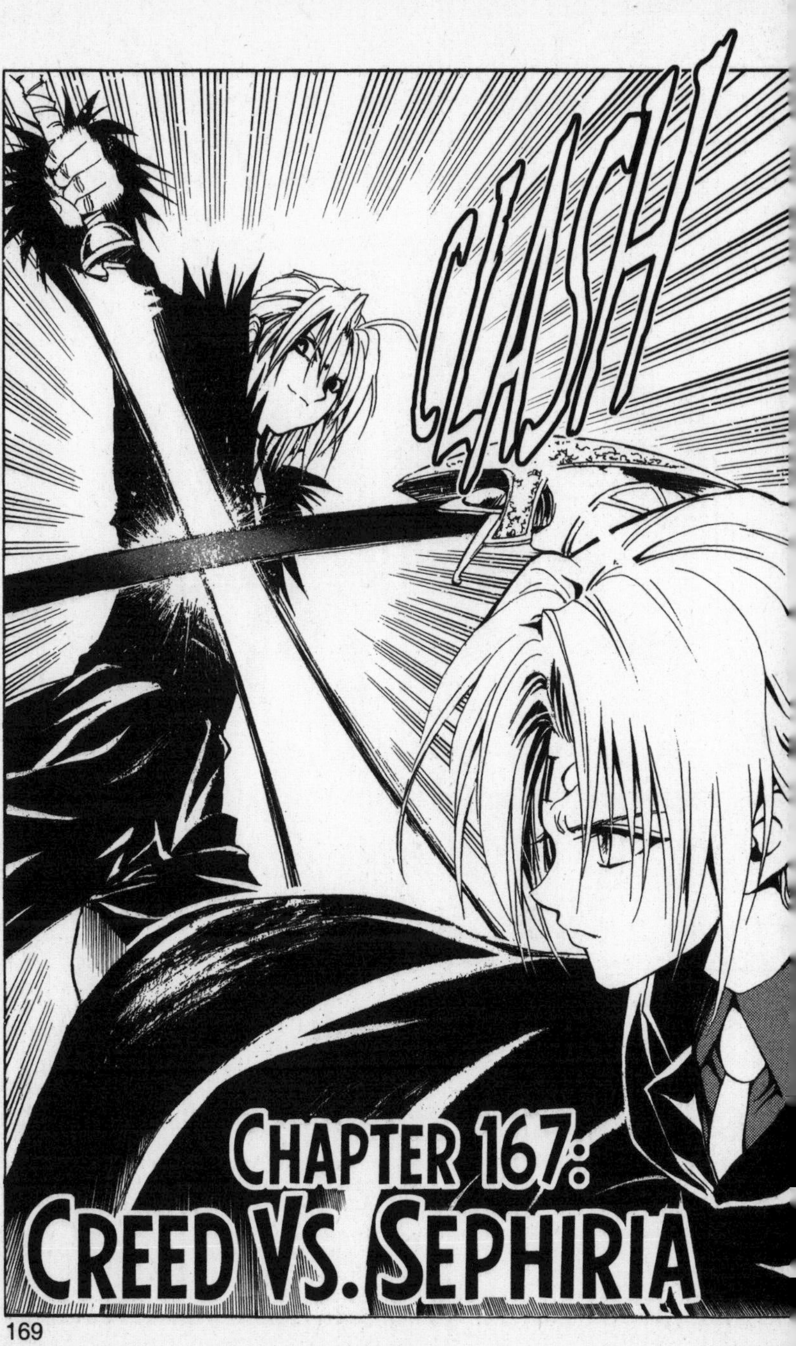
CLASH
CHAPTER 167:
CREED VS. SEPHIRIA

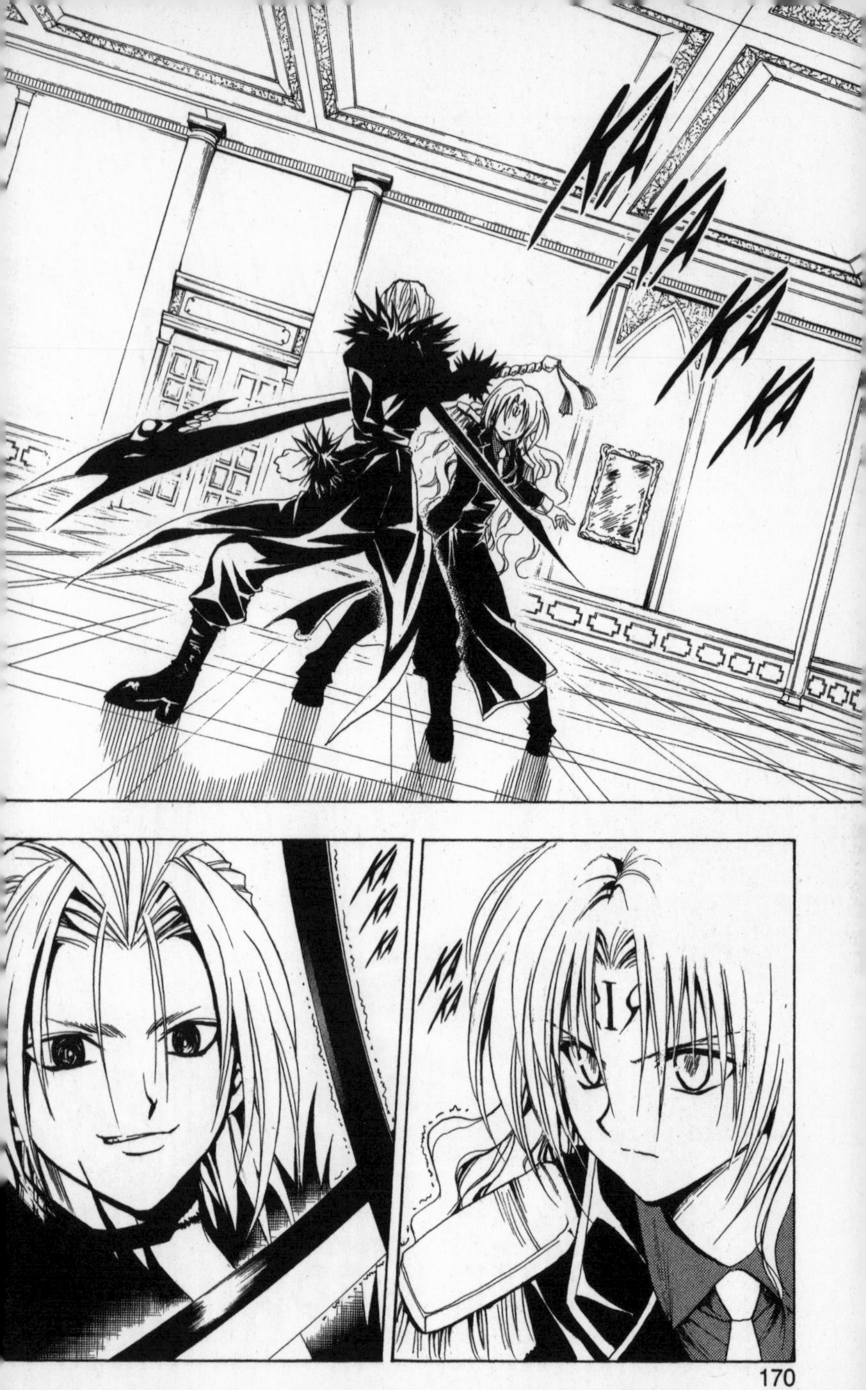
KA KA KA KA KA
KA KA KA
KA KA KA KA

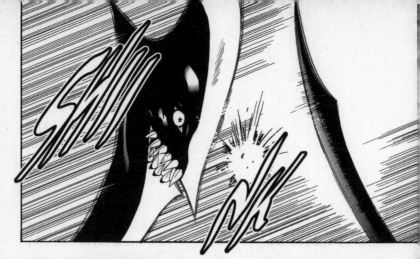

HEH. NICE FORM.

NO HESITATION OR DOUBT.

PAH

NONE.

HMPH. BUT THERE IS *ONE THING* YOU LACK...

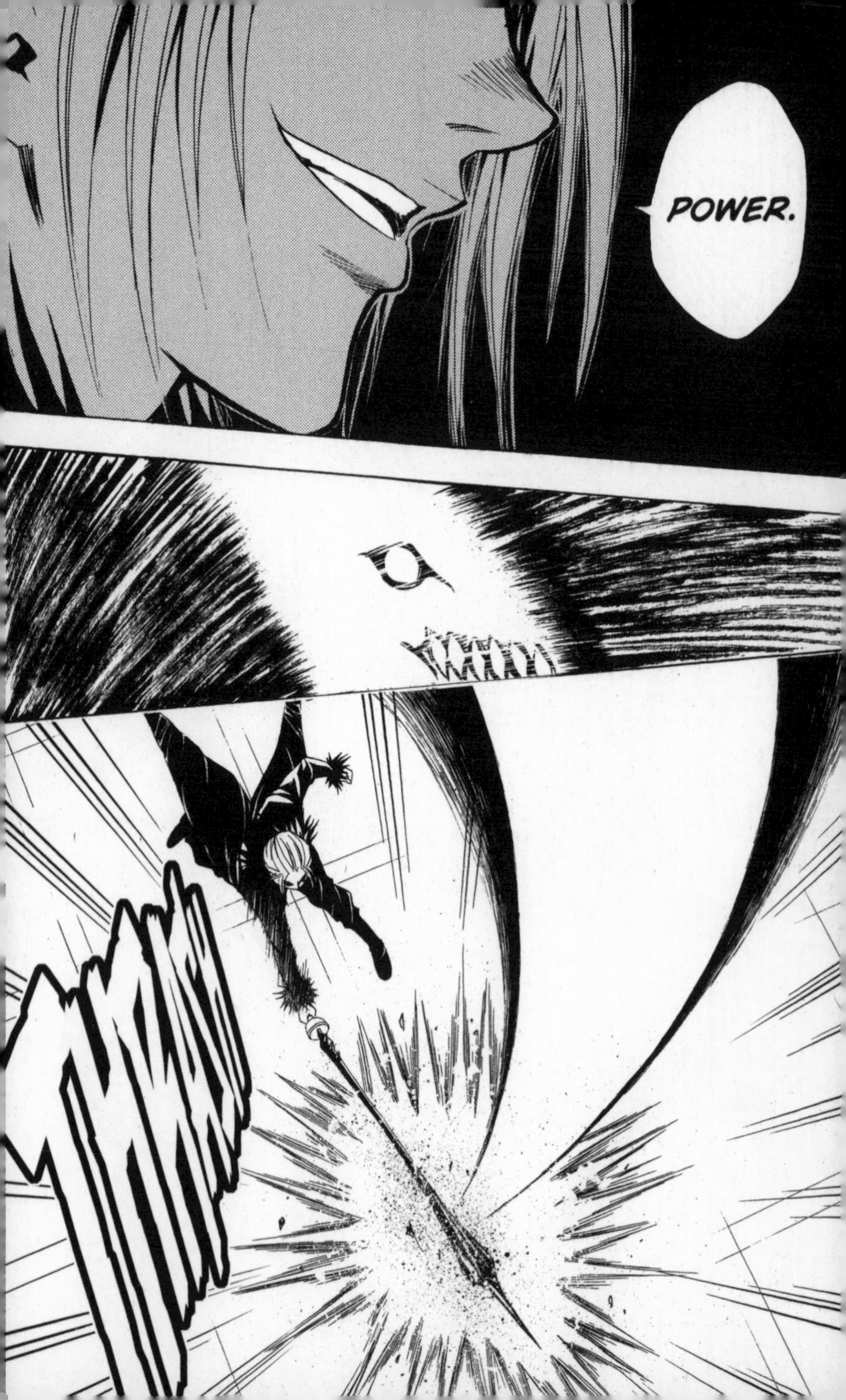
POWER.

READ THIS WAY

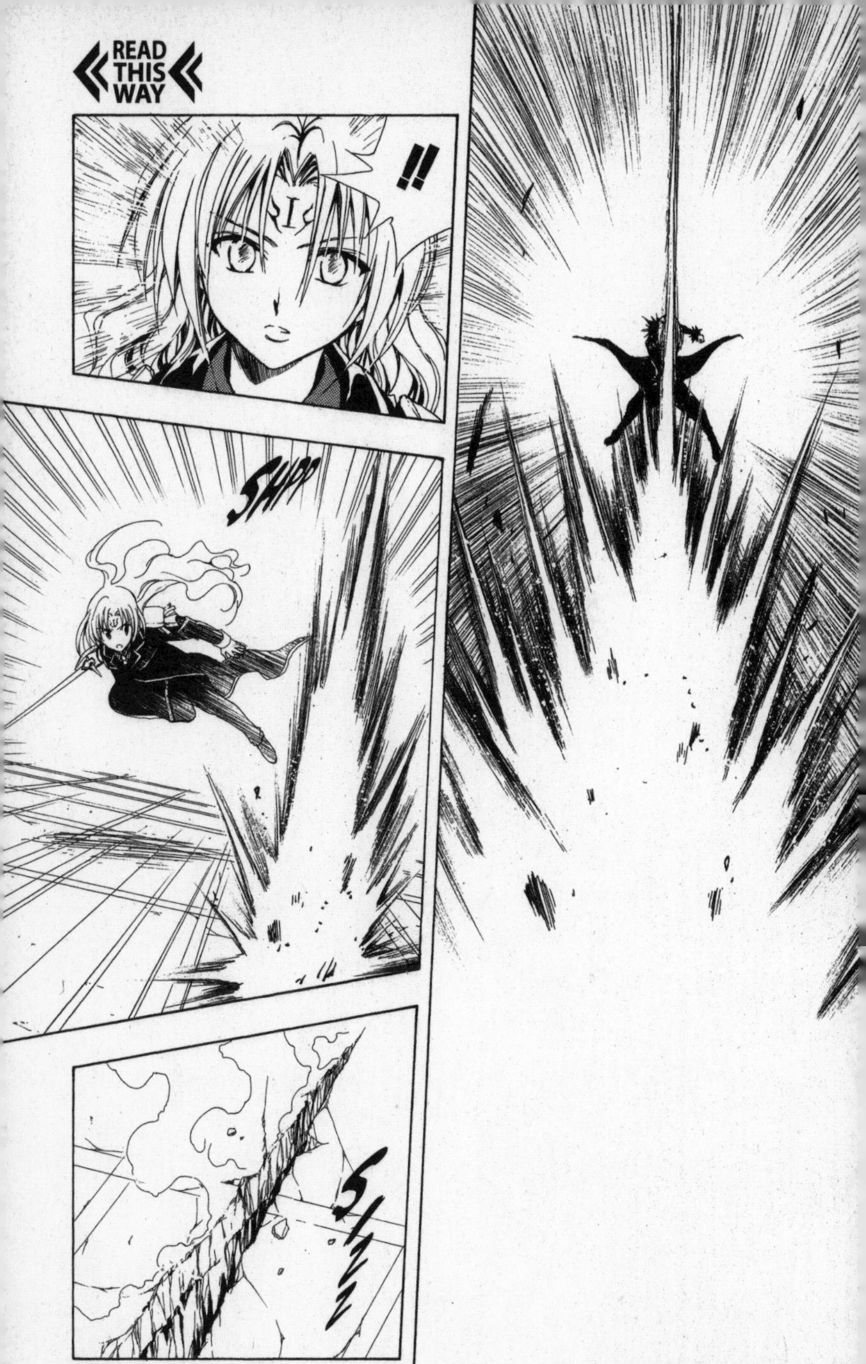
!!
SHPP

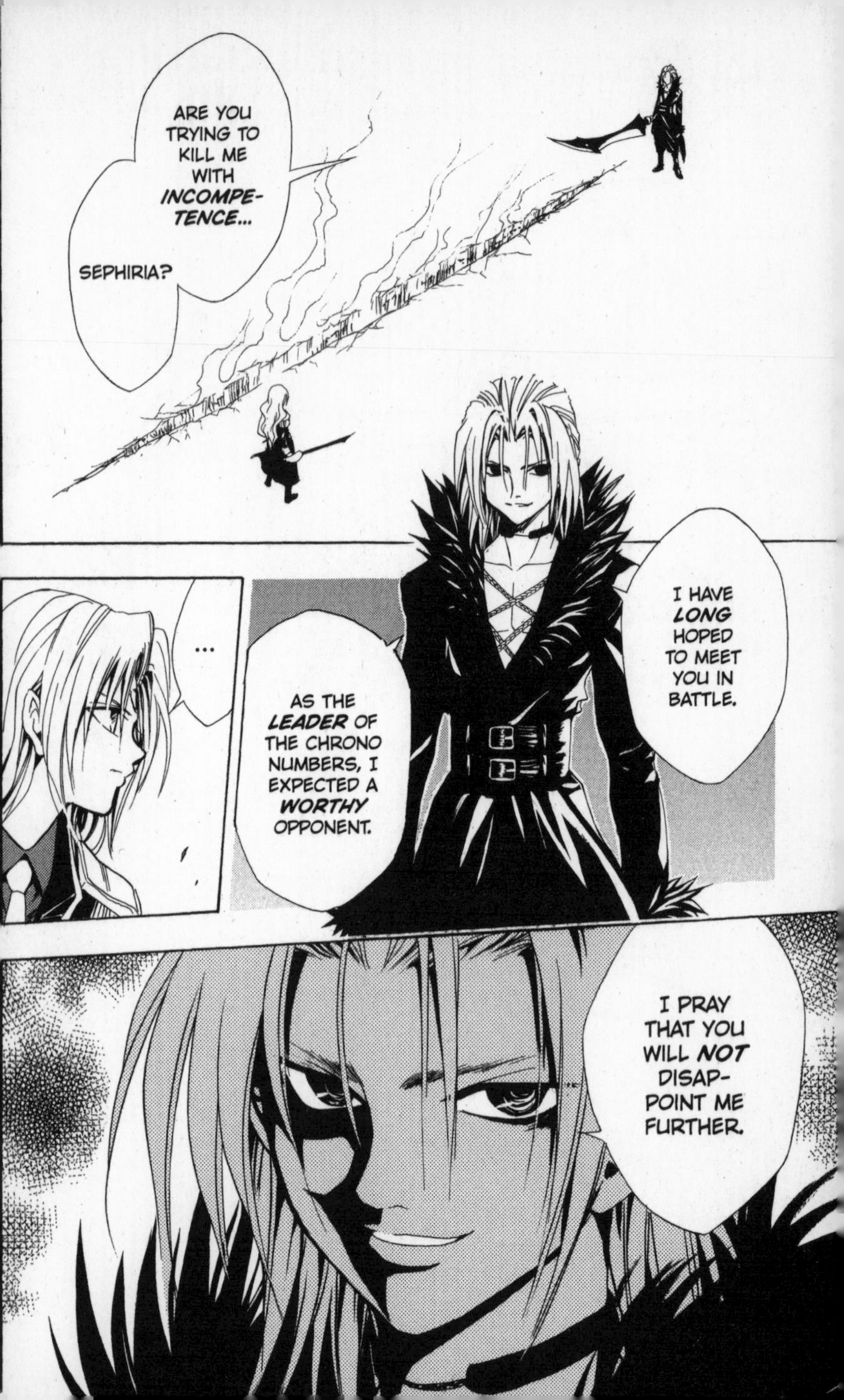
ARE YOU TRYING TO KILL ME WITH *INCOMPETENCE*...
SEPHIRIA?
I HAVE *LONG* HOPED TO MEET YOU IN BATTLE.
AS THE *LEADER* OF THE CHRONO NUMBERS, I EXPECTED A *WORTHY* OPPONENT.
...
I PRAY THAT YOU WILL *NOT* DISAPPOINT ME FURTHER.

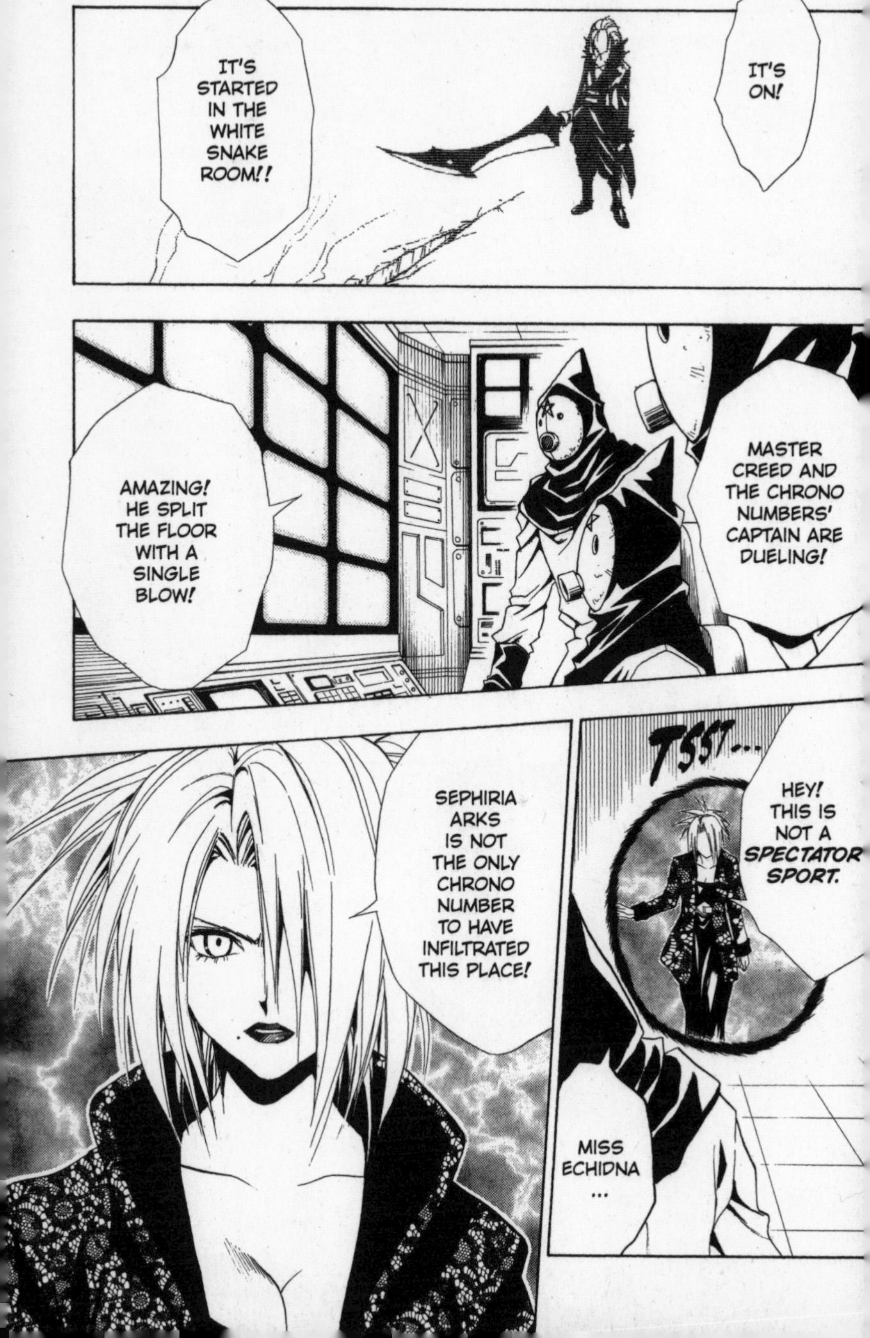
IT'S ON!
IT'S STARTED IN THE WHITE SNAKE ROOM!!
MASTER CREED AND THE CHRONO NUMBERS' CAPTAIN ARE DUELING!
AMAZING! HE SPLIT THE FLOOR WITH A SINGLE BLOW!
TSST...
HEY! THIS IS NOT A *SPECTATOR SPORT.*
MISS ECHIDNA ...
SEPHIRIA ARKS IS NOT THE ONLY CHRONO NUMBER TO HAVE INFILTRATED THIS PLACE!

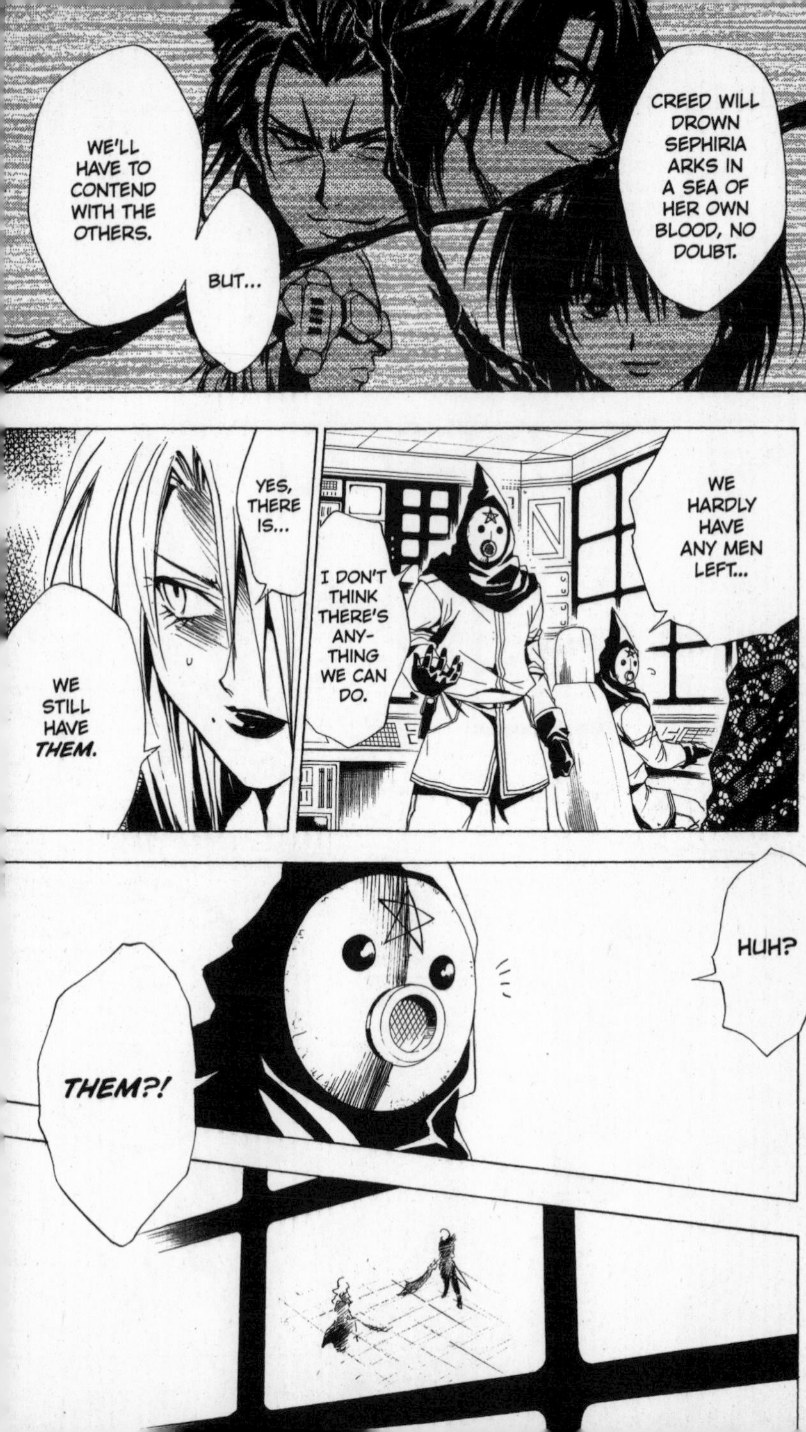
CREED WILL DROWN SEPHIRIA ARKS IN A SEA OF HER OWN BLOOD, NO DOUBT.
BUT...
WE'LL HAVE TO CONTEND WITH THE OTHERS.
WE HARDLY HAVE ANY MEN LEFT...
I DON'T THINK THERE'S ANY-THING WE CAN DO.
YES, THERE IS...
WE STILL HAVE *THEM*.
HUH?
THEM?!

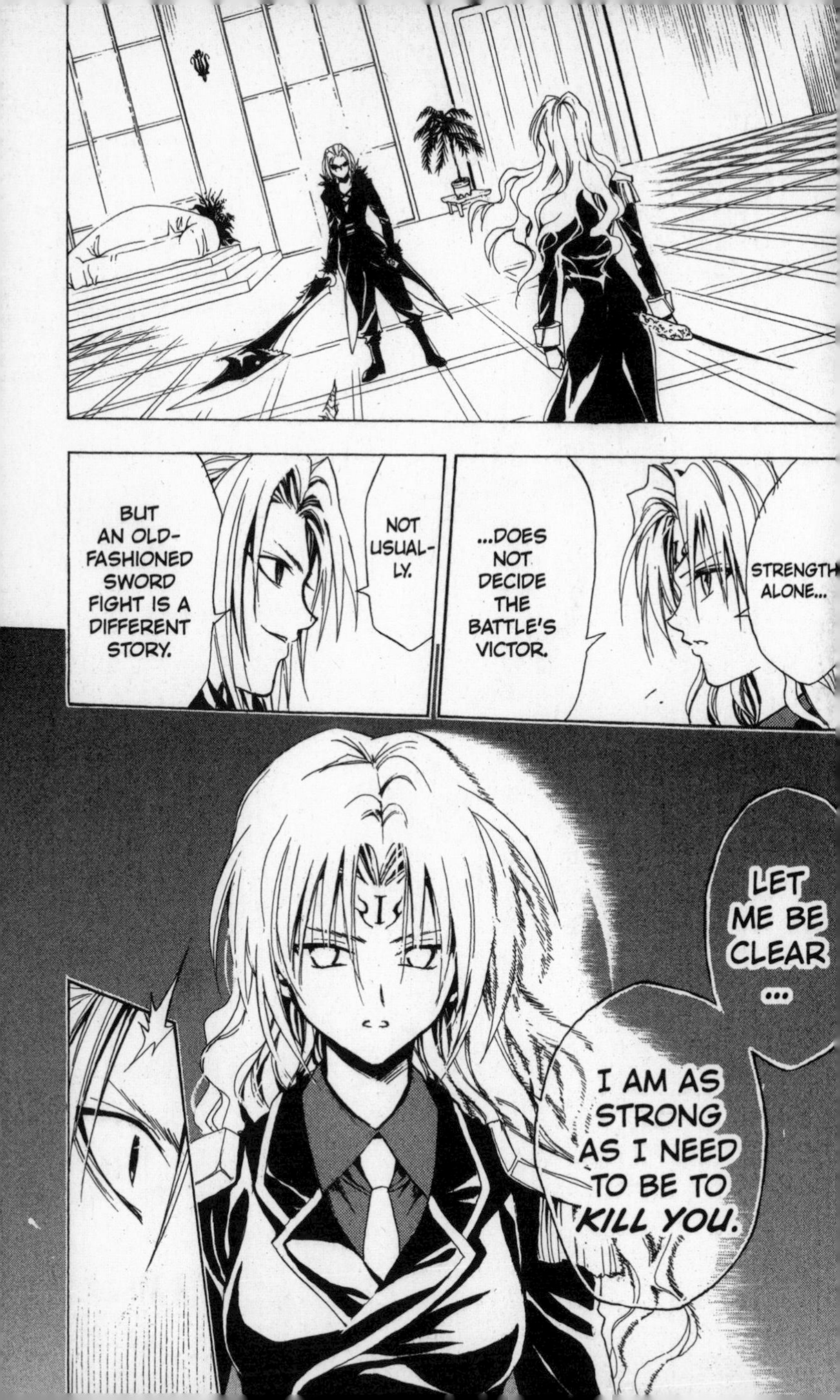
STRENGTH ALONE...
...DOES NOT DECIDE THE BATTLE'S VICTOR.
NOT USUALLY.
BUT AN OLD-FASHIONED SWORD FIGHT IS A DIFFERENT STORY.
LET ME BE CLEAR...
I AM AS STRONG AS I NEED TO BE TO *KILL YOU.*

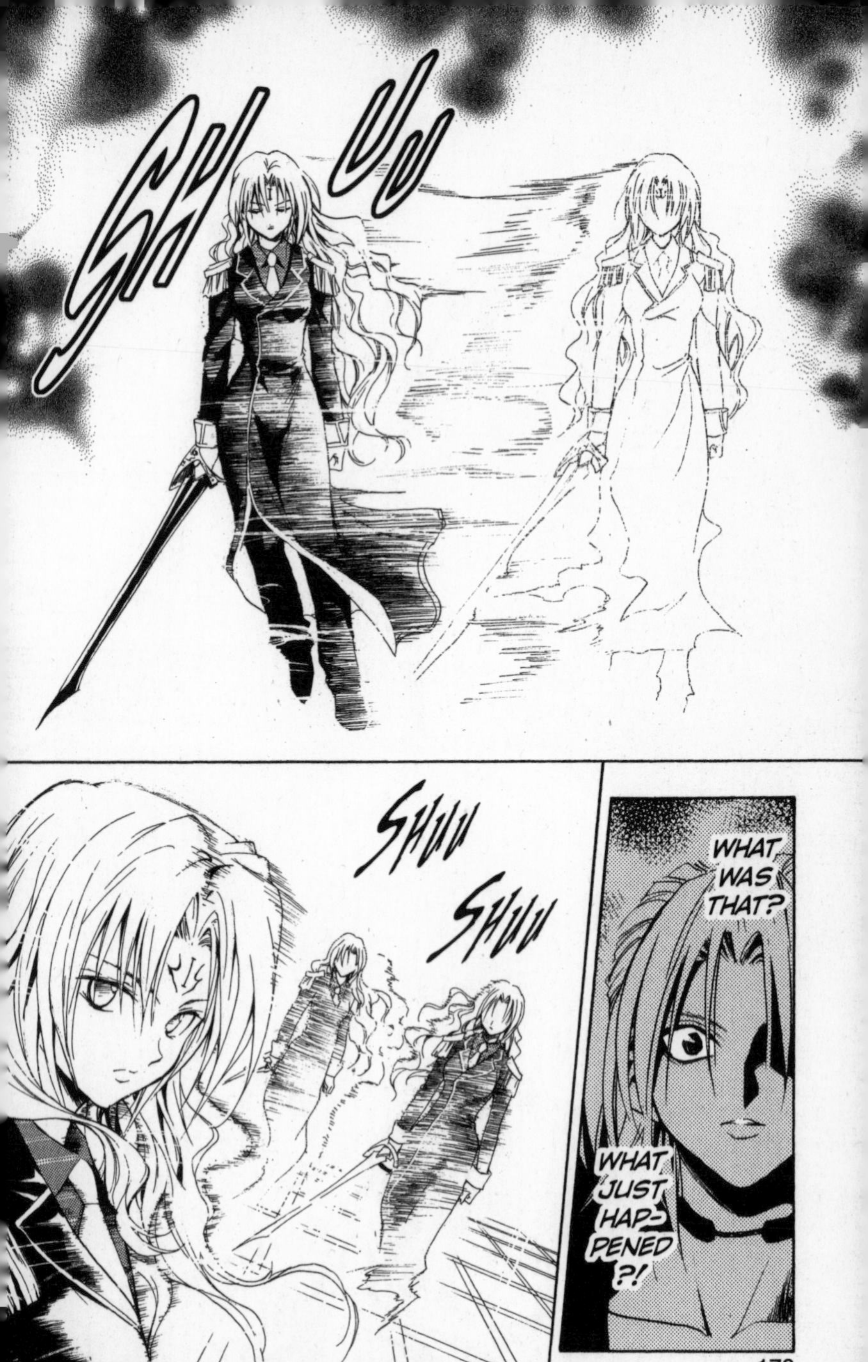
SHUU
WHAT WAS THAT?
WHAT JUST HAP-PENED?!
SHUU
SHUU

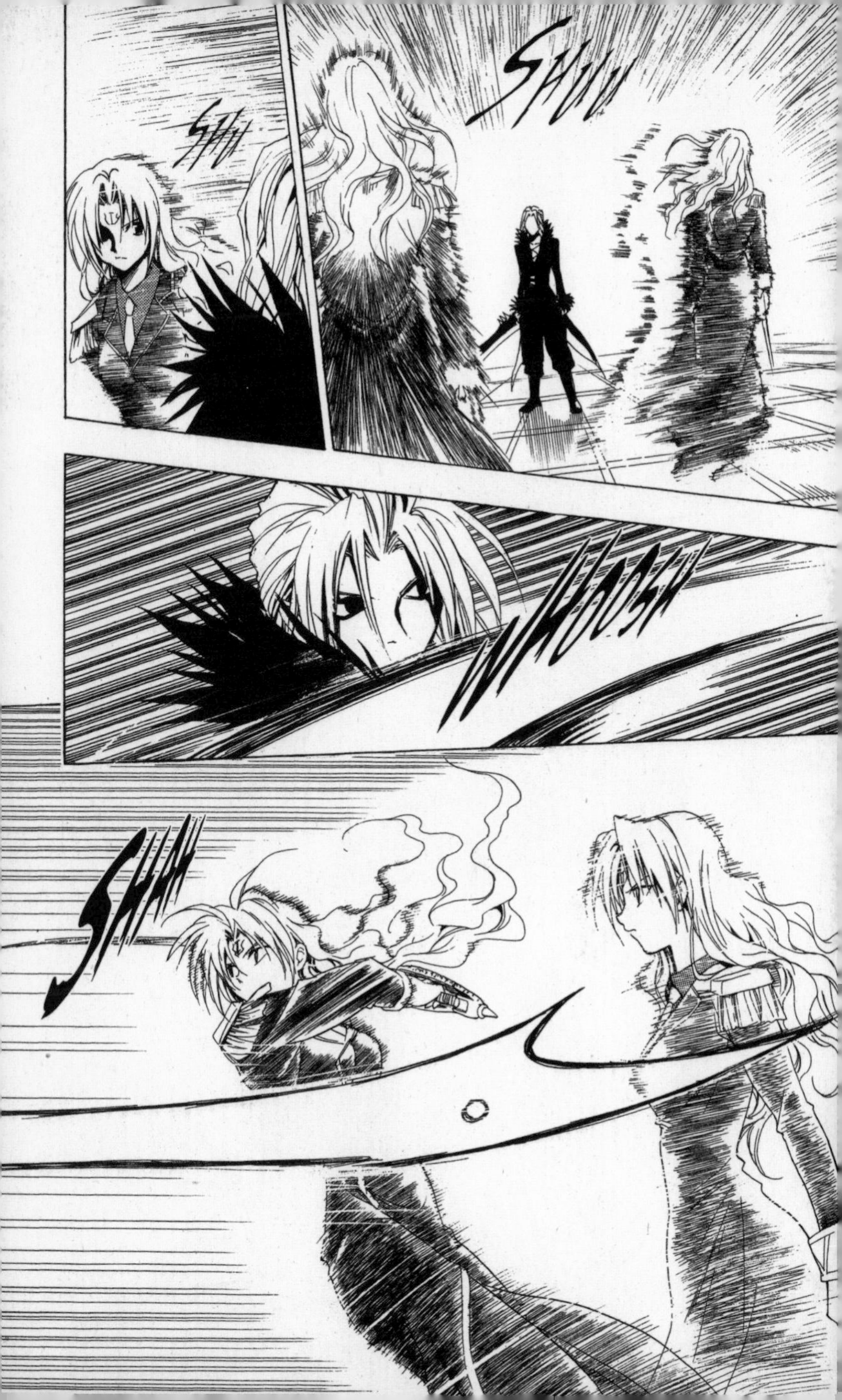
SHUU
SHU
WHOOSH
SHAH

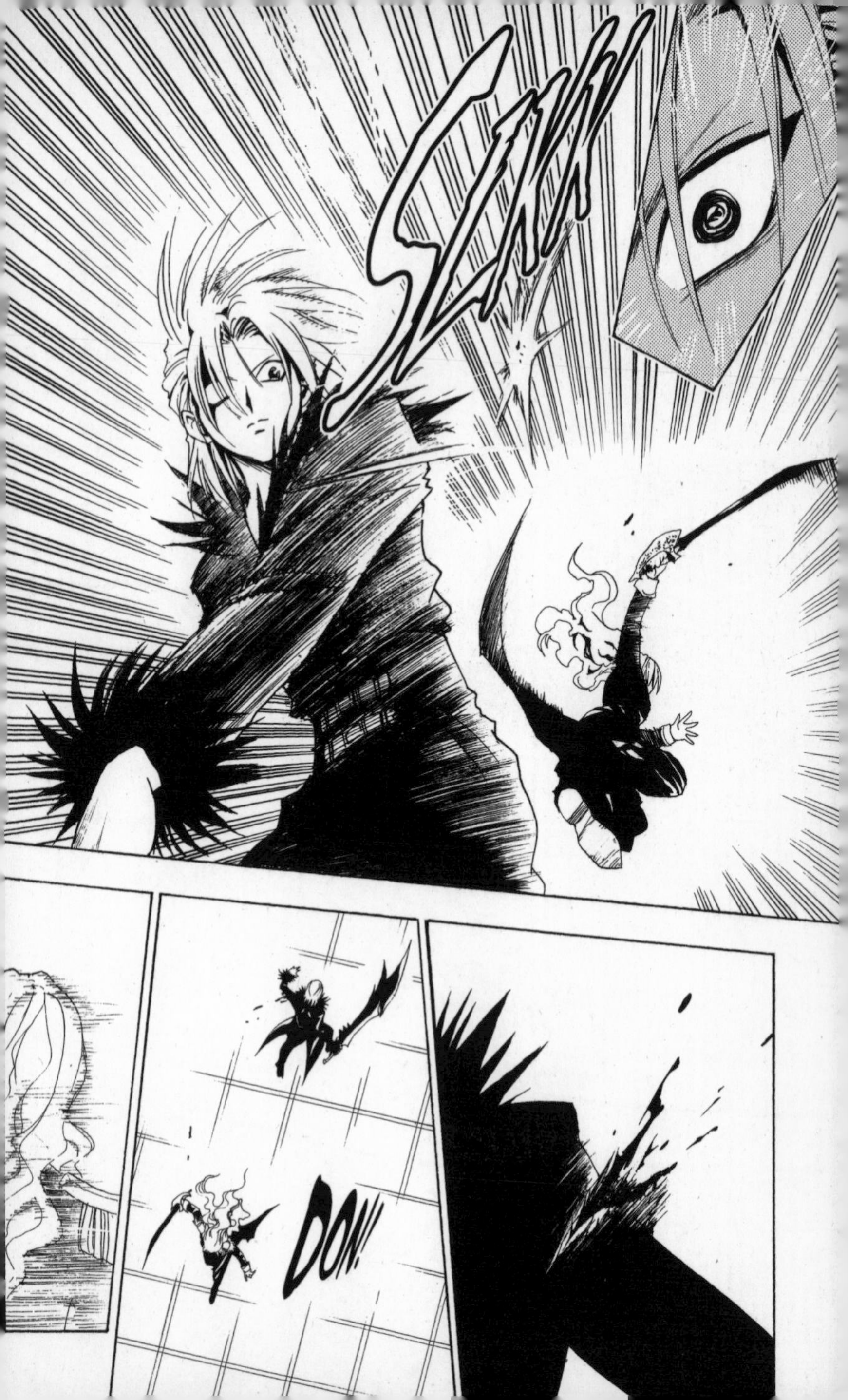
SLASH
DON!

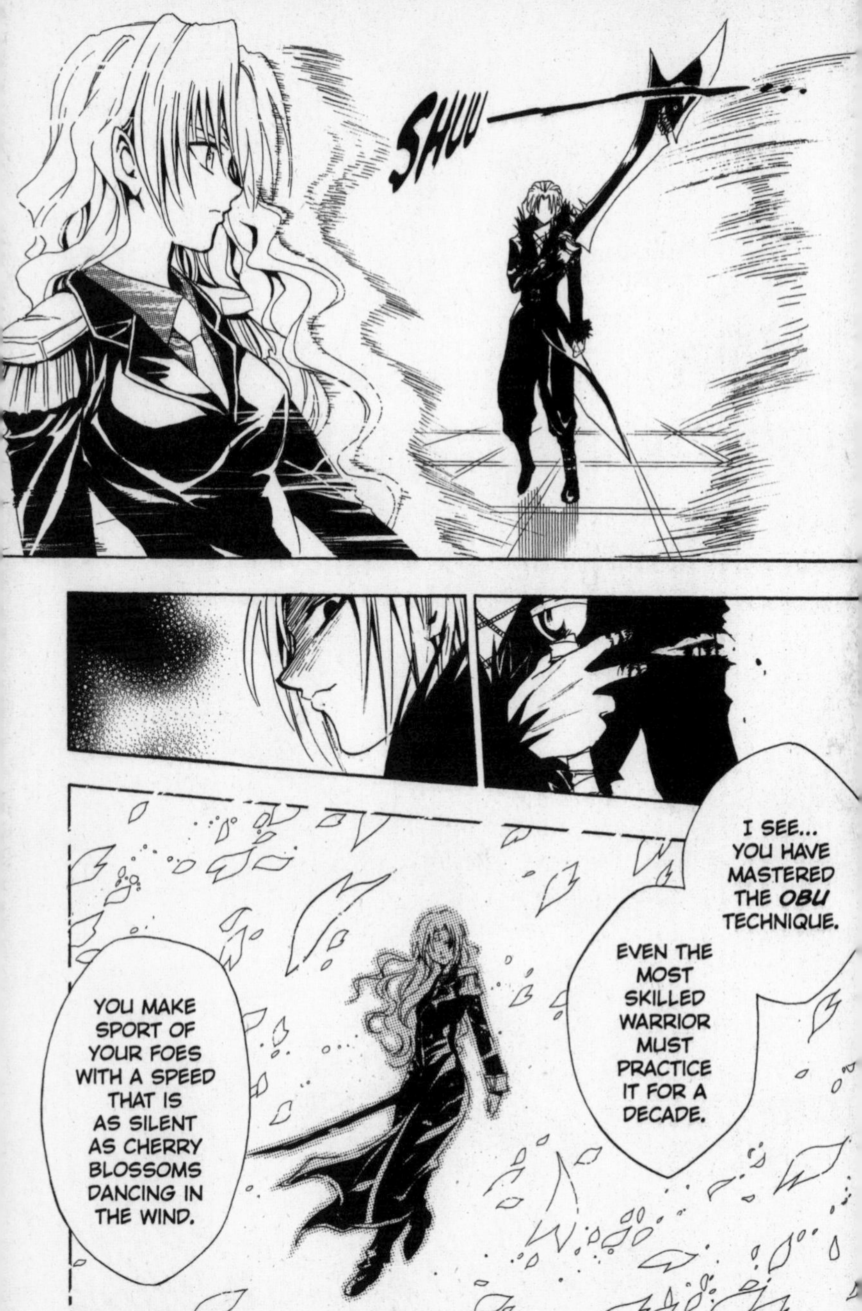
SHUU
I SEE... YOU HAVE MASTERED THE *OBU* TECHNIQUE.
EVEN THE MOST SKILLED WARRIOR MUST PRACTICE IT FOR A DECADE.
YOU MAKE SPORT OF YOUR FOES WITH A SPEED THAT IS AS SILENT AS CHERRY BLOSSOMS DANCING IN THE WIND.

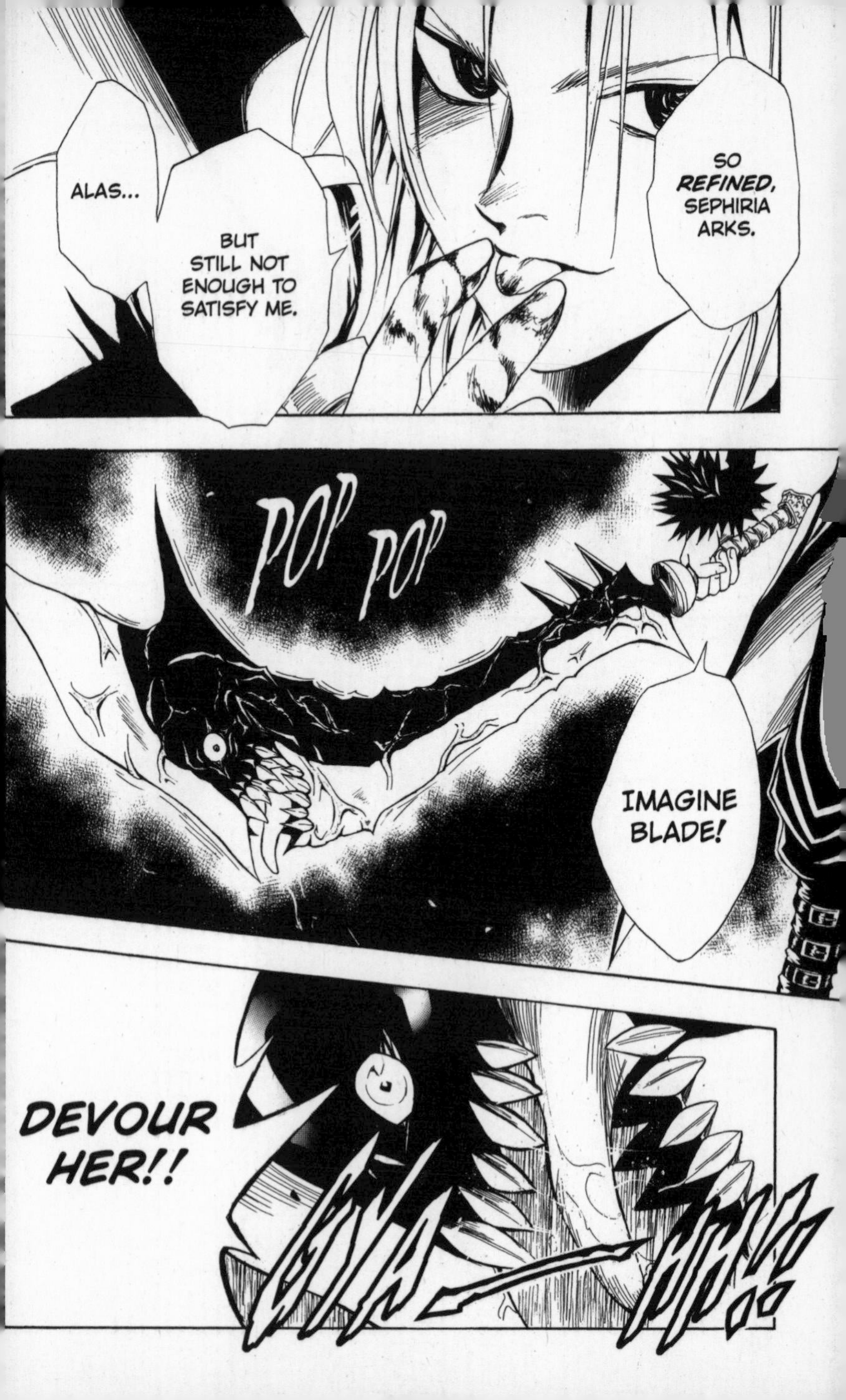
SO *REFINED*, SEPHIRIA ARKS.
ALAS...
BUT STILL NOT ENOUGH TO SATISFY ME.
POP POP
IMAGINE BLADE!
DEVOUR HER!!

READ THIS WAY

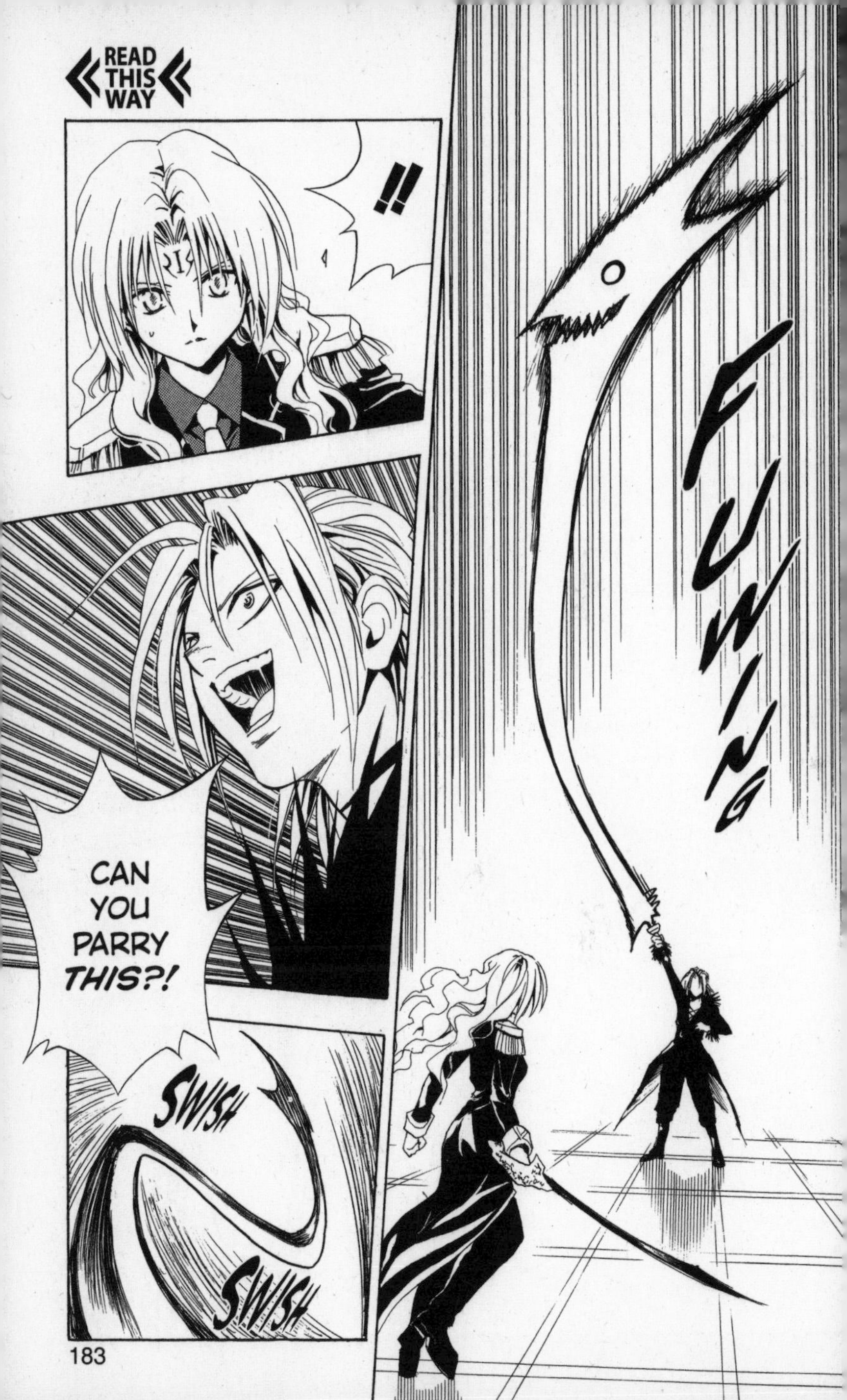

FWING
!!
CAN YOU PARRY THIS?!
SWISH
SWISH

WHOOO

SHH

?!

184

READ THIS WAY

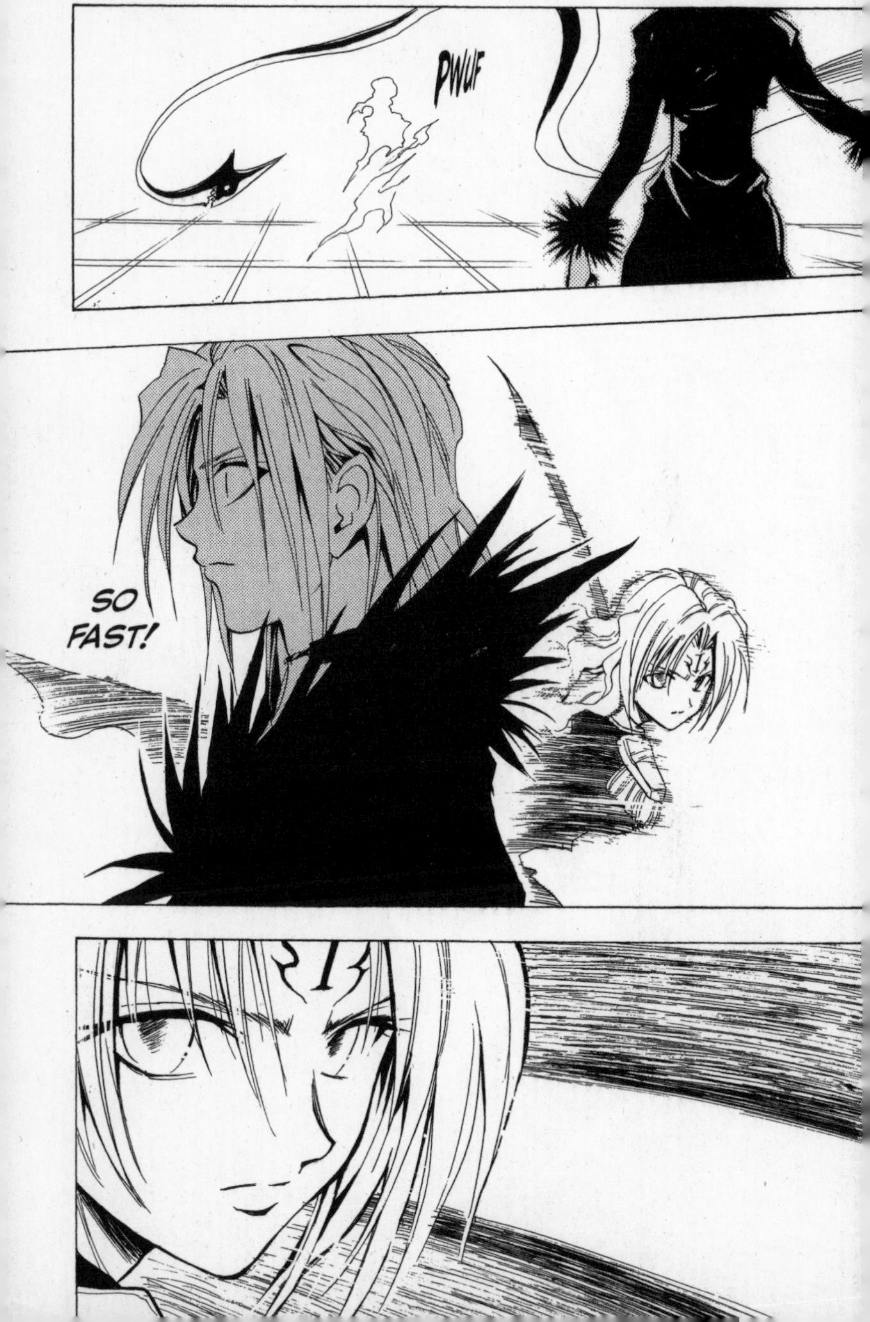
PWUF
SO FAST!

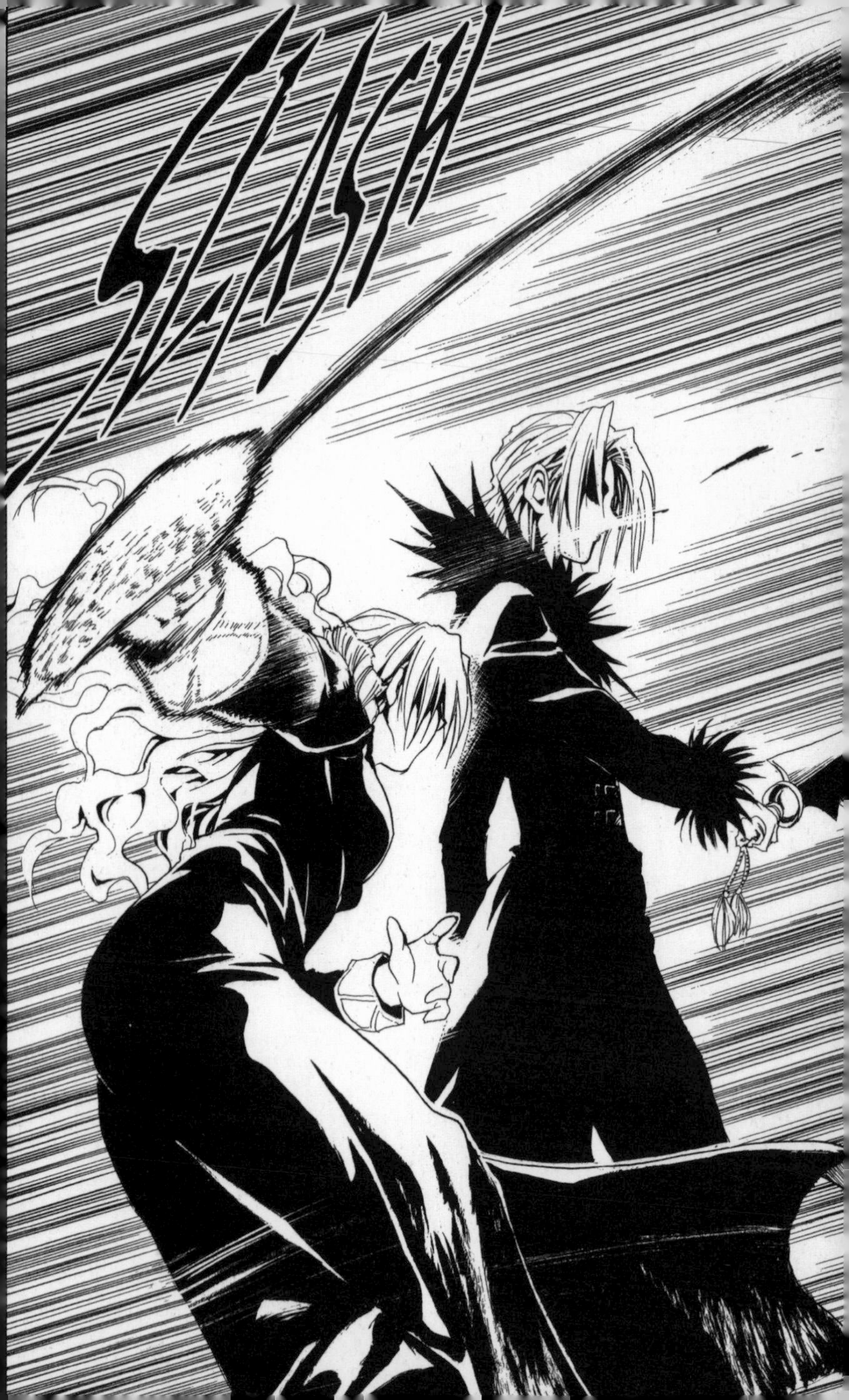
SLASH

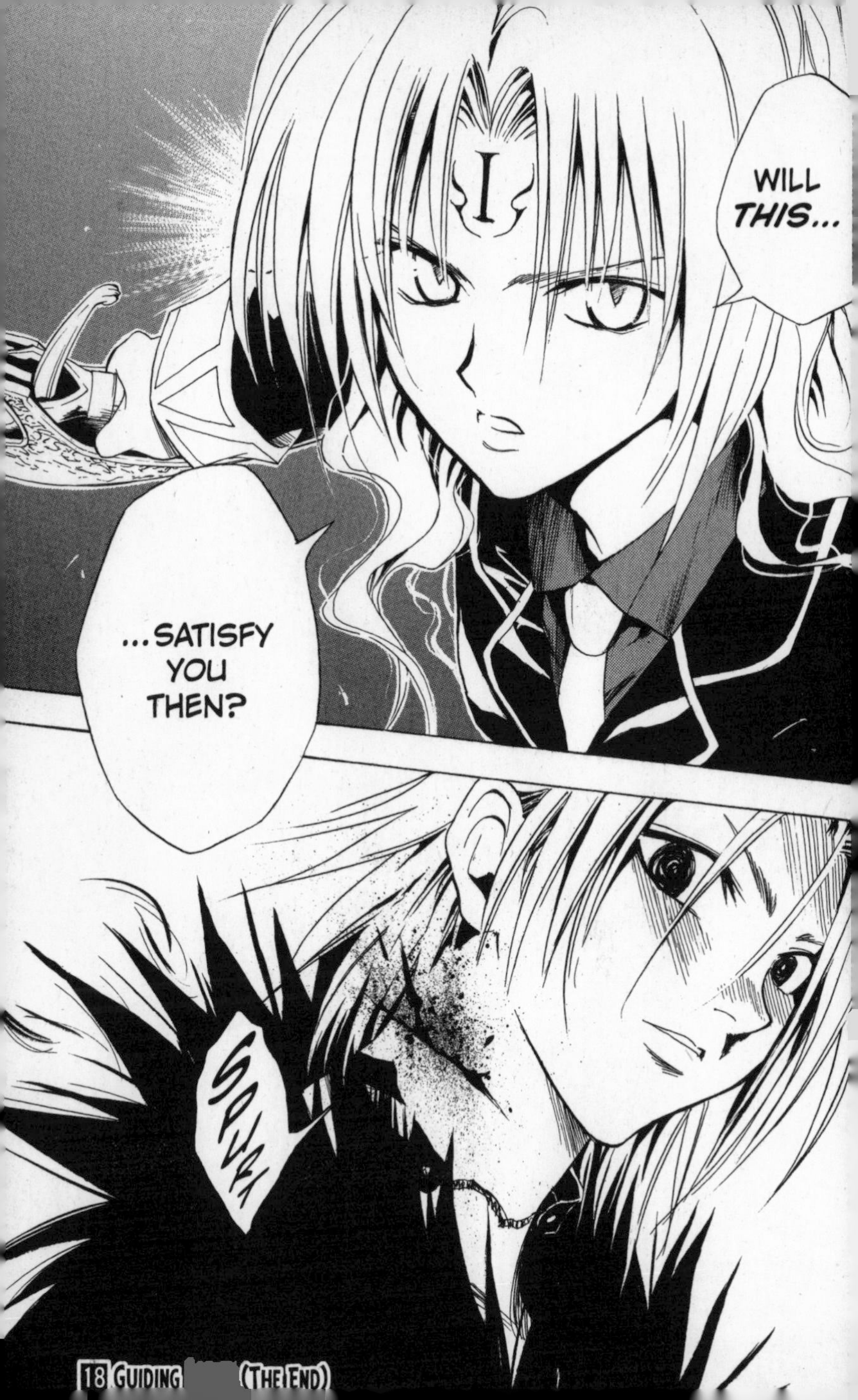
WILL THIS...
...SATISFY YOU THEN?
18 GUIDING [redacted] (THE END)

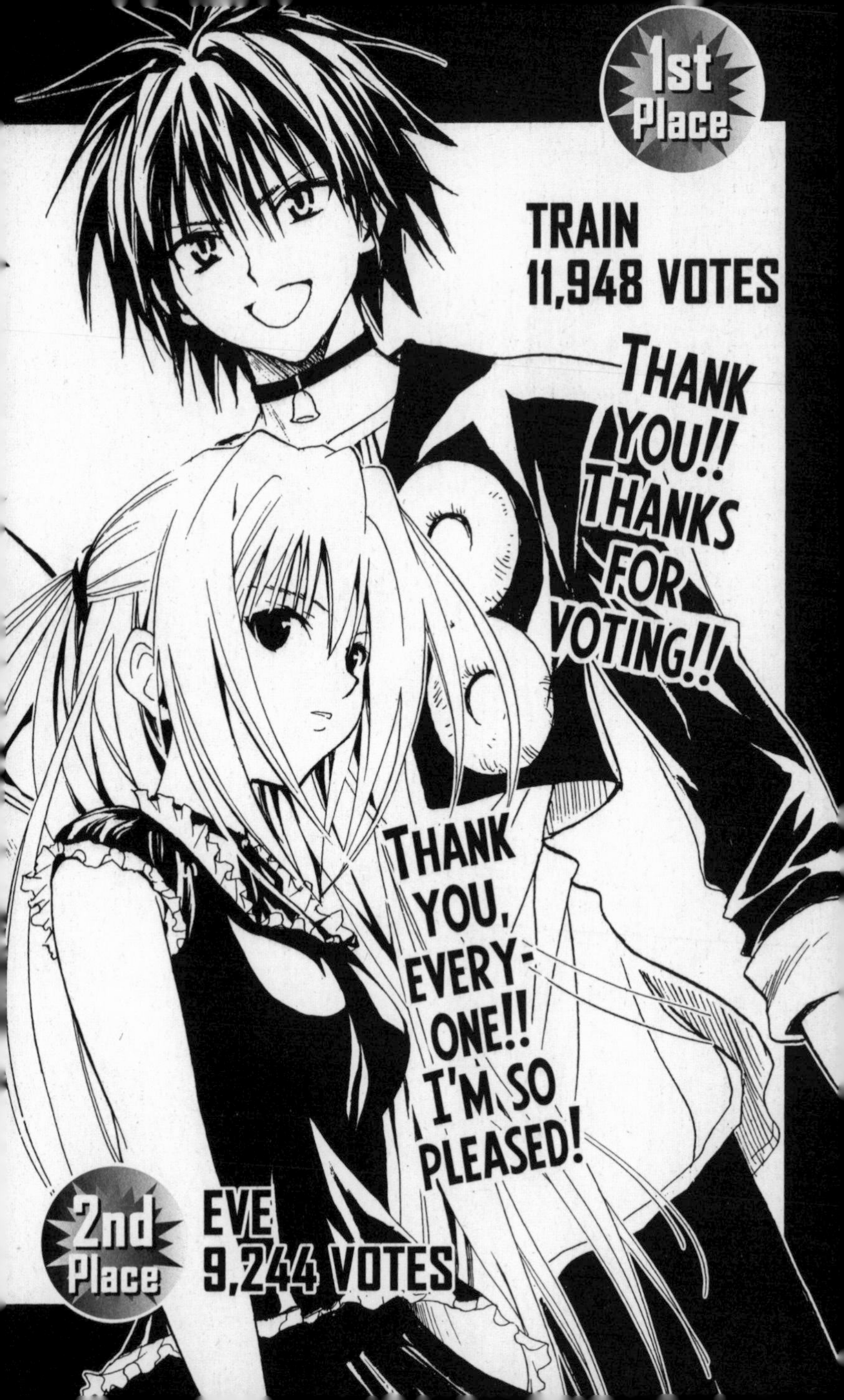
1st Place
TRAIN
11,948 VOTES
THANK YOU!! THANKS FOR VOTING!!
THANK YOU, EVERY-ONE!! I'M SO PLEASED!
2nd Place
EVE
9,244 VOTES

THE 3RD CHARACTER POPULARITY CONTEST RESULTS!!

Part1

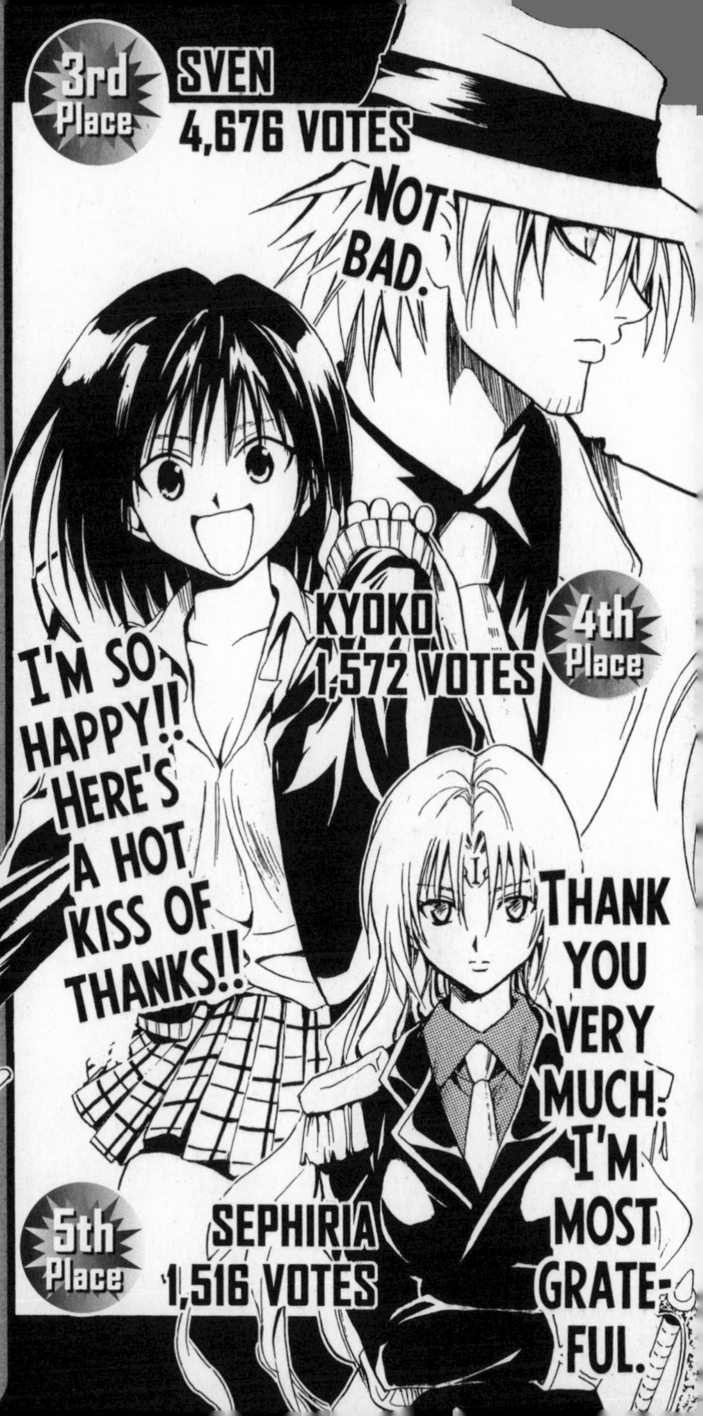

3rd Place
SVEN
4,676 VOTES
NOT BAD.
4th Place
KYOKO
1,572 VOTES
I'M SO HAPPY!! HERE'S A HOT KISS OF THANKS!!
THANK YOU VERY MUCH. I'M MOST GRATE-FUL.
5th Place
SEPHIRIA
1,516 VOTES

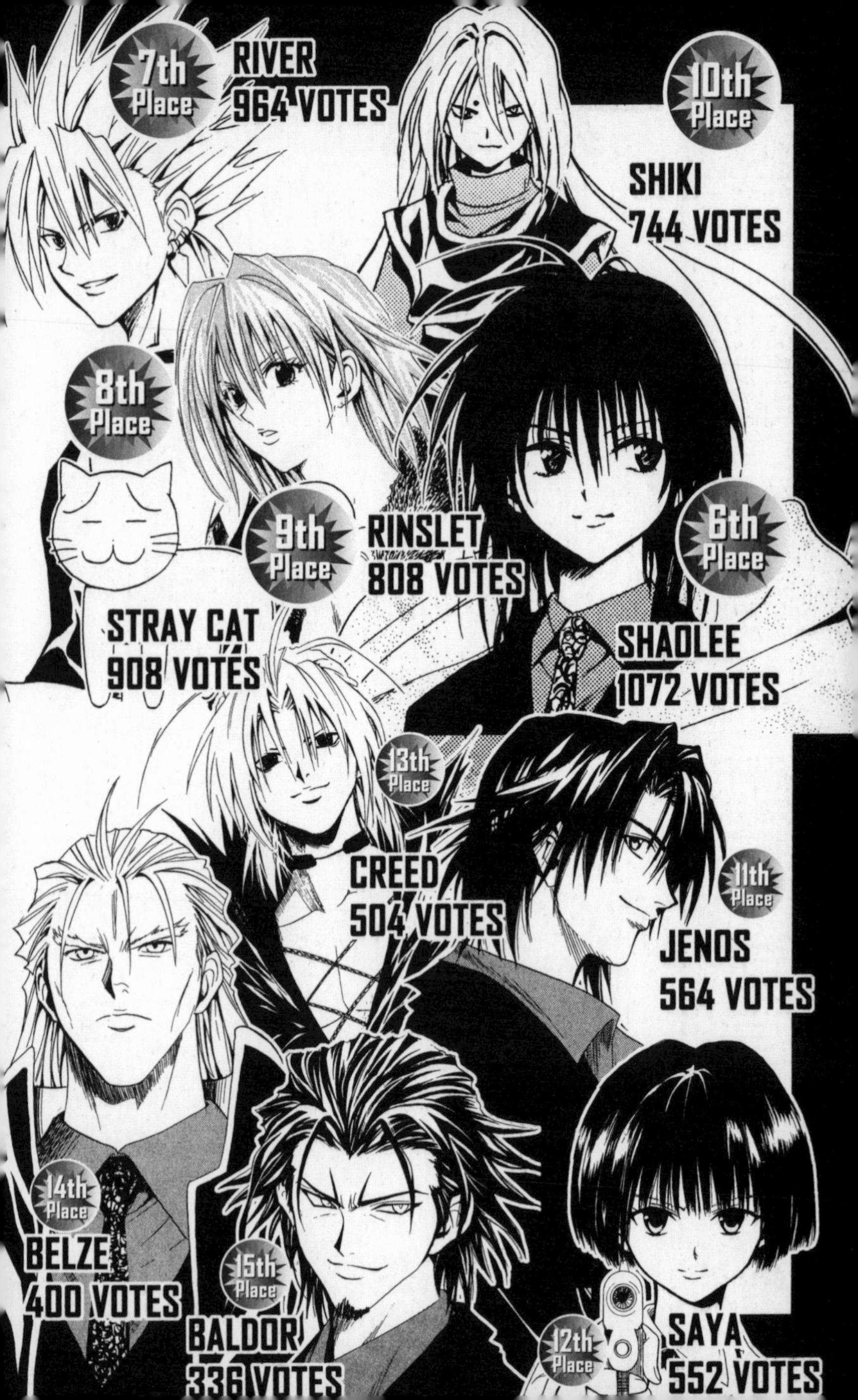
10th Place
SHIKI
744 VOTES
7th Place
RIVER
964 VOTES
6th Place
SHAOLEE
1072 VOTES
9th Place
RINSLET
808 VOTES
8th Place
STRAY CAT
908 VOTES
11th Place
JENOS
564 VOTES
13th Place
CREED
504 VOTES
12th Place
SAYA
552 VOTES
15th Place
BALDOR
336 VOTES
14th Place
BELZE
400 VOTES

THE 3RD CHARACTER POPULARITY CONTEST RESULTS!!

Part2

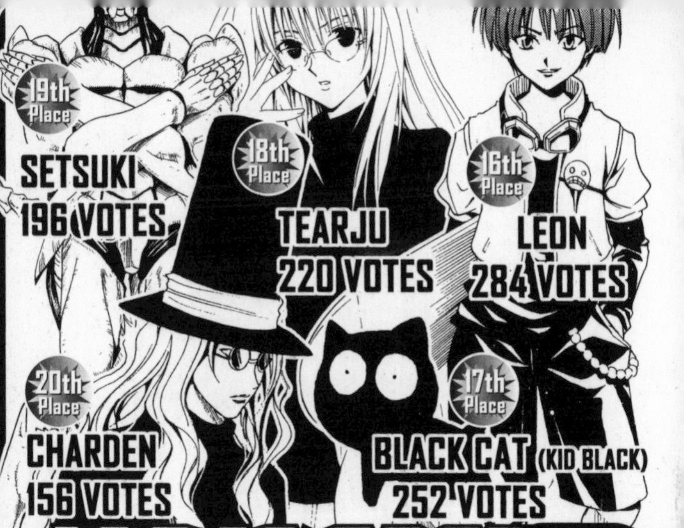
16th Place
LEON
284 VOTES
18th Place
TEARJU
220 VOTES
19th Place
SETSUKI
196 VOTES
17th Place
BLACK CAT (KID BLACK)
252 VOTES
20th Place
CHARDEN
156 VOTES

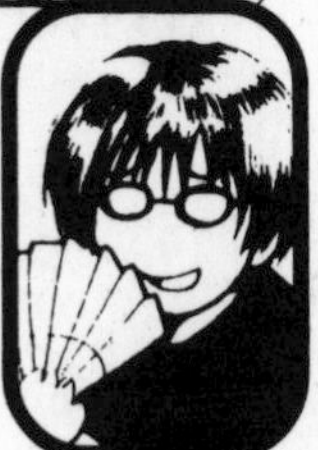

THIS IS OUR THIRD POPULARITY CONTEST TO COMMEMORATE THE THIRD YEAR OF PUBLICATION. I WAS A BIT NERVOUS, AFRAID THAT EVE MIGHT WIN MORE VOTES THAN TRAIN, BUT TRAIN HELD HIS OWN AND PROVED HE'S STILL OUR HERO. THE TOP VOTE-GETTERS WERE BASICALLY THE SAME AS THEY WERE IN THE FIRST TWO CONTESTS. AND I'M GLAD TO SEE THAT SVEN CAME IN THIRD. WHILE HE'S OFTEN RELEGATED TO THE BACKGROUND, EVE AND TRAIN'S EXPLOITS WOULD NOT BE POSSIBLE WITHOUT SVEN. MY THANKS TO EVERYONE WHO TOOK THE TIME TO VOTE!

IN THE NEXT VOLUME...

Even after being wounded by Sephiria's sword, Creed stands unscathed! What secret does he harbor in his body? Train rushes to confront Creed and settle the past, and challenges him to a final battle!

AVAILABLE MARCH 2009!

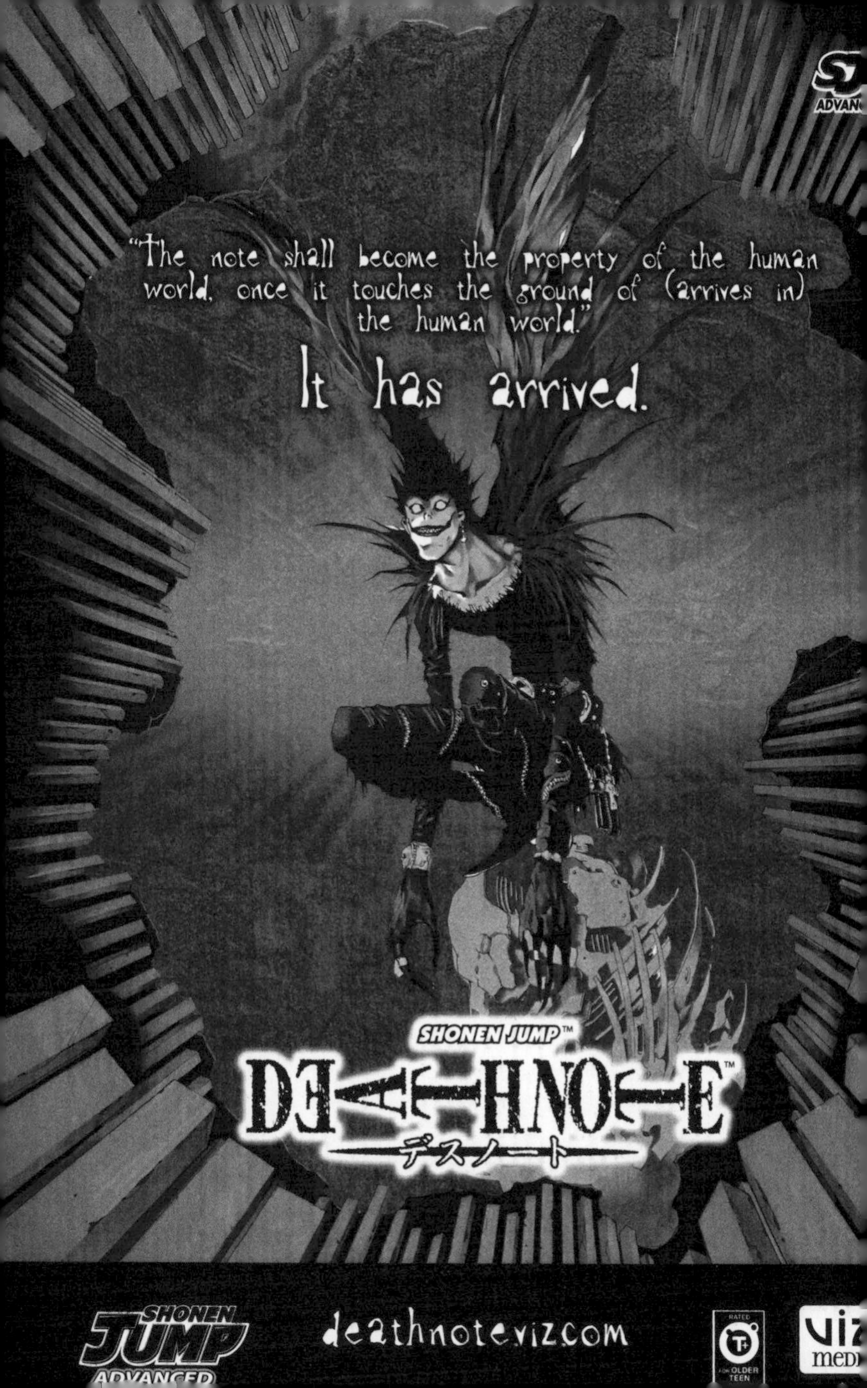
"The note shall become the property of the human world, once it touches the ground of (arrives in) the human world."
It has arrived.
SHONEN JUMP™
DEATH NOTE™
デスノート
SHONEN JUMP ADVANCED
deathnote.viz.com
RATED T+ FOR OLDER TEEN

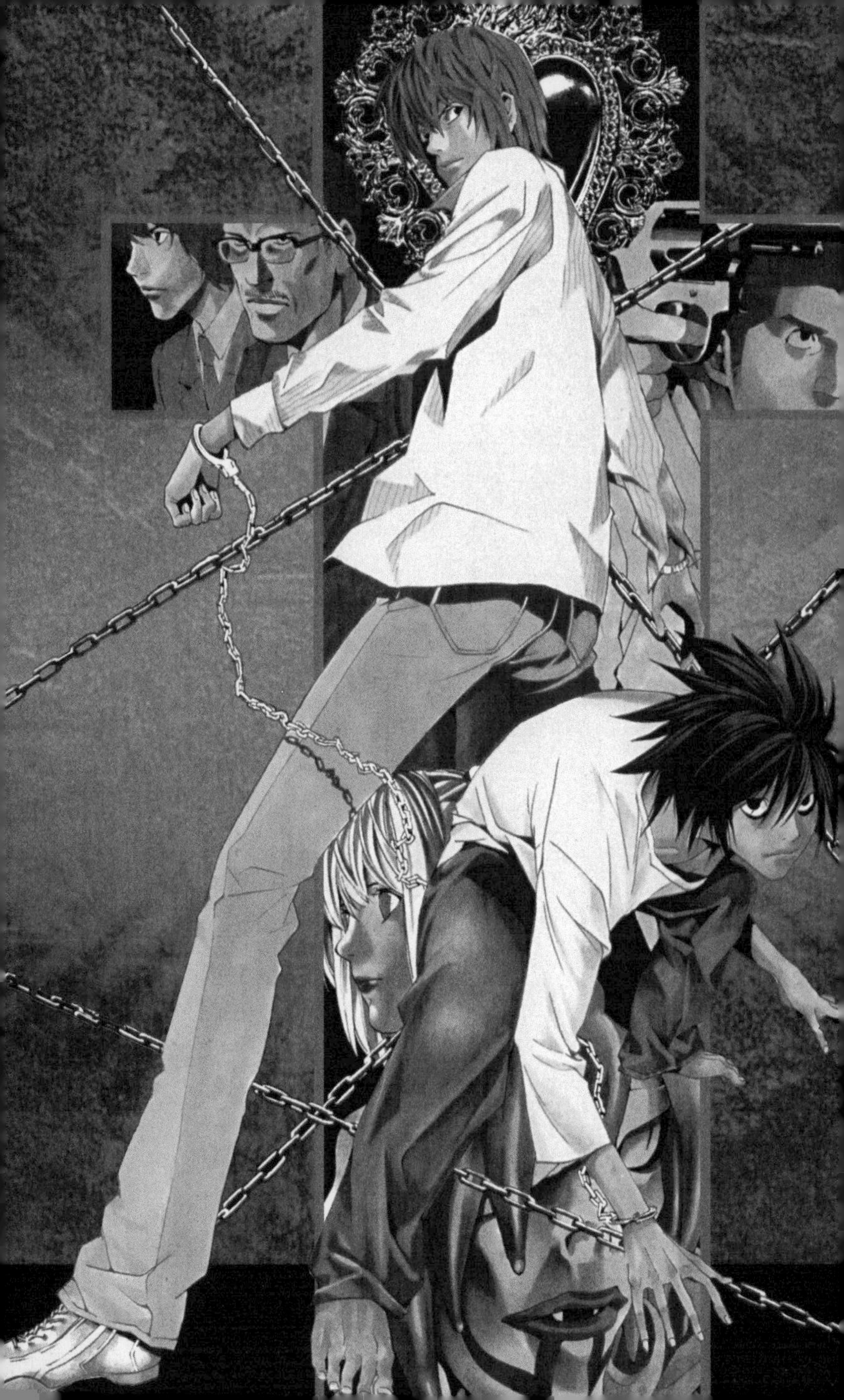

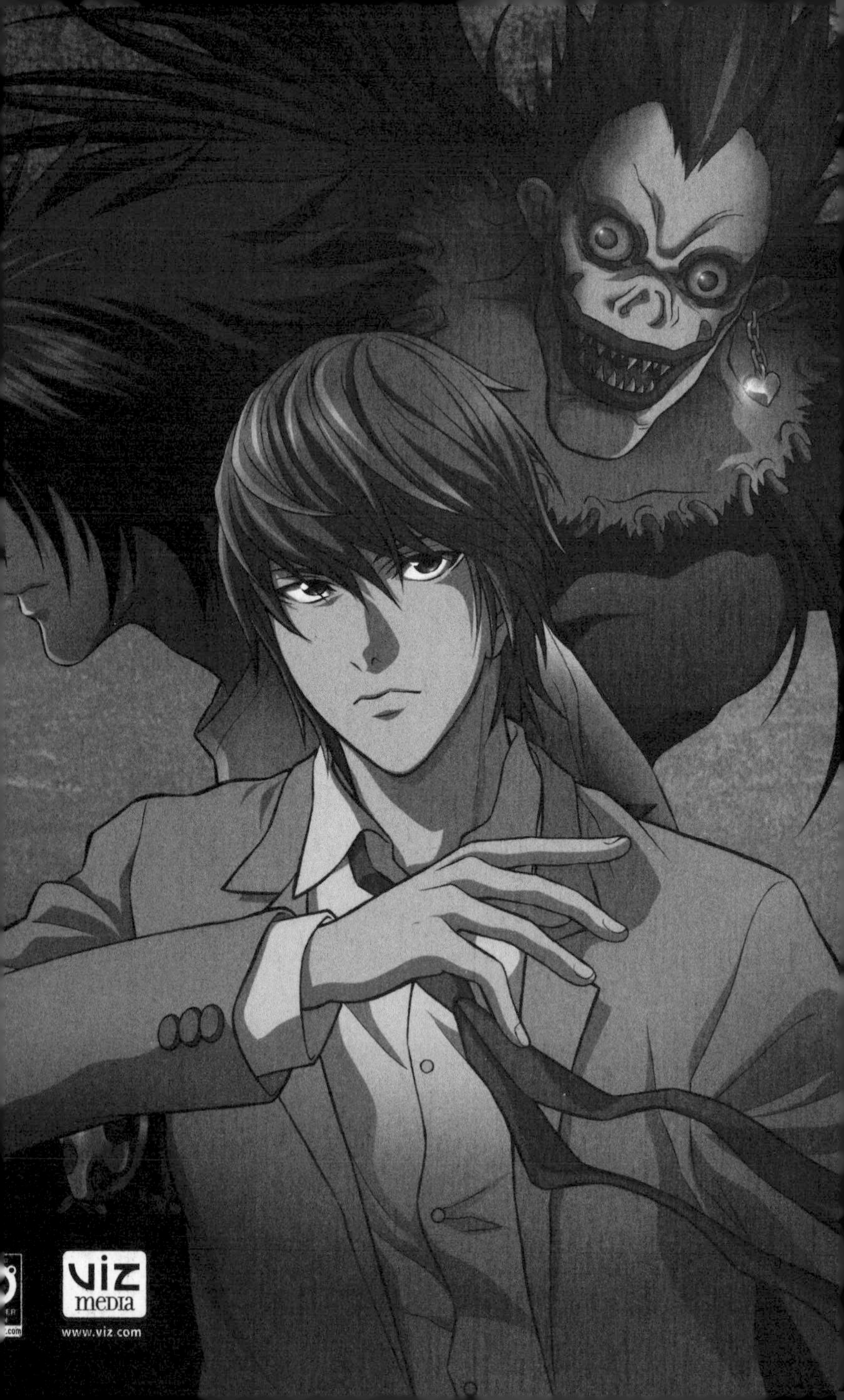
VIZ media
www.viz.com

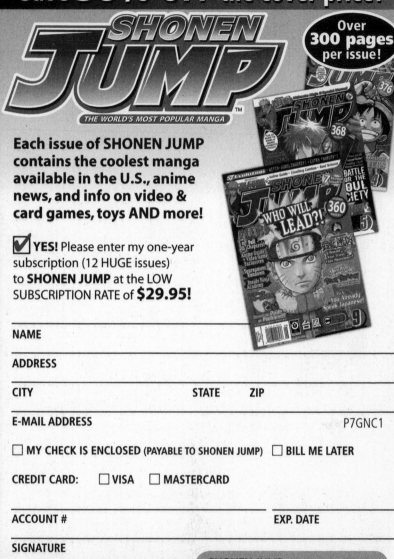